Wedded to the Cause

Ukrainian-Canadian Women and Ethnic Identity 1891–1991

Swyripa argues that ethnicity combined with gender to shape the experience of Ukrainian-Canadian women, as statelessness and national oppression in the homeland joined with a negative group stereotype and minority status in emigration to influence women's roles and options. She explores community attitudes towards the peasant immigrant pioneer, towards her daughters exposed to the opportunities, prejudices, and assimilatory pressures of the Anglo-Canadian world, towards the 'Great Women' evoked as models and sources of inspiration, and towards the familiar baba. In these stereotypes of the female figure, and in the activities of women's organizations, the community played out its many tensions: between a strong attachment to Canada and an equally strong attachment to Ukraine; between nationalists who sought to liberate Ukraine from Polish and Soviet rule and progressives who saw themselves as part of an international proletariat; between women's responsibilities as mothers and homemakers and their obligation to participate in both Canadian and community life.

Swyripa finds that the concerns of community leaders did not always coincide with those of the grassroots. The differences were best expressed in the evolution of the peasant immigrant pioneer woman as a group symbol, where the tensions between a cultural ethnic consciousness and a politicized national consciousness as the core of Ukrainian-Canadian identity were played out in the female figure.

FRANCES SWYRIPA holds a joint appointment in the Department of History and the Canadian Institute of Ukrainian Studies at the University of Alberta.

FRANCES SWYRIPA

Wedded to the Cause: Ukrainian-Canadian Women and Ethnic Identity 1891-1991

UNIVERSITY OF TORONTO PRESS
Toronto Buffalo London

© University of Toronto Press Incorporated 1993
Toronto Buffalo London
Printed in Canada

ISBN 0-8020-5008-5 (cloth)
ISBN 0-8020-6939-8 (paper)

Printed on acid-free paper

Canadian Cataloguing in Publication Data

Swyripa, Frances, 1951–
    Wedded to the cause : Ukrainian-Canadian
women and ethnic identity, 1891–1991

Includes bibliographical references and index.
ISBN 0-8020-5008 5 (bound) 0-8020-6939-8 (pbk.)

1. Ukrainian-Canadian women – History.*
2. Ukrainian-Canadian women – Social conditions.*
3. Ukrainian-Canadian women – Political activity.*
I. Title.

FC106.U5S9 1993   305.48'891791071   C92-095029-9
F1035.U5S9 1993

A version of chapter 6 first appeared as 'Baba and the Community Heroine: The Two Images of Ukrainian Pioneer Women' in *Alberta: Studies in the Arts and Sciences* 2, 1 (1989): 59–80, published by the University of Alberta Press, and is reprinted with permission. The excerpts from *Garden in the Wind* by Gabrielle Roy is used by permission of the Canadian Publishers, McClelland and Stewart, Toronto.

This book has been published with the help of a grant from the Social Science Federation of Canada, using funds provided by the Social Sciences and Humanities Research Council of Canada.

Contents

Preface

The final revisions to the manuscript for this book were completed in August and September 1991. These were a momentous two months for Ukrainians in Canada. On the one hand, as Canadians proud of their heritage, they celebrated the one hundredth anniversary of their settlement in Canada. On the other hand, as Ukrainians concerned for their homeland, they witnessed the collapse of the communist régime in the Soviet Union and Ukraine's declaration of independence. Nothing could have better brought home the political nature of this study and the fact that its subject matter is, for Ukrainian Canadians, part of their self-image and identity. History, in other words, is important for the present and the past.

Ukrainian Canadians possess a strong attachment to Canada, rooted in the peasant pioneers who settled the prairie provinces at the turn of the century. These settlers became the basis of a 'founding fathers' myth that confirmed their descendants in their Canadian birthright, to counter the legacy of low immigrant status and a negative group stereotype, and the source of an apolitical 'Ukrainian' consciousness. Ukrainian Canadians also possess a strong attachment to Ukraine, rooted in its history of statelessness and oppression under foreign rule, and, in the twentieth century, status as a Soviet republic. These conditions not only ensured continued and intense interest in the homeland; after 1917 they also produced hostile nationalist and progressive camps, the one with a mission to liberate Ukraine and preserve an endangered language and culture in Canada, the other with a mission to bring to the world's toiling masses the communist paradise enjoyed by their compatriots in the Soviet Union.

This study explores the impact of Ukrainian Canadians' self-image as Canadians and their continued involvement with Ukraine on one segment of the group – women. It distinguishes throughout between the views of the nationalist majority, who have dominated community politics and the perception of most Canadians about Ukrainian Canadians, and those of the progressives, for whom Ukrainianness has been less important than class. The nationalist perspective also receives the bulk of the attention – partly because it represented the majority view; partly because the nationalists, unlike the progressives, were themselves divided into several factions; and partly because the nationalist perspective, more than the progressive, provides insights into the relationship between ethnicity and gender. What effect do statelessness and national oppression, especially when compounded by emigration and minority status in a new country, have on women's images, roles, and options?

The nationalist agenda, predicated on the unresolved 'Ukrainian question' in Europe and on concern for Ukrainians' position in Canada, subordinated women and women's rights and issues to the interests of the group and the nation. At the same time, it guaranteed Ukrainian-Canadian women a role as actors in their own right, a role simultaneously defined by and transcending gender, and imposed an arbitrary group tie with constraints and tensions. The home, as the primary bastion of Ukrainianness, exalted the significance of the private sphere, making mothering and homemaking women's major function. Yet women were also to further the Ukrainian cause by participating in public life as 'full citizens of the nation,' and they were encouraged to pursue the education that promised upward mobility and acceptance in Canadian society. Women's community activities drew on traditional 'female' qualities and pursuits, but their sex was irrelevant to socioeconomic integration and the group achievement it represented.

The progressive agenda was based on an international proletariat and the unity of workers' interests rather than any Ukrainian blood tie. It is important to the discussion not for what it says about women and the class struggle but for what it says about the primacy of the class struggle and women's responsibilities and self-image as Ukrainians. Complicating any generalizations concerning the impact of class on gender and ethnicity is the specific Ukrainian-Canadian case: women belonged to a group whose homeland was no longer involved in the struggle but had already achieved the ideal. As a result, progressives placed less emphasis than the nationalists on women's role in preserving and promoting Ukrainianness, yet they were able to draw on their heritage and the achievements of the homeland to derive inspiration and a sense of satisfaction.

The term 'ethnic' in this book is defined in a purely Canadian context and encompasses Canadians of non-British and non-French origin, excluding Canada's aboriginal population. It implies particular, albeit changing, national-cultural traits as well as socioeconomic characteristics determined by a group's historical ranking in Canadian society. Ukrainian Canadians are 'ethnic.' They are also a 'community' and a 'group,' with a crucial distinction between the two. 'Community' refers to formal organized life and those individuals who consciously identify with Ukrainian culture, institutions, and causes, in particular the leadership elite giving shape to the community and defining goals and responsibilities for the group. 'Group' refers to all Canadians of Ukrainian origin. Regardless of their attachment to things Ukrainian, they are the people the community addresses and in whose name it presumes to speak; and they are the people whom historians and others must consider when determining the fate of the descendants of Ukrainian immigrants to Canada. The present work focuses on the 'community,' but the community focuses on the 'group,' so that what the community has to say to and about women as members of the group become its major concern.

Readers expecting an in-depth analysis of the reality of women's lives will be disappointed; so will readers expecting a history of women's organizations or a profile of their leading figures. While community activists and spokespersons are more central to the study than the women they address, they are less important than the propaganda and programs they devised for their sex. By the same token, the reality of women's lives is significant only as it has been perceived by these elites and has been seen to affect their political agenda. Those responsible for defining women's relationship to Ukrainian-Canadian group issues and concerns – women's organizations, preceded in the pioneer period by an immigrant male intelligentsia – have dictated the nature of the discussion that follows. The book deals primarily with ideas, specifically those of the 'official' Ukrainian-Canadian community as it sought to influence women on behalf of competing and incompatible blueprints inspired by Ukrainian nationalism or the class struggle. The attitudes of ordinary people – of women towards the expectations placed on them, and of descendants of the pioneers towards the peasant immigrant woman as an ethnic symbol – form a

secondary thread. Throughout, the discussion touches on the complicated interrelationship of class, gender, and ethnicity.

Ideas often resist conventional and tidy treatment reflecting a historical progression from point A to point B. Some structure and order
had to be imposed to make the topic manageable, however, even at
the risk of occasional overgeneralization or simplification and somewhat arbitrary and artificial packaging. Ultimately, the organization
and presentation of the material is based on the themes and issues that
emerged from careful reading of the sources and my interpretation
of them. These themes and issues represent either the preoccupations
of those concerned with rallying women behind nationalist and progressive banners at a particular moment or the broader trends that
became evident only with the passage of time. While there is no continuity between chapters in the customary chronological sense, there
is a logic to the arrangement, including the 'circularity' of beginning
and ending with the peasant immigrant. Each chapter can be read as
a separate essay, but all are tied together by the central thesis and its
subsidiary themes. Time and place overlap from chapter to chapter,
and, within a chapter, are frequently irrelevant; similarly, continuity
and sameness are often more important than change or difference,
and agreement more important than conflict. Region as such, for example, had little bearing on the propaganda and programs organizations directed at women, although their audiences were distributed
unevenly across Canada; and antagonistic views on the political future
of Ukraine did not have to mean conflicting views on women's roles.

Chapters 1 through 5 explore the way competing community elites
and their organizations perceived and stereotyped Ukrainian-Canadian women, defined their function within the group, and set up guidelines for their private and public lives. The discussion begins with the
'first' Ukrainian women in Canada, peasants from Galicia and Bukovyna in the Austro-Hungarian empire who, in the early 1900s, settled
among their own kind on homesteads in western Canada. Criticized
by contemporaries for ignorance and apathy, they were held to impede
their people's progress as well as the politicization that the Ukrainian
cause and class struggle required. The focus then shifts to the peasant
immigrants' daughters, exposed to the opportunities, prejudices, and
assimilatory pressures of the Anglo-Canadian world. Against the
changes in women's lives set in motion by the new environment, and
drawing on a popular stereotype of the working girl, chapter 2 describes the community's reaction to often conflicting demands on the

loyalties of a rising generation. 'Great Women' whom nationalists and progressives evoked as models and sources of inspiration form the subject of chapter 3. Chapter 4 examines the propaganda and programs of the national women's organizations the two camps established between the wars to see how they translated the message of these 'Great Women' into programs of action. Chapter 5 follows these same organizations into the postwar era and observes a process of Canadianization in their profiles, activities, and mythology. The final chapter, which documents the retrospective idealization of the peasant immigrant woman at both the formal community and the grassroots levels, draws together and illuminates several earlier themes. In so doing, it demonstrates how the tensions between a cultural ethnic consciousness and a politicized national consciousness as the core of Ukrainian-Canadian identity have been played out in the female figure.

For the greater part, the study relies on the traditional tools of the historian, notably Ukrainian-Canadian historiographical literature and official community publications. The ideological press, especially the women's pages of the large weeklies and the women's journals that replaced them, was by far the most important source, and a discussion of its usefulness can be found in the bibliographic note to this book. But the topic also lent itself to more unorthodox sources and demanded the consultation of a wide range of materials recognized for their peculiar value to women's history or having special relevance for Ukrainian Canadians and Ukrainian-Canadian women. Pottery, statuary, artwork, foods, embroidery, photographs – all have something significant to say about the place and role Ukrainian-Canadian women have occupied in their group's experience and its collective consciousness. Several of these cultural forms or expressions represent not only women's work but also women's work that has come to symbolize Ukrainian-Canadian identity.

I alone bear responsibility for the book's flaws, but support, encouragement, and motivation came from many quarters. The financial assistance of the Killam Trust, the Canadian Research Institute for the Advancement of Women, and the Canadian Foundation for Ukrainian Studies facilitated preparation of the manuscript first as a doctoral dissertation and then in book form. R.C. Macleod of the Department of History at the University of Alberta, who supervised the project during its initial stages, deserves special mention, both for his intellectual guidance and for his astute advice that a finished thesis was better than an unfinished one. Anne Marie Decore, John Foster, John-Paul Himka, Susan Jackel, and David Mills at the University of Alberta, and John Herd Thompson of McGill University, read an earlier version of the manuscript; their comments and suggestions, together with those of the anonymous readers who reviewed the manuscript for the University of Toronto Press and the Social Science Federation of Canada, were most helpful. I would also like to acknowledge Gerald Hallowell, Laura Macleod, and Rosemary Shipton of the University of Toronto Press; the Ukrainian Basilian and Redemptorist Fathers, who generously permitted access to their parish records; the staff of the University of Alberta Archives, who provided me with a home base throughout my doctoral program; John Sokolowski, a willing sounding board for many ideas; and George Richardson, whose insights, constructive criticism, and moral support are always appreciated.

Abbreviations

AUUC	Association of United Ukrainian Canadians (Tovarystvo obiednanykh ukrainskykh kanadtsiv)
ICW	International Council of Women
NCWC	National Council of Women of Canada
OUN	Organization of Ukrainian Nationalists (Orhanizatsiia ukrainskykh natsionalistiv)
SSMI	Sisters Servants of Mary Immaculate (Sestry Sluzhebnyts Presviatoi Neporochnoi Divy Marii)
UCC	Ukrainian Canadian Committee (Komitet ukraintsiv Kanady)
UCWC	Ukrainian Canadian Women's Committee (Komitet ukrainok Kanady)
UCWL	Ukrainian Catholic Women's League (Liga ukrainskykh katolytskykh zhinok Kanady)
ULFTA	Ukrainian Labour-Farmer Temple Association (Tovarystvo ukrainskyi robitnycho-farmerskyi dim)
UNF	Ukrainian National Federation (Ukrainske natsionalne obiednannia)
USRL	Ukrainian Self-Reliance League (Soiuz ukraintsiv samostiinykiv)
UWAC	Ukrainian Women's Association of Canada (Soiuz ukrainok Kanady)
UWOC	Ukrainian Women's Organization of Canada (Orhanizatsiia ukrainok Kanady im. Olhy Basarab)
WFUWO	World Federation of Ukrainian Women's Organizations (Svitova federatsiia ukrainskykh zhinochykh orhanizatsii)

WEDDED TO THE CAUSE

Introduction:
Queen Elizabeth the Ukrainian

One thousand years ago the daughter of the Saxon king, Harold, married Grand Prince Volodymyr Monomakh of Kievan Rus'. Their union, in the words of a popular Ukrainian-Canadian mythologist, 'gave the present Queen Elizabeth II of England and Canada an infusion of Ukrainian blood.'[1] That Queen Elizabeth is Ukrainian no doubt comes as a surprise to most Canadians, but to Ukrainian Canadians who accept the wisdom of the mythologists in their midst, Her Majesty's Ukrainian ancestry is both an article of faith and a fact. Not unnaturally, the connection enhances the self-image and sense of belonging of members of an ethnic group long considered inferior in a country defining itself through its British ties. Far more fascinating is the exploitation of the connection for Ukrainian political purposes. Community activists and spokespersons have evoked the blood bond between Ukrainian Canadians and the British monarch of Canada to demand recognition for their group as a full partner in Confederation, a partner who, in the interests of national-cultural survival, is guaranteed the same collective rights as the two charter peoples.[2]

This concern for survival is nurtured by Ukrainian history. Long periods under powerful neighbours unsympathetic or indifferent to the Ukrainian population separated the medieval princedom of Kievan Rus', the Cossack state of the mid seventeenth to the eighteenth century, and the Ukrainian People's Republic of 1917–20. During centuries of rule by Poland and Russia in particular, the greater part of the native nobility was alienated, the church as a national institution was stifled, the peasantry was enserfed, and expressions of cultural and political consciousness were suppressed. By the late nineteenth century, however, when the Russian empire controlled Eastern Ukraine and Austria-Hungary controlled the western provinces of Galicia, Bukovyna, and Transcarpathia, the processes of the last several hundred years were being reversed.

First, serfdom had been abolished in Austria-Hungary in 1848 and in Russia in 1861, although rural poverty and overpopulation subsequently forced hundreds of thousands of peasants to seek relief in seasonal employment or in permanent relocation overseas. Second, a national awakening that originated as a cultural revival dominated by clerical and literary figures became increasingly politicized under an activist secular intelligentsia combining national and populist goals. In the transformation of the Ukrainian peasant mass into a self-conscious nation, soon to express its new sense of peoplehood in a bid for political independence, Austria-Hungary provided a more favourable climate than autocratic Russia, where even elementary education in Ukrainian was prohibited, and Galicia emerged as the formal base of the Ukrainian national movement. In the east, nation building awaited the cataclysmic events of 1917, but in Galicia it had penetrated deeply into the countryside by the early twentieth century. A network of reading halls (*chytalni*), *prosvita* or enlightenment societies, and agricultural cooperatives spearheaded by the local priest, intelligentsia, or advanced peasants crisscrossed the province, vying for influence and control. Assisted by an expanding press, these institutions helped to weld village peasants into a larger national community, hastening their politicization and encouraging group action against socioeconomic oppression.[3]

Movement abroad was all but closed to Russian Ukrainians, so Austria-Hungary, with Galicia predominating, supplied the great majority of Ukrainian immigrants to Canada at the height of turn-of-the-century expansion and growth. As homesteaders for the prairie provinces, and as unskilled labour for railways and resource frontiers, the newcomers were expected to provide the manpower for a country engaged in physical and psychological nation building. Most settled in the parkland belt of Manitoba, Saskatchewan, and Alberta, in a series of blocs extending from east and south of Winnipeg to the large Vegreville colony outside Edmonton. Perceived as threatening because of their size and for their preservation of old-country ways and attitudes, these blocs were responsible for much of the Anglo-Canadian hostility that followed. Smaller numbers of immigrants formed Ukrainian enclaves in the working-class and immigrant districts of major Canadian cities or ventured farther afield to the mining towns of British Columbia, northern Ontario, and Sydney in Nova Scotia.

This immigration (1891–1914) of approximately 170,000 peasants, accompanied by a few members of the lay and clerical intelligentsia, gave the Ukrainian group in Canada its basic character and public image – peasant, prairie, and Western Ukrainian. Some 68,000 inter-war immigrants, again primarily peasants from Western Ukraine and again initially destined for prairie farms, reinforced the pioneer base. The 34,000 displaced persons arriving in the wake of the Second World War favoured central Canada; from Soviet as well as non-Soviet territories, and more socially diverse than their predecessors, they injected a new dimension into community life without fundamentally altering the group profile.[4]

Strong identification with Canada, rooted in the peasant pioneers' role in nation building during its most crucial phase, generated a feeling of group worth as a 'founding people' that became an important aspect of Ukrainian Canadians' ethnic consciousness. This positive self-image existed alongside a negative, often defensive sense of Ukrainianness as being different, encouraged by the prejudice of an aggressive British-Canadian society towards Ukrainians' peasant cultural baggage and reflecting the reality of their inferior position in the new homeland. Yet a solidifying sense of Ukrainianness as being different, as being 'not-Anglo-Canadian,' did not merely spell alienation. While emigration in general can sharpen national identity by throwing objective differences into relief and causing individuals to gather around familiar points of identification, it is of the utmost significance that Ukrainians' arrival in Canada occurred at a critical juncture not only in Canadian but also in Ukrainian history.

The process of nation building in Ukraine, gathering momentum as Ukrainian emigration to Canada began, accelerated under the impetus of events set in motion by the First World War. In the Russian empire, the Ukrainian People's Republic was proclaimed in Kiev following the Bolshevik seizure of power and, on 22 January 1918, the republic declared complete sovereignty. Despite widespread popular support and commitment to social and economic reforms, it faced formidable obstacles: political inexperience; invading Russian Red and White armies; anarchy and ruin in the countryside; hostility in the cities, non-Ukrainian centres of Bolshevik support; and opposition from both a rival Soviet Ukrainian government and the Hetmanate, a conservative German puppet régime installed after armistice with the Central Powers in early 1918. In Austria-Hungary, with the collapse of the Habsburg monarchy at the war's end, Galician Ukrainians established the Western Ukrainian People's Republic, unleashing a war with Polish forces claiming this ethnically Ukrainian territory for a restored Poland. In January 1919 the two Ukrainian governments merged.[5]

The united Ukrainian People's Republic proved unable to withstand combined Soviet and Polish aggression or to influence world leaders who were redrawing the map of Europe. By the early 1920s Western Ukraine had been divided among the new states of Poland, Romania, and Czechoslovakia, while the bulk of Eastern Ukraine was incorporated into the Soviet Union as the Ukrainian Soviet Socialist Republic. Socioeconomic conditions for the peasantry worsened under Soviet collectivization and Polish and Romanian colonization schemes in Galicia and Bukovyna. Intellectual purges in Soviet Ukraine and the repression of Ukrainian institutions in all three areas crippled national-cultural life and hindered the ongoing Ukrainization of the masses. The artificial famine that accompanied collectivization, together with the less devastating Polish 'pacification' of the Ukrainian countryside, threatened physical survival itself. The Second World War brought further hardship under Soviet and Nazi occupations as well as another aborted bid for independence. After 1945 all Ukrainian territories were part of the Ukrainian Soviet Socialist Republic. Until Mikhail Gorbachev's policy of *glasnost* or openness in the 1980s challenged the status quo, they were subject to centralization through Moscow, escalating Russification, the suppression of dissent and human rights, and censorship of national-cultural life.[6]

The unfinished business of Ukrainian nation building, as territorial integrity and political independence eluded twentieth-century Ukraine, had a profound impact on the evolution and expression of Ukrainian consciousness in Canada. The metamorphosis of individuals into a structured, politically focused, and articulate community was largely the work of a Ukrainian-Canadian elite. Beginning with the lay and clerical immigrant intelligentsia of the early twentieth century and a small educated stratum emerging in the new homeland, its ranks were augmented by activists from two subsequent immigrations as well as the Canadian born. Anxious to rid Ukrainians of their peasant image and encumbrances in the interests of integration into Canadian society, and to mobilize them behind general national-cultural goals and specific political ideologies, these individuals not only shared the idea of group responsibility but also assumed a leadership mantle as their prerogative. Public sentiment supported this view; several correspondents to the pioneer immigrant press, for example, complained when the more able and privileged members of the group refused the role that was rightly and necessarily theirs.[7]

Jockeying for position in the pioneer or pre-1914 Ukrainian-Canadian community were representatives of the powerful Greek Catholic church and a three-pronged opposition drawn from overlapping secular nationalist, socialist, and anti-clerical currents in late nineteenth-century Galician politics.[8] Already challenged in Galicia by the secular intelligentsia and radical villagers, the Greek Catholic church found itself further undercut by emigration. Subordination to the French-dominated Roman Catholic hierarchy, which presented its foster flock with non-Ukrainian, celibate, Latin-rite priests, alienated Ukrainians accustomed to worship in the Greek rite under married priests of their own nationality. The spiritual and political crisis that ensued opened the door to Russian Orthodox and Anglo-Canadian Methodist and Presbyterian missionaries, proselytizing for their earthly masters as well as for God. Ecclesiastical independence in 1913 helped the Greek Catholic church to consolidate as the largest religious denomination among Ukrainians in Canada, but it had been irrevocably shaken. The Vatican's disallowance of married clergy[9] introduced unfamiliar monastic priests, who lacked the secular leadership credentials of their married village counterparts; besides, they were too few in number to establish a permanent presence in dispersed and undeveloped pioneer communities. Latinisms, continued use of non-Ukrainian priests, and lack of assurance that the Greek Catholic bishop in Canada would be Ukrainian exposed the church to charges of denationalization and contributed to its failure to reassert its old authority.[10]

Anti-clerical secular nationalists, who had initially objected to trends within the Greek Catholic church without seeking a formal break, increasingly queried its undemocratic structure, the integrity of its Ukrainian character, and its ability to represent and defend Ukrainian interests. In 1918 they established the Ukrainian Greek Orthodox Church of Canada as a 'national' church that would resolve these questions. Especially attractive to the nascent middle class, the new institution soon counted a quarter of the Ukrainian Canadians among its members, and emerged as the most dynamic voice in lay matters.[11] Indigenous roots aside, other strands of Ukrainian Protestantism were quickly discredited by ties with the assimilationist Anglo-Canadian

Methodist and Presbyterian churches, as financial dependence created pressures to adopt their dogma and prejudices as well.[12] Early socialists, who also maintained ties with sectors of mainstream society dedicated to goals not specifically Ukrainian, soon abandoned their original agrarian socialism for Marxism, supporting the Bolsheviks in 1917 and, thereafter, the new Soviet state.[13]

Anglicization and Bolshevization cost Protestants and socialists many pioneer adherents, including several leading figures, as the Great War and the Ukrainian Revolution strengthened the immigrants' Ukrainian identity and pushed those grouped around the Ukrainian Catholic and Orthodox churches to the fore. Protestantism faded as a force, but the 1920s witnessed the crystallization of what would be the fundamental cleavage in Ukrainian-Canadian community life for the next seventy years. On the one side were the 'nationalists' – those who stressed upward mobility and integration coupled with Ukrainian consciousness for their people in Canada, and who championed the cause of an independent, noncommunist Ukrainian state in Europe. On the other side were the self-styled 'progressives,' pro-communist and pro-Soviet, who supported both the struggle of the international proletariat and the construction of socialism in their homeland. Concerned to educate Ukrainian Canadians in their class interests, progressives identified not with upward mobility but with the prejudice and discrimination Ukrainians encountered in Canadian society.

Leaving their homeland at a time when Ukrainian identity was still being formed, turn-of-the-century peasant immigrants were 'Ukrainized' in Canada as much as in Ukraine. For many, despite the best efforts of community leaders, their Ukrainian consciousness remained more passive than active, more cultural than political. Interwar and postwar immigrants had survived war, revolution, military defeat, foreign occupation, physical genocide, and national-cultural and political oppression. They brought an often intense nationalism together with bitter ideological differences that strengthened the nationalist community but compounded its initial religious rift. Rival factions, convinced that they alone understood and voiced their people's best interests, established nationwide networks to bring Ukrainians across Canada under their respective umbrellas. Facing a united progressive front were organizations representing Catholic and Orthodox laity, republican and monarchist sympathizers from Ukraine's aborted revolution, and, later, the anti-communist displaced persons of the Second World War. Servant and tool of their creators, Ukrainian-Canadian organizations became the vehicles through which community leaders articulated group needs and goals, translated these needs and goals into active programs for the masses, and projected a collective group image and sense of purpose onto the mainstream consciousness. Whether or not Ukrainian Canadians shared the ambitions and assumptions of their self-appointed representatives, these leaders gave them their official identity.

Philosophical disagreements over the nature of the future Ukrainian state, over Ukrainian-Canadian involvement in its realization, and over group priorities in Canada divided nationalist organizations. Yet a mutual foe in the Soviet Union and its apologists, and in the interwar masters of Western Ukraine, resulted in inevitable similarities and in repeated cooperation for the greater and common good. Separately and collectively, nationalists lent the struggle in Ukraine both material and moral assistance. Political subjugation and cultural-linguistic persecution were also held to impose a sacred duty on Ukrainians privileged to live and prosper in Canadian freedom to preserve in the new homeland what was endangered in the old. This imperative, putting national-cultural survival at the top of the domestic community agenda, underlies the exploitation of the idea of Queen Elizabeth the Ukrainian. It equally explains why Ukrainian-Canadian nationalists were in the forefront of the lobby to redefine Canada as a 'mosaic,' backed by an official multiculturalism policy that would service their group's special needs.[14] Multiculturalism, in this context, meant a political commitment to the preservation of ethnocultural communities – as microsocieties with their own inner dynamics, infrastructures, and means of self-expression and perpetuation – aided by public funds and access to government institutions and programs.[15]

The vocal and articulate majority in the Ukrainian-Canadian community, nationalists have been most adept at projecting their concerns and ambitions as those uniting and animating all Ukrainian Canadians. Understandably, their view of contemporary Ukrainian history, and their accompanying sense of group mission, were not shared by the progressive minority. Well-publicized defections aside, until events behind the Iron Curtain in the 1980s turned the progressives' traditional world upside down, loyalty to Moscow withstood changes in the party line, the intellectual and political purges and the artificial famine in Soviet Ukraine in the 1930s, and persisting Russification and intolerance of dissent. Like nationalists, progressives appealed to the timeless values and principles Ukrainian Canadians inherited from their ancestors – through their struggle for human dignity, justice, freedom, and democracy – as their contribution to the Canadian 'mosaic.'[16] But glorying in the existence and achievements of the Soviet Ukrainian state, progressives attached no urgency to group survival; they had no need for, and in fact rejected, multiculturalism as perceived and promoted by their nationalist rivals.[17] Their group mission was not Ukrainian specific. Progressives argued that exploitation and discrimination, historically in Ukraine and now in Canada, made Ukrainian Canadians apostles of equality and brotherhood; they also argued that because their homeland had a special bond with one of the world's two superpowers, progressives in particular were uniquely placed to promote international peace and goodwill.[18]

Fundamentally different interpretations of Ukrainian Canadians' relationship to Ukraine divided nationalists and progressives over the meaning of Ukrainianism in Canada, including its implications for individual group members. Yet the importance of the homeland tie made it impossible for the two factions to ignore each other and each other's propaganda and programs. The relevance and appeal of both nationalist and progressive messages hinged in part on the attitudes of mainstream Canadian society towards ethnic assimilation and ethnic group maintenance, and towards specific ethnic groups and the men, women, and children who composed them. But success ultimately rested on the degree and quality of commitment by the mass of Ukrainian Canadians to the agenda of community activists and spokespersons. For the better part of one hundred years, progressive and nationalist elites sought to popularize their points of view among successive generations of Ukrainian Canadians, monitoring their activities and instructing them in their responsibilities towards the cause whose righteousness justified this invasion of their lives. In nationalist circles in particular, membership in the Ukrainian nation and its accruing obligations were seen as involuntary. Every Ukrainian Canadian belonged to the group, and was accountable for its image and status in the larger Canadian context and for its continued commitment to Ukraine.

In the exploitation of her Ukrainian blood to ensure an environment sympathetic to nationalist goals, Queen Elizabeth's gender is irrelevant: inherited from her father, the crucial genes will be passed on in her son. But 'other' Ukrainian women in Canada – immigrants, symbolic figures imported vicariously as models and sources of inspiration, and the swelling ranks of the native born – have found the blood tie more onerous on their sex. The involuntary nature of group membership subordinated individual women and their lives to the collective experience and needs of the whole, while imposing unsolicited rules and attentions that may or may not have been welcome. The involuntary nature of group membership also meant the unquestioned acceptance of women as legitimate participants in the group experience. Those who conformed to community expectations existed as actors in their own right, both identified and vigorously identifying with what was perceived as the general good; the remainder existed as objects of community concern to be harnessed and moulded in that good's interests. Ukrainian Canadians' peculiar needs and predicament resulted in a perception of women that at once embraced and transcended their procreative function and their traditional prescribed role. The dependence of group survival on the commitment of future generations to a community agenda magnified the importance of motherhood and homemaking. But women were also expected to participate, actively and knowledgeably, in the public sphere, representing their sex within their own community and their group within mainstream circles.

The first (pre-1914) immigration of Ukrainians to Canada saw peasant men significantly outnumber peasant women, and the sexual imbalance was even more pronounced among the intelligentsia. Community life remained male dominated, even though the disinclination of major figures from the male intelligentsia in Galicia to emigrate elevated lesser individuals to positions of unprecedented influence. No leading member of the much smaller female intelligentsia emigrated, and the small size and 'village' character of the educated male immigration[19] had a direct impact on the number and background of the women, as these men's wives and daughters, available to assume the leadership of their sex. Other members of the immigrant male intelligentsia married in North America, choosing wives from their own circle or from the already acculturated, older Ukrainian immigration in the United States. Wasyl Swystun and Jaroslaw Arsenych, for example, married Pennsylvanian girls who had come to Canada as single immigrants; community activists in their own right, both Olha Swystun and Olha Arsenych (sister of Michael Luchkovich, Ukrainian Canadians' first member of parliament) taught school in the bloc settlements.[20] Emigration also separated Ukrainian peasant women from 'natural' leaders in the village, as Rome's proscription against a married Greek Catholic clergy prevented priests' wives from donning their traditional mantle in the bloc settlements of western Canada. The four Sisters Servants of Mary Immaculate who accompanied the first Ukrainian monastic priests to Canada in 1902 were an inadequate substitute; besides their youthfulness (the oldest, their superior, was twenty-six, the youngest barely twenty), the nuns worked within and for the secular community without joining it.[21]

Despite this leadership vacuum, and despite illiteracy and prejudice against women in public life, women did come together in groups to take part in community affairs. In rural and urban localities across Canada, sisterhoods cleaned and beautified parish churches and raised funds for their own and parish projects. During the First World War, for example, the sisterhood at Ss Volodymyr and Olha Church in Winnipeg bought Christmas gifts for Ukrainian 'enemy aliens' interned in nearby Brandon.[22] Women's auxiliaries served local *chytalni*, *prosvita* associations, and *narodni domy* (national halls). Women also participated in the life of these institutions as individuals, attending their lectures and concerts, acting in their plays, singing in their choirs, and cooking for their communal meals. Some, like Paranka Oleinik in rural Alberta, elected secretary of the Stry branch of the Ukrainian Social Democratic Party in the spring of 1918, occupied official positions.[23]

The most significant women's group, however, was connected with the intelligentsia and reflected the predilection of the crystallizing community elite for city life. Formed in Winnipeg in 1916 on the initiative of the recently elected MLA, Taras Ferley, the Ukrainian Women's Enlightenment Association (UWEA) represented the Ukrainian response to women's enfranchisement in Manitoba. In Ferley's words, its goal was 'to be concerned not only with childrearing and homemaking but also with the need for women to show interest in national and political affairs in order to become the equals of other citizens of their country.'[24] Although club members saw themselves as models and sources of inspiration for their unorganized and unenlightened sisters, and attempted to organize women's groups in rural Manitoba on their example,[25] more extensive organization awaited a larger pool of women with the requisite time, commitment, and talents. The UWEA has since been heralded as the predecessor of the organized Ukrainian women's movement in Canada. But while it and other groups provided a base for subsequent large-scale mobilization and activity, their efforts were modest and their influence limited. In the pioneer period, men and not women dominated discussions of women's relationship to community-defined goals.

The interwar establishment of nationwide women's organizations and the emergence of a new female leadership defined this relationship further and brought the interplay among class, gender, and ethnicity into focus. Ukrainian-Canadian women were perceived to have special needs, wants, and obligations *as Ukrainians* that justified and necessitated their organization separate from other Canadian women. They also had special needs, wants, and obligations *as women* that justified and necessitated their separate organization within community structures. However, at the same time as ethnicity and gender unified women and supplied the rationale for organization, the factionalization characteristic of Ukrainian-Canadian community life divided them along ideological lines. It pitted those whose first commitment was to the class struggle against those who identified with a captive Ukrainian nation, and it splintered the latter into hostile and competing groups. Regardless of the independence women's organizations enjoyed in their own sphere, they also functioned as affiliates of the major male-dominated institutions that defined the organized community and controlled community decision making. This situation contrasted sharply with interwar Galicia, where the Women's Union (Soiuz ukrainok) – a mass organization founded to improve the quality of village life, mobilize women in the nation's service, and seek international forums to publicize the Ukrainian cause – was unaffiliated with any male body and jealously guarded its independence in community life.[26] The fact that Ukrainian-Canadian women organized outside the Canadian mainstream and within community structures under nationalist and progressive banners confirmed at the outset the primacy of Ukrainian politics in dictating a role for their sex. Moreover, the individuals who formed the nucleus of a female organizational elite were shown to be motivated not by narrowly defined feminist goals but by the national or class goals of community agenda.

The virtual absence of an immigrant female intelligentsia ensured that leadership roles early devolved, uncontested, to a young Canadian-educated generation that had spent its formative years in the new homeland. Comparative ease of movement in mainstream society gave these women, sometimes barely out of their teens, an influence and authority among older peasant immigrants and isolated farm wives that education alone would not have warranted or their youthfulness otherwise permitted. But the new leadership was not simply the beneficiary of Canadian schooling. It was also the product of the private *bursy* or residential institutes the Ukrainian community erected in major prairie cities as centres of Ukrainian consciousness and activity. At the helm stood the Mohylianky, female students at the Petro Mohyla Institute in Saskatoon (est. 1916), who underwent aggressive Ukrainization while pursuing their studies beyond the rural school. In 1925, acknowledging their sisterhood with Ukrainian women abroad, the Mohylianky launched the first concerted campaign among Ukrainian women in Canada, raising funds for the Ukrainian National Women's Council in Prague to send a delegate to the International Council of Women meeting in Washington.[27] The following year the Mohylianky formed the Ukrainian Women's Association of Canada (UWAC) to unite Ukrainian women across the country behind the nationalist cause. Olha Swystun became the group's first president.[28] Although conceived as nondenominational, the UWAC, like the Mohyla Institute, soon identified with the new Ukrainian Greek Orthodox church. The insistence of this church on a married clergy returned to women a traditional source of female leadership, although priests' wives never supplanted the laity in the UWAC.

Interwar immigrants provided a second pool of female leaders. One such woman was twenty-three-year-old Kharytia Kononenko, who came to a Saskatchewan farm in 1923 but soon relocated to Saskatoon, where she taught and served as matron at the Mohyla Institute. Her Eastern Ukrainian and prominent family background, education, culture, and intelligence impressed students and staff alike, and she was welcomed for her influence on the national consciousness of the *bursa*'s Canadian charges.[29] Kononenko was an important participant in the gestation of the UWAC and the Mohylianky's physical link with the Ukrainian women's movement overseas, but she could not adjust to Canada and returned to Europe in 1925. More lasting in their impact were women immigrating in company with veterans of the revolutionary struggles or otherwise gravitating to the ideological organizations these men established. They formed women's branches or affiliates of the monarchist Canadian Sitch Organization and its successor, the United Hetman Organization, as well as of the republican Ukrainian War Veterans' Association and the more prominent Ukrainian National Federation (UNF) it spawned. The most important interwar 'émigré' women's group affiliated with the UNF, which was sympathetic to the militant nationalism of the right-wing Organization of Ukrainian Nationalists working underground in Galicia, although the Ukrainian Women's Organization of Canada (UWOC) dated its origins from 1930 in women's branches of the Ukrainian War Veterans' Asssociation. Except for a one-year hiatus, Anastasia Pavlychenko served as the UWOC's sole president until 1940; her husband, a European-trained plant ecologist who joined the staff of the University of Saskatchewan after upgrading his qualifications, was prominent in the UNF and undoubtedly exerted an influence on his wife, who began her community career in the UWAC. Anastasia had initially come to Canada in 1923 as a young woman of twenty to visit her elder brother, a political émigré, but stayed to make it her home.

While the Canadian-educated offspring of the peasant pioneer immigration had a prairie, often rural, background, the new immigrant leadership tended from the beginning to be urban and was as active in eastern as in western Canada. Organizational work proceeded outward and downward from the city headquarters of the UWAC and the UWOC, and from directives originating with their central executives and national conventions. National and regional organizers (like Rozha Kovalska for the UWOC in eastern Canada, and Savella Stechishin for the UWAC in the West) also visited the countryside and remote resource frontiers, along with the more accessible towns and cities, to appeal to women directly. Local initiative came from female teachers in particular; often *bursa* graduates and far superior in education to the surrounding women, they enjoyed their greatest influence in the bloc settlements. With some four thousand members compared with the UWOC's six hundred on the eve of the Second World War, the moderate UWAC was by far the more attractive nationalist alternative. It drew its strength from the peasant pioneer immigration in the prairie provinces, where most of the hundred or more branches were located in the bloc settlements at rural crossroads communities marked by their Ukrainian church and hall, and perhaps by a school or country store.[30] Fourteen of twenty-seven UWOC branches, in contrast, were located in Ontario, reinforcing the contention that it addressed interwar immigrants, perhaps already with an urban background, who chose to live in major industrial centres or resource towns.[31]

In the 1920s and 1930s, Ukrainian Catholic women stood on the periphery of the nationwide organization of nationalist women under female activists. Although local sisterhoods had existed since the pioneer period and women were active in the interwar Ukrainian Catholic Brotherhood, the Ukrainian Catholic Women's League of Canada

(UCWL) was not formed until 1944. Impetus came from women's increased wartime responsibilities and the growing feeling among a second generation that parish work alone was too confining.[32] Mary Dyma, the first UCWL president, typified this outlook. A promising gymnasium graduate, her studies in Galicia interrupted by war and revolution, and by humanitarian work among military and civilian casualties, she had come to Canada in 1920 at the invitation of an aunt. Dyma received her BA from the University of Manitoba three years later; active in Winnipeg municipal politics and mainstream women's circles, she unsuccessfully ran for the provincial legislature in 1936. The distribution pattern of UCWL members and branches initially copied that of the UWAC, pointing to the same origins and similar constituencies in the peasant pioneer immigration. The UCWL grew quickly, however, to become the largest of all Ukrainian-Canadian women's organizations, with some six thousand members in the mid 1980s.[33]

Between the wars, progressive women never organized independently of the main male-dominated Ukrainian Labour-Farmer Temple Association (ULFTA). Both the Women's Section of the ULFTA, established in 1922, and its branches owed much to male organizers, instructors, and agitators representing the authority of the Central Executive Committee, and a female elite never took control of the organization of women's groups as in the nationalist community.[34] The life story of an activist like Mary Vinohradova, who served on the national executive of the Women's Section from its inception and repeatedly toured the country on its behalf, illustrates the appeal of the progressive call to the class struggle: she had fewer than three years' schooling in Galicia before she was kept home to babysit, followed by field labour for the local landlord at the age of ten, jobs as a domestic, cook, and chambermaid after her emigration to Canada in 1912, and work as a daily help and seamstress after her marriage until she was forced by ill health to stop in 1939.[35] Half of the Women's Section's reputed two thousand members in the late 1930s lived in Ontario, British Columbia, and Quebec, reflecting the relevance of the progressive message to a urban proletariat putting down and pulling up roots in factory and resource towns according to the dictates of the marketplace. Another four hundred came from the Winnipeg area. Alberta was the only province to recruit farm women on any scale.[36]

Stalin's support of Hitler in the early stages of the Second World War led to the banning of the ULFTA, although progressives regrouped after Germany invaded the Soviet Union and the latter became Canada's ally. The ULFTA's postwar successor, the Association of United Ukrainian Canadians, preserved the idea of separate women's branches. In nationalist circles, the war brought women closer together. In 1940 the nationalist community created an *ad hoc* superstructure, the Ukrainian Canadian Committee (UCC), to coordinate the Ukrainian-Canadian war effort and to speak with a united voice on behalf of the Ukrainian nation in Europe. Women's organizations, to their chagrin, were excluded as independent participants,[37] and their delegates attended the first UCC congress in 1943 through their male counterparts. The UWAC, the UWOC, the UCWL, and the women's section of the now-defunct United Hetman Organization formed a parallel Ukrainian Canadian Women's Committee (UCWC) in 1944. When the UCC was made permanent after the war, the UCWC continued its separate existence.

The Second World War also precipitated a stream of anti-communist refugees. Some newcomers eschewed separate women's organizations altogether and joined the mixed scouting association, Plast, which sprang up in cities where this third immigration congregated in large numbers. Those with right-wing sympathies either strengthened UWOC branches or joined the Women's Association of the more extremist Canadian League for the Liberation of Ukraine, founded by displaced persons supporting the Bandera wing of the Organization of Ukrainian Nationalists in Europe. Women who rejected right-wing politics faced a novel situation. Religion, in Greek Catholic Galicia, had not fractured a broad coalition like the Women's Union. In Canada, however, nationalist women mirrored the Catholic-Orthodox split dividing the Ukrainian-Canadian community, and the fact that the newcomers found the Orthodox UWAC a less comfortable home than the Catholic UCWL coloured the two organizations' postwar profiles and fortunes.

From their inception, the goal of Ukrainian-Canadian women's organizations was to politicize their sex, rallying women behind either the national or the class struggle and instructing them in their roles and responsibilities in aid of the cause. To this end, dedicated activists visited hundreds of localities to propagandize the grassroots and draw previously unorganized individuals into a common network under a central authority. The ideological press issued by the national offices of different organizations reached greater numbers more regularly and more effectively, and, augmented by circulars, special printed lectures, and activity or discussion suggestions, became the principal communications link between the leadership and the rank and file. The effect of nationwide organization was to broaden women's horizons and increase the scope of their activities; at the same time, it encouraged conformity in their thinking and behaviour. Nationwide organization also enhanced women's sense of belonging to a larger Ukrainian community, within Canada and throughout the world, and emphasized the international content of other ties – Catholicism and communism. The great majority of Ukrainian-Canadian women never responded to the command to organize, even if they consciously identified with nationalist or progressive objectives. Together but from opposite sides of the coin, the thoughts and actions of female activists and the grassroots response to them measured the degree of identification by Ukrainian-Canadian women with the interests of their community, particularly as it envisaged a role for their sex.

The interplay between elite and popular concepts of women and their role in the Ukrainian-Canadian experience showed that the masses shared visions and prejudices with community leaders, evidence of both the latters' rapport with the popular mind and the success of their propaganda. The exclusiveness of other visions and prejudices, however, revealed the frequent irrelevance of the community's ambitions and perspectives to those whom it claimed to represent. Traditionally, Ukrainian-Canadian women were the involuntary (although not necessarily unwilling) focus of community expectations, pressures, and dictates that stressed the primacy of their role in the home yet demanded their participation in community life. Later, women became the involuntary (although again not necessarily unwilling) focus of a popular sentiment in which the female figure symbolized the essence of the Ukrainian-Canadian identity – a cultural ethnic consciousness that attested to the gulf separating the politicized community from the grassroots. Two group myths constructed around the turn-of-the-century peasant immigrant woman in western Canada, one of them popular and regionally based, the other national in scope and cultivated by the formal community, reflected incompatible views of both Ukrainian Canadians' Ukrainian heritage and their role in Canadian nation building.

Whether cultivated and exploited by community elites (male or female) as part of a political message, or expressing spontaneous grassroots emotions, the images, roles, and myths created about and for Ukrainian-Canadian women over the past century said relatively little about their lives. Intended to serve the prejudices and self-interests of their creators, they were often divorced from the reality and practical options of ordinary women, and from women's own attitudes towards group membership and its impositions. But the images, roles, and myths created about and for Ukrainian-Canadian women said a great deal about the way Ukrainian Canadians at elite and grassroots levels saw themselves, and about the way they identified women with the issues and concerns of their group. In the history of Ukrainian women in Canada, questions of ethnicity and class have been more important than 'women's rights,' with questions of gender subordinated to and interpreted within the context of the perceived needs of the ethnic group and/or class to which women belonged. Because of this dominance of ethnicity and class over gender, the present study neither places women at the centre of their past nor adopts as its framework 'female' issues and concerns related to women's position in society. Instead, it places Ukrainian Canadians at the centre, with the issues and concerns that formed their collective consciousness and purpose as the underlying and unifying theme.

1

Failing to Measure Up:
The Peasant Immigrant

On an isolated homestead in northern Alberta old Marta Yaramko puttered in her flower garden, distracted by the needling pain that she sensed signalled her death. As she laboured, thoughts of immortality, good and evil, human hope and futility crowded her head, and she marvelled that she, a simple Ukrainian peasant woman, dared to contemplate such lofty themes. She thought, too, about her own life with only her flowers and the constant wind as companions, alienated from the past of her parents, the self of her youth, and the future of her children alike. 'She was a part of Canada, of course,' Marta reflected:

> Somewhere, carefully tucked away, she even kept her naturalization certificate. To get it she had merely to declare before a witness that she loved the country and would be loyal to it. But Canada seemed to her less a country than an immense map with strange cut-outs, especially in the North; or was it no more than a sky, a deep and dream-filled waiting, a future in suspense? Sometimes it seemed her life had been spent on the edge of the country, in some vague zone of wind and loneliness that Canada might yet embrace. For how could those in Volyn, now reduced to a handful, old and complaining, have reached out and touched it? They were no longer quite Ukrainian but not quite Canadian either, poor lost folk, so discouraged it seemed there was no way they could help themselves except by disappearing.
>
> She raised a baffled gaze to the sky, wide and immense ... 'Will you ever tell us why we came so far, what wind blew us here, what

we're doing here, the poor of Ukraine, in these farthest prairies of Canada?'[1]

Gabrielle Roy's poignant tale of Marta's search for purpose and identity in the solitude of her marriage, her immigrant condition, and an overwhelming landscape captures the marginality of the Ukrainian women who settled western Canada in the opening decades of the twentieth century.

During this first period of Ukrainian settlement (1891–1920), which peasants from Galicia and Bukovyna dominated, most female immigrants came not on their own to try their luck in a new country but as members of family units – wives, mothers, daughters, sisters. Until 1910, only one-fifth of arrivals were adult women, slightly more than one-half adult males; over the next four years, when family migration declined, adult males made up 72.8 per cent of all arrivals.[2] Women's dependent and minority status, together with a settlement pattern that isolated them from Canadian society, reduced their visibility. While single men roamed the country in search of work, families tended to homestead, so that the vast majority of women (97.5 per cent in 1911) resided in the bloc settlements of the prairie provinces. Here males outnumbered females by a slim margin of 5 to 4, compared with 4 to 1 and 9 to 1, respectively, for the resource towns and cities of Ontario and British Columbia.[3] The bloc surrounded Ukrainians with their own kind, and encouraged a lifestyle that preserved their language, peasant customs, and gender roles. Although the immigrant generation experienced the trauma of uprooting and bore the brunt of pioneering in a strange and virgin land, in many respects it was less challenged and changed by the new environment than its offspring. And women were less challenged and changed than men. While circumstances forced the male pioneer to compete and seek work and to conduct business in an often hostile 'English' world, his wife remained on the farm.

Cut off from Canadian society, already separated from the ancestral village, Ukrainian peasant immigrant women were indeed invisible, isolated, and marginalized. Yet by reinforcing and even exaggerating their peasant cultural baggage, isolation and marginalization conspired to make them noticed. Since women were perceived to be more backward than men, they stood in greater need of 'modernization' and 'emancipation' if Ukrainians were to fulfil the ambitions others had for them. Rival elites – one Anglo-Canadian, the other Ukrainian – each anxious to win the mass of Ukrainian peasant immigrants to its world view, cast a critical eye on the peasant immigrant woman. This is not to say that women dominated the discussions or the agenda of these elites, for they did not, but female images and roles were dictated by the priorities and prejudices of outside interests, and not by the peasant immigrant woman herself. These interests did not necessarily address her needs and concerns, as women were defined first and foremost in terms of their group membership and their effect on group fortunes. Whether the peasant immigrant woman had her own plans for the future or not, or felt strongly about her lot one way or the other, she would not be left to her own devices.

To middle-class Anglo-Canadian nation builders, the group fortunes at stake were their own, and the issue was how Ukrainian peasant immigrant women (as Ukrainians and as women) affected their vision of Canada. To the Ukrainian immigrant intelligentsia, group membership and group fortunes were understood to be Ukrainian, although precisely what that meant was interpreted differently by different factions in the infant community. How the Greek Catholic church, secular nationalists, Protestants, and socialists perceived the peasant immigrant woman depended in the first instance on their respective world views, rooted in the religious-political divisions of late nineteenth-century Galicia, as they attempted to secure and define Ukrainians' place in the new country. In the process, they were influenced by the peasant immigrants' old-country heritage, the peculiarities of the Canadian environment, and developments in the homeland that heightened the national consciousness of some and the class consciousness of others. How these groups perceived the peasant immigrant woman depended in the second instance on women's specific relationship to their ideologies and goals, as gender was seen to give them special roles and responsibilities. Subsequent generations of community activists, intent on identifying the mass of Ukrainian Canadians with their propaganda and programs, would build on the base provided by the pioneer intelligentsia.

A few short weeks before stopping at the Immigration Hall in Winnipeg on the last stage of her journey to a Canadian homestead, the Ukrainian peasant immigrant woman had been part of a well-defined village society. At the same time, the social and economic crisis that was forcing the desperate and ambitious overseas had undermined its traditional lifestyle and rocked the old order. The influence of the Polish landlord, the Greek Catholic priest, and the Jewish innkeeper, shopkeeper, moneylender, and leaseholder was challenged as local reading clubs (*chytalni*), cooperatives, and loan societies sought to enlighten and awaken the national consciousness of the peasantry and to put commerce into Ukrainians' own hands. But the church and the tavern remained major village institutions – the one encouraging submission to God and priest, the other to alcohol in a province where alcoholism was rampant[4] – and they, together with their new opposition, dominated social life. If the peasant needed work, either because he was landless or because of a shortfall in his farming operation, he still looked first to the manor. His wife and children earned a fraction of what he did labouring in the fields, while his children often tended flocks and herds or his daughters became manor servants in return for room and board.[5] Ukrainian peasant girls also worked for wealthier village Jews and as domestics in Polish and Jewish homes in larger urban centres, employment that immigrants to Canada would equate with moral corruption and sexual exploitation.[6] Village girls returning from work in the city were bearers of modernization, although they became sources of tension when they lorded it over their peers, flaunting their foreign phrases, for example, and making fun of the peasants' clothes.

Life's cycles, the seasons, and holy days dictated the rhythms of village life, their observance regulated by ancient rituals and superstitions fused with Christianity. Although its hold was weakening, the peasants' belief system governed individual actions, prescribing behaviour for every situation, and provided different members of society with specific roles and responsibilities. Those assigned to women emphasized their sex's association with evil, fertility, and the hearth. Pestilence and other scourges assumed female personae in peasant lore; village 'witches' were blamed for damaging storms and dry cows; and, since all peasant societies distrust the successful, the woman always able to find mushrooms was held to be in league with the devil. Taboos and rituals in the interests of her household's health, happiness, and prosperity permeated the peasant woman's daily routines; others, equally elaborate and with similar ends, guided her through the major female passages of marriage and childbirth. In some regions, the peasant wife ensured a bountiful harvest by sprinkling the unsown fields, her husband, the plough, and cattle with a palm leaf dipped in holy water, then casting the remains, mixed with an egg, into the furrow.

She also ensured her family's safety; a mother guarded against the evil eye, for example, by sucking out suspected bewitchment from her child's forehead and spitting it, with the correct incantation, into the four corners of the room.[7] Until modernization and education robbed her society of its belief in the efficacy of magic, the need to appease the spirits, and the effectiveness of taboos and rituals for 'good' to triumph over 'evil,' the peasant woman had considerable power. On her knowledge and actions (but also on her failure to do the right thing) rested the fortunes of her household.

In the nonspiritual world, a woman was indispensable to the peasant family unit, not only responsible for the house, children, and garden but also expected to contribute to the farming operation. As such, marriage was considered inevitable, and carried prestige as the induction into adulthood; 'single people,' the saying went, 'are not human beings.' Although military service delayed marriage for males, a girl married in her late teens or early twenties: in 1904, 27.9 per cent of Ukrainian brides in Galicia were under twenty years of age, 59.4 per cent under twenty-four.[8] Since a wedding entailed the formal exchange of family property, it was not simply a private commitment between bride and groom but engaged the interest of the entire village. Ukrainian proverbs testified to the importance of the peasant woman: 'Being without a wife is like being without hands.' They also indicated that women were ultimately lesser beings ('A woman is long in hair, short in mind') and male property ('An unbeaten wife is like an unsharpened scythe').[9] Women's inferior status in Ukrainian peasant society had numerous expressions. The land a woman received as part of her dowry, for example, was controlled by her husband even if registered in her name. A wife traditionally walked behind her mate, a practice condemned by immigrants in Canada who claimed that the English, and even Ukrainian children, derisively referred to it as the 'Galician style' of walking. Finally, sexual transgressions were punished more severely in the case of the woman than the man.[10]

Although the argument has recently been made that conditions among the Ukrainian peasantry were not as bad as they have traditionally been painted and in some respects actually saw improvement, poverty and its companions were a fact of life.[11] Almost 90 per cent of Ukrainian peasant women in late nineteenth-century Galicia were illiterate. High infant mortality (210/1000 between 1904 and 1909), aided by disease, malnutrition, and uninformed childcare, accompanied a birth rate (46/1000) exceeding that in Austria as a whole by more than seven births per thousand.[12] Basic cooking, a starch-rich diet, and casual ideas about hygiene attested to and reinforced the peasants' low standard of living, but they also reflected the housewife's lack of skills and nutritional knowledge and the limited resources available. Yet life had its amusements, its vanities, and its beauty. Women took pride in the coral that highlighted their strings of beads. Girls gathered on winter evenings to tell their fortunes; they decorated special eggs to offer young men of their fancy on Easter morning; they danced in the village on Sunday; and they joined in community celebrations like Ivan Kupalo or midsummer night's eve, when free love received popular sanction. Peasant folk art gave women a fulfilling creative outlet. Moreover, their handicrafts were increasingly extolled and encouraged in intelligentsia circles, both for their national significance and for their profitability as a cottage industry; this success enhanced women's self-esteem and won male converts to the idea of female education.[13]

That female education should even be an issue, or that the lot of Ukrainian peasant women should receive attention, emerged in part from the general campaign to enlighten and politicize the Galician village. These issues were also a concern of the new women's organizations among the female intelligentsia and the more conservative circles of townswomen and priests' wives and daughters. Despite often different priorities and ideas about women's place in society, these women's groups supported female education and deemed it necessary for the Ukrainian cause. Demand for access to institutions of higher learning benefited the privileged few; emphasis on self-help and agitation for practical education and enlightenment among peasant women (including home economics and handicrafts instruction), outreach to urban domestics, and the organization of female workers focused on the masses. Natalia Kobrynska, the nationally oriented socialist and feminist who founded the Ukrainian women's movement in 1884, also spearheaded the establishment of rural daycare centres and communal kitchens to help peasant women as a growing money economy obliged them to work outside the home without relieving their domestic responsibilities. Concrete results prior to 1914 were modest, but claims of a significant breakthrough in peasant attitudes were made.[14] Proof of successful politicization were the village women who participated, albeit in limited fashion, in their local reading club. Between 1897 and 1910, approximately 5 per cent of *chytalnia* membership was female, although it declined proportionately over the period, tended to be ephemeral, and was heavily weighted in favour of unmarried girls (while male recruits remained in the club after marriage, women did not). That women were not more active has been attributed to the patriarchal nature of Ukrainian peasant society, women's greater isolation and thus less openness to innovation, and the indifference of the male leadership of the national movement in Lviv to their involvement, partly because of sexism and partly because women lacked the vote.[15]

In sum, the Ukrainian women who immigrated to Canada in the years before 1920 were exposed to complex and often contradictory influences representing alternately 'tradition' and stability and 'modernization' and change. Experiences were not identical, however, and the specific cultural baggage of individual women reflected this difference. Nor did the new country constitute a microcosm of the old. Although letters to the pioneer press testified to literacy among women together with a keen interest in issues affecting their group and their sex, Canada attracted few female activists. The vast majority of arrivals were peasants – unworldly, steeped in superstition and ritual although not immune to the changes underway in their villages, and accustomed to a mean and frugal existence. They were essential to the functioning of the family as the basic unit of production and consumption, yet they were regarded as inferior beings subject to the authority of their menfolk. This cultural baggage would be the vehicle through which women coped with and adapted to new and strange surroundings. It would also serve as the basis of the negative stereotype of the Ukrainian peasant immigrant woman that fueled the demand, among both Anglo-Canadians and the Ukrainian immigrant intelligentsia, for reform.

Her reputation at the hands of an Anglo-Canadian and Ukrainian immigrant elite was probably far from the mind of the woman, caught up in the emotional turmoil and events of the moment, who stepped off the wagon onto a quarter section of Canadian land. Perhaps the decision to emigrate had been hers,[16] but like all emigrants, whether looking forward to their adventure or not, she had bid farewell to loved ones and everything familiar and dear. If she joined a husband already working or farming in Canada, she had borne additional burdens as head of the family responsible for the mechanics of the voyage and her children's well-being. In all likelihood, she had taken her first train ride and boat trip (in the hold of a transatlantic steamer), seen her first street lights, encountered her first cook stove, and bought

Ukrainian peasant immigrant in the sheepskin coat and headshawl that symbolized her 'foreignness' and inferiority to Anglo-Canadians. St Julien, Saskatchewan, 1921

her first loaf of the 'English' bread that seemed so tasteless. In all
likelihood, too, if she had ignored the advice of the immigrant intelligentsia to avoid stares and ridicule by changing into 'clothes of the
world' before reaching North America, she had suffered indignities
for the peasant attire that made her an exotic sight on a Canadian
railway platform.[17] She had travelled a thousand miles through the
rock and forest of the Canadian Shield and crossed a plain that appeared almost as unpeopled and endless. Fresh from her first trial with
the myriads of mosquitoes that the immigrants would say sucked more
Ukrainian blood than the landlords they had escaped, she now looked
out on the mixture of prairie and bush that was to be her new home.

Canadian pioneering conditions promoted both change and continuity in women's lives. For at least one woman, the shock of a river-
bank dugout accommodating four adults and ten children ended any
illusions of Canada as a paradise as painted by earlier emigrants.[18]
Homestead regulations required each family to live on its quarter
section, so despite their Ukrainian character and the efforts of villagers
and kin to settle together, the blocs lacked the closeness and support
networks of old-country village life and failed to replicate old-country
communities. One effect was to exaggerate loneliness. Life in Canada
was materially good but pervaded by homesickness, a settler commented in 1903, citing the suicide of a sixty-year-old widow who lacked
the money to return home.[19] Sometimes the wilderness won. In 1916
the bones of a Ukrainian woman were found in the Shoal Lake district
of Manitoba, almost six years after she went into the bush to look for
her cattle, leaving two babies at home. The skeleton was identified by
the woman's beads and cross and by the pitchfork taken as protection
against wolves. Her husband had been away working at the time.[20]

The homesickness, isolation, and workload of the immigrant wife
intensified when cash shortages forced her husband to leave the homestead in search of paid work. Years later, a pioneer recalled how such
women braved the mosquitoes and mud, lifting their skirts 'clear up
to ... [their] armpits' to walk twenty miles with a basket of eggs to his
rural post office and store in hopes of a letter and to buy a few basic
supplies. Wives in another district hoping for mail from their husbands
assembled weekly at their local post office on a prearranged date so
they could use the opportunity for much needed socializing.[21] Visiting
via the footpaths that were soon worn from homestead to homestead,
occasional trips to town, and attendance at church services or events

Homesick mothers with children visiting the nearby Methodist mission to have their pictures taken to send home. Rural Alberta, nd

in the local Ukrainian hall helped to combat individual loneliness while cultivating a larger sense of community.

Emigration and the physical isolation of the homestead placed unaccustomed emphasis on the nuclear family.[22] Women who no longer lived with or near their husbands' families, as was customary in the peasant village, became their own mistresses with their domestic power increased. Yet pioneering conditions preserved and reinforced women's traditional role within the family socioeconomic unit. The poverty, simple tools, and subsistence agriculture characteristic of Ukrainian homesteading put a premium on physical labour and ensured that women remained essential to survival. All family members were expected to pull their weight, and cases were recorded of settlers who brought their mothers to Canada as part of an extended family and later abandoned them when they became too old to work.[23] In

That all-important letter from absent loved ones. Wahstao Methodist
Mission, Alberta, 1909–14

some ways, the position of Ukrainian peasant women worsened as
pioneering required them to perform heavier work and spend more
time in the fields than they had been used to in the old country. A
1917 government investigation into conditions in rural Ukrainian districts in the prairie provinces discovered that two-thirds of women
surveyed regularly worked on the land; nearly all children were given
farmyard chores as soon as they were old enough, and a good proportion worked in the fields as well.[24] While such labour undoubtedly
helped progress on the Ukrainian homestead, it did nothing for a
woman's health, her childcare, or her housekeeping. As evidence of
the detrimental impact of farm work on women's domestic responsibilities, the investigators also found that Ukrainian families ate more
varied food in winter because the housewife had more time to prepare
it.[25]

   This investigation was headed by James S. Woodsworth, the Methodist minister and social reformer behind All People's Mission in North

Market day, breaking the isolation of the homestead and providing women with an opportunity to socialize. Sheho, Saskatchewan, 1909

End Winnipeg whose book, *Strangers Within Our Gates* (1909), had expressed his concerns about the effects of immigration on the Canadian fabric. Analysis of the data from just two districts, both in Saskatchewan and settled at approximately the same time, reveals that Ukrainian agricultural progress had a direct bearing on home life. At Prince Albert, northeast of Saskatoon, over 90 per cent of the farms were a quarter section or less, with less than 10 per cent of their acreage broken; in the Hafford area east of North Battleford, only a third of the farms were a quarter section or less, almost half of the land was broken, and livestock was significantly more numerous. Hafford boasted better general hygienic and sanitary conditions in the home, superior clothing and furniture, and more solidly built and slightly larger houses. School attendance, another measure of prosperity in that families no longer required their children's labour, was higher.[26] Two-thirds of all families in the survey lived in homes of two rooms or less. The housewife received generally good marks for the home's cleanliness, although the verdict on the quality and neatness of her family's clothing, and on the home's furnishings, was more mixed. In half the districts, a majority of homes grew flowers in the

Cutting wheat with a sickle. If there were no older siblings to babysit, young children accompanied their mothers to the fields. Stuartburn, Manitoba, 1918

house and/or garden, but in only a minority of cases was evidence of women's handicrafts, either embroidered items or woven rugs, mentioned. Unlike men in the survey, over 90 per cent of women could not speak English, and virtually none were able to read and write it; 70 per cent were totally illiterate. Over half of all homes had no books and subscribed to no newspaper. Access to medical care was limited: in the Stuartburn colony in southeastern Manitoba only one mother out of eighty-five had had a doctor or midwife present at her last delivery. Most homes also remained without the labour-saving devices and technology that would ease women's workload and isolation; few had cream separators, few had telephones, and few shopped through the mail-order catalogue.[27]

Regardless of the objectivity and competence of its investigators,

Family outside partially plastered dwelling. Both preparation and application of the plaster, primarily a mixture of clay and straw or cut slough grass, were typically women's work. Lamont, Alberta, c.1920

who included the Ukrainian Wasyl Swystun, the Woodsworth survey contains the only 'scientific' and quantifiable data specifically addressing conditions among Ukrainian peasant immigrant women to be gathered by their contemporaries. It is important for this reason alone. The glimpse into women's lives that it provides is important for another reason as well. Just as her old-country legacy underlay the image of the peasant immigrant woman that emerged among both Anglo-Canadians and the Ukrainian immigrant intelligentsia, so was that image predicated upon the reality that existed in the bloc settlements, as the Canadian environment perpetuated or modified women's traditional status and roles. This is not to say that the image accurately mirrored the reality or that it was based upon empirical as opposed to impressionistic or biased evidence. In fact, reality itself was less important than what it was perceived to be. The perception of reality was also less important than how this perception was manipulated or interpreted to nurture an image of women that both revealed and served the prejudices and interests of the image's creators. The reasons why her contemporaries bothered with the Ukrainian peasant immigrant woman are as central to the issue of women's relationship to community elites as what the elites had to say.

While the focus of this study is the Ukrainian community and the propaganda and programs rival nationalist and progressive elites directed at women in the name of the Ukrainian nation or the class struggle, it would be a mistake to ignore the propaganda and programs of another competitor for the bodies and souls of Ukrainian-Canadian women. The reaction of middle-class Anglo-Canadian nation builders to Ukrainians' cultural baggage, and to the peasant immigrant woman in particular, formed part of the reality with which the latter had to cope and which contributed to her public stereotype. How Anglo-Canadians saw the peasant immigrant woman, and sought to use and transform her in the interests of Canadian nation building, also affected Ukrainian leaders. Not only were they sensitive to the dominant Anglo-Canadian image and influenced by it in their own attitudes, but nationalists had also to recognize and counter the threat that assimilation posed to their own agenda. Similar prejudices, tactics, and activities on the part of Ukrainian nationalists and Anglo-Canadian nation builders – albeit on behalf of different and conflicting ends – showed that women's subordination to the interests of the nation was not peculiar to Ukrainians or to suppressed peoples and minorities.

Bloc settlement, the Ukrainian language and way of life it sustained, and the special isolation women's immobility produced effectively segregated the Ukrainian peasant immigrant woman from Anglo-Canadian society. Less exposed to discrimination, exploitation, and direct assimilative pressures than her husband and children, she was shielded from the uglier aspects of Anglo-Canadian nativism. At the same time, her sheltered existence prolonged unwanted 'peasantness' and 'Ukrainianness' and delayed 'modernization' and 'emancipation,' causing anxiety among turn-of-the-century nation builders, worried about the impact of non-British immigration on Anglo-Canadian standards and ideals, who believed in the family, with the woman at its heart, as the basis of a healthy society. Ukrainian attitudes and practices as they pertained to the treatment of women, and to women's own behaviour and outlook, were a concern of middle-class missionaries, educators, and assorted women's groups committed to social reform and the preservation of Canada's British heritage. Their image of Ukrainian womanhood reflected the immigrants' peasant origins and the pioneering conditions in which they lived, but it was also limited by them. Anglo-Canadian women, for example, were ignorant of the Ukrainian women's movement that in some respects (as in Kobrynska's theoretical contribution to feminist socialism) was as concerned with ideas as with action. Although they spoke confidently of their opinions and impressions, Anglo-Canadians of both sexes were handicapped in their impartiality by a sense of superiority, and by the language and cultural barrier that confined them to often uncomprehending observation. The result was a distorted and incomplete picture of Ukrainian womanhood – one that betrayed the class and ethnic biases of its creators – as uniformly passive, helpless, downtrodden, and lacking a native tradition of self-help for change.

This image, for it did not appear in any one place or in coherent form, can best be reconstructed from published works from the period intended for public consumption: travelogues, feature articles, books, and missionary and teacher reports. The Anglo-Canadians who wrote about Ukrainians and the peasant immigrant woman did so not for private satisfaction but for political ends. Those ends went beyond describing strange and exotic customs to eager audiences; writers sought to expose, publicize, and, if need be, sensationalize Ukrainians' shortcomings in order to impress readers with the urgency of reform and to rally them in support. The features of 'typical' Ukrainian immigrant life that the literature highlighted were perceived as both fundamentally evil and destabilizing to Canadian society: peasant housekeeping standards, domestic violence, child brides bartered like commodities, and male superiority, especially in the husband-wife relationship, that demanded obedience and servility from women regarded as little more than domestic drudges and beasts of burden. The peasant woman herself was characterized as indifferent to personal appearance and improvement, given to idle and malicious gossip, and, like 'foreign' men, fond of settling disputes with physical force, which confirmed her lack of femininity.[28] Regardless of the accuracy of this image, it was incompatible with the middle-class Anglo-Canadian ideal of women as angels of the hearth – pure and delicate, respected and respectable, loving and loved.

If Anglo-Canadians found Ukrainians' treatment of women indefensible, they also found it incomprehensible. Indignation and condemnation seldom took into account the social and economic organization of peasant society, or the impact of emigration and immigration on members of that society, that lay behind gender roles in the bloc settlements.[29] To some minds, the treatment of women verified Slavic inferiority. 'No wonder the Canadian farmer speaks of the "bohunk" or "the heathen" ... fit only for the roughest work,' an English woman touring the West in the late 1920s exclaimed, citing the case of a Ukrainian widower who compared the death of his wife to the loss of his best cow.[30] A Saskatchewan school inspector reported how he had 'seen a poor Galician mother lying at death's door, the result of premature delivery – brought on by doing a man's work in clearing land. Only a threat that a charge of manslaughter would be laid if she died influenced the man to go 20 miles for a doctor.'[31] In reporting the beating of a woman by two men in the Vegreville colony east of Edmonton in 1916, the *Edmonton Bulletin* ventured the opinion that such things 'hardly appeal to a "white" man ... [but are] ... fairly common among the foreigners.'[32] And when a young wife from the same area committed suicide after maltreatment, the investigating officer suggested she had overreacted. 'Wife beating,' he said, 'is so common among these people, that I dont believe that ... [X] ... was any more cruel to his wife than the average Galician is, especially considering his having grounds for suspicions of her fidelity. I believe many of the Galician women in that district stand as much if not more beating than she, without any thoughts of suicide, or even much resentment.'[33] The proceedings at one inquest into the death of a woman from injuries inflicted by her spouse would have done little to reassure uneasy Anglo-Canadians. The husband, witnesses testified, had said he 'cared about as much for his wife as he did for last year's snow' and beat her 'for fun'; the husband himself denied ever abusing his wife, 'excepting several times I hit her with a strap.'[34]

Wife-beating perhaps epitomized to Anglo-Canadians the presumed coarseness of Ukrainian peasant life, but the 'Galician wedding' came a close second. A several-day event combining Byzantine-rite Catholic ritual and ancient pagan customs with much merrymaking could only upset teetotalling Protestants who abhored pageantry and excess as much as they admired restraint and temperance. The image of a drunken orgy ending in a bloody brawl and the courts was popularized by countless reports and editorials in the Anglo-Canadian press, and by the Presbyterian clergyman and novelist, Ralph Connor, whose fictional description of the sordid activities connected with Anka's wedding in the 'foreign colony' in North End Winnipeg received wide exposure.[35] Teachers and missionaries stationed in the blocs, attending as guests and writing for audiences back home, also contributed to the popular image of the Galician wedding. Most voiced disapproval of the alcohol and fights that marred festivities; some complained of dancing that was 'contorted' and 'crude,' or made time-honoured rituals seem silly and vulgar; others merely described a quaint and exotic event for peers fascinated by 'primitive' and 'foreign' cultures.[36] Some guests noted the clean tablecloths and the presence of plates, knives, forks, and spoons; others deplored the communal glasses and bowls and the lack of cutlery, and expressed horror at the food.[37] Prepared to observe but reluctant to participate, such wedding guests were outsiders to the end. If the 'odoriferous aroma of cigarette-smoke, whisky fumes, [and] perspiring humanity' did not chase them homeward, the feeling that 'things were getting a little bit too exciting' certainly would.[38]

But the barbarities of the wedding paled beside the marriage they celebrated. The dominant image was of a child bride arbitrarily married to a man more her father's age than her own in a business transaction where she was as much a commodity as her dowry, and condemned thereafter to bearing fifteen or sixteen children.[39] In the words of one female teacher, who failed to appreciate the economic basis of marriage in peasant societies, Ukrainian parents happily sold their young daughters to any man, 'regardless of age or character,' provided he met their price of 'two cows or four pigs.'[40] A Methodist minister in east-central Alberta pursued the implications. 'A large percentage of such marriages are happy,' he wrote, 'but in some cases they are not; love has not come in. Then, where the bride is so very young – fourteen or fifteen is the usual age – the offspring is often puny and weak and has not the vitality to survive the environment into which it comes.'[41] In that they penalized the next generation, Ukrainian attitudes towards women went from being inherently wrong to threatening Canada's future. This threat convinced Anglo-Canadians that they were justified in supplanting the home and family, enlisting the state if necessary, to protect and prepare Ukrainian girls for Canadian wifehood and motherhood. In 1913, for example, the Woman's Canadian Club of Calgary petitioned the Alberta government to prohibit marriage of Ukrainian girls before the age of seventeen, and asked that it establish residential schools where they could be taught domestic science. That same year, the Woman's Christian Temperance Union proposed publishing, for distribution east of Edmonton, Ukrainian-language leaflets outlining the evils of child marriage.[42]

Besides the ideas and attitudes that made up their invisible baggage,

Ukrainian peasant immigrants brought a material culture that also raised eyebrows in Anglo-Canadian circles. Their clothing immediately set Ukrainians apart from other settlers, and women in particular were attached to their native dress (one wife reportedly threatened to drown herself if her husband so much as cut his hair).[43] Women appeared in the literature in gaily coloured folk costumes or, more commonly, as multilayered and bulky in sheepskin coats and headshawls over poor homespun, their feet bare or thrust into heavy boots. This picture was a world away from that of the wife of the premier of Alberta, attending a reception 'smartly gowned in royal blue charmeuse' finished with a chic 'black chapeau trimmed with royal blue willow plume.'[44] With allowances for the unavailability of traditional materials in the new setting, Ukrainian immigrants also attempted to recreate what they could of their physical environment. The outwardly picturesque peasant cottages, thatched and whitewashed, that appeared on the western landscape fascinated Anglo-Canadians, who could still be censorious of the life inside. One of the more charitable descriptions, painstaking in its detail for curious readers, was by a visitor to the Vegreville colony in 1915:

> The houses which the Russians [sic] built in the early days of the colony were invariably divided into two rooms, one only of which has an outdoor entrance. This was perhaps only one-third the size of the other room, and had no means of heating. In the corner of the larger room was built a mud stove. Often on top of this the family drew their blankets over them, and slept when the weather was cold. Since only one room was heated the whole family must perforce live in that one room. Necessarily conditions were rather primitive.
>
> In addition to the stove the furnishings, in these early houses, were liable to include only a couple of wide bunks built of rough lumber, a small table fashioned from the same, and a stationary bench along one side of the room. This was almost sure to be placed so high that an adult must perch on it with feet dangling.
>
> The decorations of the room consisted of a row of ikons, or sacred pictures, placed close to the ceiling on the east wall. Clustering around the picture there was sure to be some cunningly devised flowers, fashioned of tissue-paper as gaudy in hue as were the pictures themselves. Since the walls of the room were limewashed the pictures, against the glistening whiteness, proved very effective. The

floor of the room was of clay, and in some of the houses was straw-strewn.[45]

Other descriptions were less generous:

On approaching one of the dwellings one is in dire danger of being torn to pieces by a pack of wolfish, hungry-looking dogs. Should he escape these and open the door, several chickens start out noisily under his feet, and he beholds an old hen nestling under the stove. In another corner a turkey is mothering her brood, and a family of kittens are playing on the earthen floor. A youngster or two are perched on the bed; three or four unkempt, dirty urchins cling to their mother's skirts and gaze curiously at the newcomer. The whole establishment reeks with a strong peculiar Russian [sic] odor. If it is about their meal time, the home-made table is freighted with an un-limited supply of murky tea. The most noticeable feature of the dwelling and its occupants is the lack of cleanliness everywhere in evidence.[46]

However these outside commentators judged the condition of the Ukrainian pioneer home, it was a reflection on the housekeeping abil-ities and mothering skills of the peasant immigrant woman. The con-sequences were serious when she failed to measure up. To middle-class Anglo-Canadian nation builders convinced that the family was the backbone of society, mothers and homemakers could not be al-lowed to remain 'peasant' and 'Ukrainian' if being so aversely affected Canadian values and standards of living. Whether the culprit was her lack of opportunity to learn English and Anglo-Canadian ways, or the restrictions of her society against women, the unassimilated Ukrainian peasant immigrant woman hurt not just her own family but Canada itself.

'Peasantness' and 'Ukrainianness' also attracted the attention of the Ukrainian immigrant intelligentsia. Reactions to the treatment of women in Ukrainian peasant society, and to the peasant immigrant woman's own attitudes and behaviour, were inextricably linked with what pioneer nationalists in particular saw as a more fundamental problem facing Ukrainians in Canada. On the one hand, they believed, the immigrants' peasant cultural baggage imperilled their group's prospects for upward mobility and integration into Canadian life. In

Ukrainian farm in the Vegreville bloc, east-central Alberta, late 1920s.
Despite widespread replacement of traditional peasant architecture with
Canadian-style buildings between the wars, the thatched and whitewashed
cottage did not disappear.

Baking bread in a typical Ukrainian outdoor clay oven or *pich*. Fraserwood,
Manitoba, 1916

Taking child to be christened. The baby bottle barely visible in the folds of the generous wrap suggests that convenience appealed to hardworking nursing mothers. Ladywood, Manitoba, 1921

this, nationalists shared a bias and goal with their Anglo-Canadian counterparts, even if the latter harboured reservations about Ukrainians' suitability as citizens of their country. On the other hand, and here Anglo-Canadian nation builders and Ukrainians parted company, nationalists also concluded that the immigrants' peasant cultural baggage imperilled the political consciousness that was to bind members of the group together in a distinct and separate Ukrainian-Canadian community. While nationalist criticism of the status quo and demands for reform echoed the response of mainstream society to the Ukrainian peasant immigrant, both hinged on plans for the future that did not always coincide with those of Anglo-Canadians.

Owing to this difference of purpose, women's 'peasantness' and 'Ukrainianness' were not always understood in Ukrainian circles as they were in Anglo-Canadian. Like Anglo-Canadians, the emerging community elite viewed the ignorance, apathy, and low standard of living that prevailed among Ukrainian peasant women in Europe –

and which pioneer conditions in Canada sustained and even exaggerated – with disfavour. But the 'peasantness' that came under attack did not automatically include the ritualized folkways that identified the immigrants as Ukrainian. It was this matter of the Ukrainian peasant immigrant woman's 'Ukrainianness' that most divided Ukrainian and Anglo-Canadian elites, and would separate nationalists (Greek Catholic and secular) from both Protestants and socialists in the immigrant community. If women's immobility and isolation in ethnically exclusive blocs retarded Canadianization, they also, especially to crystallizing nationalist ranks, retarded Ukrainization. The fault with the peasant immigrant woman's 'Ukrainianness' from this perspective lay not in its so-called foreignness but in its passivity. True, the absence of mainstream contacts dulled a sense of differentness and inferiority emerging from her group's ambiguous reception and lowly position in Canadian society; but the Ukrainian milieu, informal and formal, that enveloped her also dulled a sense of differentness expressed in a politicized Ukrainian national consciousness.

Since women lived outside the dominant prairie culture – with family fellowship, friendships, and community activities limited to other Ukrainians – they were not apt to perceive their behaviour or routines as 'ethnic.' Seldom confronted with their ethnicity, they had neither to grapple with the implications of belonging to a disadvantaged minority nor to make conscious decisions or observations concerning their relationship to their group.[47] The passivity of the peasant immigrant woman's Ukrainianness became an issue to the embryonic nationalist community for the same reason that her entire cultural baggage alarmed Anglo-Canadians. Because of their roles as mothers and homemakers, Ukrainian women were perceived to be crucial to the prosperity, status, and Ukrainian identity of their group. While activists acknowledged the peasant immigrant's daughters as their primary focus and the essential force to harness in shaping the future, they realized they had to begin with the peasant immigrant herself. She held the key to her family's upward mobility and its sentiments towards things Ukrainian; she also held the key to her daughters' attitudes towards their familial and group responsibilities. Unenlightened women, blind or indifferent to their national and social obligations as members of a larger community, were both an embarrassment and an encumbrance. They added to the Ukrainian group's unfavourable image among Anglo-Canadians, obstructed the progress nec-

Two-storey frame house attests to 'Canadianization' and agricultural prosperity, although gardening remained labour intensive and women's responsibility. Nd

essary for it to better itself, and jeopardized the quality of its Ukrainian consciousness and commitment.

Attitudes towards the peasant immigrant woman crystallized in conjunction with developments in the larger Ukrainian community as antagonistic ideological factions sought to reconcile the immigrants' old-country heritage with the opportunities and impositions of the new country. Thus, the world view of the immigrant intelligentsia as it pertained to Ukrainians' prospects for life in Canada and their relationship to the homeland is crucial to understanding how and why women came to be seen as they were. The source for this world view is the pioneer press, particularly the official mouthpieces of the Greek Catholic church and its secular nationalist, Protestant, and socialist opponents. Read by the literate to the illiterate in homes and halls throughout Canada, the press helped to unite individuals and colonies scattered across half a continent into a community identified by common Ukrainian origins and interests. It also provided an elite in that community with a forum from which to air its views about its compatriots and to agitate where it thought necessary for reform. Two themes preoccupied the pioneer press: *temnota* (ignorance) and *baiduzhnist* (apathy), equated with the peasant immigrants' old-country legacy; and *prosvita* (enlightenment) and *postup* (progress), promoted as their hope for the future. In apportioning blame for the former and defining the latter, Catholics, secular nationalists, Protestants, and socialists not only established their boundaries with each other but also decreed how Ukrainians in Canada should live. The thinking of these years, particularly how an emerging leadership elite first defined and then proposed to solve the problems facing Ukrainians in Canada, would have tremendous implications both for Ukrainian Canadians as a whole and for women as members of the group.

Protestants blamed the evils plaguing Ukrainian peasant society on what they described as an authoritarian, immoral, and uncaring church that bound its flock to Rome by keeping it ignorant and oppressed.[48] Progressives blamed Ukrainian 'priests and patriots' who used their Ukrainian patriotism with its slogan, '*svii do svoho*' (buy Ukrainian – literally 'each to his own') as a camouflage to exploit the masses, and to turn the peasants against farmers and workers of other nationalities.[49] Both the Greek Catholic church and secular nationalists, the two most important groups to this study, perceived admitted deficiencies in Ukrainian peasant and immigrant life as national issues. Ukrainians had their faults because they were a dark and ignorant mass, wrote a correspondent to *Kanadiiskyi farmer* (Canadian farmer); and they were a dark and ignorant mass because of centuries of slavery under foreign masters who knew how to hold a people in subjugation.[50] National oppression was also synonymous with socioeconomic oppression, since the Ukrainian's long-time political overlord in Galicia was his social and economic superior as well. The Polish landowner (and his Jewish agent) received the brunt of the blame in clerical and secular nationalist circles for the shortcomings of the peasant immigrant in Canada, particularly his addiction to alcohol that reflected the landlord's monopoly of liquor production and sale and the Jew's role as vendor.[51]

To all factions, alcohol was the major scourge of the peasantry in Galicia and of immigrants in Canada alike, responsible for physical debilitation, material poverty, and demoralization.[52] But alcohol abuse also had ideological implications. Protestants faulted a church that neither provided uplifting leadership nor condemned a crippling evil. The drunken 'Catholic' Ukrainian wedding upset them as much as it did Anglo-Canadians, epitomizing what they characterized as the moral and spiritual bankruptcy of church teachings and incense-burning, icon-kissing priests.[53] Socialists condemned both alcohol and illiteracy as instruments of the exploiters of the toiling masses, employed to ensure their bondage while justifying their poverty and backwardness. Clerical and secular nationalist circles tied alcoholism directly to national oppression. Drawing a parallel between the Easter season and the national renaissance in Ukraine to urge a new temperate beginning on its readers, the official organ of the Greek Catholic church, *Kanadyiskyi rusyn* (Canadian Ruthenian), identified alcohol as the primary reason why a 'talented and brave' people lay in foreign captivity: Ukraine's enemies understood well that a sober people never betrayed itself.[54]

In an important psychological sense that helps to explain the intelligentsia's harsh assessment of its fellow immigrants, emigration magnified peasant ignorance and apathy and made enlightenment and progress imperative. Canada brought Ukrainians into contact with what the intelligensia described as 'civilized and cultured' peoples who would be their competitors and judges. Within their own world, it was the Jewish immigrant with his business acumen, professional aspirations, and educational drive who offered the most unfavourable comparison. But 'the English' were the yardstick by which Ukrainians ultimately measured themselves and knew that they, in turn, would be measured, and many were only too aware of their people's image as 'stupid and crazy Galicians.' Ignorance so clung to the peasant immigrant, wrote one sensitive critic, that he was oblivious to the shame conscious Ukrainians suffered on his behalf.[55] Unseemly behaviour was also seen to represent a mindset that prevented the reform needed to make Ukrainians the respected equals of their fellow Canadians. For example, certain critics drew on the old-country economic relationship between the Ukrainian peasant and the Jew, where the latter's position as innkeeper, shopkeeper, and moneylender had caused widespread indebtedness and ill will.[56] One individual accused Ukrainian immigrants of being so locked into ruinous old-country relationships that in Canada they volunteered for victimization by patronizing Jewish merchants rather than their own businessmen. Others complained that Ukrainian immigrants preferred the bar and poolroom to the elevated atmosphere of the *chytalnia*, spending a fortune on beer and whiskey but begrudging a dime for the books and newspapers that represented their emancipation.[57]

Once emigration removed the perceived Polish and Jewish yokes, secular nationalists and their clerical counterparts faced an awkward situation in identifying the peasant immigrants' legacy of darkness with national oppression. Letters, editorials, and articles in the pioneer press repeatedly expressed impatience with a people that was seemingly unwilling, in a country with new freedom and opportunity, to help itself. In Canada, they concluded, Ukrainians had no one else to blame for the ignorance, apathy, and disorderliness that made them as much objects of rule and ridicule as in Galicia.[58] It was this admission that made perceived indifference or hostility to education a major issue. One disgruntled immigrant described the great majority of Ukrainians in Canada as little better than savages or cattle, content with full stomachs and oblivious to either greater material comforts or finer sentiments.[59] Without literacy, broad knowledge, and facility in English, it was argued, the peasant immigrant generation sentenced its successors to permanent inferiority, forever manual labourers and the servants of others, scorned by the cultured and exploited by the unscrupulous.[60] Parents who measured progress solely by a paycheque or quarter sections of land and plucked their children from school to work, or denied them the higher training increasingly equated with success in Canada, were deemed as harmful as parents who crippled their children by drunkenness, quarrelling, or passive complacency.[61] To Greek Catholic and secular nationalist leaders, literacy, books, newspapers, and higher education represented vehicles of upward social mobility.

Ukrainian Protestants and progressives also insisted on formal education and informed parenting to raise Ukrainians to the level of other Canadians.[62] But the 'enlightenment' they promoted in the name of 'progress' had ideological ends. To Protestants, immigrants had two choices: they could persist in their centuries-old dream of darkness, alcohol, and ruin; or they could embrace the sober Christian life that went hand in hand with Western Protestantism, culture, and democracy.[63] Progressives conceded that Canada had eliminated many evils of Galician society. It still, however, served capitalist interests, and it compounded class exploitation with ethnic discrimination. Moreover, Ukrainians had to contend with their own so-called leaders who were motivated not by genuine concern for the welfare of the masses but by the desire for selfish material gain.[64] True enlightenment, progressives argued, lay in class consciousness and struggle.

For both progressives and Protestants, enlightenment and progress entailed discarding old-country practices and values that the Greek Catholic clergy and secular nationalists considered integral to Ukrainianness. The Protestant equation of Greek Catholicism and Ukrainian peasant custom with immigrant debauchery, violence and backwardness challenged religious and folk customs considered fundamental to Ukrainian national identity. In condemning the superstitions and customs of their ancestors as unsuitable for twentieth-century Canada, and a further excuse to keep the masses enslaved and ignorant,[65] progressives rejected not just peasantness but the religion and secular nationalism that valued Ukrainian folk culture for political reasons. The progressives' own definition of Ukrainianness took into account the discrimination and exploitation their people faced in Canada as Ukrainians, making the question of class consciousness also one of national consciousness. Protestants accused their Greek Catholic and secular nationalist opponents of a ghetto-like mentality and dismissed their own assimilationist label, yet underscored their mainstream ties and obligations by opposing public bilingual schools on the prairies on the grounds that the schools catered to unwanted traditions and influences. Nevertheless, Protestants termed their mother tongue 'their greatest national treasure,' and although critical of the aggressive Ukrainianism of the nationalists, identified true enlightenment and progress with Ukrainian group goals – a better quality of life in Canada and nationhood at home.[66]

'Progress' and 'enlightenment' as understood by pioneer Greek Catholic and secular nationalist leaders eschewed the idea of freedom from old-country Ukrainian traditions and institutions. Instead, they were to be preserved and enhanced through a new consciousness binding and animating the masses. To become the equals of the 'cultured and civilized' peoples of Canada, according to this view, Ukrainians had to acquire self-knowledge and self-respect. And if these qualities came on one level from introspection on the part of the individual,

Pictures of Taras Shevchenko, Ukraine's national poet, and Ivan Franko, writer and activist, hang on the wall of a consciously Ukrainian home. A modern stove represents material progress. Redwater, Alberta, 1920

they came on a second, more important, level from collective pride in and active identification with the history, culture, and aspirations of the people and nation to which Ukrainians in Canada belonged.[67] Questions concerning the precise nature of this Ukrainianness, however, simultaneously united and divided these two influential factions in the Ukrainian immigrant community.

To the Greek Catholic clergy, who argued that patriotism was impossible without God, the Greek Catholic religion and rite were as

Far from the peasant stereotype. Rural Manitoba, 1917

integral to Ukrainians' national identity and soul as their language. 'Remember,' *Kanadyiskyi rusyn* warned, 'that he who fails to heed the kingdom of God and his own people turns God and his people away from him.'[68] Thus, Ukrainians in Canada who abandoned their church – whether through ignorance, becoming the hirelings of the assimilationist English, or because of a misguided national consciousness – divorced themselves from the vital interests of their people and their nation.[69] Language and faith as cornerstones of a politicized Ukrainian national consciousness, and as fundamental components of individual personal integrity, were to have far-reaching and long-term implications. At the time, the indissoluble bond linking language, Greek Catholicism, and Ukrainianness influenced the church's instructions to its immigrant flock, particularly parents and mothers, and it brought intervention in the educational field. After 1916, when escalating Anglo-Canadian nativism closed public bilingual schools on the prairies, the church turned to private Ukrainian schools, *bursy* (residential institutes), and *ridni shkoly* (Saturday and vacation schools) to preserve Ukrainians' language, faith, and culture.[70]

Such institutions demonstrated the importance attached to com-

munity socialization of Ukrainian-Canadian youth. The insistence of
the Greek Catholic bishop that they be Catholic as well as Ukrainian,
however, created a permanent schism with the secular nationalists,
focused around the Petro Mohyla Institute in Saskatoon.[71] Although
their rival networks would subsequently gravitate to the new Ukrainian
Greek Orthodox church, secular nationalists initially insisted that community institutions be nondenominational and all-Ukrainian. They also
realized that the abolition of public bilingual schools threw Ukrainians
onto their own resources if they wanted to preserve their language
and culture in Canada and resist assimilation by the English. Without
enlightenment to cultivate a politicized Ukrainian consciousness, it was
charged, the peasant immigrants' ignorance, helplessness, and passivity
before Anglo-Canadian overtures threatened national ruin. In Europe,
Kanadiiskyi farmer wrote, Ukrainians had responded to attempted Polonization with a national renaissance, but in Canada where they enjoyed full freedom, Anglicization met with indifference.[72]

The relationship between enlightenment and progress and Ukrainian group goals was illustrated by a list of 'commandments' appearing
anonymously in mid 1914 in *Ukrainskyi holos* (Ukrainian voice), organ
of the secular nationalists, particularly bilingual teachers, and future
mouthpiece for the Ukrainian Greek Orthodox church. Men were to
use their franchise to vote for candidates sympathetic to pro-Ukrainian
issues like bilingual schools. Parents were to ensure that their children
spoke and could read and write their native language, provide them
with Ukrainian playmates, and teach them the proverbs, songs, beliefs,
and customs of their people. Families were to revive lapsing national
traditions, subscribe to patriotic newspapers, read Ukrainian books,
decorate their homes with scenes from Ukrainian history, and maintain ties with other Ukrainian families. As conscious and conscientious
members of the Ukrainian nation, they were to attend Ukrainian concerts and patriotic celebrations, patronize Ukrainian businesses, join
Ukrainian organizations, and lend financial and moral support to
worthy causes in their native land.[73] The formula for living outlined
in these 'commandments' was to become entrenched in nationalist
thought. As expressions of the essence of Ukrainianness in the new
country, both formula and 'commandments' also revealed that parental attitudes and the home environment would be pivotal to the success
or failure of the community agenda.

Emigration itself exaggerated the importance of parents and the
home in raising patriotic Ukrainian youth, as institutions and individ-

Showing off their needlework. Kolokreeka Methodist Mission, rural
Alberta, nd

uals ready to assume the burden in the old country when the family
unit defaulted were either absent or weak. The Greek Catholic prelate,
Metropolitan Andrei Sheptytsky of Lviv, impressed on Ukrainian parents in Canada their holy duty in rearing their children; they could
not presume to rely on the priest or teacher as in Galicia, because the
priest and teacher did not always exist.[74] For both pioneer Greek
Catholic and secular nationalist leaders, public bilingual schools helped
to compensate for the drawbacks of emigration. But the removal of
state mechanisms for maintaining language and culture increased pressures on the home. Greek Catholic circles no longer admonished peasant immigrants to support bilingual and Catholic schools wherever
possible, and stressed home upbringing instead. The home was to
defuse the denationalizing influences of both the Anglo-Canadian and
the Latin-rite Catholic school systems, just as it was to counter the
propaganda of higher educational institutions like teacher colleges on
the grounds that they sought to divorce Ukrainian students from their
faith and nation.[75] Writing to *Ukrainskyi holos* in December 1915, a

woman complained that Anglo-Canadians shed tears for war-ravaged Belgian women and children but stripped Ukrainian women of their treasured language and stole their sons and daughters; her sex, she said, had to shoulder its domestic and maternal responsibilities, and answer the challenge to Ukrainians' national existence that the abolition of bilingual schools presented.[76]

The Great War, whose passions lay behind growing Anglo-Canadian intransigence towards bilingual schools as disloyal, was a watershed in the immigrants' evolving sense of themselves as Canadians and Ukrainians. They found their enemy alien status, given because of their Austrian birthplace, insulting and unjust when they had done so much for Canada, and an unequivocal statement that they remained outsiders. Ukrainian leaders insisted on their people's loyalty, appealed to their role in nation building to attack disenfranchisement, internment, and threats of deportation, and defended against Anglo-Canadian criticism many of the features of Ukrainian peasant and immigrant life that they themselves condemned. Education and progress became all the more important as Ukrainians emphasized the duties of Canadian citizenship, and as they responded to the urgent Ukrainian tasks that the collapse of the Russian and Austro-Hungarian empires set in motion.[77] As Ukrainians overseas joined other subject peoples of Eastern Europe fighting for national sovereignty, Ukrainians in Canada wanted to help. A committed elite, however, could do little if ignorance and apathy continued to hold sway over the masses.

How an educated elite reacted to and characterized its peasant immigrant compatriots, taking into account their old-country heritage and the Canadian environment, determined not only how the peasant immigrant woman was perceived but also that she merited discussion at all. Women's images and roles emerged from and were dictated by what Catholics, secular nationalists, Protestants, and socialists considered good or bad in Ukrainian immigrant life, and by what they considered necessary for the future. Attitudes towards the peasant immigrant woman reflected a faction's general prejudices, confirming that women were to be treated as members of the larger group, and the idea that women, by virtue of their sex, required special attention. The world view of the pioneer intelligentsia is significant in two further respects. First, excluding the increasingly marginalized Protestants, the years before 1920 identified the issues that would subsequently occupy and plague nationalists and progressives as they sought to accommodate 'Ukrainian' with 'Canadian' and class interests with national interests. In the decades that followed, a female leadership elite, as part of the organized community, functioned within these parameters and under the same assumptions in addressing its sex. Second, the opinions and prejudices of the peasant immigrants' contemporaries constrasted sharply with the myth making of their successors. Not only did this reinterpretation demonstrate the changing needs of a community elite; more importantly from the perspective of the present discussion, it elevated the peasant immigrant woman to unprecedented heights in the process.

The least motivated by Ukrainian group ambitions, progressives approached the peasant immigrant woman from the perspective of interrelated class and female oppression, with her condition on both accounts to be alleviated by a fundamental restructuring of society. Progressives harshly criticized women's treatment in their homeland, particularly the apparent conviction of the Ukrainian peasant (and his wife) that abuse and degradation were his right, thinking moulded and endorsed by a church that preached 'Women, fear your husbands.' The immigrant in Canada, progressives declared, remained a slave to his heritage. As master of the house he was loath to take an 'old woman's advice' (*babska rada*), regardless of how intelligent or useful it might be; he was incredulous that the vote of a mere woman (*baba*) could equal that of a man, so that his wife's indifference to her new rights and responsibilities was the fruit of his active discouragement as much as her own ignorance; and he kept his women in domestic bondage and darkness while bourgeois women profited from expanded opportunities to strengthen the ranks of the enemy.[78]

As victims of the present order, Ukrainian peasant immigrant women were expected by the progressives to participate in the liberation of both their sex and the toiling masses, making enlightenment through the cultivation of class consciousness a priority. Otherwise, they would remain forever as they were now: reading only their prayerbooks, if anything, for fear of what the priest would say. That Anglo-Canadian nativism did not join class and gender discrimination in the pioneer socialist press no doubt reflected the rural peasant woman's limited contact with mainstream society. A letter to the socialist *Robochyi narod* (Working people), however, implied that the predicament of Ukrainian working girls was particularly bad, partly because of their disinclination to join workers' organizations but also because of conditions they faced in the workplace.[79] Others, too, identified with an urban population. Women laboured long hard hours and for low wages, a comrade told her sisters in 1914; they constituted one-half of the human race, suffered together with male workers, bore and reared children, and therefore had to join men in the struggle for a better future. Progressives also reminded women that just as mothering was their most important task, so the home was not an island. Responsible for the class consciousness and welfare of the next generation, women had to teach their children by their own example and take an intelligent interest in all aspects of society affecting their well-being.[80]

Protestants attributed ignorance among Ukrainian peasant women, widespread neglect, and the poverty of their families to the unhealthy grip of the Greek Catholic church and its priests. They also blamed 'Catholic' prejudices for channelling women's energies into useless church decoration instead of community and social work, and 'Catholic' morality for sanctioning sexual exploitation. Sordid incidents – like the story of a girl seduced and 'sold' by an illiterate immigrant with a wife in the old country – were related with relish in the press to show the perniciousness of the immigrants' Galician Catholic upbringing. In fact, *Ranok* taxed the Greek Catholic bishop with deliberately promoting immorality when he permitted a deserted husband with three children to advertise in *Kanadyiskyi rusyn* for a replacement for his wife.[81] Only evangelical Christianity, Protestants argued, would liberate Ukrainians from the superstition and tyranny that blighted both sexes. Secular nationalists accused Protestants of assimilating Ukrainian girls to the Anglo-Canadian world; Protestants retaliated with the accusation that nationalists fostered religious indifference and demoralization among Ukrainian-Canadian youth, and were 'un-Canadian' in the admonition to mothers to raise good Ukrainians. The propaganda of Ukrainian Protestants reflected their English ties, but, unlike Anglo-Canadian missionaries, they did not see that religious conversion had to separate the convert from the Ukrainian people. One goal of Protestant *bursy*, for example, was to train female leaders of enlightenment and national consciousness for their sex.[82]

Women and women's issues warranted little space in the official organ of the Greek Catholic church, with female oppression in Ukrainian peasant society not a concern at all. Yet women were not totally overlooked or treated unsympathetically, and, despite significant differences, such as less emphasis on female education, the church at times sounded like its rivals. Discussions of alcoholism, for example, invariably painted women and children as victims, both for the material poverty and for the physical and emotional abuse male drunkenness inflicted on the family.[83] In spiritual matters, the church insisted on a Christian (Catholic) ceremony for marriage as a sacred institution; it also stressed the importance of love between husband and wife, with the man as the benevolent but unquestioned head of the family, the woman his obedient helpmate. From Galicia, Metropolitan Sheptytsky advised prospective grooms in Canada to choose as brides girls who would make good Christian wives and mothers – devout, conscientious, thrifty, industrious, self-sacrificing, and prepared for responsibility however disagreeable.[84]

Despite this reiteration of traditional and subordinate roles for women and the implied dominance of religious over secular priorities, the Greek Catholic press addressed broader questions. A women's column was introduced in *Kanadyiskyi rusyn* in 1915 under the editorship of Halyna Sushko, placing its hopes in 'our patriotic womanhood.' While never a bold forum for opinion, it published news from the international feminist movement and articles on women throughout the world, along with domestic advice for the peasant immigrant in Canada.[85] Although expected to operate within 'emancipated' parameters determined by specifically female functions and qualities, in effect transferring their domestic roles into the community, women were also to assume responsibilities outside the family: engaging in social work among the less fortunate, donating their dairy and garden produce to Ukrainian Catholic *bursy*, and taking an active part in church and national life. Both this service to the larger community and women's primary function within the home, it was argued, required mass enlightenment to cultivate a sense of positive self-worth and national commitment that would transform the ignorant and apathetic into useful members of society and good citizens.[86] In identifying Ukrainian women with their group in this fashion, the church made a statement about the individual's responsibility towards Ukrainian national-cultural goals. Secular nationalists made the same statement more forcefully.

To the pioneer nationalist intelligentsia, both the crises and realities of pioneering and immigrant adjustment and the fate of women as persons or members of a disadvantaged sex were secondary to the impact of peasant attitudes and behaviour on Ukrainian fortunes. Concern was less for the abused wife or neglected child than for the bad impression made on Anglo-Canadians, less for the workload of farm women than for their abandoning of traditional Ukrainian dishes in favour of labour-saving canned goods.[87] Sensitivity to Anglo-Canadian opinion and the desire to create 'civilized and cultured' beings proud of their national origins inevitably highlighted, and perhaps exaggerated, the negative and unpleasant in the peasant immigrant lifestyle. The objective, however, was not to flatter the moral and the upright but to get the errant to recognize and correct their ways. Women's sins and omissions, in that they aggravated Ukrainians' negative image and retarded national-cultural growth, were regarded as especially serious because of the peculiar place women came to occupy in the community agenda.

Nevertheless, pioneer nationalists addressed the issues of female oppression and women's rights as human beings. Letters and articles in the press, their authors frequently women, framed these issues as both universal and Ukrainian questions. They compared male opposition to female suffrage with strong nations' subjugation of the weak, holding them in ignorance for easier exploitation. They challenged a social order that forced women to marry for economic survival, making them the slaves of masters who used the power of the physically strong to dominate the weak in unions where 'despotism reigned as in Russia.' They defended women's work and intelligence, protesting that all human beings had comparable needs, abilities, and value. They insisted on a woman's right to justice and relief from an abusive husband, and on society's duty to condemn domestic tyranny. Ukrainian immigrant women deserted their husbands not out of perversity, it was explained, but because of the drunkenness, laziness, lovelessness, and lack of respect. Only when both sexes were equally enlightened and mutually supportive, with men respecting women as persons and women conscious of their personhood, would Ukrainians realize true progress. Ukrainian women in Canada were encouraged to appreciate their human worth and to assert themselves in their own interests and those of the greater community.[88]

In 1912 women's right to equality with men was debated in the local *chytalnia* in Ethelbert, Manitoba, and, to the 'loud applause of the women, girls and many men,' decided in favour of the affirmative. The four debaters, who were all male, presented standard arguments. Women would exert a moral and human influence on public life; women in public life would neglect their homes and children, leading to moral corruption.[89] But even in the elite circles to which discussion of the woman question was confined, the idea of women as full citizens of the community met resistance. The Third National Convention of Ukrainians in Canada in 1919, for example, saw Olha Swystun and

Anna Bychinska criticize their male colleagues who claimed to be patriots with noble ideas yet were reluctant to promote education for women and accept them as equals in public national life.[90] By 1920, interest in female emancipation as a principle had been largely supplanted by the more pressing identification of Ukrainian women with nationalist plans for the Ukrainian-Canadian group. Henceforth enlightenment and progress would refer not to individual autonomy but to women's ability to further community objectives – upward mobility and the maintenance of Ukrainian culture in Canada, and aid to Ukraine abroad. This connection had, in fact, always existed. Since before the turn of the century, the peasant immigrant woman's perceived ignorance and backwardness had been considered obstacles to those same objectives.

Echoing the contradictory attitudes of the contemporary women's movement in English Canada, although outside its debates and activities, secular nationalists considered women simultaneously superior and inferior to men. On the one hand, they had been less demoralized by their Galician upbringing than Ukrainian men and were thus better equipped to respond to Canadian opportunities for reform and improvement. Nationalists who supported female suffrage also argued, like mainstream advocates (and the socialists), that women's moral superiority and maternal sensibilities would eradicate political corruption and cure a variety of social ills.[91] On the other hand, those opposed to authoritarianism and Latinization in the Greek Catholic church singled out the peasant immigrant woman as the mainstay of an untenable status quo. Less enlightened and conscious than her menfolk, she was more likely to succumb not only to the propaganda of French Catholic interlopers but also to the calumniations of her own priests against the 'godlessness' of *Ukrainskyi holos* and its backers. *Ukrainskyi holos* accused the church of exploiting women's ignorance to maintain its traditional grip on the peasantry; and, warning enlightened men that priests would try to control them through their wives, it insisted on women's enlightenment too.[92]

Although fewer in number than their male counterparts, a more transitory sight on Canadian streets, and less addicted to the alcohol that gave Ukrainian men such a bad reputation, female immigrants were also observed to contribute to their group's poor image. According to the Reverend Nestor Dmytriw, who toured the West in 1897, it began in the immigration sheds; there, he said, women's slovenliness and the foul habits of their unsupervised children, urinating and defecating in public, helped make Ukrainians 'worse than Indians' in Anglo-Canadian eyes. Critics charged that some women drank with their husbands, even urging their children to join. Others stole without shame, whether from the Canadian merchant or their fellow immigrant: one mortified man, the newspaper report claimed, hanged himself when his wife was convicted of stealing $94 from a drunken countrymen. Committing lesser crimes but still an embarrassment were the women who went to town barefoot, or underlined their empty-headedness and lack of culture with unrestrained and foolish chatter.[93] Those disturbed by the unflattering figure their people cut in the new land did not spare the peasant woman their censure, and they left little doubt as to the culprit. Peasantness was at fault, and peasantness would have to go.

But attitudes were ultimately more complex and ambiguous as conflicting prejudices and priorities moderated Ukrainians' sensitivity to both Anglo-Canadian opinion and their own heritage. Anglo-Canadians might refuse to let their wives and daughters work on the land because Ukrainian women, who were a lower breed, did so;[94] but in Ukrainian circles, the homesteader's poverty and his leaders' desire for socioeconomic progress prompted defence of the peasant immigrant woman's labour, despite its scandalizing the English.[95] And despite their admiration of the cultured English woman, Ukrainians' pride in their hardworking peasants accompanied disdain for the pampered wife of the Anglo-Canadian, in what amounted to a rejection of the Victorian ideal of femininity. During the Great War, when the Anglo-Canadian press praised women's physical labour and sacrifice, Ukrainians noted that the toil the leisured English woman was just discovering had long been familiar to Ukrainian women. They were stronger and healthier for their exertions, the more beautiful for being without powder and perfume, and no less cultured for all that they could not play the piano and, like the great Tolstoi, went barefoot in summer.[96] Ukrainians' greatest defence of their womenfolk came in the wartime debate over female suffrage. Anglo-Canadians closed ranks to exclude 'foreigners' and 'enemy aliens,' on the grounds that to give the vote to downtrodden women ignorant of Canadian institutions would insult intelligent, patriotic Anglo-Canadian women. With the reminder that they, unlike the English, had entered Canada not with sabres and cannons but by invitation, Ukrainians retaliated: the 'foreign' woman raising a new generation of Canadians not only loved her country but had contributed more to it by her labour than many an English woman.[97]

Both defence and criticism of the Ukrainian woman's more visible peasant traits, affecting as they did her people's image and reception in the new homeland, were influenced by external factors, notably Anglo-Canadian opinion. In many respects, the problem was peculiar to the adult immigrant and would disappear in her 'Canadian' daughters. This was not the case when nationalists turned to their own community. Here the peasant immigrant woman's attitudes and behaviour were seen to have long-term repercussions, detrimental to the nationalists' crystallizing Ukrainian agenda. Events overseas, as Ukrainians attempted and then failed to establish their own state, complicated the ramifications of immigrant and minority status in Canada to define women's specifically 'female' relationship to their group for years to come. The unresolved Ukrainian question ensured that women would not be allowed to remain private individuals, with loyalties and horizons limited to the immediate family. Nor would they be allowed to become 'Canadian' without the conscious counterpull of forces that tied them to the homeland and to each other. At the same time, emigration and Canada's growing antipathy to expressions of Ukrainian consciousness, reflected in the abolition of bilingual schools, magnified the significance of the family as the primary bastion of Ukrainianness.[98] The traditional functions and responsibilities of mothers and homemakers acquired new status as a result, to give women a higher profile than they had experienced in the past. Childrearing simultaneously became something that women consciously did rather than simply let happen. As the group's reproducers as well as guardians and transmitters of its identity, however, women were restricted in their options and freedom of movement to what advanced the nationalist cause. Since women in their traditional roles were important to the future direction and content of Ukrainian-Canadian life, their own lives became legitimate matters of community inspection and supervision.

Maintenance of culture and service to the homeland through a politicized Ukrainian consciousness depended to a large extent on the quality of the base provided by the peasant immigrant generation. The image of an ignorant and apathetic woman in the clutches of her dark heritage – whether unaware of and indifferent to her failings and responsibilities, or actively hostile to self-improvement and

Ukrainian goals – had frightening implications. Unable to lead by example or to inculcate patriotic sentiments and greater ambition in her husband and children, she obstructed the spiritual growth and material progress of her family and group.[99] To those wishing to transform the masses into upwardly mobile Ukrainian patriots, it was more important to rail against her kind than it was to commend the woman quietly working for her parish or hall or keeping a good home. Yet the latter made for good propaganda. In early 1914, under the heading 'Exemplary Mother,' *Ukrainskyi holos* printed a plea for books from an impoverished farm wife who had found the time to teach her eight children to read. Like this woman, the accompanying editorial proclaimed, the exemplary Ukrainian mother did not forget in the midst of poverty that her children needed books and learning to ensure a bright future; moreover, the home was the first and most important school, teaching respect for work, truth, knowledge, and all things Ukrainian.[100]

Physical survival may once have been considered enough and, indeed, absorbed a person's energies, but to community activists committed to upward mobility in Canada and to national-cultural goals linked to nation building in Ukraine, it was enough no longer. Women were responsible for maintaining Ukrainian homes, raising their children in Canada in the Ukrainian language and culture and in a Ukrainian spirit, and imparting the values that dedicated the next generation to enlightenment and progress. The 'Ukrainianness' that the Ukrainian peasant immigrant woman embodied in her 'peasantness,' and the 'peasantness' that characterized her 'Ukrainianness,' would secure neither objective. A lifestyle and outlook that penalized Ukrainians in a country that classified its citizens by their ethnic origins was as unsatisfactory as a Ukrainian identity, passive and unconscious, erected on folk customs. Both acceptance and respectability as Canadians and group-imposed obligations as Ukrainians demanded that women, like men, be enlightened and conscious members of their community. What the bloc settlements preserved and perpetuated by size and inertia alone, and by the physical and social constraints they placed on women, was not what the future required.

Yet the isolated pioneer on her homestead, while perhaps unpoliticized and unmotivated, possessed one unassailable quality: she was also unassimilated. Unfavourable comparisons of town and country demonstrated how important this distinction became in community thinking. Rural Ukrainians were held to value their language and

culture more highly, while assimilation proceeded quickly among urban Ukrainians, helped by mothers failing to inculcate a meaningful
Ukrainianness rooted in language in their children.[101] To nationalists,
'the street' not only demoralized Ukrainian youth in the absolute sense,
exposing them to the corrupting influence of unsavoury individuals
and the moving pictures, for example, but also alienated them from
their Ukrainian heritage and community.[102] The assimilation 'the
street' symbolized made it a worse evil to Ukrainians than to Anglo-
Canadian social reformers, who also feared its corrupting influences,
and it exaggerated the role of the home, especially of women as mothers, in rearing young Ukrainian Canadians in their own tradition.
From this perspective, the ignorant and apathetic peasant immigrant
outside the bloc, helpless against the assimilatory forces and demoralization of the larger society, was more of a millstone around the
collective group neck than her sister safely ensconced among her own
kind, despite the often oppressive weight of old-country attitudes and
practices.

How women, for better or worse, were perceived by factions in the
Ukrainian-Canadian community would be refined over the next several decades, but by 1920 the mould had been cast. Different goals
aside, reflected in their understanding of enlightenment and progress,
both progressives and nationalists had rejected the peasant immigrant
woman's peasantness, although nationalists had to separate and salvage
the desirable 'Ukrainian' from the undesirable 'peasant' in her heritage. Because of their traditional roles as mothers and homemakers,
women were central to both camps (but to nationalists in particular),
for success hinged on the outlook of the next, Canadian-born and
-raised generation; each camp also expected women to participate actively and intelligently, as members of the larger collective, in community life. Women's special relationship to the propaganda and
programs of an emerging elite had subjected the peasant immigrant
to scrutiny – and that scrutiny would only intensify among her daughters, both those who remained inside the bloc and those who ventured
outside.
　'The people of foreign countries who come to Canada after having
reached maturity – the middle-aged and the aged – will never become
true Canadian citizens, imbued with the highest Anglo-Saxon ideals,'
wrote a proponent of assimilation in 1918, referring to the Ukrainian
woman's mud-bake oven, Easter egg painting and foreign speech and

dress. Rather, her children were 'the material upon which Canadians as nationbuilders must work.'[103] Adult immigrants represented an essentially lost generation to the emerging Ukrainian community leadership as well. Among those formulating and articulating Ukrainians' goals and needs, both as citizens of the new country and as members of the Ukrainian nation, the immigrants' daughters would command greater attention. Handicapped at the outset by the shortcomings of their own mothers, themselves prospective mothers responsible for upcoming Ukrainian-Canadian youth, they were also the first generation of women to have sustained intercourse with the Anglo-Canadian world, exposed to its baser attractions and assimilatory pressures as well as to its opportunities. How they responded and the degree to which the community would be able to direct their responses were crucial to the future.

2

Jeopardizing the Future:
Alienated and Rebellious Daughters

'Nasha Meri.' The world turns and is turning upside down and in a single year our Maria Perih has turned into Meri Porydzh – forgetting Ukrainian and limited to 'yes' and 'no' in English.[1]

> Just look at such a girl. She plants on her head a hat that an intelligent girl wouldn't even touch. She wears gaudy clothes that are as wide as a haystack. She says that it's the style – but it's well known that no one is interested in fashion like ignorant and stupid women and girls. It's the most important thing in the world to them, but they're the ones who have the least understanding of real beauty.

What's more, you see how such a girl puts on powder, by the shovelful. And it runs down her face, disgusting to look at.

Third, the gum. Wherever she goes – in the street, on the street-car, in church – she munches like a cow in the pasture.

Fourth, to top it off, the English language. Having learned a little English, she doesn't even bother with her own language. Everything in English, especially how she twists her mouth and laughs. Already you have the complete Katie ...

You don't call such a girl anything else, for she's no longer our intelligent, honourable, thinking girl – the daughter of her parents and the daughter of her people; likewise, she isn't a proper English girl; she falls into the category of those who live in darkness ... and consort only with ... low and characterless people.[2]

Nasha Meri and Katie – together they symbolized the Ukrainian immigrant girl in young womanhood and her Canadian-born sister testing the freedoms and attractions of the new country. Her bastardization of her name a sign of alienation and moral ruin, Katie (Keidi) emerged as a type in the nationalist press early in the century. Nasha Meri (Our Mary), as the group possessiveness in her name implies, met with greater tolerance, although sharing many of Katie's faults. She appeared between the wars, her creator the satirist-humorist Jacob Maydanyk – more famous for his lovable but roguish Shtif Tabachniuk, whose escapades, words of wisdom, and correspondence with his wife in the old country enlivened newspaper columns and provoked impassioned responses from readers. As he coped with unfamiliar surroundings, Vuiko Shtif (Uncle Steve) provided his fellow immigrants with an often unflattering picture of themselves while easing their trauma with laughter and practical advice.[3] Despite differences, all three characters displayed undesirable effects of uprooting and transplanting as Ukrainians groped to reconcile the ways of two worlds. The larger issues Nasha Meri and Katie in particular represented spanned overlapping generations, beginning with the first Ukrainian girl to become a domestic in an English home and including the Depression teacher who changed her name to improve her chances for a job.

Guilty of rejecting traditional restraints and values, and of succumbing to the vulgar and superficial in the Canadian lifestyle, Nasha Meri and Katie were the female counterparts of 'Jack,' the maladjusted Ukrainian young man whose education began on the railway gang and finished in the bar and pool hall. Their numbers and visibility, as well

as their frequent rowdiness, earned the Jacks great publicity and no-
toriety,[4] yet the nationalist community came to regard Nasha Meri
and Katie as a more serious problem. Adolescents and young women
today, such girls were tomorrow's mothers and homemakers, and in
this role would determine not only the level at which the next generation integrated into Canadian society but also the quality of its
Ukrainianness. If the ignorance and apathy of the adult peasant immigrant demonstrated the need for enlightenment and reform among
women, nationalists thought, the behaviour identified with Nasha Meri
and Katie demonstrated the consequences of external change without
the necessary inner transformation to make judicious use of Canada's
opportunities.

Nasha Meri and Katie personified female rebellion against traditional demanding and subservient roles, parental expectations, and
community directives in the name of the larger good. They raised the
questions of intermarriage, language loss, and alienation from Ukrainian institutional life, and they bore eloquent testimony to the difficulties of competing with the material attractions of North American
society for the allegiance of Ukrainian-Canadian youth. As symbols
for those Ukrainian girls who indiscriminately embraced new ideas
and new independence, Nasha Meri and Katie represented a reality
that was the exception rather than the rule through the years when
the stereotype was cultivated. But the pressures and choices they represented would persist and multiply to challenge women's ties to the
group and jeopardize the nationalist agenda. That agenda was already
complicated, quite apart from the weight of homogenizing Canadian
influences, by its own internal contradictions: young women as Ukrainians had to be retained and groomed against enticements from the
larger society, but as Canadians they had to be encouraged to exploit
its benefits and integrate with it. From the nationalist perspective,
broadened horizons that represented personal emancipation carried
a hidden danger of potential emancipation from group ties and loyalties, at a time when Ukrainians were desperately seeking respectability and a secure foothold in the new homeland while they strongly
sympathized with the aspirations of the old.

Nasha Meri and Katie illustrated the negative results of the inter-
action of Ukrainian immigrant and Anglo-Canadian worlds. As such,
they were identified not with the bloc settlement but with the city and
resource town, wherever in Canada that might be, and in particular
with those women and girls who worked outside the familial home for

Daughter in stylish 'English' clothes, reflecting the impact of the new world on the younger generation. Rural Alberta, c.1915

a living. This group included single immigrants, whether they arrived before or between the wars, and the daughters of homesteaders/farmers and male wage-earners in the same prewar and interwar periods. The three major areas where the Canadian environment influenced Ukrainian tradition and the nationalist agenda – the workplace, education, and marriage – give some sense of the actual direction and scope of change in women's lives up to the end of the Second World War. The stereotype of the working girl symbolized by Nasha Meri and Katie flourished against this backdrop, although it emerged in the pioneer period when the issues Nasha Meri and Katie represented were first articulated. Marginal to this debate, the progressives approached the working girl in ways that bore some similarity to the nationalist position but differed in important respects.

The contradictions in the goal of nationalist activists – to urge young Ukrainian women to use Canada's advantages in the interests of enlightenment and progress, while securing influence over them in the interests of Ukrainianness – touched upon a more fundamental dilemma: the ambiguous reaction of Ukrainian pioneer leaders to the concept of Canada as a 'free country.' On the one hand, they recognized and applauded the democratic institutions and ideals that provided Ukrainians with political, educational, and cultural opportunities, as individuals and as a group, unknown in the homeland. The idea that Canada was the deliberate choice of Ukrainian emigrants yearning for such freedoms, and that an expression of gratitude and loyalty was due to the country that furnished them, would become part and parcel of a Ukrainian-Canadian group myth.[5] The new environment was also perceived to contest and erode traditional social controls and values deemed responsible for the ignorance and backwardness that contributed to the peasant immigrants' negative image and low status. Progressives and Protestants, as well as the secular nationalist intelligentsia, agreed that in a 'free country' priests could not dictate to their flocks or live like lords, 'above the people and the state.'[6] Nor could parents dictate to their children, or husbands to their wives. In fact, argued one progressive well into the interwar years, the woman who beat her husband for losing their savings at cards was acting within her rights in a 'free country.'[7]

On the other hand, the phrase 'fri kontri' as used in the ideological press, beginning with the pioneer era, denoted distrust of the effects of democratic ideals and institutions as interpreted at the popular level by unenlightened and impressionable Ukrainian immigrants. The British Columbia woman accused of profiting from a 'free country' to defy the laws of God and man and leave her husband for a common-law relationship won no approval for her actions. Nor did the young men in Fort William, Ontario, who in 1911 relieved a party of single immigrant girls of their luggage and money and plied them with liquor, saying that this was Canada and everything came cheap; en route to farms near Biggar, Saskatchewan, the girls had been attracted by the promise of a better life in a free country.[8] The grassroots understanding of Canada that such incidents were seen to represent aroused concern at elite levels for two reasons. They seemed to justify doubts about Ukrainians' ability to escape their dark heritage and handle Canadian freedom, and they implied a popular perception of the Canadian frontier as an unrestrained liberating and liberalizing influence. To nationalists, if either suspicion proved correct, the new homeland would release Ukrainian immigrants not only from the old-country controls and values that the emerging leadership had rejected for inhibiting progress and enlightenment, but also those it upheld as embodying the essence of the metropolitan heritage to be preserved and nurtured.

In their ambiguous assessment of the impact of Canadian freedom on Ukrainian immigrants, Ukrainian pioneer leaders echoed the sentiments of contemporary Anglo-Canadian nation builders. Although Anglo-Canadians spoke on behalf of different group goals and metropolitan ties, those of Britishness and Protestantism, they too expected Canadian freedom to liberate Ukrainians from their legacy of backwardness and ignorance. Using the Ukrainian Protestant press to denounce self-serving priests who held the Ukrainian people in ignorance and submission, Presbyterian clergyman and historian George Bryce stressed Ukrainians' right in a free country to think for themselves; he also attacked priests for resisting female education on the grounds that it made girls 'proud or independent or saucy.'[9] But Anglo-Canadians, too, feared the potentially destabilizing effects of freedom on susceptible peasants. Non-English-speaking immigrants little understood 'the institutions of freedom to which they have come,' it was said. 'If they had been worthy of freedom, or capable of making right use of it, they would have fought for it in the land from which they came, or died fighting for it – as Scotchmen and Irishmen and Englishmen and Americans have fought and bled for freedom wherever they have lived. A people unused to freedom suddenly plunged in freedom need not surprise us if they run amuck.'[10] Electoral corruption, crime, violence, immorality, atheism – these were perceived as the price paid when Ukrainians were allowed to sample Canadian freedom without proper guidance in the 'right' choices. To Anglo-Canadian nation builders, the opportunities their country promised Ukrainian immigrants did not extend to being permitted to chart their own course if it threatened Canada's social fabric and political institutions. In the final analysis, Canadian freedom was to weaken traditional Ukrainian bonds, values, and community mechanisms not so much for the sake of individual Ukrainians as for the sake of Anglo-Canadians' ambitions for their nation.

Ukrainians who also feared that Canadian freedom would cause vulnerable immigrants to 'run amuck' blamed the situation on their history of oppression coupled with the wholesale abandonment of traditional values and restraints. But unlike Anglo-Canadian nation builders, who wanted to replace Ukrainians' old-country heritage with their own, nationalist activists and spokespersons wished to reform while reinforcing a sense of Ukrainian group membership and responsibility. To men and women anxious to see their people accepted and prosperous and committed to Ukrainian national-cultural goals, Nasha Meri and Katie (together with their male companion Jack) embodied the perils of thrusting Ukrainian youth, the group's future, unsupervised and unprepared, into the life of the new country. Lacking all propriety and social conscience, they not only became a laughingstock themselves but further blackened an already unflattering group image and played into the hands of those who would divorce them from their past.

But if Nasha Meri and Katie symbolized an extreme and represented something of a panic reaction to an imagined rather than an actual threat, they did not emerge in a vacuum. The conditions Ukrainians encountered in Canada made inevitable the conflicts and dilemmas they expressed. First, poverty forced both turn-of-the-century homesteaders and working-class families to send their daughters out to work, removing adolescents from parental and community supervision – to experiment with new ideas, new activities, and new relationships that not infrequently existed uneasily with the old. By the 1920s and 1930s, the same poverty forced the rural girl attending high school in town to pay for her room and board by working as a home help during term and as a general home and farm hand in the summer. Throughout the lengthy period under discussion, there were also girls and women who came to Canada alone and had to earn their own living. Between 1905 and 1914, almost one-third of Ukrainian female immigrants listed themselves as servants, and in the 1920s (Canada closed its doors to immigrants during the Depression) the figure was closer to two-thirds.[11] The second and third spheres where Canadian conditions had an impact were education and marriage. Whether Ukrainian community leaders insisted on the need for general enlightenment or not, Canadian school attendance laws swelled the number of Ukrainian girls in educational institutions and increased their length of stay. By introducing girls to new lifestyles and providing the means to pursue them, education fostered independence and choice, combining with other developments either to postpone marriage or to create viable alternatives. Access to marriage itself became a matter for the Canadian state, as minimum age and age of majority laws challenged tradition and parental control. Jobs, school, and marriage – not necessarily in that order, not always in combination, and not for everyone – would be both cause of and witness to massive change in the collective profile of Ukrainian women as a 'Canadian' generation left the peasant immigrant behind. Even as individual lives were transformed, however, the biases of Anglo-Canadian society towards women and Ukrainians, and ingrained attitudes among Ukrainians themselves, interfered on all fronts to influence the direction of change and to limit its scope.

Like Ukrainian males seeking paid employment, Ukrainian girls obliged to support themselves or to contribute financially to the well-being of the family unit initially had few skills to offer potential employers. Low-paying and low-status jobs – in service in private English or Jewish homes, as chambermaids and waitresses in hotels and restaurants, and as workers in Canadian factories – reflected this handicap, together with unfamiliarity with English and with Canadian ways. The girls' employers saw their new help as a mixed blessing. The sturdy Galician servant freed her mistress from hard work and menial tasks, but ignorant of the 'implement[s] of modern indoor warfare,' she had to be taught not only Anglo-Canadian standards of cleanliness and home management but also the use of strange household appliances and gadgets. Some matrons simply gave up on 'untrainable' foreign maids.[12] The first concerted effort to help working girls adapt came in 1901 when the Roman Catholic Oblate Fathers in Edmonton organized the Ruthenian Young Ladies Club, a night school conducted by the Faithful Companions of Jesus, where some forty working girls learned English, their catechism, and needlework. When the Ukrainian Sisters Servants of Mary Immaculate arrived a year later, they added Ukrainian music and handicrafts to the curriculum. This circle gave the Sisters Servants their first Canadian recruit.[13]

The jobs in which Ukrainian girls were clustered corresponded to their people's intended station in Canadian society, as Anglo-Canadians deliberately solicited and groomed them for the occupations held to be ideally suited to their talents and Ukrainian origins. To train servants for 'good' middle-class Anglo-Canadian homes, through classes in household economics and English, was one of the functions of the Ruthenian (Ukrainian) Girls' Home opened in Edmonton in 1909 by the Woman's Missionary Society of the Methodist church. Interwar legislation designed to restrict and regulate East European immigration was more sinister; by exempting agricultural workers and domestics, the Railways Agreement of 1925 earmarked large numbers of Ukrainian women for a specific and humble location in the Cana-

Job opportunities in the pioneer bloc settlement. Rural store clerk,
Wahstao, Alberta, 1918

dian social and economic hierarchy. In 1931, 64.2 per cent of the
Ukrainian immigrant female labour force was in service and 24.8 per
cent in agriculture.[14]

In 1902 a traveller in the West spoke of Canadian optimism concerning the potential of Ukrainian immigrants. 'They speedily discard
their sheepskins and other distinctive clothing,' he said. 'Especially is
this the case with the girls, many of whom are in domestic service in
Edmonton, and whose taste for the millinery and dry-goods of the Far
West is undoubted. They are usually shorter and of heavier build than
our slim Canadian girls, and such is their desire to assimilate with their
new surroundings they may even soon hold the conviction that type-
writing and the business college are the chief end of woman.'[15] If
business college became the dream, it remained far from the reality.
Prior to the Second World War, only a small minority of Ukrainian
women participated in the paid labour force in a given year, although
the overall proportion increased significantly from one-twenty-fifth of
those over the age of fifteen in 1921 to between one-tenth and one-
fifth in 1941. A shortage of technical training and skills was still very
much in evidence as most women worked in the service industry (66.9
per cent) or agriculture (16.5 per cent), although the manufacturing

Skilled job opportunities in the bloc settlement. Seamstress in tailor shop. Smoky Lake, Alberta, 1949

sector (7.3 per cent) showed some movement into semi-skilled occupations. Data gathered in Montreal in the 1930s showed few employed Ukrainian women in the city's many factories, the great majority being servants in Jewish homes; moreover, most worked only until they married, since husbands thought working wives lowered their status, even though the women reported feeling useless in an urban environment with only housekeeping to do. Movement into the professions was even more modest. The number of teachers doubled (from 273 to 553) between 1931 and 1941 and the number of nurses almost quadrupled (from 66 to 231), but teachers and nurses formed only 3.6 per cent and 1.5 per cent of the Ukrainian female labour force, respectively; nuns constituted the next largest category of 'professionals.'[16]

Entry into the professions, however gradual or uneven, and however limited by the choices available to women, was a sign of higher education, at least for the privileged few who became part of a Ukrainian-Canadian middle class. The epitomization of progress and the group benefits of enlightenment, its ranks supplied the women who worked between the wars to organize their sex within the nationalist framework. New roles were also a sign of decreasing sociocultural distance

Most professionally minded Ukrainian-Canadian women chose teaching, the
great majority finding employment in schools in the bloc settlements.
Smoky Lake, Alberta, 1942

between Ukrainians and the Canadian mainstream, as the former adopted mainstream customs and values and the latter, as a result, repressed its anti-Ukrainian sentiments. Two Alberta women were an early example of this type of acculturation; Miss Sophie Howka and Mrs Tomashewsky, the *Lamont Tribune* announced in 1916, had opened a dressmaking and millinery business in nearby Mundare.[17] Acculturation and 'English' education could also throw Ukrainian girls into the limelight, when they were called upon to serve as court interpreters, sometimes to the displeasure of Ukrainian men but to Anglo-Canadian praise for a job well done.[18] But the interwar years provided the most prominent examples of women acting as bridges between mainstream agencies and their own people: Hanna Romanchych and Savella Stechishin, activists in the newly established Ukrainian Women's Association of Canada. Forced to abandon university because of depression and her father's refusal to further finance her education,[19] the Manitoba-born Romanchych was retained by the Alberta Women's Bureau in the Department of Agriculture to lecture on domestic science to Ukrainian women in the Vegreville bloc. Stechishin, who had come to Canada in 1913 as a young child, settling with her family at Krydor, Saskatchewan, provided a similar service in rural Saskatchewan through the extension department of the university in Saskatoon. The holder of a degree in home economics, she had continued her education after marriage to the principal of Mohyla Institute, where she herself had been a student and subsequently served as dean of women. Both Romanchych and Stechishin had a large audience. The great majority of the first Canadian generation of Ukrainian women remained on the farm – to work, marry, and bear and rear children as their mothers had done before them.

Farm girls who did go to the city, regardless of how temporarily, joined single immigrants and the daughters of urban labourers as wage-earners. The nature of their work was unlike that of the married woman who ran a boarding-house or washed clothes and cooked meals for her bachelor countrymen[20] in that it involved them with mainstream society, even if they were isolated in a private English home. This way of life fitted with the goal of the nationalist agenda promoting maintenance of Ukrainian culture within the context of full participation in Canadian life. But the trio of Nasha Meri, Katie, and Jack – both as they were understood to represent an actual or potential reality (job ghettoization and unseemly behaviour) and in that they served to express communal concerns – stood as proof that this hope

Helping with chores on the homestead. Rural Manitoba, 1926

was doomed without widespread enlightenment. Why, asked a former Mohylianka in 1923, pointing the finger at parents who saw only marriage in a girl's future, did thousands of Ukrainian girls work in hotels and for Jewish mistresses when the Jews sent their daughters to university?[21] The Jews, it will be remembered, were Ukrainians' old-country yardstick for measuring progress and upward mobility in Canada. But the woman also drew on other comparisons. Why, she continued, did ethnic groups in Saskatchewan smaller in size than the Ukrainian have a greater proportion of girls in university? Ukrainians could boast only one woman student in all of Canada.[22]

Support for the nationalist community's agitation on behalf of education came from mainstream society as compulsory attendance regulations by the 1920s ensured at least elementary and some secondary schooling. In 1921 only half of foreign-born Ukrainian females in Canada were illiterate, as girls arriving as young children entered Canadian schools. Ten years later, literacy requirements for new immigrants had helped drop the figure to a third, by which time illiteracy among native-born Canadians was lower for Ukrainian than for Canadian women as a whole. By the Second World War virtually all

Farm wife and hired girl working in the fields during threshing. Rural
Alberta, c.1925

school-aged Ukrainian girls attended educational institutions, although they were slightly less likely to do so in rural than in urban
areas.[23]

But to Ukrainian community activists and spokespersons, *prosvita*
(enlightenment) referred not simply to knowledge obtained from formal academic instruction but to education in the broadest sense, and
thus it embraced more than the public school. Enlightenment meant
expanded intellectual horizons to make Ukrainians competitive with
the 'cultured and civilized' peoples of the world; it meant an awakened
national consciousness; and it meant taking an interest in local, national, and international affairs. To this end, beginning with the peasant immigrant generation and continuing through the interwar years,
Ukrainian leaders insisted on education and enlightenment for girls
as well as for boys; and, they believed, if the girl sent to work in the
city needed improving, so did her sister who stayed on the farm.

Indifference or hostility to book learning in general was only one
of the problems identified to be tackled. The other was ingrained
attitudes that trivialized women's intellectual needs. If Ukrainian-
Canadian women were to be useful members of society concerned for
their group's image, their families' spiritual and material progress,
and the Ukrainian goals of a community elite, they had to be intelligent

First day at school. Rural Alberta, c.1920

mothers and homemakers and intelligent public citizens. Between the wars, a nationalist female elite that understood the 'true' meaning of enlightenment and presumed to speak both for and to its sex would argue that the importance of women as mothers made female education necessary.[24] Such a position was already accepted community wisdom by 1920. No longer, would-be reformers said, could Ukrainians presume that girls were adequately prepared for life if they knew how to cook, sew, clean, and milk cows and valued hard work. No longer could physical appearance be ranked above things of the mind or spirit. No longer could it be argued that schooling, while necessary for doctors or lawyers, was irrelevant to girls whose future lay in marriage as farm wives. And no longer could women be allowed to stagnate within the four walls of their houses, preoccupied with their petty cares and routines and oblivious to the world outside.[25] If they did, they condemned their families and people to a second-rate existence.

Early twentieth-century Anglo-Canadians also propagandized specifically for the education of Ukrainian girls. Like Ukrainian community leaders, they objected to the popular wisdom that early and inevitable marriage and motherhood precluded the need for intellectual development. Looking back in her autobiography, women's rights activist, Nellie McClung, complained of the Ukrainian settler's reluctance to educate his daughters. 'Many a promising pupil,' she wrote, 'had her education cut short when some grizzled old widower thought a good strong red-cheeked young girl would be right handy around the house and it would be cheaper to marry her than to have to pay her wages ... Women and children did not count for much in the grim battle for existence.'[26] But while Ukrainian leaders defined female enlightenment (as opposed to education) primarily in terms of Ukrainian group objectives, Anglo-Canadians understood it to mean liberation from the Ukrainian woman's traditional oppression and her assimilation in the service of their own group. This type of enlightenment the public school could achieve. Writing about 'our new immigrants – "the Galicians"' in 1898, the anonymous author of one article had defined the purpose of education as being 'to break up the old habits and prejudices begot of centuries of oppressive darkness, and to assimilate ... [Ukrainians] as soon as may be, not only in language but in all other respects with our own people. Freedom they will surely have, but enlightenment is as necessary as freedom, and without this, however laborious, they cannot advance much beyond their present primitive condition.'[27]

That enlightenment meant more than simply the bookish knowledge imparted by the school, with the assimilated Ukrainian girl put to Anglo-Canadian uses, was illustrated by the 1915 prohibition referendum in the Vegreville bloc. Missionary-organized children, 'trained and led' by Ukrainian girls drilled in Methodism, paraded outside a rural poll to get Ukrainian men to sign temperance pledges.[28] Furthermore, in their campaign to liberate Ukrainian girls from the sexual oppression that had weighed upon their mothers, Anglo-Canadians showed themselves willing to ignore their own preaching when it served their purpose. What received disapproval when equated with undesirable Ukrainian peasant custom could be applauded when Anglo-Canadian interests were at stake. In her report to the Woman's Missionary Society in 1915, a Methodist worker in rural Alberta wrote:

Last winter we had the experience of deciding the delicate question of a marriage proposal for our maid. After several suitors had come, a young Methodist Ruthenian came along and asked for Pokeetza in the presence of Miss Yarwood and myself. Being assured that Pokeetza would make a good wife for the right man, Kepha promised to love her and treat her well. The conclusion was that in about two weeks they were married at her home by Rev. C.H. Lawford, M.D., Miss Yarwood and myself having the honor of being bridesmaids.[29]

A second report to church headquarters provided more background to the story. The successful suitor was one of four Methodist converts homesteading together. 'After batching for a month or so,' the young men 'decided that a woman was needed at the head of the house; they debated the question and decided that Kepha was to go forth in search of a wife. Paketza was found.'[30] From all appearances, this particular mission servant was as peripheral to her betrothal as the peasant bride that Anglo-Canadians sought to befriend was to hers. The difference was that Anglo-Protestant missionaries had replaced the peasant girl's parents as the decision makers.

From the perspective of a Ukrainian community leadership committed to national-cultural survival as well as to integration, so called 'enlightenment' through an aggressively assimilationist school system or mission centre could create as many problems as it solved. It provided Ukrainian-Canadian women with necessary knowledge but it militated against the Ukrainian consciousness that nationalists' definition of enlightenment entailed. 'Education' in its Anglo-Canadian meaning facilitated assimilation to Anglo-Canadian ideals and attitudes; the practical knowledge that came with it also enabled young Ukrainian women to eschew traditional roles for their sex, jeopardizing the hold that Ukrainian custom and community sanctions had exerted over their mothers. The school itself usurped much of the mother's role as childrearer, threatening her ability to raise Ukrainian daughters.

Marriage was the third area where the Canadian environment had a significant impact and joined forces with the imperatives of the Ukrainian community to affect both attitudes and practices. The issues that would dominate discussions about marriage had all been raised by 1910. One episode, particularly important because it was initiated by Ukrainians themselves, aired and brought together the principal points of view in the debate. In late 1905 *Kanadiiskyi farmer* reported the claim of a Mrs Chisholm, addressing the Woman's Christian Temperance Union in Hamilton, Ontario, that for twenty-five or thirty dollars Ukrainian immigrants routinely sold their thirteen- and fourteen-year-old daughters in marriage. With the tongue-in-cheek observation that temperance convention or not, the woman's remarks had to have been inspired by diabolical drink, a barrage of letters denounced as a 'scandalous slur' false and ignorant remarks designed to cast the Ukrainian people in a negative light. One author claimed that part of Mrs Chisholm's problem arose from her misunderstanding of an important wedding ritual where the groom displayed his affluence by presenting the bride's parents with a gift of money – often exceeded in value, it was pointed out, by the dowry he received in return. But these letters also had another side that tempered the message of outrage and injustice. Ukrainians often deserved their bad reputation, some of Mrs Chisholm's detractors conceded; and they had to face the fact that prevailing attitudes towards marriage, particularly among the rising generation of young women, left much to be desired. Correspondents also addressed prospective brides and grooms directly. A bachelor, obviously unhappy with his single condition after thirteen years in Canada, advised young women to exchange ignorance for education and organization, to choose their male companions wisely, and to curb their new-found passion for hats and put the savings in mutual aid associations, for no one cared about penniless widows whose husbands were killed on the job. He told men to marry literate women, for their wives would be mothers entrusted with moulding their children.[31]

The Chisholm episode is significant, both for its articulation of a common Anglo-Canadian prejudice and for the nature of the Ukrainian reaction it provoked. As the prewar immigrant community surveyed peasant attitudes and practices for their impact on the quality of Ukrainian-Canadian life, the criteria governing a girl's induction into wifehood and thus motherhood became a target. Critics of the status quo condemned early and arranged marriages as immoral, unnatural, and illegal; an impediment to progress, they were the mark of an uncultured people and backward parents. Critics also decried what was described as the coldness and stupor of family life when marriages were loveless or spouses unenlightened. They fretted about the emotional and intellectual unpreparedness of adolescents for marital responsibilities, and they expressed concern for the health of both mother and child when a woman faced repeated pregnancy before full physical maturity.[32] The conclusion to be drawn from such worries is that Ukrainian children, the hope of the future, were not to be penalized by mothers forced into marriage and motherhood before they were ready. If a girl's right in a 'free country' to decide when and whom she married was held to be one consideration, clearly the effect of adolescent and loveless marriage on Ukrainian prospects was another.

Critics also offered remedies. Ukrainians' own priests, teachers, and other enlightened compatriots were urged to promote reform in the colonies by using their influence at the personal level; priests, for example, were told they should simply refuse to marry the overly young. Others used a medical approach, alerting intending couples to the dangers of consanguinity and venereal and other diseases that could affect the health of their offspring. The press introduced columns on childrearing and homemaking, combining material of an ideological nature with practical information on topics ranging from personal hygiene to food preparation and infant care. Increasingly, too, Ukrainians wishing guidance in matters of sex and the heart could turn to 'experts' for help. In 1913 the Ukrainian Bookstore in Winnipeg published a guide to writing love letters, a middle-class social convention undoubtedly of no little novelty to newly literate peasants, and by the Second World War its catalogue carried several Ukrainian-language titles on feminine health and hygiene.[33]

Both Anglo-Canadian and Ukrainian nationalist elites were preoccupied with their private agenda – the future of Canada, ethnic-group status and survival – that carried their own prejudices and perceptions of reality to govern calls for reform. Neither group examined the relationship between Ukrainian marriage practices and the pragmatic needs of a modernizing peasant society in an emigration/immigration situation. Had they done so, they might have realized that much of what they observed and criticized was abnormal and temporary. An imbalanced sex ratio with a surplus of adult males joined forces with the demands of homesteading to exaggerate and exploit the traditional peasant concept of marriage as an economic necessity. 'Bride-wanted' advertisements in the Ukrainian immigrant press represent one response of bachelors deprived of a traditional source of potential wives to a novel and unnatural situation, particularly for men who lived away from the bloc settlements. Letters to the press from men working in

Eldest daughter ready for a husband. Rural Alberta, nd

Lethbridge and Vancouver, for example, spoke of the loneliness without Ukrainian girls, and tried to entice them with promises of plenty of well-paid jobs in service or the local hotels.[34]

The 'bride wanted' advertisements appearing in *Kanadiiskyi farmer* between 1906 and 1920 also provide insight into what men thought was necessary for success in the new country. Losing importance with free homestead land, more-or-less steady wages or some savings, and the scarcity of women, a dowry was never a universal requirement, although some diehards went so far as to specify the amount of money or land they expected. Material considerations in general were increasingly replaced or supplemented by other criteria, reflecting views ordinary immigrants shared with the community elite. Would-be grooms wanted women of good character who possessed good housekeeping skills, could read and write, had some knowledge of English, and, suggesting unwelcome rebellion on the part of Ukrainian girls in Canada, were willing to do farm work. But unlike men who wrote to *Kanadiiskyi farmer* as part of an embryonic community elite, these men cared little about the religion or national consciousness of their mail-order brides, and some were as happy to marry Poles as they were Ukrainians.

Had either Anglo-Canadian or Ukrainian elites analysed the reality

Groom with his bride's dowry of household goods. Rural Alberta, 1926

of Ukrainian marriages in the bloc settlements of western Canada, they would also have realized that many of their assumptions and prejudices were unwarranted. One cannot, of course, measure the incidence of romantic love as the basis of matrimony, plot the fortunes of arranged marriage as a fact of life, or evaluate the intellectual and spiritual content of individual relationships. Unlike the situation with education and the workplace, however, where Anglo-Canadian institutions dominated and Ukrainians were often only one of many nationalities, the data exists to examine in detail the accuracy of many stereotypes, and to explore change and continuity in Ukrainian marriage patterns from the turn of the century through the Second World War. Providing a 'pure' Ukrainian sample, the data in question comes from the parish registers of the Ukrainian Basilian Fathers, dispatched to Canada in 1902 by Metropolitan Sheptytsky and settling in east-

Outdoor wedding on the homestead, nd

central Alberta where for many years they served a large mission field from their headquarters in Mundare.[35]

Even a cursory examination of the material in these records reveals the impact of uprooting and relocation. Despite the tendency of kin and villagers to settle in identifiable pockets,[36] emigration offered new choice in marriage partners and a new gene pool. In 1908 only 13 per cent of contracting parties came from the same village; fully one-half of all marriages over the next three years involved people who came not only from different villages but also from different districts in Galicia; and by 1920, when forty of sixty-nine marriages involved partners who were both Galician born, 72.5 per cent of contracting parties came from different districts. Marriage entries also support the contention that circumstances encouraged speedy engagements, unions that stressed economic considerations ahead of love, speedy remarriage on the death of a spouse, and young brides. One young widower, for example, initiated proceedings to marry presumably his first choice in mid February but, later in the month, settled on his dead wife's seventeen-year-old sister. The precariousness of peasant immigrant life and the practical necessity of a complete family unit were further hinted at by the unusually high proportion of weddings in 1919, after

Young mother and baby. From a Woman's Missionary Society album,
captioned 'A New Madonna.' Wahstao Methodist Mission, Alberta,
1909–14

the Spanish influenza epidemic, involving widows (25.8 per cent) and
widowers (28.0 per cent).

In its own sphere, the church's authority remained intact. The Basilians continued to enforce the two great fasting periods before Easter
and Christmas, so that November, after harvest, and the winter months,
before Lent and spring planting, were the two favoured times for
weddings. In 1915 half of all weddings occurred in November, January, and February. By 1945 less than a third did so; and the summer
months (June–August), perhaps reflecting adoption of the mainstream
idea of the 'June bride,' became the preferred season for nuptials. By

Farm mother posing with her twins, nd

1945 weddings had also shifted from a majority on Sunday, traditionally chosen because the peasant was free from labour for the landlord,
to Saturday, the off-day in North American urban industrialized society. Sunday weddings were unusual among the Ukrainians' Anglo-
Canadian neighbours; in thirty-nine years, only nine of 347 marriages
solemnized by ministers of the Vegreville United (Methodist) Church
took place on that day; Wednesdays and Fridays, fasting days in the
Greek Catholic calendar, were more popular.[37] Comparison of the
Basilian sample with a Toronto parish, also Greek Catholic, suggests
that Ukrainians settling in Canadian cities made the Sunday to Sat-

urday shift much sooner.[38] To farmers who ordered their lives around the natural cycles of the seasons, the rhythm of the urban work week was long irrelevant, and Saturday awaited the 1960s to triumph as the unrivalled day on which to celebrate weddings in the Vegreville bloc.[39]

Belying the Anglo-Canadian stereotype of the older groom, most Greek Catholic men in the Mundare mission field married in their mid to late twenties throughout the period under discussion. They tended to be younger, in fact, than the Alberta average. Moreover, in the crucial prewar years when the image of the 'child bride' crystallized and flourished, the average age of marriage for spinsters (as all previously unmarried brides, regardless of age, were identified) ranged from 17.3 to 18.5; fourteen-year-olds were a rarity, and seldom did one-third of brides in any year marry at sixteen or younger. But while refuting Anglo-Canadian stereotypes in their extreme, this picture leaves untouched the basic complaint, shared by the Ukrainian community elite, that Ukrainian girls in the bloc settlements of western Canada married too young. Through the First World War, at least three-quarters of brides married by the Basilian Fathers in Mundare were under twenty years of age. The question to be asked is whether this reflected the norms of Ukrainian peasant society transplanted to Canada, or whether it reflected the peculiar emigrant/immigrant experience of Ukrainian homesteaders in the prairie provinces.

The latter is more probable. In prewar Galicia, fewer than one-third of Ukrainian brides were under twenty years of age (see chapter 1). Alberta reported roughly the same fraction of brides marrying under twenty in this period; and in Anglo-American and Scandinavian areas of the province, comparatively prosperous and with different cultural baggage, age of marriage for both brides and grooms was significantly higher than in the Vegreville bloc.[40] Other findings warn against generalization even in terms of Ukrainian settlement. A second Galician and Greek Catholic sample, from Yorkton-Canora in southeastern Saskatchewan,[41] also shows generally older brides and grooms than the Basilian sample. It suggests that decisions on marriage were influenced by local variables like time of settlement, quality of land, and opportunities for agricultural expansion or employment.

Areas of Canada outside the prairies point even more strongly to the impact of provincial or regional cultures on Ukrainian marriage patterns. In Ontario, where Ukrainian men far outnumbered women, where family settlement with marriageable daughters was not the norm, and where economic insecurity argued as much against a wife as home-

88 Wedded to the Cause

steading argued for one, only a fraction of brides ever married at sixteen or earlier. And during the First World War, when girls in the Basilian sample were marrying around their seventeenth and eighteenth birthdays, their counterparts in Toronto, many of whom undoubtedly worked for their living, married closer to twenty.[42] At the height of the Depression in the mid 1930s, up to a third of Greek Catholic brides in Toronto married in their late twenties, a third of grooms in their early thirties. Delayed marriage in a time of widespread unemployment was much less evident among rural Ukrainians in the Vegreville bloc, cushioned by their social and physical environment despite the general economic hardship. This does not mean that nothing happened in east-central Alberta. In the early 1920s a rapid and permanent drop in the proportion of brides who were sixteen or younger, from 30.0 to 4.8 per cent, benefited the seventeen to nineteen age group in particular. By the end of the Second World War, half to three-quarters of brides in the Basilian sample were in their twenties.

Postponement of marriage, like increased emphasis on love, was a product of agricultural progress that made the peasant concept of marriage, reinforced by the demands of homesteading, obsolete. Less positive factors affecting the timing of marriage, specifically the Depression and the disappearance of free arable land in the original bloc, had the same result. Postponement also reflected 'Canadian' influences – more time in school, state matrimonial laws, perhaps a job or even a career. The changes that occurred in the interwar profile of brides in the Vegreville bloc were spectacular, with far-reaching implications for the women concerned. The changes were less impressive when compared with Alberta as a whole, where brides showed the same trend towards later marriage, but remained concentrated in higher age categories.[43] Nationally, Ukrainian women also tended to be more married than their all-Canadian counterparts.[44] That Ukrainian brides in the Vegreville bloc remained comparatively young points to the persistence of old attitudes together with cash shortages that continued to make a wife an important asset on the Ukrainian farm. One interwar study would argue that a wife's intensive and unpaid labour allowed the Ukrainian farmer to prosper and expand at the expense of his Anglo-Canadian neighbour who hired help.[45]

On the surface, even before the accelerated pace of change after the Second World War, the Ukrainian-Canadian woman of 1945 was unrecognizable as the descendant of the peasant immigrant of the

Changing times and pastimes. Ukrainian-Canadian youth indistinguishable from their mainstream counterparts. Rural Alberta, 1938

1890s. No doubt the latter's contemporaries, both Anglo-Canadian and Ukrainian, who had agitated for reform would be pleased. In other respects neither elite could feel that the battle was won. True, the changing profile of Ukrainian-Canadian women registered the revolution in women's lives that emigration had inaugurated – evidence of 'progress,' 'enlightenment,' and 'emancipation.' But throughout the interwar years, significant socioeconomic and cultural differences continued to distinguish Ukrainian-Canadian from other Canadian women.[46] The differences reflected in part Ukrainians' immigrant entrance status and Anglo-Canadian prejudices, limiting women's mobility in the larger society. In part they reflected the persistence of Ukrainian linguistic and cultural points of identification and traditional Ukrainian attitudes towards women. Moreover, what the mainstream applauded as a positive sign of assimilation, Ukrainians deplored as the leading wedge of denationalization; what the mainstream deplored as unhealthy ghettoization, Ukrainians applauded as a positive sign of national-cultural survival.

With few exceptions, the Ukrainian Catholic bride in east-central Alberta in 1945 had married within her group, and in the great majority of cases she had married within her faith.[47] Nationwide, some three-quarters of Ukrainian-Canadian women still belonged to the Ukrainian Catholic or Orthodox churches; over 90 per cent still spoke Ukrainian as their mother tongue; and, despite a significant decline in religious endogamy, some two-thirds still married Ukrainian Catholic or Orthodox husbands.[48] Most adult Ukrainian women, if now the beneficiaries of formal education, delayed marriage, and exposure to 'civilization' through the school and workplace, remained the Ukrainian-speaking, church-going wives of Ukrainian farmers. The community apprehension that participation in Canadian life, while highly desirable, would bring social disorganization and alienate Ukrainian women from their group appeared overdrawn and premature.

The apprehension was very real, however, and went back to the beginning of the century. While perceived to be of questionable value to her family or people as she stood, the ignorant and apathetic farm girl remained in a milieu and under authorities able to direct change along desirable channels. She, in a sense, was safe. The truly frightening spectacle was the urban working girl removed from traditional constraining and guiding influences. She failed her family and people not by ignorance and apathy alone but by ignorance and apathy culminating in outright rebellion against the values, traditions, loyalties, and obligations that bound Ukrainians and Ukrainian society together. To be sure, not all working girls deserved the mantle of Nasha Meri and Katie. Emilia Polianchuk, a hotel worker in Fernie, British Columbia, where her father was employed in the mines, promised readers of *Kanadiiskyi farmer* that she would not forget the 'dear Ruthenian songs' and she pined to hear a real 'Ruthenian church service.' Disregarding the dearth of qualified candidates, a worker's wife wrote to *Ukrainskyi holos* in 1919 to criticize the inertia of those women equipped and obliged by education and privilege to lead their sex: the wives of doctors, lawyers, priests, politicians, businessmen, and teachers, and teachers themselves. Such individuals, she said, ought to have been in the vanguard of organizing women for national purposes.[49] Her Ukrainian servant singing the songs of her people, presumably as she worked, had stimulated the interest in Ukrainian culture that led Florence Randal Livesay to publish *Songs of Ukraina* in 1916. Critics of the working girl also carefully excluded the 'honourable industrious' girls who were a 'credit to their people' from their remarks, and Ukrainians liked to boast of their domestics' good reputations.[50]

But the fact remained that the Anglo-Canadian city embodied the community's worst fears for the future. Expressing these fears, an unflattering stereotype of the working girl, ultimately symbolized by Nasha Meri and Katie, first emerged in nationalist literature shortly after Ukrainians arrived in Canada. The progressive equivalent, largely an interwar phenomenon, expressed some of the same complaints but demonstrated less concern for the girl's Ukrainianness and considerably more concern for the person herself.

To the girls caught by its magnetism, the city represented material amenities and North American popular culture; it brought freedom from often circumscribed and isolated life on the homestead, and promised financial independence and escape from unwanted filial obligations, female roles, and parental authority. At the same time, inexperience, lack of marketable skills, and a nativistic host society convinced of its superiority exacerbated the girls' female condition, limiting their options and subjecting them to exploitation, prejudice, and discrimination. This reality gave progressives, as champions of the downtrodden, their motivation and program. Fear and disorientation in unfamiliar surroundings could also crush any sense of adventure. Two homesteaders' daughters sent by their families to find jobs in Neepawa, Manitoba, were ample proof. Terrified of missing the second train, as they had the first, they sat on a railway bench for one and a half days, refusing the brakemen's offer of food because it might be poisoned (one of the girls had lived in Canada for a year and knew about such things).[51] Nor did their peasant background and the Ukrainian immigrants' rudimentary sense of identity help unsophisticated and inwardly insecure youth cope with an alien milieu that often made them ashamed of and eager to transcend their origins while erecting barriers against it.

From the nationalist standpoint, the personal confusion of the flesh-and-blood Ukrainian girl in the city was less disconcerting than the impact of her actions and reactions on her group's fortunes. In one sense typical of all immigrant youth caught between two worlds, the

citified adolescent as immortalized in Nasha Meri and Katie and popularized by the nationalist press cannot be separated from the role the
nationalist community defined for its women. Themselves the embodiment of the unacceptable, Nasha Meri and Katie were intended
to leave little doubt as to what women's attitudes and behaviour should
be.

An Austrian government representative touring Canada in 1904
remarked on the popularity of Ukrainian domestics in Edmonton hotels and private homes. He also noted their taste for urban luxury and
added a comment about their hats, which were so expensive and over-
stated that society ladies had switched to cheaper styles to avoid being
mistaken for their servants.[52] As the Ukrainian community watched
what was happening among its young women, hats attracted an in-
ordinate amount of attention.

On one level, the flamboyant hats that found such favour with their
wearers symbolized the externals in the Anglo-Canadian lifestyle – the
face powder, the chewing gum, the fashions – that Ukrainian leaders
deplored as the excesses and vulgar choices of ignorant, directionless
girls. Cutting pathetic figures in their paint and finery, they possessed
all the wrong priorities. Only stupid girls, wrote an irate observer of
the city scene in 1907, thought that a big hat with a peacock feather
increased their intelligence; they should be reading the Ukrainian
press and interesting themselves in Ukrainian affairs instead.[53] Promoting a different set of priorities, an interwar progressive voiced
similar views on powder and lipstick, when women should be spending
their money on the progressive magazine, *Robitnytsia* (Workingwoman), to develop their class consciousness. A Catholic contemporary
spoke on behalf of yet other values. Feminine fixation with powder,
perfume, and external beauty, he cautioned, should not obscure the
need for a beautiful soul too.[54]

On a second level, clothing symbolized an assimilation with Anglo-
Canadian attitudes and ideals. Contemporary Anglo-Canadians fondly
saw the discarding of their 'quaint Galician garb' by Ukrainian girls
as the outward manifestation of an inner revolution in which they
identified with superior Anglo-Canadian values and standards.[55] In
much the same way, Ukrainian nationalist leaders regarded 'English'
dress as the outward manifestation of an inner alienation from the
Ukrainian-Canadian group. For both the Ukrainian community anxious to keep Ukrainian girls under its influence and for the girls who
wore them, hats marked the substitution of a particularly important

Ukrainian cultural symbol for one with none of the same meaning behind it. An important ritual in the Ukrainian peasant wedding was the bride's exchange of her maiden's wreath for the headshawl of a married woman, after initially refusing the kerchief to show her resistance to leaving girlhood.[56] If in their preference for hats Nasha Meri and Katie were making a statement of freedom and independence, perhaps they were also rejecting women's traditional status and roles that the headscarf symbolized. Any such statement need not have been as conscious or militant as the community elite might have feared, but the implications were serious nonetheless.

A further expression of emancipation was the lifestyle that Nasha Meri and Katie equated with the city. After the isolation and physical toil of the farm, and after an often equally hard day's work for the English businessman or mistress, they fancied a 'gud taim' (good time). As their notion of a 'gud taim,' dances and the moving pictures offered stiff competition to church services and lectures, whether those of the Ukrainian or the Anglo-Canadian community. In their reaction to the working girl's lifestyle and values, Ukrainian nationalists expressed attitudes remarkably like those of their Anglo-Canadian competitors. In part this reflected similar nation-building goals despite their different ends, but it also reflected the prejudices of an aspiring Ukrainian middle class towards working-class culture.[57]

Both Anglo-Canadians and Ukrainians were censorious of the working girl's entertainment choices and intent on providing uplifting alternatives. Urban temptations and vices, as much as the need for assimilation in the interests of nation building, led middle-class Anglo-Canadians to advocate live-in domestic service, with its supervised immersion in Anglo-Canadian home life, as the ideal employment for Ukrainian girls. This was the argument of the matron of the Ruthenian Girls' Home in her annual report for 1914. She also lamented the reluctance of the home's girls to attend its compulsory evening classes and worship services and their preference for the night life of the Edmonton street.[58] In the hierarchy of evils awaiting to snare unsuspecting girls, alcohol, cigarettes, and prostitution loomed as far worse dangers than lipstick, powder, and perfume.

For their part, the demoralization and loss of control the city represented made the Ukrainian immigrant intelligentsia, like its counterpart in late nineteenth-century Galicia,[59] reluctant to see girls go out to work in any capacity. Most assuredly, supervised immersion in Anglo-Canadian home life with its goal of assimilation was not the antidote to 'the street,' and Ukrainian pioneer leaders were as wary of service in even the best of homes as they were of the restaurant, hotel, or factory environment.[60] How the working girl chose to occupy her leisure hours received few accolades. It joined the clothes, the obsession with expensive things, and the sweet tooth that craved ice cream and cake to cement her reputation as frivolous, vulgar, and worthless. Next on the list came the affected mannerisms and pretentious imitation of what the girls construed to be the airs of an English 'lady,' picked up in the street or in their employers' homes, which bespoke of a more serious alienation.[61] Youth's misguided emulation of a superior class not its own was also condemned in Jack. But Jack, unlike Nasha Meri and Katie, worked not in an English environment but on crews dominated by his own kind or by other immigrants, and, rather than imitate an English 'gentleman,' he tried to play the Galician '*pan*' (lord).[62]

If letters and articles in the nationalist press attributed the Nasha Meri and Katie phenomenon to any one cause, it was careless or indifferent upbringing at the hands of ignorant and unprogressive parents who needed guidance themselves. Such parents were observed to be lacking in self-respect and a positive identity, without their own sustaining values and principles, and mindless of the higher things in life. This made them singularly ill-equipped to inspire their daughters, already handicapped by an irrational and impressionable female nature,[63] to greater heights. The meagre spiritual resources these girls received before being shoved, often far too young, into the foreign world explained the irresponsibility, fascination with trinkets and questionable pastimes, and disdain of books and learning. Without proper instruction, it was argued, inexperienced and rudderless girls naturally and inevitably gravitated towards the worst in Canadian society, by which standards they became 'civilized.'[64]

That Nasha Meri and Katie's priorities and extravagances, indeed their very fate, could also have reflected their condition as members of an immigrant group assigned to the fringes of Canadian society was little appreciated in either Anglo-Canadian or Ukrainian nationalist circles. Only the progressives explored the relationship between the working girl's options and fate, and the class, ethnic, and gender hierarchies of which she was a part. Progressives also accused nationalists of indifference to the human plight of these girls, being concerned only for their ability to sing patriotic songs and their willingness to hand over their money for patriotic causes.[65]

Exactly where the nationalist community stood is illustrated by the response to a letter that appeared in *Kanadiiskyi farmer* in 1909. The original missive, possibly the work of the editor who published it, was ostensibly from 'Meri' to her parents in the old country, who, bewildered by its anglicisms, had sent it to *Kanadiiskyi farmer* for translation. Meri reports that she is having a 'gud taim' and proceeds to describe her adventures. 'We see clearly from this letter,' states the editor in his commentary, zeroing in on what he saw as the crux of the problem, 'what our girls working in private English homes, hotels and factories come to. Excluding the more conscious ones, they become victims like the author of this letter. It would be timely to reflect on the danger looming over such girls. First parents and then all those who desire true cultural consciousness among our youth ought to be watchful of such developments in our "cultural" life and direct these Meris onto the correct path. As Shevchenko says, "Learn from others but do not forsake your own." '66 The solution to this predicament was enlightened leadership by members of Nasha Meri and Katie's own sex. If Ukrainians had a female intelligentsia, lamented an article in *Ukrainskyi holos* in 1910, working girls in Winnipeg would not fritter away their free hours in idleness and frivolous amusements but be busy with worthwhile projects in women's organizations under the intelligentsia's tutelage and guidance.67 Between the wars, Mohyla graduates in particular, and the educated in general, were understood to have a missionary role, instructing farm women in both practical housekeeping and Ukrainian matters, and raising the national consciousness of urban female workers.68

Public censure and ridicule for conduct harmful to the Ukrainian group image and goals, plus admonition to the delinquent to reform, were commonplace in the pioneer nationalist press, and their barbs were by no means confined to Nasha Meri and Katie. Publicizing instances of adolescent waywardness among both sexes, of drunkenness and violence, of child abuse, of bigamy by men with wives in the old country, of marital infidelity, and of 'instant' bachelors and widowers playing fast and loose made examples of the guilty.69 On occasion the moral lesson was unmistakably direct. Dmytro Hunkevych wrote *Zhertvy temnoty* (Victims of darkness), he explained in his afterword to the play, in order to expose the evils waiting to ensnare Ukrainian immigrants in Canada, their ignorance making them easy targets for the scum of Canadian society. *Zhertvy temnoty* was a warning to male sojourners against alcohol and bad company and the temptation to abandon their families, and to girls against over-hasty marriage and a lifetime of regret.[70]

If the pioneer nationalist press is to be believed, Nasha Meri and Katie's march towards 'civilization' in the absence of traditional and stabilizing influences culminated in moral depravity. First there were the unsavoury characters (Jacks – here a type, without regard to nationality) the girls both attracted and found attractive, and the seamy underworld the men represented. Then came the girls' own immodesty and sexual promiscuity, as poor judgment and gullibility, bad upbringing, and a weak female nature collaborated to make them the willing and shameless prey of the low type of men they pursued and were pursued by in turn. The behaviour of another group of Ukrainian women was viewed even more dimly: in 1902 an immigrant who had quickly absorbed the prejudices of the new country charged that older Ukrainian prostitutes in Edmonton were so lacking in national pride and self-respect that they competed for the favour of the city's Métis.[71] In pioneer nationalist literature, Nasha Meri and Katie seduced and abandoned were fallen women who should pay and be ostracized for their crime. Years later, a short story set in rural Alberta during the Second World War took this attitude to task; its sympathies were with the young unwed mother ostracized by local townsfolk for having transcended the bounds of morality and race (and cast aspersions on her Canadian loyalty) by forming a liaison with a Japanese worker.[72]

In contrast to the nationalists, progressives saw the seduced and abandoned girl as more sinned against than sinning, and their literature emphasized the sexual exploitation and ethnic discrimination that led to her ruin. One of novelist Vera Lysenko's favourite themes, for example, was the Ukrainian working-class girl seduced by her English boss or the dandified scoundrel whose shady activities eventually destroyed her too.[73] The sexually defenceless working girl as portrayed in the progressive press was just as often victimized by her fellow Ukrainian. In one tale the seducer, who had reneged on his promise of marriage, was saved in court when his friends testified to intercourse with the girl; denied justice, the poor unfortunate then gave birth to her illegitimate child, only to be left an orphan when the shock of visiting her hospital bedside killed her mother. The moral of the tale came in the author's admonition to women to raise their daughters well and watch over them, for a daughter's affliction affected her mother no less.[74]

Intertwined with the moral issue revolving around Nasha Meri and Katie's preference in men was the insistence that they be English.

Writers to the nationalist press maintained that the crude, unscrupulous types they chased had already been rejected by more discerning English girls; and that to lovers who neither loved nor respected them, Nasha Meri and Katie were merely objects to be used and cast aside. Then after humiliation and desertion, according to the scenario, they settled for 'second best' and married Ukrainian husbands.[75] Critics also complained that city life ruined young women as farm wives. Expecting to be pampered, too spoiled to work, and sulky when their whims went ungratified, they were an encumbrance to hardworking husbands striving to get ahead. Most Ukrainian bachelors, according to an Alberta settler disgusted that Ukrainian girls would rather be English men's servants than their own mistresses, simply ignored their kind and picked willing farm wives from among new batches of immigrants.[76]

The status and assimilation with the Anglo-Canadian world that Nasha Meri and Katie sought through marriage to English men also drew sharp criticism for its alienation from things Ukrainian. An early correspondent to the socialist *Chervonyi prapor* (Red flag) deplored the lack of national pride it revealed.[77] Concerned as they were for Ukrainianness, nationalist spokespersons were more vocal. They also identified a second evil, condemning as 'enemies of their children' spiritually bankrupt parents, consumed by material greed, who forced their daughters to marry Anglo-Canadians for the status it afforded.[78] Intermarriage might be a stepping stone to wealth or acceptance but it was also the harbinger of national suicide, beginning with the family unit. The 'first' marriage between a Ukrainian and an Anglo-Saxon, celebrated in Dauphin, Manitoba, in 1897, elicited this comment from the officiating priest:

> 'Assimilation!' trumpeted the Canadian newspapers. If only our culture could flourish at such a high level that the children of mixed marriages would retain the Ruthenian characteristics, then a race of people would rise of whom we could be justly proud before the world. Otherwise, our women and the generations born of mixed marriages will be doomed in the sea of English civilization. But, on the other hand, they will not be beggars or slaves without a sense of human dignity, but they will be fully human. And that is all that matters. Or is it?[79]

Undeniably, the group suffered when it lost its future mothers to a rival culture bent on assimilating them and their children to its supposed superior way of life. But the priest raised an equally valid and related question. Was completeness as a human being possible, even if 'the English' represented undreamed-of heights of civilization, for the Ukrainian man or woman alienated from the group into which he or she was born? To a community committed to survival, the answer was obviously no. And just as obviously, mixed marriage was the principal culprit and leading wedge, an indulgence of weak characters lacking in self-respect. Nasha Meri and Katie, along with their sex and class, were not the only guilty parties. How many young men, *Ukrainskyi holos* asked, intoning that true Ukrainians married their own, thought that an English wife spelled entry into better society? The spectre of intermarriage among males became an argument for the education of Ukrainian girls – to ensure that the educated Ukrainian young man did not look to foreign nationalities for a compatible bride in Canada as he did in Galicia.[80]

One of Jacob Maydanyk's cartoon strips opened with Nasha Meri the flapper scornfully rejecting her mother's humble offer of a dish of *pyrohy* or Ukrainian dumplings. The second panel showed her arm-deep in dishwater as her employer, arms folded, sat watching. In the last panel she was again at home, hungrily devouring the once-spurned *pyrohy* while her mother in her kerchief thanked God.[81] The cartoon touched another community concern that had arisen shortly after Ukrainians arrived in Canada. Summoning all the combined pathos and rebuke they could muster, letters to the pioneer press recited instance after instance of haughty and tight-fisted working girls rejecting their 'Galician' parents. They publicly humiliated their fathers by cutting them dead in the street as it were, leaving the grieving men, anxious to spare the girls' mothers their pain, to make their way home.[82] As early as 1897 the Greek Catholic priest, Nestor Dmytriw, had observed how farm girls employed in Edmonton were ashamed of their parents' squalor and the 'foreignness' that contributed to their reputation as ignorant and backward peasants.[83]

In wishing to escape the same fate and associations, such daughters were not unlike other young immigrant women of their generation straining against old-country heritages, although Ukrainians' negative image and low status undoubtedly added to their shame and alienation. Dmytriw himself was not entirely critical of such girls (more apt than their male counterparts to absorb the Canadian traits most essential for Ukrainian progress),[84] but the coalescing nationalist leadership was less generous than the itinerant priest. Membership in the family

was neither voluntary nor to be taken lightly, and the refusal of working girls to honour their parents, part with their wages, or return to
help on the homestead was interpreted as an unforgivable act of de-
fiance and alienation. The danger that exposure to the Anglo-Canadian world would estrange Ukrainian girls from their parents struck
at the heart of denationalization, for it implied repudiation not only
of filial responsibility and 'peasantness' but of everything, including
the all-important Ukrainian cultural heritage, for which the peasant
immigrant generation stood. When Nasha Meri and Katie chose the
marketplace over rural married life and its workload, spent their pay-
cheques on themselves, rejected the values and bonds their parents
represented, wore flashy clothes and went to dances instead of church,
and experimented with new moral standards, they were asserting independence.

In reality, the working girl's independence was often more symbolic
than real, as prejudice and discrimination confined her to a bottom
rung in Canadian society. Moreover, tradition proved more ingrained
than perhaps many girls wished to admit or a community elite feared:
one teacher in rural Saskatchewan in the 1920s, for example, remarked on the reappearance of the headscarf for a funeral, suggesting
the tenacity of community sanctions when faced with something as big
as death.[85] But however restricted by forces beyond their control,
economic earning power promised emancipation from what, to some,
were suffocating roles for women in Ukrainian peasant society and
unwanted community obligations. The few men and women who actually addressed the 'woman question' in the pioneer press had stressed
that only a fundamental change in Ukrainian society and attitudes,
with men and women equally enlightened and mutually supportive,
would end women's subjugation and inaugurate true progress. They
had also insisted on education as the key to genuine economic freedom,
liberating women from the need to marry in order to survive.[86] At
their end of the scale, and feminists in their own right, the real girls
who unwittingly acted as models for Nasha Meri and Katie were probably neither given to theorizing nor interested in the comprehensive
reform of society. In affirming their right to choose their own lifestyle,
they often failed miserably, made questionable decisions, and looked
ridiculous; but they knew what they wanted and would take full advantage of money in their pockets, new surroundings and opportunities, and a new freedom of movement to attain it.

In their portrayal of the Ukrainian working girl and her rural sister, progressives emphasized the oppression, exploitation, and discrimination that either stimulated the girls' class consciousness or proved that such stimulation was the end to which the progressive leadership and the girls themselves should devote their energies.[87] Ideological constraints and impositions aside, this approach recognized the girls' humanity. Nasha Meri and Katie emerged from nationalist circles, however, and the point is not how many working girls actually conformed to the stereotype but what the stereotype said about its creators.[88] Hats, face powder, chewing gum, and affected mannerisms were embarrassing and did nothing for Ukrainians' reputation, but they constituted minor irritants compared with the alienation from the Ukrainian people that a penchant for English men and the rejection of parental values and filial obligations signified. The fate of the Ukrainian working girl herself paled beside the long-term repercussions of her denationalization, and it was the purpose of exposing and combatting denationalization that Nasha Meri and Katie ultimately served. They also had a predecessor, the Polonized 'Wanda' (who shared their lesser sins as well) invented by the secular intelligentsia in Galicia.[89] In Canada the issue of denationalization reached well beyond improperly raised and unsupervised working girls to penetrate the ranks of the new middle class, proving that education and enlightenment were not synonymous. Female teachers were criticized for their imperfect Ukrainian, shame of their origins, and preoccupation with dances, belying the contemporary and subsequent image of patriotic servants of their people. For his part, 'Jack' could be a member of the Canadian-educated intelligentsia, identified with the assimilation that attended immersion in the English world, as well as an unskilled and maladjusted worker.[90]

Nothing in the moral deterioration of youth lured by the attractions of the new country and the independence it represented was so ominous as alienation from the Ukrainian community. Herein lies the explanation for the deeper significance of Nasha Meri and Katie over Jack. Women, for better or worse, were crucial to the future of the Ukrainian-Canadian group in a way to which men could not aspire, and when they renounced their own membership in the Ukrainian nation, they renounced that of the next generation too. Nasha Meri and Katie acted as wilful agents in the assimilation of their children when in their traditional roles as mothers and homemakers they refused to speak Ukrainian, discouraged their families' participation in Ukrainian community life, and failed to maintain Ukrainian homes.

After centuries of resisting Polonization and Russification, it was charged, Ukrainians had to watch mothers in Canada raise enemies of their people.[91]

In the effects of denationalization, a new generation raised in indifference or hostility to things Ukrainian and the larger social good, Nasha Meri and Katie had their rural counterpart. The farm girl removed from school at an early age for marriage faced a life of hard work, little intellectual challenge, and few opportunities for socializing or community involvement. Absorbed by her immediate surroundings and uninterested in improvement, she was perceived, like her peasant immigrant mother before her, as an obstacle to socioeconomic and national progress. Her kind escaped 'denationalization' as associated with Nasha Meri and Katie, but if the Canadian urban environment and its distractions helped to alienate working girls from their Ukrainian roots, the Ukrainian bloc settlements also had their drawbacks. Without enlightened leadership and organization, they could not guarantee that the Ukrainian milieu they sustained by sheer preponderance and inertia would instil a politicized national consciousness and sense of community commitment in the farm girl or her offspring.

An article appearing in *Ukrainskyi holos* in 1916 made the lesson of Nasha Meri and Katie clear. The author, a man, had attended a Ukrainian gathering where two girls made a spectacle of themselves with their English conversation, affectations, and rudeness. To the delight of the crowd, they were soundly chastised by a young bachelor, exuding national pride, who showed them how repugnant they were to intelligent men and lectured them on their conduct and shame of their language and people. While one girl burst into tears, her companion became angry, saying 'Come on, Katie, I want to go.' But Katie (her real name was Nastia) stayed, comforted by a group of girls welcoming her back to the fold and by the young bachelor moralizing that the sin was not stumbling but failing to get up. Today, the author concluded, Nastia was a decent girl, happily devoted to her saviour, while the real Katie had undoubtedly (and deservedly) gone from bad to worse.[92]

As Nastia demonstrates, Katie could be saved and her rewards were great – marriage to an intelligent, patriotic Ukrainian young man and happiness and security within the bosom of her people. Present too is the suggestion that the community would be forgiving of its prodigal daughters. Both the possibility of Katie's redemption and the use of her patriotic foil to advertise the benefits of identification with things Ukrainian were admissions that the community needed these girls. An entirely negative image and an intransigent message were counter-productive if Ukrainian community leaders hoped to harness the rising generation of young women in what they defined as the group's interests.

With the consolidation of organized community life and the hardening of ideological lines between the wars, the question of community influence over individuals grew in importance as nationalist and progressive elites sought to popularize their perceptions of what was best for Ukraine and for Ukrainians in Canada. The existence of a Soviet Ukrainian state diluted the sense of urgency in progressive circles, although the building of communism and the ongoing class struggle ensured continuing and keen interest in mobilizing Ukrainian Canadians under their banner. Among nationalists, an ambivalent reception in Canada had earlier necessitated monitoring individual behaviour in the interests of image, status, and material progress. Now military and political defeat and the insecurity of national-cultural life in the homeland necessitated motivating individuals in the interests of group survival and duty to Ukraine. From the perspective of both camps, neither Nasha Meri and Katie in their mutiny nor their rural sister in her cocoon could act as propagandists for community objectives, raising their children as Ukrainian patriots or class-conscious revolutionaries. Nor would they themselves participate actively and consciously in the life of their community, contributing directly to its welfare. What such young women needed were 'Great Women' to act as models and sources of inspiration.

3

Models for Their Sex:
Princess Olha and the Cossack Mother

The ignorant and apathetic peasant immigrant woman and her re-
bellious rudderless daughters were, of course, anti-heroines. In fact,
much of Nasha Meri and Katie's force as a community stereotype
stemmed from their contrast with the patriotic Ukrainian speaker who
won the admiration of the upright, nationally conscious young man.
Together Nasha Meri and Katie and their patriotic foil established
the values and standards of behaviour that were acceptable for their
sex in Canada and those that were not. They were figments of the
imagination, who could be juggled and rewritten at will, not actual
women. The one entirely negative, the other never to be tested or
forced to prove herself in the real world, their propagandistic potential
was limited. Only concrete heroines, 'Great Women' who had done
great things for the cause, be it the Ukrainian nation or the class
struggle, could sufficiently excite and motivate Ukrainian-Canadian
women to enlist them in its service too.

In the search for these Great Women, the pioneer intelligentsia was
soon surpassed by the women's organizations that emerged between
the wars to dominate organized women's life in both nationalist and
progressive communities. Beginning with the 1920s, Great Women
became a permanent and integral part of women's organizational
propaganda and programs, expressed in an increasingly elaborate ritualistic construct with them at its centre. The identity of these individuals, and the uses to which they were put, not only defined an ideal
for Ukrainian-Canadian women but also illuminated the mythical world
in which Ukrainian-Canadian women's organizations operated. The
most significant features of both phenomena were the extent to which

they depended on Ukraine for stimulation and nourishment, and the fact that while they constituted a celebration of women by and for women, they were not peculiar to women. Collective group symbols drawn from landmark events and from the outstanding figures in Ukrainian history characterized Ukrainan-Canadian community life since it had been transported across the ocean by turn-of-the-century immigrants.

In 1908 Ukrainian settlers south of what became Riding Mountain National Park received a post office and officially registered their small community. They called it Olha, after the medieval princess who ruled Kievan Rus' (945–62), wisely and well, during her son's minority.[1] Olha, Manitoba, joined a handful of pioneer Ukrainian settlements and school districts across the prairie provinces bearing famous names from Ukraine's past and present – Jaroslav, Khmelnytsky, Bohdan, Mazeppa, Shashkevych, Kulish, Szevczenko, Taras, Franko, Myroslaw, Petlura. All immigrant groups of the period christened their new homes after people and places in the old country, but in Ukrainians' case the exercise went beyond simple nostalgia. To name a school after Bohdan Khmelnytsky, leader of the great Cossack revolution of 1648, or after Myroslav Sichynsky, the student who in 1908 assassinated the Polish governor of Galicia, were political acts. They demonstrated a consciousness of Ukrainian history, especially those individuals popularly seen to have championed Ukrainians' best interests; and they showed continued emotional involvement with developments in the homeland.

Olha was the sole woman honoured in this homage to national political, literary, and cultural figures. One of the major twentieth-century Ukrainian historians would subsequently describe her as 'a prototype of later Ukrainian women of the Cossack period who, as wives of hetmans and colonels, in the absence of their husbands at war, ruled the country, issued *universals* (manifestos), and took, on the whole, an active part in politics.'[2] But Olha's legacy transcended place as well as time. In the propaganda and programs of Ukrainian nationalists in Canada in particular, the medieval princess became a prototype of service and activity for succeeding generations of Ukrainian-Canadian women. As a public figure, wife, mother, and saint (for her role in converting Rus' to Christianity), she embodied the virtues that were to inspire and guide them as they coped with the implications of membership in the Ukrainian nation. After Olha came a long line of women, continually lengthened and assiduously cultivated by a leadership elite to act as models and sources of inspiration for their Canadian sisters. The line eventually extended from the princess's royal contemporaries to Soviet dissidents of the 1980s.

Between the wars, escalating religious and ideological divisions within the Ukrainian-Canadian community precluded a consensus as to the identity and message of these Great Women. Progressives, for example, lauded women's expanded roles in the Soviet Union, while nationalistic interwar immigrants pledged to honour the memory of the female martyrs and heroines of the independence struggles. Whether representing the fundamental nationalist-progressive split, the Catholic-Orthodox rivalry, or one of several secular threads within nationalist circles, a faction's attitudes towards women's roles and responsibilities were affected by two factors. One was its ambitions for the Ukrainian-Canadian group – as part of a larger Ukrainian nation, and as a minority in Canada anxious to improve its status while preserving its national-cultural identity. The second, not always in harmony with the first, was the faction's broader mandate and orientation. The internationalism of the Catholic faith and class struggle, for example, tied Ukrainian-Canadian women to like-thinking women around the world regardless of nationality. Reflecting the different and frequently conflicting aims of their sponsors, the Great Women held up for Ukrainian women in Canada to emulate wore many faces – maternal, militaristic, domestic, organizational, literary, Christian, revolutionary.

The ideal Ukrainian woman who took shape in community literature, particularly under the aegis of the new national women's organizations, bore the stamp of the camp from which she emerged and which she was expected to serve. While reflecting ideological differences among women's organizations, she transcended geography by offering women in widely dispersed local branches a common image with which to identify and a common goal for which to strive. She also demonstrated remarkable staying power, linking women of different immigrations and generations. Only certain Great Women from whom the ideal was fashioned became common property. Behind the manipulation of their legacies this sharing entailed, and in the exclusiveness of other models and sources of inspiration, lay conflicting conceptions of Ukrainianness and the obligations Ukrainian group membership imposed on women.

In drawing up a code of conduct and a course of action for Ukrainian-Canadian women, the pioneer generation of nationalist activists and spokespersons was hampered by two factors. First, the absence of a distinct and satisfying Ukrainian 'way of life' as a point of departure and reference deprived Ukrainians of a mechanism for defining individual and collective roles and responsibilities. Second, the contradictions in nationalists' ambitions for their group precluded a well-articulated, clearcut, and unambiguous statement of direction. Thus, what women could or would be called on to do in the name of their group was contingent upon the larger issue of establishing guidelines for Ukrainian-Canadian life, particularly for their community life, in general. It rested in the final analysis on crystallizing ideas and agreement concerning the nature of Ukrainianness and its expression in Canada.

The first obstacle can best be illustrated through a comparison with two contemporary immigrant groups who shared important similarities – a sense of diaspora and mission – with Ukrainians. Jews and Mennonites brought with them to Canada a body of law and tradition, respectively, that contained an all-encompassing and group-sanctioned formula for living and a blueprint for survival. Both provided a focus and rationale for a positive group identity. Outside the formal rituals and official doctrines of the church, Ukrainians' sole old-country guide to 'being Ukrainian' or to a 'Ukrainian way of life' came from their peasant lifestyle. Individuals who had emigrated to escape the deficiencies of that system found in it no formula or blueprint for the future. Moreover, nationalist leaders rejected outright its unprogressive socioeconomic underpinnings as an impediment to upward mobility and acceptance. At the same time, the modernization they championed, and which Canadian education and popular culture encouraged, made alienation from the world view that had governed the Ukrainian peasants' actions and psyche inevitable. Nor could the immigrants' peasant cultural baggage furnish the politicized Ukrainian consciousness that was only just reaching their villages in Ukraine when they left, but which community propaganda and programs in Canada came to demand. To the nationalist elite in particular, as events brought group survival in Canada and active support of the homeland to the fore, Ukrainianness could not be limited to the rote practice of a faith or folk culture, or unthinking loyalty to a mother tongue.

At the same time, Ukrainianness was not to be erected on a Ukrainian 'way of life.' From the beginning, nationalists sought full participation in Canadian social, economic, political, and cultural life and recognition by the host society as its equals. They considered themselves a 'group' because of partnership in the Ukrainian nation, which carried certain obligations and needs. They were not to be a 'group' because of external socioeconomic influences and prejudices dictating their status, and they harboured no desire to maintain a lifestyle that was distinct from that of other Canadians. Canada's materialism and individualism might challenge the core of Mennonite identity, but Ukrainians could adapt to Canada and be fully Canadian while remaining Ukrainian. However, to propagandize for progress and integration while insisting on the right and necessity to survive as a distinct national-cultural entity created its own problems. Ukrainians had to convince mainstream society of the justice of their position while resisting assimilative pressures. They had also to tread a fine line between participation in Canadian life and Ukrainian particularism, in that pursuit of the former could jeopardize the community control necessary for the latter. And they had to define what precisely being Ukrainian in Canada meant.

When the pioneer intelligentsia and later the nationwide women's organizations set about popularizing the ideas that came to underlie the nationalist agenda, the models chosen to inspire and instruct Ukrainian-Canadian women were revealing. They neither offered guidance in reconciling the tensions and conflicts nationalists' 'Canadian' and 'Ukrainian' goals created nor helped women to adapt to Canadian society. That the cultivation of a womanly ideal should so ignore the reality of women's lives and their immediate surroundings casts doubt on both its potential as a practical alternative for women and the judgment of the leadership elite. More importantly, it illustrates that events outside and not inside Canada dictated nationalist priorities. Models had one function – to assist women in fulfilling their duties as Ukrainians. For this reason, although non-Ukrainians had important lessons to teach, they could not replace Ukrainians' own Great Women in significance and emotional appeal. And Ukrainian heroines came from Ukraine, not Canada. The peasant nature of both prewar and interwar immigrations, with women occupying a subordinate and inferior position, was not conducive to the creation of exceptional figures, just as the Canadian environment could not produce larger-than-life rivals for their sisters in the homeland.

Yet from the nationalist standpoint, and representing a situation all the more sinister because they worked for diametrically opposed ends, Canada produced other kinds of rivals – the women of the host society. Ukrainians' failure to cull heroines from the ranks of contemporary

Canadian women or from Canada's past was in one respect a consequence of marginality and alienation from mainstream women's circles. On a deeper level, it registered nationalists' realization, even
subconsciously, that such women threatened survival as Ukrainians
understood it. In the campaign to assimilate Ukrainians to Anglo-
Canadian values and standards, early twentieth-century nation builders
considered their womenfolk important ammunition. Although the
Ukrainian community would find much good in Anglo-Canadian
women – qualities to admire and desire in its own wives, mothers, and
community activists – it stopped well short of making them into cultural or political icons. The host society had no such qualms in mobilizing its women as models and sources of inspiration for their
Ukrainian counterparts. The interests of class and ethnicity cut across
gender as middle-class Anglo-Canadian women made their group their
first loyalty, and, in turn were used by their group to preserve its
influence, status, and way of life.

'The foreign women, in too many instances, have few or no opportunities for the development of womanhood according to Anglo-
Saxon ideals,' wrote the prominent educator, James T.M. Anderson,
in 1918, 'but are little better than slaves, who toil laboriously at the
beck and call of inconsiderate husbands, whose lack of proper respect
for womanhood is a heritage of darker ages. Great work lies ahead of
us, as Canadians, to see that these women are given an opportunity
to learn our language and to become familiar with ideals of womanhood and motherhood.'[3] Anderson, elected Conservative premier of
Saskatchewan in 1929 by exploiting the popularity of the anti-Catholic,
anti-'foreigner' Ku Klux Klan, was an ardent and long-time assimilationist. Whatever role genuine altruism played in such concern for the
quality of Ukrainian womanhood and motherhood, self-interest played
an equal if not greater role. The ideal woman of contemporary Anglo-
Canadian propaganda – pure and noble, maternal and domestic, delicate and ornamental – had little in common with the stereotype of
loveless marriage, physical abuse, and exploited labour that were perceived to be the lot of Ukrainian peasant women, or with the latters'
reputation as indifferent housekeepers and mothers. The size of the
Ukrainian immigration generated fears that such women, if left alone,
would endanger the future of Canadian citizenship. But converted to
Anglo-Canadian ideas of proper womanly conduct and imbued with
the British and Protestant principles underpinning the Canadian nation, Ukrainian mothers and homemakers became powerful agents for

change and assimilation.[4] The 'emancipation' Anglo-Canadians advocated for Ukrainian women and girls reflected this thinking, as did the programs devised for their uplifting and enlightenment. Their goal was not to assist members of a peasant immigrant society in transition. It was to divorce them from that world, to be recreated in the image of the middle-class Anglo-Canadian wife and mother and employed in her group's interests.

Anderson's solution to the problem of assimilating Ukrainian women and girls to Anglo-Canadian mores and standards of behaviour, a view shared by social reformers of all hues, was to place 'the best type of our Canadian womanhood' in their midst. Not the conventional heroines of British or Canadian history but ordinary teachers, missionaries, and community workers labouring in the bloc settlements were to be the models and sources of inspiration for Ukrainian women as they underwent 'Canadianization.' Well-publicized successes and none-too-subtle propaganda appealing to Anglo-Canadians' patriotism underscored not only the challenge and urgency of 'foreign work' but also its rewards, and were intended to enlist Anglo-Canadian women in its service. One propagandistic piece, winner of a Woman's Christian Temperance Union short-story contest, featured a beloved Anglo-Canadian teacher in the Ukrainian bloc in east-central Alberta who had lectured on the evils of tobacco and alcohol and taught the girls to sew 'Canadian' dresses. A daughter's duty to nurse a sick mother, however, obliged her to resign her position, and in the students' plea for a replacement 'to teach us to be Eengleesh and make Canadian tings,' the author's message to female readers was unmistakable.[5] Operating from isolated teacherages, or from one of the school homes or medical missions established by the Presbyterians and Methodists, the women who answered the call agreed that theirs was a special duty and a unique opportunity to acquaint the non-English-speaking with everything good in Canadian womanhood. With an image of 'fathers carrying the load and walking hand in hand down the trail with the mothers,' a Saskatchewan teacher explained her tactics:

> My house on the school grounds was invaluable in helping me towards realizing the hopes I had for the district. Girls stayed with me and learned cleanliness in cooking and preparing simple wholesome dishes. I was extremely particular about the care of my own hair and person, the cleanliness of the teacherage and cooking utensils. It had the effect of making them realize there was something sadly

'The best type of Canadian womanhood.' Schoolteacher serving her country in the Ukrainian colony east of Edmonton, c.1915

lacking in their way of living, and the marked improvement in their homes exceeded all my expectations. They copied me as closely as it was possible for them to do in eating, table manners, housekeeping, cooking, dress and actions. For that reason I tried to do my best. I polished my shack with greater care to receive a mother in a sheepskin coat and shawl than I would clean my home in preparation for afternoon tea.[6]

The adult peasant immigrant was already set in her ways and often beyond reach. Sporadic English, sewing, cooking, hygiene, childcare, and Bible classes nevertheless sought to mitigate the linguistic-cultural isolation and poor home environment perceived to handicap her children and retard their assimilation. The peasant immigrant's daughters called for more drastic intervention, with Anglo-Canadians prepared to supplant the home and family to guarantee the proper training of future wives, mothers, and homemakers. Rural missions with their captive audience were particularly well equipped to create female am-

Methodist missionaries hosting their Ukrainian neighbours at a party for a worker leaving on furlough. Kolokreeka, Alberta, 1923

bassadors of British-Canadian civilization and values, although in the long run the returns proved to be modest: through the First World War, for example, the Presbyterian school homes handled fewer than five hundred students of both sexes, with only a handful of converts.[7]

The homes' aggressive evangelization and 'Canadianization,' together with hands-on instruction in household economics, where girls assisted in the domestic tasks of the institution, had two objectives. The lesser, reflecting the ethnic and class hierarchy promoted by Anglo-Canadian social reformers, was to produce servants for English mistresses; the greater, reflecting the more intangible concerns of nation building, was to create 'good little homemakers in their mother's home, and later creditable wives for the rising generation of Austrian Canadian young men.'[8] In the Ruthenian Girls' Home in Edmonton, these priorities were reversed. The missionaries also hoped that many of their girls would become teachers, nurses, and deaconesses. Their great triumph, personifying the rewards of their labour, was Annie Korzak, raised by the missionaries after being sent by her parents for treatment in their hospital; she trained as a nurse and married a Scottish farmer. Korzak did not live up to expectations as a role model for other Ukrainian girls, however, and attract them into Protestant-

ism and missionary work.[9] The first Ukrainian girl to train as a dea-
coness at Manitoba College (1928) did so not because of missionary
influence but because of her evangelical family background from Galicia.[10]

Taking their cue from the wag who quipped that Ukrainian girls
needed a course in 'filial disobedience and rights and privileges of this
free country,'[11] the female missionaries and teachers who undertook
to instruct the maturing generation in dress, deportment, and domestic skills also considered the more fundamental question of the
position of women in Ukrainian immigrant society. Methodist propaganda promoted the Ruthenian Girls' Home as a sanctuary from
unbearable conditions,[12] but this was at best a stop-gap solution. More
importantly, Ukrainian girls had to be taught to rebel against overwork
and abuse, tyrannical fathers, early forced marriages, and domineering
husbands who neither loved nor respected them; they had to be convinced of their right to and the need for education; and they had to
be made to appreciate their own worth. Once again, the best of Anglo-
Canadian womanhood showed the way. 'The Home-trained girl,' pronounced an employer of Ukrainian servants in speaking of the missionaries' achievements, 'has invariably the Canadian woman's
viewpoint of the self-respect and independency of womanhood as distinguished from the Slav idea of subserviency. They would much rather
earn their own living among Anglo Saxons than go home to be literally
given away, by parents, as wives to some men for whom they have no
love. This may be undermining discipline in the Slav home, as some
see it, but it is unquestionably the Canadian ideal and has the approval
of many enlightened Slav parents.'[13] Despite such optimism, Anglo-
Canadians could not be assured of success. In a prize-winning short
story written in 1914, a teacher trying to convert her star pupil to
book learning and women's emancipation betrayed the sense of helplessness, disenchantment, and bitterness when these women proved
impotent against the weight of centuries-old habits and attitudes. Her
protégé rejected business college to marry a local Ukrainian hero and
ex-convict, explaining 'I am not like you – I am only a woman, you
know.'[14] According to a caustic commentator on life in the Ukrainian
bloc in Alberta where the story was set, no other ending would have
been plausible.[15]

Anglo-Canadian proselytization, religious and secular, persisted into
the 1930s, albeit with retrenchment as Ukrainian teachers replaced
Anglo-Canadian instructors and expanding Ukrainian institutions ir-

reversibly eclipsed Protestant mission centres. As models of Anglo-Canadian superiority able to influence Ukrainian women and girls, the teachers and missionaries were limited by their small numbers and isolation, cultural alienation, attitudes, and social composition. Often young, single women from middle-class homes in the East, less acclimatized to the rigours of pioneer life than their Ukrainian targets, they were hardly experienced authorities on marriage and maternity and certainly could not illustrate the ideal wife and mother in action. Evidence by 1940 would also suggest that Ukrainian girls were less likely to imitate Anglo-Canadian teachers than Ukrainian teachers.[16] At the time, Ukrainians harshly condemned the assimilation and self-contempt the missionaries in particular encouraged, so that young girls shouted in their bad English, 'Mother, you are a dirty Galician. I am Canadian. I hate you.'[17] Subsequent Ukrainian-Canadian literature has questioned the picture of self-sacrificing virtue and charity of contemporary Anglo-Canadian propaganda, portraying these women as self-centred, aloof, demanding, and prejudiced.[18]

This image must be tempered by the compassion and sisterhood at times revealed by the missionaries' own archives. Preserved in their photograph albums from Wahstao (Methodist) mission in Alberta, for example, are the following pictures: 'A New Madonna,' a tiny framed cameo of a Ukrainian girl holding her baby; 'Mothers and babies asked Miss McLean to take their pictures to send home'; and 'A woman for her mail,' capturing for posterity the smiling subject posed with her all-important letter.[19] Inevitably, however, the interests of class and race that propelled Anglo-Canadian women into foreign work qualified the enlightenment and emancipation they advocated for their foreign sisters. Ukrainian women were not to be the equals of the Anglo-Canadian women they were told to emulate, but 'liberated' only as far as the status accorded Ukrainians as a whole in Canadian society permitted. The early twentieth-century campaign for female suffrage made this abundantly clear when Anglo-Canadian women sought their own enfranchisement to neutralize the corrupting influence of the foreign male electorate and to reinforce British solidarity during the Great War.[20]

As saleswomen for Anglo-Canadianism or North American values, individual teachers and missionaries would be surpassed by more pervasive and powerful influences – the school itself, the mail-order catalogue, the workplace, mass advertising, and the mass media – whose mixed messages often clashed with those of early twentieth-century flagbearers. To their counterparts among the emerging Ukrainian community leadership, which also defined 'emancipation' for Ukrainian women and girls in narrow terms, these women represented the same unwanted end as the baser attractions of Canadian society that lured Nasha Meri and Katie to their downfall. Nationalists recognized that the enlightenment and progress they advocated for their women-folk to further Ukrainian group interests was not the same as that advocated by Anglo-Canadian assimilationists; and they recognized the dangers (as well as the benefits) that exposure to the Anglo-Canadian world entailed. Always quick to acknowledge public appreciation and favourable exposure of their culture, Ukrainians applauded when Florence Randal Livesay published her *Songs of Ukraina* in 1916.[21] Wary of assimilation, however, they held up no great Canadian women, either from the past or from the best type of Canadian womanhood toiling in their midst for the greater national good, for Ukrainian-Canadian women to venerate and imitate.

Yet attitudes towards Anglo-Canadian women were more ambivalent than this implies. While faulting Ukrainian women for adopting English fads, foods, and speech (to the exclusion of their own language), and condemning the deeper alienation they symbolized, pioneer Ukrainian leaders coveted the upward mobility and integration such things represented. Critical as they were of the peasant immigrant and her daughters, they also saw Anglo-Canadian women as examples of female deportment, household management, initiative, organization, and national service. Unlike Ukrainian girls, it was charged, English girls read widely and put their knowledge to good use; unlike Ukrainian housewives, English housewives spent their days industriously and reared their children well; and unlike Ukrainian women, English women knew how to value and serve their people (in the process showing Ukrainian women how to participate in Canadian national and political life).[22] If their assimilatory goal and rhetoric could be circumvented, and their positive qualities divorced from exclusivist WASP associations, Anglo-Canadian women indeed had much to teach Ukrainian women: self-improvement, a social conscience, and national commitment would make them better Ukrainians. Ultimately, however, as models and sources of inspiration for that role, Anglo-Canadian women were inadequate. Not only did the individualism they promoted conflict with the prescribed task of Great Women to mould and channel collective behaviour, but the qualities they championed proved too constricting.

Whether this would have been the case had events in Ukraine unfolded differently will never be known. What is certain is that developments overseas made the cultivation and exploitation of an ideal important and dictated the forms that it took. For Ukrainian-Canadian nationalists, Ukraine's unsuccessful bid for independence in 1917–20 focused attention on national-cultural oppression under its partitioners and the continuing struggle for a sovereign and united Ukrainian state. For Ukrainian-Canadian progressives, the establishment of Soviet power brought the all-consuming task of constructing a communist paradise in their homeland. In both cases the Anglo-Canadian womanly ideal, domestic and passive, had little to offer by way of inspiration or example. Ukraine required strong active women convinced of the rightness of their cause and prepared to work tirelessly on its behalf, shouldering a public responsibility and role in addition to their primary function in the home. For models and inspiration, the interwar Ukrainian-Canadian community needed women exhibiting greater vision than Anglo-Canadian maternal feminists and suffragists, and called to greater effort and sacrifice than Anglo-Canadian schoolteachers or missionaries in the Ukrainian colonies. Nationalists found such women in places like contemporary Ireland, locked in combat with the forces of British imperialism, and in Eastern Europe, among the very peoples competing with Ukrainians for their national existence. Progressives found them wherever the toiling masses fought for their rights. Above all, both factions found such women in Ukraine, among the fictional heroines of propagandistic literature and among the flesh-and-blood heroines of history itself.

The women progressives chose as models and sources of inspiration reflected their identification with both the international proletariat and the communist experiment underway in the Soviet Union. In the process, class was shown to dominate over women's common ethnicity with other Ukrainians, whether in Canada or in the homeland, and over gender distinctions that restricted them to their own sex. Women's branches of the Ukrainian Labour-Farmer Temple Association (ULFTA), for example, bore the names of such 'great female revolutionaries' as Rosa Luxemburg, Aleksandra Kollontai, and Klara Zetkin. They also, and in contrast to nationalist women's organizations that chose only women as their patronesses, were named after men in the revolutionary movement – men like the Ukrainians Stepan Melnychuk and Petro Sheremeta and including Lenin himself.[23] *Holos robitnytsi* (Workingwoman's voice) and *Robitnytsia*, the official organs of the Women's Section of the ULFTA, regularly carried articles on these individuals, particularly on the anniversaries of their deaths, to acquaint Ukrainian-Canadian women with the leaders and martyrs of their movement and to motivate them on its behalf. Stories about the often anonymous heroines of the class struggle throughout the world (Germany, China, Spain during the Civil War), the heroines, both fictional and real, of the 1917 Revolution, and the new Soviet woman had the same goal.[24]

Like their nationalist opponents, progressive women were expected to serve their cause as mothers and as public activists, and to subordinate themselves to the larger group to which they belonged. Marxists' emphasis on the essential and overriding unity of workers' interests worldwide determined that this sense of group and group responsibility would be based on class and not on Ukrainianness. Events in Ukraine only reinforced this order of priorities. Supporters of the new Soviet Ukrainian state were necessarily (and significantly) less obsessed with national oppression and related issues than nationalists, although they too condemned interwar Polish, Czech, and Romanian régimes in Western Ukraine. As a result, progressive women faced fewer demands as Ukrainians than as women in nationalist circles, even when Catholicism provided an international perspective comparable to communism. Victory instead of defeat in 1917, with both national and sociopolitical objectives realized in Soviet Ukraine, tempered the urgency and altered the focus of the demands they did face.

As the losers of 1917–20, nationalists could not relax and rest on their laurels; they had to continue the fight. To do so, and to do so effectively, required that the mass of Ukrainian Canadians be emotionally aroused on behalf of the homeland and convinced of the justice of its case. A leadership elite sought to accomplish this through an appeal to Ukrainian history – the trials and tribulations of the Ukrainian people throughout the centuries, its heroic struggles and achievements, and the example of those who had served and made sacrifices for it. To avoid repeating the failures of 1917–20, nationalists had also to try to understand the reasons for defeat. Again a leadership elite turned to history. These two imperatives determined how nationalist women came to see their sex not only in relation to the tasks facing their homeland in the present but also in relation to its fluctuating fortunes in the past. Nationalists' interpretation of Ukrainian history and of women's role, including the role of Great

Women, offered an explanation for both the positive and the negative in the Ukrainian experience. It also told contemporary women what they had to do to enable their people to realize its aspirations. This particular interpretation was neither of Ukrainian Canadians' making nor unique to them, but was cultivated overseas in interwar Western Ukrainian and émigré circles. It became part (and remained part) of the political mythology of nationalists of both sexes throughout the West, illustrating both the importance and the exploitation of history to console and to animate subject peoples.

In 1988 a historian of the Ukrainian women's movement attributed the nonparticipation of Ukrainian women, compared with their Polish counterparts, in the battle over Galicia to chauvinistic Ukrainian male attitudes. During the revolutionary period itself, women in Western Ukraine had voiced similar complaints, criticizing their sex for inactivity and their society for refusing to use women's talents effectively, first by discouraging public involvement and then by relegating them to a kitchen role.[25] In emigration in North America, women also castigated their sex for its deficiencies at a time when Ukraine needed conscious, zealous women. At the height of the liberation struggle in 1919 and well before interwar immigrants brought its legacy to Canada, articles in *Ukrainskyi holos* pointed out that in the conflict for control of Galicia, Polish women were shouldering arms, proud to show their men how to murder and enslave their Ukrainian enemies. But Ukrainian immigrant women, according to these same articles, 'cowered like mice in their holes.' Indifferent to the fate of their nation, they watched passively as their children were assimilated and the rest of their community responded to Polish actions in Galicia with telegrams of protest and the Red Cross work women's talents so suited.[26] Between the wars, Ukrainian-Canadian women's organizations contended that women deserved much of the blame for Ukrainians' failure to create their own state in 1917–20. Neither had the great mass of women sufficiently supported their nation's struggle themselves, either on the homefront or in battle, nor had they imbued their children with the patriotic fervour necessary for victory. At fault, according to the more moderate Ukrainian Women's Association of Canada (UWAC) representing Orthodox laity, was women's lack of enlightenment and consciousness.[27] More militant in its nationalism, the Ukrainian Women's Organization of Canada (UWOC) charged that a Ukrainian state would exist if its sex had grasped the fundamental principle of 'Nation above all' and acted accordingly. Next time, UWOC leaders warned, whether at home or in emigration, Ukrainian women could not be caught unprepared.[28]

The UWOC was the major women's organization in the interwar nationalist community to be identified with the second immigration, specifically the veterans of the defeated republican armies with their émigré mentality. Both the UWAC and the Ukrainian Catholic sisterhoods that preceded the Ukrainian Catholic Women's League (UCWL) were, of course, augmented by interwar immigrants, but they had their roots in the period of initial settlement and were spearheaded by the Canadian born or raised. They too believed that being Ukrainian imposed special group obligations, with the individual mobilized for and subordinated to the collective good. And like the UWOC, they insisted that the unresolved Ukrainian question obliged women to assume an active role in the community and national life. But their nationalism lacked the extremism of the UWOC and focused on the Ukrainian group in Canada as much as on Ukraine in Europe. The female images organized Orthodox and Catholic laity cultivated were less militant, less militaristic, and less dogmatic than those promoted by their right-wing sisters.

The women the UWOC chose as models and inspiration reflected the brand of nationalism it and the Ukrainian National Federation shared with the Organization of Ukrainian Nationalists in Galicia, waging a violent underground campaign against Polish occupation. Hierarchical, militaristic, and totalitarian, its ideology preached the primacy of the nation, with all resources – material, spiritual, and human – mobilized in its service; the state was the highest form of evolution in the struggle of each national organism for existence.[29] Statelessness imposed special burdens and obligations. For Ukrainian women it meant that motherhood and homemaking, their 'natural' functions, were not enough. Besides rearing 'fresh cadres of young nationalist warriors,'[30] they too had to be ready to die for their country, participating actively and directly in the liberation struggle and in Ukrainian national life. For models and inspiration, the UWOC turned to women of action and fanatical commitment to the national idea: Joan of Arc, the undisputed archetype of the willing soldier-martyr for her nation; Spartan mothers whose maternal sacrifice, ordering their sons into battle, was the epitome of national devotion; Italian unification fighters who died with 'long live Italy' on their lips; their successors who gave their wedding rings to finance Mussolini's Abyssinian war; and Nazi mothers who admonished small boys when they cried on scraping their knees that their nation's soldiers had lost entire legs without a whimper.[31] Even though the interwar Polish state was anathema, the UWOC held up Polish women who had fought for Poland's rebirth, and had exhorted and shamed their menfolk to do likewise, as models of female service and sacrifice for their nation. Ukrainians needed women like them, identifying unflinchingly with their nation's struggle, if they hoped for success when the war to undo the injustices of Versailles gave them their second chance.[32]

In combining a public role with women's first role in the nursery, the UWOC was not proposing anything novel. Nations have always asked more from their citizens in times of crisis without intending to formalize these changes on return to normalcy. Nazi ideology, for example, placed extra demands on German women while the movement was struggling, but Hitler's consolidation of power saw them eased back into their traditional stabilizing role in the family; then again, as Germany prepared for war, they were recruited into the labour force to liberate males for military needs.[33] Canada's wartime approach was similar: officially sponsored entry for women into the workplace during manpower shortages, and officially encouraged exit to resume their proper place in the home when demobilized veterans needed jobs.[34] Women in both countries were impressed with the necessity of sacrifice for their nation during emergency, and women in both countries acquiesced in the return to domesticity at its end. The UWOC was to be no different. With the achievement of a free and united independent Ukrainian state, wrote Rozha Kovalska, one of the movement's principal interwar organizers, women would be released from their labours into the bosom of the family. As models for Ukrainian women as their nation struggled for statehood, Kovalska chose women from French, Italian, and German history. She distinguished, however, between their past roles during crisis and the present: Italian women under fascism had abjured the need for the vote, French women were the most pampered in the world, and German women were devoted to the kitchen, their children, and the church.[35]

The blame that interwar nationalist women assumed for Ukraine's failure to establish a viable state in 1917–20 was mitigated by the view of history they popularized and which flourished thereafter in nationalist circles. Reassessing women's place and role in the Ukrainian experience, it absolved contemporary women of direct responsibility for their shortcomings while enhancing their self-esteem and giving them their own heroines to admire and emulate. The crux of the argument was that in periods when Ukrainians controlled their own destiny – notably under the Kievan princes and Cossacks and in the Ukrainian People's Republic – the position of women in the family and community reflected the egalitarianism towards which 'natural' Ukrainian society inclined. For proof of female equality, proponents pointed to the matriarchy believed to exist in ancient Ukrainian culture; to the property rights guaranteed women in the eleventh-century law code, *Rus'ka pravda*; to a common root for the words for wife (*druzhyna*) and friend (*druh*); to the liberty and initiative of Cossack women on the steppe frontier, particularly compared with their contemporaries in Western Europe; and to the legal equality granted women by Ukrainian statesmen in 1917 (rights granted, it was stressed, without women having to fight for them as in other countries). Lastly, defenders of egalitarianism in 'natural' Ukrainian society pointed to the extraordinary few – warriors, powers behind the throne, rulers during a husband's absence or a son's minority – who offered concrete examples of women's high status.[36]

The interpretation of Ukrainian history put forward by interwar nationalists and their successors also explained women's weakness in the great test of the twentieth century. To identify Ukrainian women of the past with their nation's struggles and interests, modern definitions of nationalism and national consciousness had to be projected onto their thoughts and actions. This occurred both with famous Kievan and Cossack women and with the great mass of mothers during Cossackdom, routinely portrayed as having raised Ukrainian patriots and freedom fighters. If the failure of 1917–20 was due to too few mothers being aware of their national responsibilities, as nationalist women contended, this multitude of faultless Cossack mothers should have guaranteed Ukraine its independence in the seventeenth century. But the troublesome implications of such logic were avoided, as nationalist women proceeded directly from 'masters in our own house' to subjugation. 'Later,' said Stephanie Sawchuk, addressing the first congress of the Ukrainian Canadian Committee in 1943 on behalf of the UWOC, 'the heroism of our women, so nobly demonstrated throughout the princedom and Cossack periods, was crushed into submission, and a period of slavery and general depression followed. This broke both the spirit and the national consciousness of the Ukrainian woman. The aggressors transformed her into a deaf and dumb slave. These conquerors knew that as long as the Ukrainian woman remained oppressed and degraded, they had nothing to fear. They knew that an enslaved woman could not rear her children to be good patriots who could be expected to fight for their nation.'[37] National oppression, in other words, transformed Ukrainian women into victims. Instead of the rights, equality, and active role they had enjoyed in 'natural' Ukrainian society, they were confined to the home, denied education, and spiritually stifled; and to enhance the masters' grip, Ukrainian men were encouraged to regard them as weak and inferior – as *durni baby* (dumb broads).[38] With one stroke of the pen, Ukrainian women were exonerated for their performance in the national-liberation struggle, and Ukrainians as a whole for their treatment of women in nineteenth-century Ukrainian peasant society. Dispensing with rulers and warriors, this perspective also exalted motherhood as woman's greatest function in national life, for on the quality of the Ukrainianness of mothers rested the fate of the nation.

Succeeding generations of apathetic and servile women would have boded ill for the future had not individuals, rejecting the submission of the masses and the opportunism of those assimilating with the enemy, kept alive the ideas of freedom and struggle. Stephanie Sawchuk continued:

> As a result of these conditions, there appeared noted poetesses, writers and organizers, who began to arouse the Ukrainian woman from her deep slumber in slavery, for they were aware of the fact that if this was allowed to continue the Ukrainian nation would perish. Although full of difficulties and obstacles, this vital work of the pioneers of our Ukrainian movement was very successful. At the commencement of hostilities during the Ukrainian nation's war of liberation, 1917–20, we see the Ukrainian mother trembling for the fate of her children; but realizing that the enslavement of her people is unbearable and that destruction is threatening them, she does not keep her sons at her side although she loves them so dearly. With heroic sacrifices she arms her sons, hides her emotions from them lest they too weaken, and sends them off to battle for freedom. In addition, many women themselves pick up arms and fight for the rebirth of the Ukrainian state. The rich fertile soil of Ukraine is strewn with the white bones of many heroic mothers.[39]

Defeat, then, had been due less to the weakness or absence of the dedicated than to the indifference and hostility of those who outnumbered them. In 1931 an angry veteran in Edmonton took exception to the claims of a local speaker that Ukrainians had no state because their women had failed as mothers and as active patriots; he took equal exception to the women in the audience who applauded the speaker, insisting that women who were aware of Ukraine's many heroines, past and present, would not acquiesce in their own humiliation.[40]

The image of women's place and role in Ukrainian life that the nationalist interpretation of Ukrainian history championed was simplistic and self-serving, relying in part on the inconclusiveness of the sources for much of Ukrainian pre- and early history, an exaggeration of the exceptional, careful selection of the evidence, and the avoidance of problematic issues, including fundamental questions of class and gender.[41] Widowed regents and hetmans' wives, for example, owed their prominent roles to their privileged position and male connections, not to women's right to govern. A brochure issued for the millennium of the death of the Kievan princess Olha in 1969, which women's organizations across Canada celebrated with special events, illustrates the manipulation involved. The accompanying biographical sketch (accredited to the émigré historian Natalia Polonska-Vasylenko) not only elevated Olha to 'empress' of a 'young but mighty state' but also refrained from mentioning that her rule was a regency.[42] In the twentieth century, chauvinistic male attitudes in the Ukrainian People's Republic, even within government, restricted what women could do, despite their formal equality. Prejudice against women outlived their election to the Central Rada in Kiev and representation on its executive council. As the Rada's activities and its reliance on specialists grew, women's effective participation declined, and they became concentrated in traditional female areas of welfare and education.[43]

Exaggeration of the exceptional and selection of the evidence, to nurture what became articles of faith, enabled the nationalist version of Ukrainian history to realize a final goal – to act as a propagandistic weapon and psychological prop for twentieth-century Ukrainian women. History showed that their ancestors had been valued, self-respecting members of their society. Identifying intimately with their people and its struggles, they had been honourable participants in nation building, had performed great deeds, and had made great sacrifices. The conclusions to be drawn were obvious. The heroines of Ukraine's past gave Ukrainian women in Canada the right to be proud of their foremothers; they also imposed an obligation to follow in their footsteps.[44]

Between the wars the women's pages in *Ukrainskyi holos* and *Novyi shliakh* (New pathway), maintained by the UWAC and the UWOC, respectively, began to feature famous women from Ukrainian history in what would become a permanent practice in the women's organizational press. The Great Ukrainian Women evoked as models and sources of inspiration for interwar Ukrainian women in Canada (and who continued to speak to their postwar successors) were often faceless – the sacrificing mother, the unknown warrior, the unsung community worker.[45] More frequently, they were specific individuals, beginning with the prototype in Princess Olha. She was joined by lesser noble women of the period like Anna Iaroslavna, married to Henry I of France and acclaimed by her admirers as the sole literate in the French court, an able regent and a patroness of Rus' culture.[46] Later figures were chosen to demonstrate the independent spirit and wide-ranging influence of Ukrainian women. They included the fifteenth-century Marta Boretska, who fought valiantly to defend Novgorod from the Muscovites; and the sixteenth-century slave Roxolana, who, when the Crimean Tatar vassals of the Ottoman Empire made their living slave-hunting in Ukraine, used the considerable power she wielded as the favourite wife of Suleiman the Magnificent to help her captured countrymen. The memory of Roxolana was said to forbid succeeding generations of Ukrainian women, also in bondage or outside their native land, from being traitors to their people.[47]

The rise of Cossackdom as a response to the Tatar challenge on the steppe frontier and to Polish domination after 1569 produced its own heroines in the interests of Ukrainian autonomy. They included Hanna, wife of hetman Bohdan Khmelnytsky, who issued universals in the commander-in-chief's absence; Olena Zavisna, the wife of a Cossack captain, who inflicted great injury on her town's besiegers and chose death for herself and her children over capture by the Poles; and Maria Mahdalyna, the abbess, benefactress, and mother of Ivan Mazepa, who gave her hetman son wise counsel and supported Ukrainian cultural causes.[48] In the nineteenth century, Great Women came from the national renaissance and embryonic women's movement – literary figures like Olha Kobylianska and Lesia Ukrainka; the feminist Natalia Kobrynska; and Olena Pchilka, both a writer and a women's activist. Their twentieth-century successors, often the contemporaries of the women they were expected to motivate, reflected the physical demands of nation building. In early 1917, *Kanadyiskyi rusyn* quoted Olena Stepaniv (quartermaster in the paramilitary Ukrainian Sich Sharpshooters, taken prisoner and exiled to Siberia) invoking the image of Zavisna to appeal to young women in Galicia to revive their tradition of activism and to participate in national-political life.[49] The women, besides Stepaniv herself, who answered such a call included soldiers like Sofia Halechko, ensign in the Ukrainian Sich Sharpshooters; and martyrs like Olha Basarab, intelligence courier in the Ukrainian Military Organization, brutally murdered by the Poles in 1924, and Vira Babenko, liaison officer with the exiled government of the Ukrainian People's Republic, captured and killed by the Bolsheviks in 1921.[50]

Collectively, these women were the spiritual mothers and mentors of Ukrainian women in Canada, saluted annually on their anniversaries with concerts (*sviata*) and articles in the press. Subordinating their personal concerns to their nation, they had gained immortality by their commitment and idealism, and by their willingness to endure arrest, torture, and even death. They stretched across the centuries in an endless chain to unite Ukrainian women in a common sisterhood. In 1902 a Ukrainian immigrant in Lethbridge, appealing to the 'Immaculate Virgin, Mother of the Ukrainian nation' for help and guidance, reminded his countrywomen in America that they held the fate of their nation in their hands. In the tradition of Olha, Boretska, and brave Cossack women, they were to leave a glorious legacy, raising their children as good Ukrainians and hastening the day of deliverance from Polish and Russian domination.[51]

Despite similarities in purpose and general outlook, factions in the nationalist community were frequently able to share their heroines only by highlighting or suppressing different qualities. The same process permitted the progressive community also to share many of the same heroines before events of the twentieth century created two distinct and antagonistic streams. Progressives' use of Great Ukrainian Women expressed not only their class consciousness but also their Ukrainianness, in ways parallel to yet incompatible with those of their nationalist adversaries as the two disagreed over what was good for Ukraine. Between the wars, the dedicated Soviet Ukrainian male was the role model for Soviet Ukrainian women,[52] but progressives in Canada did not dismiss the latter out of hand. Their pantheon of twentieth-century Ukrainian heroines embraced the anonymous women of awakening consciousness, revolutionary fervour, and toil for Soviet glory – whether in agriculture, industry, the Communist party, or war. Wedding the sociopolitical with the national, such heroines identified Ukrainian women in Canada as heirs, by reason of their sex, to the struggles and achievements of the Soviet Ukrainian state.[53] Between the wars, the Women's Section of the ULFTA also maintained ties with communist sympathizers in Galicia, in a reverse relationship where the section was perceived as the model and source of inspiration for women in the homeland.[54]

Using several prominent women whose symbolic importance spanned interwar and postwar periods as an example, it is possible to show how progressives and nationalists, as well as different nationalist factions, interpreted Great Women's 'Ukrainian' legacies. Because of her multiple roles, domestic and public, secular and religious, Princess Olha offered something to everyone. Even the progressives, advancing a view of women in Ukrainian history akin to that of the nationalists, took her to illustrate the important role played by women in national political life before foreign domination denied them 'the most elementary rights, even those few conceded to men.'[55] Nationalist mythology, projecting modern concepts onto Kievan Rus', made Olha purposefully Ukrainian; both her public and religious roles, and her roles as wife and mother/grandmother, were interpreted to reflect and serve that Ukrainianness. A devoted wife, Olha ministered to her family's happiness and counselled her husband wisely in matters of state. After avenging his murder at enemy hands, she governed justly and firmly during the minority of her son, the future Sviatoslav the Conqueror, who expanded his princedom and thus increased its stature. Finally, her personal conversion to Christianity paved the way for the conversion of Rus' under the grandson, Volodymyr the Great, she raised in the faith that became a cornerstone of Ukrainian national identity.[56] Ukrainian Catholic and Orthodox churches revere Olha as a national saint (her feast day is observed on 11/24 July), and the millennium of Christianity in Rus' in 1988 focused attention in the wider Ukrainian-Canadian nationalist community on her and her grandson. To nationalist women, Olha has been above all an inspiring example of one who effectively combined family and community duties in the national interest.

Three other women – Kobrynska, Ukrainka, and Basarab – were regarded as examples of public activism alone. Only Kobrynska (1851–1920), the nationally oriented socialist and feminist who spearheaded the Ukrainian women's movement in Galicia in 1884, became identified specifically with women's issues. Interwar progressives dismissed her as a nationalist 'society lady' indifferent to the plight of workers and peasants, and called on working women to recognize Rosa

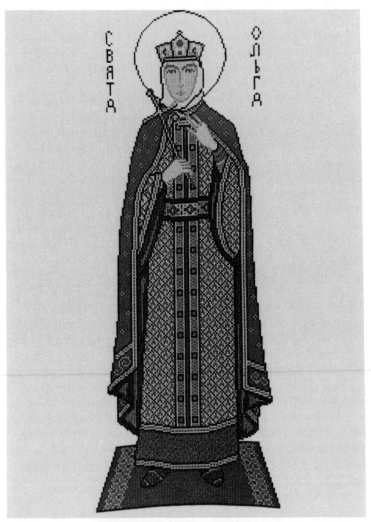

Postcard of Saint Olha embroidered in cross-stitch by Ann Hluchaniuk. Issued by the UWAC to commemorate the 'millennium of the baptism of Ukraine into the Holy Orthodox Faith, 988–1988' (reverse)

Luxemburg as their leader instead.[57] Kobrynska's changing fortunes in the Soviet Union subsequently transformed her into a democrat who had 'actively defended women's right to economic independence

Natalia Kobrynska, 1851–1920. Founder of the Ukrainian women's movement in Galicia in 1884; both her father and her husband were Greek Catholic priests.

and equality with man in work and education.' Tying Kobrynska's feminism to her socialism, postwar progressives suggested that her ideas, familiar to the first female immigrants in Canada, were what propelled them into the progressive movement. As the movement's women pioneers, these immigrants and their female descendants became Kobrynska's spiritual heirs.[58] Those outside progressive circles downplayed Kobrynska's socialism and tied her feminism to her nationalism. To nationalists, her message was two-fold. On the one hand, political and community rights as well as educational and economic rights for women could be fully realized only in an independent Ukrainian state. On the other hand (and despite the preceding argument), national oppression required an 'emancipated' or enlightened womanhood committed to the well-being and liberty of the Ukrainian people.[59] In 1939 the UWOC claimed that the national consciousness and sacrifice Ukrainian women had exhibited in the liberation and resistance struggles of the twentieth century bore testimony to the successful labours of pioneers like Kobrynska, 'a true Ukrainian patriot'; Ukrainian women in Canada ought to 'follow in her footsteps and work for the good of their people and fatherland.'[60] This sentiment would endure among nationalist women.

Kobrynska's co-worker in the women's movement, the writer Olena Pchilka, was acclaimed as much for her domestic as her public role. Her 'inspired motherhood'[61] gave Ukrainians their great poet, Lesia Ukrainka (1871–1913), whose works became a catalyst to uncompromising struggle for freedom, truth, and justice. Following the official Soviet line, and without specifically suggesting her as a model for women, interwar progressives stressed Ukrainka's social conscience and humanitarianism, casting her as a revolutionary, while suppressing the nationalistic component of her works.[62] To nationalists, who saw Ukrainka's universal and non-Ukrainian themes as analogies for the subjugation and struggle of nineteenth-century Ukraine, her message of the necessity to fight for the national idea was both an inspiration and a challenge. The poet's words inciting a captive people to insurrection, wrote the UWOC on the twenty-fifth anniversary of her death in 1938, must continue to spur men and women to make the ultimate sacrifice that Ukraine might be free.[63] To the UWOC, conscious national commitment among Ukrainian women began only with individuals like Ukrainka, distinguishing them from earlier heroines like Olha who inherited their position.[64] Some years later, the UWAC expressed Ukrainka's legacy in less militant but equally Ukrainian terms: 'To love one's country, people and culture, to be courageous, to hope when there is no hope, are some of the mottoes expressed by Lesia Ukrainka, which if practiced by every Ukrainian woman, should assist us greatly in our striving for the independence of Ukraine.'[65]

In 1893 Ukrainka had been nonplussed when Kobrynska asked her to contribute to a projected women's almanac: 'She suggested that I work on topics such as the "role of women in the Ukrainian national renaissance." I do not even know how to go about starting on this subject.'[66] The poet would undoubtedly have been bemused had she known the fate that awaited her in the mythology of nationalist women. In addition, Ukrainka more than any other Ukrainian woman, perhaps because the qualities she stood for were traditionally more 'masculine' than 'feminine,' moved from an example for her sex alone to an all-Ukrainian national symbol – incontrovertible proof that service to the cause overrode the gender of the servant. Ukrainka's official obituary by the historian and future president of the Ukrainian People's Republic, Mykhailo Hrushevsky, in the Galician daily *Dilo* (reprinted in

Lesia Ukrainka, 1871–1913. Poet and daughter of the writer and women's activist, Olena Pchilka; she died prematurely, of tuberculosis.

Kanadyiskyi rusyn, 6 September 1913), attached little significance to her as a woman. Instead, it paid tribute to the Ukrainian patriot and poet.[67]

In contrast, Ukrainka's spiritual daughter, Olha Basarab (1889–1924), became predominantly a woman's model and source of inspiration, although news of her death at Polish hands sparked a widespread emotional outpouring among Ukrainians in the West that transcended political differences. Progressives, like the nationalists, opposed Poland's control of Galicia, and until hardening ideological lines put her outside their orbit, they acknowledged Basarab's heroism. At least two newly formed women's branches of the ULFTA (Medicine Hat and Fedorah, both in Alberta) were named in her honour.[68] Cath-

Olha Levytska Basarab, 1889–1924. Underground activist arrested and killed by the Poles, whose control of Galicia was internationally recognized in 1923

olic and Orthodox communities used Basarab's torture and death to protest Polish atrocities and rule in Galicia, and women in the two camps would continue to acknowledge her as a national heroine and example of patriotism.[69] Basarab appealed most, however, to interwar immigrants, particularly to women's groups affiliated with veterans of the defeated republican armies. When these women provided the nucleus for the UWOC and it chose Basarab as its patroness, they left little doubt as to the difference between their nationalism and that of the UWAC, which named its clubs after literary figures of the national renaissance. To the UWOC, Basarab was Ukraine's Joan of Arc, the paragon of national service and sacrifice, whose ultimate commitment to the national idea and unfinished work imposed a sacred obligation on the living, in Ukraine and abroad.[70] In 1936 the UWOC published

Oleksander Luhovy's *Olha Basarabova*, a five-act drama focusing on Basarab's martyrdom that was popular in Ukrainian National Federation halls. Attending a Montreal production of the play, a university sociologist (non-Ukrainian) described the performance as 'exceedingly well done and good entertainment in the Ukrainian fashion.' He noted, too, how the audience wept at Basarab's torture and death.[71]

One final Great Woman must be discussed. Non-Ukrainian but carefully Ukrainized, the property of nationalist women alone, she illustrated the contrast between the activist nationalism of the UWOC and the more passive nationalism of Catholic and Orthodox women's organizations. The patroness of Ukrainian Catholic women in Canada, formally adopted by the UCWL following its formation during the Second World War, was Mary, the Holy Mother of God. Today, past presidents receive a reproduction of the miraculous icon of the Mother of God of Pochaiv. Accredited with saving her town from the Turks, she is renowned for her power of healing and love of the Ukrainian people and continues to attract pilgrims, primarily women.[72] The UCWL chose as its official hymn, 'O spomahai nas Divo Mariie' (Oh, help us, Virgin Mary), once described as a 'prayer of supplication' for Mary's intercession with Christ to assist members in fulfilling their responsibilities, which were to support and promote the Catholic faith, Ukrainian culture, Canadian citizenship, and Christian charity.[73]

In keeping with their church's teaching, Ukrainian Catholic women proved the most reluctant to suggest that woman's first priority as mother and homemaker be supplemented by a public role dictated by her group's needs. They were also the most inclined to define that public role as an extension of her domestic and maternal responsibilities and in terms of innate gender differences; charitable works, for example, have long been perceived as ideal outlets for women's 'natural' nurturing talents.[74] The Ukrainian Catholic religious order, the Sisters Servants of Mary Immaculate, is the most visible evidence of this thinking; continuing the thrust of their work in Galicia, the nuns have been involved in charity (orphanages, hospitals, senior citizen homes) since their arrival in 1902.[75] The UCWL's emphasis on Mary reflected its endorsement of woman's place in the home and family and of the womanly ideal she represented – piety, humility, compliance, self-sacrifice, motherly love, and wifely devotion.[76] Mary, of course, acted in this fashion as a model for all Catholic women, regardless of their rite. Nor were Ukrainian Catholics alone in such an image and its use as a model and source of inspiration for Ukrainian-

Reproduction of the miraculous icon of the Mother of God of Pochaiv, presented to past presidents of the UCWL

Canadian women. The Mother of God, a Ukrainian Orthodox priest told his followers in 1940, 'is the model for all mothers in all times. She shows them how to raise their children, sacrifice themselves for them, and remain by them even in the worst moments. Learn from Her, mothers, how to dedicate yourselves to your children. For God has given each of you a great and important task, and that is to bear and to rear children.'[77]

Mary had a second function. In art work as far apart as the wall paintings of prairie country churches and the mass-produced ceramic Madonna figurines of the 1980s, a modest row of Ukrainian embroidery trimmed her robes. In Nativity scenes in the nationalist press, she wore a Ukrainian folk costume; she carried what resembled a Ukrainian *rushnyk* (an embroidered towel draped around holy pictures and used in rites of passage like betrothal and marriage); the manger pillow was edged with Ukrainian designs; and mother and child were surrounded by such traditional Ukrainian symbols as the *didukh*, the sunflower, and the onion-domed church. A sheaf of wheat believed to contain the souls of departed ancestors, the *didukh* was traditionally brought into the house on Christmas Eve and then burned in the field on New Year's Eve to return the souls to the soil. The message in this artwork became explicit in a popular icon marking the Feast of the Protecting Veil of the Mother of God (observed on 1/14 October) in the Ukrainian Catholic women's press. An appropriately Ukrainized Mary extended her veil over two couples representing Eastern and Western Ukraine; they knelt before a flag-flanked *tryzub* or trident, the major symbol of the Ukrainian national movement and emblem of the Ukrainian People's Republic, and prayed for her intercession for their nation.[78] Mary, the Mother of God, was also Mary, the Mother of Ukraine.

This idea had distant origins and deep roots. While Louis IX of France dedicated his nation to Mary's service, his contemporaries, the Christian princes of Kievan Rus', placed their more vulnerable state under her protection. The subsequent course of Ukrainian history further encouraged the notion of Mary as protectress of Ukraine. Besides being incorporated into church ritual, it became a persistent literary and political theme, and in the twentieth century served frustrated nationalists as both a comfort and a tool.[79] As the Mother of Ukraine or the Madonna Ukrainized, Mary bore special significance for women. In so doing, she not only separated Ukrainian Catholic from other Catholic women but also underlined the secular concerns that united Ukrainians of Catholic and Orthodox faiths despite their denominational differences. In the propaganda of nationalist Ukrainian-Canadian women's organizations, Mary was an example of sacrifice and service for Ukrainian mothers. Like the grieving but proud mother beneath the Cross, knowing that her son suffered for a Great Idea, the kingdom of God on earth, so Ukrainian mothers, believing in the righteousness of their own great idea, the resurrection of the Ukrain-

Ukrainized Madonna and child by Olexa Bulavitsky. One of several
Christmas illustrations in the Ukrainian-Canadian press

ian nation, must exhibit great selflessness. Those who did shared not
only Mary's sorrow but also her glory.[80]

Just how important were women as mothers was established beyond
a doubt in 1928 when Ukrainian nationalists in Canada (followed by
Galicia in 1929) adopted Mothers' Day for community observance.
Mothers' Day propaganda, like its counterpart in mainstream society,
eulogized motherhood in the abstract and waxed eloquent over a
mother's love and selflessness for her family. But Ukrainian mothers
were understood to have a second family, their nation; and it was this
role, as mothers of Ukraine, that prompted the Ukrainization of the
holiday. Its primary purpose, as the official organ of the Ukrainian
Greek Orthodox church explained, was to remind Ukrainian mothers
of their responsibilities, beginning with raising their children as good

Twentieth-century icon of the Mother of God as the Mother of Ukraine. Composition based on the icon of Mary the Protectress in the Church of the Protection of Mary of the last Zaporozhian Host

Ukrainians.[81] Mothers' Day literature not only advised Ukrainian mothers of their responsibilities; it also honoured, as examples for contemporary Ukrainian women, the Great Mothers of their nation's past and present, ranging from famous individuals like Olena Pchilka to the nameless thousands whose children perished in Polish or Soviet prisons. These women had reared conscious Ukrainian patriots prepared to serve their nation and who loved its language and traditions. They had sent their sons and daughters into battle, watched them suffer under foreign domination, and silently borne the pain of their sacrifice. They had recognized their all-important task within the home, for a strong Ukrainian family was the core of a strong Ukrainian nation. And they had realized they had to shoulder the additional burden of community service: 'When the Ukrainian mother fails to interest herself in national work and be a member of her community,' a UWAC editorial asked, 'how can she be an example for her children?'[82]

Ukrainian Catholic women in particular associated Mothers' Day with the Mother of God, as May was Mary's month in the Catholic church; and in 1956 the UCWL set aside a day to honour the Mother of God as its patroness. But the exploitation of mother symbolism in the nationalist community was more secular than religious, although infusing its secularism with religious significance, and ultimately identified women with their nation. It did so directly for the 'mothers of Ukraine' addressed on Mothers' Day. Between the wars, however, single or childless women like Babenko and Basarab also became mothers of Ukraine by virtue of their sacrifice for their country.[83] Ukraine itself became the mother – to orphans of her liberation struggles[84] and to the women to whom community propaganda was directed. In 1929, on the occasion of the first observance of Mothers' Day in Galicia, the Ukrainian Catholic *Kanadiiskyi ukrainets* (Canadian Ukrainian) published an article by the Women's Union activist, Olena Kysilewska. In it she stressed the responsibility of Ukrainian mothers not only to their biological families but also to their 'Great Holy Mother' Ukraine, raising conscious sons and daughters in her service.[85] The Ukrainian Protestant press specified both sexes when it urged Ukrainians in North America to help their brothers and sisters overseas, because Ukrainians everywhere were all children of one mother, Ukraine.[86] Speaking literally rather than figuratively, an Orthodox priest reminded Ukrainian children that they had the same duty to love and revere Mother Ukraine as they did their own mothers and the Mother of God.[87] As

Mothers' Day cover for the UWAC magazine, *Promin*. The lithograph, entitled *Mother*, is by Olena Kulchytska.

the distinction among Ukrainian mothers, mothers of Ukraine, and Mother Ukraine (*Ukraina* itself is feminine) became blurred, their common motherhood established a special and inescapable bond between Ukrainian women and their nation. At the same time, the local women's groups named 'Daughters of Ukraine' suggested a hierarchy in the relationship, making the nation dominant.

Inspirational message for Ukrainian mothers to introduce the children's corner, UWOC page in *Novyi shliakh*, early 1940s

Ukrainians are a people with a long folk memory and tenacious folk tradition, and it is at the folk level, not the elite level, that continuity in Ukrainian history is found. The possibility of a connection between the politically motivated mother symbolism of the twentieth century and an early pagan earth mother mythology should not be dismissed out of hand. Persisting threads in the symbolic role of the female figure in Russia and Ukraine from prehistoric times to the present have been the subject of recent scholarship.[88] Ukrainian-Canadian women, for their part, located the origins of Ukrainian esteem for the mother and the identification of Ukraine with the mother figure in the matriarchy thought to exist in ancient times.[89] The most gratifying link between them and their role as Ukrainian mothers and Ukraine as the mother was more recent – found in the poetry of their nation's great genius, the former serf Taras Shevchenko (1814–1861).

Shevchenko's favourite theme of the seduced peasant girl and unwed mother as the embodiment of cruelty, injustice, and the suffering of the innocent was perceived by Ukrainian-Canadian nationalists and progressives alike as an indictment of women's oppression. Progressives, like the Soviets, considered Shevchenko a social revolutionary whose concerns for the common people were addressed to humanity in general and to the tsarist régime in particular; his role as a national revolutionary on behalf of the oppressed Ukrainian nation was downplayed. The major progressive statement on Shevchenko argued that nationalists falsified the poet's legacy by turning him 'from a revolutionary democrat into a servant of the gentry who called on "the whole Ukrainian nation," both aristocrat and serf, to conciliation – to class compromise.'[90] In progressive mythology, the peasant girl's rape was the class crime of her landlord master.[91]

Among nationalists, Shevchenko's wronged woman merged with Ukraine, and her rape, which was attributed to Russian soldiers and landlords enjoying free licence, became a symbol for Ukraine's rape by Russia. The poet's own experience, in which his loving and beloved mother was replaced by a cruel stepmother, was also seen as an analogy for Ukraine and tsarist (Soviet) Russia. Shevchenko's equation of Ukraine with the mother (for him, the orphan, specifically, and for his people as a whole), and with a woman's violation, suffering, sacrifice, and strength, was extremely important to nationalist Ukrainian women. That their people's mouthpiece and greatest national symbol should employ a feminine metaphor to express its plight and yearnings reinforced women's unique and intimate relationship with their nation, and facilitated the popular legitimization of a female perspective in Ukrainian history. At the same time, Shevchenko's admiration for the Ukrainian mother, particularly the inner strength, love, and sacrifice that shone through her degradation and humiliation, placed an obligation on subsequent generations of women to earn his respect also.[92]

In both nationalist and progressive traditions, and particularly in the former, the cultivation of inspirational models for women became an ongoing process closely connected to formal community ritual. For example, while interwar progressives criticized Mothers' Day as bourgeois, when thousands of working mothers suffered under capitalist exploitation and were truly honoured only in the Soviet Union, their successors inserted the appropriate ideological content and adopted the holiday.[93] In the nationalist camp, as women marked Ukrainka's birth and Basarab's death in February, the month became identified with all Ukrainian heroines and was incorporated as such into the national-political rites of community life. Embracing humble and anonymous as well as important individuals, the heroines' ranks were expanded from the interwar years to accommodate new figures. The Second World War furnished another February martyr. In 1942 the poet and activist Olena Teliha was arrested and tortured to death by Nazi authorities in Kiev, eliciting, as the legend goes, reluctant praise from her tormentors for her bravery.[94] Although the incorporation of Western Ukraine by the Soviet sector after 1945 deprived nationalists of most points of contact and identification, they continued to draw strength for their mission from opponents of the régime. Postwar additions to their pantheon of Great Women ranged from the five hundred women mowed down by Soviet tanks in 1954 for protesting conditions in the prison camps to well-known female dissidents and the wives of prominent political prisoners.[95]

Shevchenko's anniversary is celebrated every year by Ukrainians throughout the world in March, the month in which he was born and died. Ukrainians in Canada are no exception. Organized women use the occasion to restate the relevance of his poetry for their sex and to incorporate him into a fixed calendar of events – heroine month in February for nationalists, Mothers' Day in May, and the anniversaries of the births and deaths of famous Ukrainian women for both nationalists and progressives. Concerts, speeches, and motivational literature duly acknowledge the courage, sacrifice, and vision of the individuals commemorated and stress the lessons for their successors as women publicly honour their sex and rededicate themselves to the cause. The connections their propaganda makes, in the spirit of Shevchenko's epistle, between the dead and the living and the unborn, whether in Ukraine or outside its borders, locate Ukrainian-Canadian women in a continuum. Heirs to the Great Women of Ukraine at one end, they share sisterhood with their contemporaries in the diaspora and the homeland at the other. The ties are direct and made explicit for women with whom they sympathize ideologically. The ties often remain unstated or unrecognized, or are expressed in negative terms, when ideological differences divide women, but they exist nevertheless. The fact that the dictatorship of the proletariat was first achieved in Ukraine kept the homeland firmly in progressive sights despite the movement's emphasis on the primacy of the class struggle over the national or ethnic group, and it gave nationalists their *raison d'être*.

If models and sources of inspiration united nationalist and progressive women by constituting at once a common bond of Ukrainianness and a source of friction when the same figures were bent to conflicting ends, they also provided each camp with a feminine ideal. Sometimes, Great Women transcended gender to become national figures whose life work was an example and inspiration not only to women but to all Ukrainians. Or they became international figures with something to say to the exploited and downtrodden of both sexes and all nations. More often, Great Women spoke specifically to their own sex – not to motivate women on their own behalf by drawing attention to male-female tensions or inequality, but to align them with like-thinking men behind something larger than themselves. The heroines exalted in the women's press had demonstrated active, conscious, and enlightened commitment to Ukraine, if they were nationalist, or to the class struggle, if they were progressive. Combining the militant and activist with the maternal and traditionally feminine to define women's roles and responsibilities, their message was mixed. But even heroic wives and mothers – who raised Ukrainian patriots to give to their nation or new cadres to fill revolutionary ranks, and who likewise supported and prodded their husbands – directed their femaleness to serving the cause.

The creation of a complex of models and sources of inspiration for Ukrainian-Canadian women was initially the work of an interwar generation that included immigrants fresh from the revolutionary upheaval in Ukraine as well as the Canadian born and/or raised. The complex was subsequently refined and the ranks of Great Women augmented under the influence of current affairs in Ukraine and displaced persons settling in Canada after the Second World War. In neither the nationalist nor the progressive community, however, could a leadership elite be content with an emotional appeal to larger-than-life figures whose circumstances were far removed from those of Ukrainian women in Canada. An interwar play that featured a Ukrainian-Canadian nurse wounded on the Galician front[96] undoubtedly gave Ukrainian women in Canada a sense of both participation in the events of the revolutionary years and the need to uphold a fine tradition of commitment, but it had little to do with the reality of their lives or their practical options. The legacy of Great Women had to be interpreted in a Canadian setting and translated into concrete programs of action.

4

Putting the Models to Work: Organizational Propaganda and Programs

To die for an idea, spokespersons for Ukrainian-Canadian women's organizations insisted, was not the only type of heroism; to live and work for that idea was equally heroic.[1] Such an attitude was necessary for the message of the Great Women of Ukraine to have any relevance in Canada. The woman working in her Sudbury kitchen or behind a bazaar table in her prairie hall could not be another Olha Basarab dying a martyr's death or the twentieth-century reincarnation of the Cossack mother giving her sons to her nation. Nor could she share the experience of her contemporary sisters in Ukraine – either the hardship, sorrow, and suffering lamented by the nationalists or the exhilaration of building the new Soviet society envied by the progressives.

Physical separation from Ukraine was felt most keenly by self-styled political immigrants, having to justify choosing the path free from personal danger, discomfort, and sacrifice. While progressives viewed Canada not as a utopia, however flawed, from which to further their cause but as a target of that cause, nationalists stressed the unparalleled scope for Ukrainian work that living in Canada offered. Implicit in the moral and material support of Ukrainian institutions in Canada as the basis of group survival, and explicit in the moral and material aid to be extended to Ukraine and Ukrainians abroad, was the assumption that Canadian democracy and socioeconomic opportunities made these activities possible. But Canada did more than furnish an environment for Ukrainian work. Nationalists insisted upon the duty of Ukrainian Canadians to exploit conditions unavailable to Ukrainians elsewhere, using their rights and privileges and relative prosperity as citizens of a 'free country' to preserve and nurture their culture in

Canada and to assist a beleaguered homeland. Indifference and assimilation were held to be indefensible when Ukrainians in Ukraine had struggled through centuries of foreign occupation and oppression to keep their language and traditions – their national soul – alive. During heroine month in February 1976, Ukrainian-Canadian women were reminded that they lived in a free country, where they could act as ambassadors for an enslaved Ukraine and themselves become heroines. No one demanded their life's blood, only minor sacrifices and will.[2]

How was the ideal of the heroic mother and community activist to be achieved in practice? Put more baldly, what were women actually expected to do? The propaganda and programs that nationalist and progressive women's organizations devised for members as Ukrainian and class-conscious women living not in the homeland but on Canadian soil addressed these questions. The activities they prescribed not only subordinated their sex to the service of the self-imposed missions of their respective communities but also defined women's role in terms that emphasized gender differences. These differences gave men and women separate spheres, and they exploited so-called 'female' qualities to place homemaking and motherhood above community work and to dictate the form that community work took. As the large-scale organization of Ukrainian-Canadian women coincided with the interwar years, these years were crucial to the niche women carved for themselves in the public and private spheres.

'Consciousness-raising' to Ukrainian-Canadian women's organizations did not mean personal growth and emancipation of the individual woman for her benefit alone. Rather, its purpose was to make the individual conform to an ideal community stereotype, directing her energies in public and private life to community goals that were deemed to represent her interests as well. Progressives sought a 'new woman' politicized as one of the toiling masses, nationalists a Ukrainian fully aware of her national obligations. Both camps recognized the importance of the printed word to give the ideal maximum exposure, and both camps stressed the importance of self-education, constantly urging the rank-and-file to improve themselves. Between the wars, progressive women identified the moment when they began to read, attend lectures, and participate in discussion groups as the moment when they stopped being the appendages and communal kitchen of male branches of the Ukrainian Labour-Farmer Temple Association (ULFTA) and started to act independently.[3] How organized women (and their male counterparts) understood women's emancipation, and the independence and fulfilment it brought, was predicated on how women were seen in relation to the larger nationalist and progressive communities, and was responsible for how they defined and arranged their priorities.

A founder of the Women's Union, the mass women's organization in interwar Galicia, and its head from 1928 to 1939, made a telling observation about the role of women in Ukrainian society. 'The Ukrainian women's movement,' Milena Rudnytska remarked, 'was never an egotistic movement concerned with narrowly conceived women's interests. We always emphasized *responsibility* rather than *rights*, and when we demanded 'rights' for ourselves, we did so out of the profound conviction that without them we could not serve our People as active and useful citizens. We always understood these rights as the right to public service, as the right to serve the Nation. Service to the Nation was, and continues to be, one of the guiding precepts of the Ukrainian women's movement, a precept from which the movement drew its strength and moral satisfaction.'[4] Rudnytska's words were printed as a substitute for a dedication page in the golden jubilee history of the Ukrainian Women's Association of Canada (UWAC). They express the thinking of her interwar contemporaries, the women at the forefront of the nationalist mobilization of Ukrainian women in Canada. Such a view subordinated female issues to Ukrainian issues, and interpreted personal fulfilment in terms of community or group service. It summoned women to organize, and it dictated the form of their organization – within community structures, outside the Canadian mainstream, under a nationally conscious and centralized leadership, and separately from men. Within these parameters, women would control their own sphere, in the execution of their peculiar responsibilities; an ideological elite, working with and through local branches, would transform its unenlightened and uneducated sisters into self-reliant, focused individuals ready to take their place as full citizens of the nation.

Emphasis on enlightenment and education for women to acquit their group obligations, and the role in public life through their organizations that these obligations imposed, implied support of women's emancipation from traditional subordinate and domestic roles. Indeed, the Ukrainian-Canadian women leading the organizational drive among their sex constantly stressed the need to extend their sphere beyond

UWOC branch members in Ukrainian folk costume. Timmins, Ontario, 1930s

children, the kitchen, and the church.[5] Ukraine's predicament and the pressures this placed on national-cultural survival in Canada put the interests of the nation first; these same priorities, however, also guaranteed support for female rights and an expanded sphere for women if they would advance the Ukrainian cause. Women, as one-half the nation, had to expect to shoulder the burdens of group membership, participating alongside men as intelligent, active, and conscious members of their community.[6] In practice, the radicalism in 'active on every front' and 'arm in arm with men,' proved more apparent than real. Both men and women acquiesced in limits to women's participation in community life, confirming a division of labour and power between the sexes.

With its militant form of nationalism and glorification of physical martyrdom, the Ukrainian Women's Organization of Canada (UWOC) might reasonably have been expected to be the most unreserved champion of women's rights. Instead, it viewed an expanded role for its sex

Some of the prairie farm women who gave the UWAC its interwar strength.
Natalia Kobrynska branch, Spedden, Alberta, 1938

as a sacrifice in an unnatural situation, one no longer required when
Ukraine lay secure in its own state.[7] In the meantime, to the extent
that centuries of national subjugation had made Ukrainian women
feel inferior to men, unprepared to shoulder equal (although not necessarily identical) burdens and responsibilities, they had to be emancipated – developing their full potential to aid in the emancipation of
Ukraine. If women's emancipation was understood in terms of national
service, Ukraine was also the reason for rejecting a feminist 'women's
rights' definition. The cause, interwar UWOC literature maintained,
demanded cooperation between the sexes, not the distractions and
divisiveness of gender-based conflict stirred by misguided women at-
tempting to assert their superiority or promote their selfish and narrow interests.[8] For an organization that had as its slogan, 'Nation above
all,' the logic in this position was obvious.

UWAC circles (and men associated with them) also equated 'emancipated' Ukrainian women with nationally conscious patriots and
stressed their necessity for the future of the Ukrainian nation.[9] Savella
Stechishin's brother-in-law offered the opinion that Ukrainians' atti-

tudes towards women, symbolized in the contemptuous use of the word
baba (old woman), had made them servants of others instead of masters
in their own house, and he tied women's emancipation to Ukraine's
need for mothers who raised 'free citizens not slaves.'[10] Savella herself
told the UWAC founding convention in 1926:

> Our women's movement in Canada and in Ukraine should have one
> objective: to help Ukrainian women develop intellectually, to pre-
> pare them for civic, domestic and public life. The preparation of
> our women to be good mothers is a matter of far greater impor-
> tance than politics, electoral rights or office-holding.
>
> Today, when our homeland, church and schools are in the hands
> of foreign conquerors, the women of Halychyna [Galicia] and cen-
> tral Ukraine must pay particular attention to the upbringing of chil-
> dren. Only the home remains in our hands and the home must
> provide a national upbringing.[11]

In 1943, addressing the first congress of the new nationalist umbrella
organization, the Ukrainian Canadian Committee (UCC), on the role
of women in the life of the nation, a second UWAC activist went further.
The international women's movement, Natalia Kohuska contended,
had campaigned for women's democratic rights as human beings to
enable them to fulfil their 'natural' function in society, which was to
bear and rear children.[12]

The Ukrainian Catholic Women's League (UCWL) did not exist
between the wars to contribute to the discussion of the relationship
between women's rights and the nation's rights. In light of the pro-
nouncements of their clergy in the postwar period, it would be surprising if Catholic women either voiced or received any different
message. Speaking to UCWL members in 1973, a priest put their priorities into perspective. Unlike women who did not know what they
wanted and sought a panacea in 'women's liberation,' the self-sacrificing and industrious Ukrainian woman had always known what she
wanted: to be a good Christian, a good companion to her husband, a
good mother, a good parishioner, and a good daughter of her church
and her people.[13]

From the preceding examples, it should be apparent that the quality
of Ukrainian-Canadian motherhood was crucial to the establishment
and aims of all three nationalist women's organizations. Mothering
was also a primary focus. The decisions taken at their national con-

ventions – the highest authority for each of the UWAC, the UWOC, and the UCWL and the best barometer of their priorities and concerns – made this clear. So did their literature. One 1946 circular, for example, advised against participation in UWAC activities until a woman's children and home were properly Ukrainized.[14] Forbidden to infringe on women's domestic responsibilities, community work was itself defined in language that emphasized women's 'maternal' and 'feminine' qualities and socially prescribed roles. Just as they were responsible for the well-being of their immediate biological families, Ukrainian-Canadian women were told, so they had a duty towards their larger family and blood tie, the Ukrainian nation.[15] This equation of the nation with the family had two repercussions. On the one hand, it justified women's community involvement and obliged them to undertake such a role; on the other hand, it automatically directed their activity towards traditional female pursuits – children and education, the church, charity, and handicrafts. Once again, the radicalism in the surface message was muted.

Nationalist women's organizations, as participants in public community life, admitted through their propaganda and programs that they perceived gender to guarantee women a separate sphere, special roles and responsibilities as members of their group, and special talents to bring to their work.[16] The foci of Ukrainian-Canadian women's organizations were not unusual for their sex and corresponded to those of women's volunteer groups in mainstream Canada. The difference was that the activities of mainstream women complemented or supplemented the functions of the state, while those of Ukrainian women represented the only areas of initiative available to a minority group concerned for the quality and direction of life in its society. This fact magnified the importance of 'women's work' in the Ukrainian-Canadian community to give a concrete focus and relevance to women's activities that the politicking and rhetoric of its male leadership lacked.

The organization of progressive women proceeded from other criteria than service to a captive Ukrainian nation. The Women's Section of the ULFTA aimed to cultivate the class consciousness of Ukrainian-Canadian working and farm women, prisoners of an exploitative capitalist system, so they would rise to fight for their rights as part of an international revolutionary movement. Already in the pioneer period, Ukrainian socialists had stressed organization as the answer to the sexual, ethnic, and economic discrimination Ukrainian immigrant girls encountered in the marketplace. They also complained of the girls' own indifference to their situation, pointing to the small numbers of women in Ukrainian Social Democratic Party branches as proof.[17] The campaign to mobilize women intensified under the socialists' interwar communist successors as more women entered the workforce and the Great Depression further battered an already powerless proletariat.

As rallying points with an ulterior political motive, the interwar progressive women's magazine *Robitnytsia* published dozens of heart-wrenching tales depicting the lives of working and farm women. In one of these stories, her father's joblessness and mother's illness forced young Meri to enter the employ of the exacting Mrs Johns: the woman hired only Catholics (because they were obedient) and worked her servants seventeen hours a day. In another story, a worker's daughter's dreams of a singing career and boys with Ford cars were shattered by harsh reality. Forced out of school to work, the girl lost her first position after refusing her employer's sexual advances, then was fired again after ruining her health in a demanding job in a hotel, and landed in the street; there she saw her old school chum working as a prostitute and woke up to her future; she returned home, warned her younger sister against reading 'true' stories and living in a fantasy world, and found salvation in the labour temple.[18] Invariably, these tales were accompanied by the admonition to organize and to engage in organized struggle – through the Women's Section of the ULFTA, local unions, and the Communist Party of Canada – for the Soviet order where both sexes were free and equal. Women, it was felt, particularly needed organization: not only was their class consciousness more rudimentary than men's, but they had been taught by poverty-stricken parents to be submissive.[19] The plight of farm women, popularly regarded as more ignorant and oppressed than their city counterparts, whom they greatly outnumbered, was perceived to be especially bad. A backbreaking workload and poverty joined the vagaries of world markets to enslave them to the land and to giant corporations, without the weapons of unionization and the strike to which their wage-earning sisters had access.[20]

Two touchstones of the interwar progressive movement were its self-professed commitment to female equality and its insistence that female oppression had been eradicated in its circles. Neither issue, however, was ever far from the surface. The very existence of the Women's Section of the ULFTA indicated that women, because of peculiar needs and tasks, were to be treated differently. Furthermore,

the origins of the Women's Section, in committees to aid famine victims in the Soviet Union (Ukraine and the Volga region) in 1921–2
on the grounds that women were best suited to this work,[21] identified
them firmly with stereotyped nurturing roles. The humanitarian origins
and work of organized progressive women – on behalf of victims of
the class struggle, social injustice, imperialist war, and natural disaster
– would in subsequent years become part of progressive mythology.[22]
Between the wars, attitudes within the progressive community concerning women's roles and the female condition were complex, and
despite the officially held position, equality often remained an elusive
and contentious ideal.

A series of articles in *Robitnytsia* in 1928–9 revealed the volatility of
the issue. They also demonstrated how interrelated were the questions
of women's organization and male chauvinism within progressive ranks.
The catalyst was the statement that women were by nature physically
and mentally inferior to and dependent on men, making meaningful
participation in community life impossible and organization unnec-
essary since men bore all oppression on their behalf. The ensuing
debate attracted letters from readers in Galicia and other parts of the
world as well as Canada and the United States. While angry respondents pointed out that millions of working and farm women knew
socioeconomic oppression first hand, women in particular drew attention to their extra burden as outside labour did not reduce their domestic responsibilities, and oppression by their own men made 'slaves
of slaves.' Only through organization, these women insisted, would
women gain the consciousness and confidence to become true comrades in the workers' struggle; men who objected to their enlightenment and involvement served bourgeois sexist propaganda designed
to keep workers weak and divided. Female respondents also insisted
on separate branches so that women could speak and act freely, undergo
the politicization preliminary to direct participation in the revolutionary movement, and transcend a purely kitchen function.[23]

That women should raise such points was a good indication that
their entry into organized community life did not always proceed
smoothly and that male prejudice was a problem. Independent sources
substantiate this contention. In 1929, looking in from the outside, a
Communist Party of Canada activist criticized the attitudes of many
Ukrainian communist men. 'They say,' he wrote, that 'a woman talks
too much and can't be trusted and [it is] enuf if their husbands are in
the party. In Lethbridge ... they even suspended one from the meet-

ings.'[24] Women themselves objected to what they perceived as obstructive male attitudes. In 1923 *Holos robitnytsi* (*Robitnytsia*'s predecessor) had received several letters from women complaining that their husbands wanted them neither to participate in the Women's Section of the ULFTA nor to read its magazine. Taking their complaints seriously, the editor, Matthew Popowich, responded with a piece entitled 'Rabyni rabiv' (Slaves of slaves).[25]

In reality, the Women's Section and branches of the ULFTA never escaped an initial reliance on male initiative and guidance. Men edited their magazines,[26] authored much of their educational and discussion literature, organized their branches, and instructed them politically. On occasion, some of these men complained of indifference and apathy hampering their work. One instructor, writing to *Robitnytsia* from Vancouver, expressed his frustration at lecturing to women's branches of the ULFTA: poor attendance, tardiness, and the lack of questions and discussion, whether from shyness or lack of interest, made his preparatory work seem like a waste of time.[27] All the same, women accepted, sought out, and relied on men's help. The female organizer who criticized the behaviour of male instructors (men who taught discipline, she said, should not bang their fists and shout)[28] was exceptional. Far more typical was the regularity with which progressive women, singly and in their national conventions, repeatedly appealed to their male comrades for both practical help and inspiration.[29]

Nor were female indifference and apathy and male opposition strangers to the nationalist community. Few women joined the Ukrainian Catholic sisterhood formed in Morecambe, Alberta, in 1940, it was explained, 'because not everyone understood that not just men had to work in the parish and lead it, but that women too ought to make their contribution.'[30] In 1933 a UWAC activist referred to other difficulties facing women's organizations in rural areas. In twentieth-century Canada, and even among those claiming to be patriots, she said, Ukrainian men still regarded women as unpaid workers who were created to sit at home except when it came to things like taking the Easter *paska* (bread) to church for the priest to bless.[31] As for men being actively involved in the organization of women, the role performed by male organizers and instructors in the progressive camp had no equivalent in the interwar nationalist community. War veterans and other émigré spokesmen did, however, sometimes participate in the establishment of what became UWOC branches and address their meetings, and the local Orthodox priest was known to exert his in-

Members of the UCWL, St Josaphat's Cathedral, with their spiritual adviser. Toronto, 1962

fluence on the UWAC.[32] The closest parallel with the progressives came with the establishment of the UCWL and reflected the hierarchical nature of the Catholic church and the paternalistic relationship of its priests with their flocks. The parish priest initiated the formation of many UCWL locals; a branch's zeal often fluctuated with the arrival and departure of an activist priest; and branch photographs invariably grouped the women around the priest who acted as their spiritual adviser. More significantly, Neil Savaryn, future bishop of the Edmonton eparchy, wrote the UCWL's constitution; it stipulated that the approval of the spiritual adviser was required for a branch to fold and the approval of the hierarchy was necessary before the organization could disband.[33]

Despite the call by a leadership elite among both nationalists and progressives for women to become full members of their community, the cause they were to serve was not always sufficient to overcome ingrained male (and female) biases. Yet women did enter the public sphere. Once it was established that they should organize separately and focus on traditional female tasks, women's organizations had their basic agenda. Fleshing out that agenda became the next order of busi-

UWAC women in their embroidered blouses. The painted backdrop to the stage behind them, depicting an old-country village scene, was typical of Ukrainian halls. Olha Kobylianska branch, Smoky Lake, Alberta, 1941

ness. The public sphere offered greater scope in terms of mobilization, activity, and coordination, and greater possibility for wielding an influence. Women worked collectively and in tandem with a leadership elite, reinforcing each other's commitment and their organization's goals. The private sphere, in contrast, was isolated and outside organizations' direct control; a leadership elite could do no more than hope that women would take its propaganda and programs to heart. Nevertheless, advising Ukrainian-Canadian women in the private sphere as wives, mothers, and homemakers became an important part of organizations' work. It acknowledged their acceptance of the idea that woman's influence was vital to the Ukrainian or class consciousness of the home and family.

Progressives were less inclined than nationalists to dictate to women in the private sphere and the criteria were different. This was especially true of marriage. Although a class-conscious husband was preferable to one who was not, progressive women did not have to marry Ukrainians. In nationalist circles, in contrast, the involuntary nature of the Ukrainian blood tie and its obligations justified, as the community's right and duty, intimate intrusion into women's private lives, beginning with the dictate that they marry Ukrainians. Nationalists liked to emphasize their people's great love and respect for freedom, yet a leadership elite was prepared to deny it to the group's members as individuals in the interests of the freedom of Ukrainians as a whole.[34] While a class-conscious home could be maintained without a Ukrainian husband, a Ukrainian home needed two partners united by their common Ukrainianness.

The instruction given progressive women as mothers also differed from that received by nationalist women. An idealized image of the noble mother was always part of progressive propaganda. Whether exploited and oppressed or struggling to break her chains, she selflessly worked for the welfare of her children and the success of the cause. Writer Myroslav Irchan, who emigrated to the Soviet Union in 1929 and disappeared in the purges of the 1930s, presented a traditionalist view of women: only mothers could raise sons for the struggle, and wives were the moral support and strength of their husbands.[35] The importance of class-conscious mothers in rearing class-conscious children, alerted and educated in their task through progressive women's organizations, was also part of progressive propaganda. For instance, progressive mothers exercised vigilance against the influence of servants of capitalism like the bourgeois public school and Hollywood, just as they exercised vigilance against the general demoralization of 'the street.'[36] In addition, class-conscious wives and mothers attacked the workers' own great albatross – the twin evils of alcohol and illiteracy – by setting an example for their husbands and children.[37]

But the progressive vision of a perfect Soviet society in Ukraine precluded the need for Ukrainian mothers in Canada to preserve an endangered Ukrainian culture and inculcate an activist Ukrainian consciousness in their children. Only rarely did national shame, with alienation from the Ukrainian language and the progressive child's Ukrainian parents, figure as an undesirable consequence of 'the street' or North American socialization.[38] Thus, while the progressive press, like the nationalist, regularly printed practical information on childcare, health, and homemaking, it did not include a mother's role in the home in the interests of Ukrainianness as part of its message. Because the preservation of Ukrainianness was cultural, and did not have the political urgency it bore in nationalist circles, progressives placed less emphasis on mothering in the socialization of youth.

The centralized, hierarchial, male-dominated character of the progressive movement, together with its ideological priorities and rigidity,

Youthfulness and commitment. Members of the Women's Section of the
ULFTA, posed with copies of the progressive magazine, *Holos robitnytsi*.
Kitchener, Ontario, 1920s

also affected the status accorded to women's mothering role. The first
loyalty of progressive women was to an international community in
which economic class (and not Ukrainianness) constituted the motivating factor and unifying focus. Pitting the exploited against the exploiters, it ensured that the workplace and the political arena, and not
the home, would be the battleground where victory was won or lost.
'Workers of the world unite' was a call to public action. As a result,
legitimate organizational activity and direct participation in the class
struggle overshadowed women's roles as mothers. Also, as teachers of
class consciousness or Ukrainian culture, mothers were overshadowed
by the discipline and trained cadres, overwhelmingly male, of the labour temple and special ULFTA youth schools (*robitnychi ditochi shkoly*).
For these reasons, strengthened by their realistic attitude towards
working wives and mothers (although deploring the conditions under
which they worked), the progressives neither agitated for primarily
domestic roles for Ukrainian-Canadian women nor saw women's

organizations largely as vehicles for improving the quality of their motherhood.

In nationalist circles, in contrast, the first goal of women's organizations was to prepare Ukrainian-Canadian women to be good Ukrainian mothers and homemakers, and to involve them in the formal Ukrainization of youth.[39] Enhancing women's self-esteem and importance, the prestige and urgency attached to motherhood also carried great pressures, placing the success or failure of community objectives squarely on women's shoulders. At its most basic, being a good Ukrainian mother and homemaker meant utilizing Canada's material advantages and the ideas of the 'experts' concerning household management and childcare to raise healthy, moral, industrious members of society, and to improve Ukrainian Canadians' status and reputation. The interwar UWAC, for example, urged women to modernize their homes so that their children would not be ashamed; and in her columns in *Ukrainskyi holos*, the organization's own expert, home economist Savella Stechishin, gave advice on interior decorating based on the fashions and researches of the larger society.[40] Assimilation by the Anglo-Canadian culture that North American goods and technology represented was to be avoided. Above all, being a good Ukrainian mother and homemaker meant ensuring the Ukrainian character and commitment of the rising generation. From the time *Ukrainskyi holos* published its ten commandments for readers in 1914, the instructions given Ukrainian-Canadian women on how to raise Ukrainian children and maintain Ukrainian homes changed in detail but not in essentials. Published in 1947 as an inspirational and practical guide 'to help the home raise youth as worthy citizens of Canada and true children of the Ukrainian people,'[41] the UWAC booklet, *Na storozhi kultury* (Guarding culture), took interwar wisdom into the postwar world.

According to the voluminous literature in the women's organizational press, good Ukrainian mothers possessed the following characteristics. They began by giving their children Ukrainian names and speaking to them in Ukrainian. They sang the little ones Ukrainian songs, told them Ukrainian tales and proverbs, and read them Ukrainian stories. They taught the older ones to read and write their mother tongue, bought them Ukrainian books and periodicals, and schooled them in Ukrainian history, culture, and national aspirations. They ensured that they had Ukrainian playmates and that the youngsters spoke Ukrainian together. To guarantee formal socialization in a

Ukrainian milieu and spirit, they took their children to church and community events; sent them to *ridna shkola*, Sunday school, and youth organizations; and (in the postwar years) enrolled them in public-school Ukrainian language courses or bilingual programs. They encouraged their higher education in the interests of upward mobility and socio-economic progress. As mothers of future mothers, they paid particular attention to the upbringing of their daughters.

While good Ukrainian mothers looked after the inner child, good Ukrainian homemakers were expected to provide the proper physical environment.[42] The pioneer immigrant intelligentsia had early rejected 'peasantness' as a way of life and an interwar elite further encouraged modernization and Canadianization in the home. This left Ukrainianness as largely symbolic, drawing on the peasants' folk art to politicize what had initially been forms of cultural and artistic expression. Good Ukrainian homemakers covered the walls of their home with Ukrainian *kylymy* (rugs), *rushnyky*-draped icons, pictures of Ukrainian heroes and heroines, and (in the postwar years) works by Ukrainian and Ukrainian-Canadian artists. They displayed glass bowls of Easter eggs; they put embroidered runners and cushions on their furniture (a postwar generation would also have them accent their family's clothes with Ukrainian embroidery motifs). They cooked Ukrainian food. Good Ukrainian homemakers were also expected to augment the visible symbols of Ukrainianness with a Ukrainian patriotic, cultural, and religious atmosphere. As home managers, they heeded the call '*svii do svoho*' and patronized Ukrainian businessmen and professionals. Knowledgeable about their heritage, they maintained Ukrainian national and religious customs within the family, celebrating major holidays like Christmas and Easter in the traditional fashion and reciting traditional prayers. They read the Ukrainian press and literature, improving their Ukrainian language skills if necessary; and they followed Ukrainian affairs with intelligent interest, so that at the supper table they could introduce Ukrainian topics and lead informed discussions with their husbands and children – whom they encouraged to read Ukrainian material and follow Ukrainian affairs on their own.

The Ukrainian family sustained by the nationalist Ukrainian-Canadian 'super mom' during the interwar and postwar periods was not distinguished by intangible 'ethnic values' fostering a distinctive lifestyle that set it apart from other Canadian families. Instead, it was distinguished by politicized Ukrainianness, structured around carefully cultivated symbols and practices that did not interfere with full participation in Canadian society. How, then, was the Ukrainian-Canadian child's Canadian consciousness understood and explained? The pioneer intelligentsia had argued that self-knowledge and self-respect as Ukrainians were necessary to make Ukrainian immigrants the equals of other Canadians, complete human beings capable of a useful contribution to society. Lord Tweedsmuir, as governor general of Canada, appeared to endorse that sentiment in 1936, telling a Ukrainian gathering, 'You will all be better Canadians for being also good Ukrainians.' His speech actually referred just to handicrafts, folksongs, dances, and legends – the popular and apolitical components of the Canadian mosaic – but Ukrainian-Canadian nationalists adopted that one sentence as their Magna Carta. It guaranteed their right to group survival in Canada and it offically sanctioned their peculiar definition of 'Canadian.'[43]

Organized nationalist women exploited this view in the interests of their own sphere: Tweedsmuir's dictum not only justified their work to Ukrainize youth, but commanded them to undertake it. The understanding that good Canadian citizenship rested on Ukrainian consciousness[44] enabled women's organizations to advise Ukrainian-Canadian mothers that in rearing conscious Ukrainians they were rearing worthy citizens of Canada, and thus worked for the good of the Canadian nation as much as for their own people. Underlying the argument for Ukrainianness as the basis for Canadianness was the assumption that just as the Ukrainian child was born into the group and could not escape its obligations, so he or she had an unalienable right to his or her national language, culture, traditions, and political security. For the Ukrainian mother in Canada to deny her children their birthright would be to deny them full personhood. Bent to serve Ukrainian purposes, the nationalist understanding of 'Canadian' demonstrated the community's willingness to enlist Canada and Canadianism in the Ukrainian political interest. The public sphere demonstrated this more clearly, in the moral and material aid to Ukrainian causes and Ukraine that nationalist women's organizations saw as part of their mandate.

The first issue to be addressed in women's life in the public sphere, however, is more basic and concerns the relationship between an elite, distinguished from the mass of women by its self-appointed leadership role, and the grassroots. How successful was the interwar organizational drive to transform Ukrainian-Canadian women into politically conscious activists as part of national and international networks of like-thinking women? Allowing for inflated numbers by competing organizations anxious to present a vigorous image, membership figures show that approximately one-tenth of Ukrainian-Canadian women over the age of nineteen belonged to the Women's Section of the ULFTA, the UWAC, and the UWOC between the wars.[45] To this must be added members of women's branches of the monarchist United Hetman Organization, members of unaffiliated local groups, progressive women in the main local ULFTA branch or fraternal Workers Benevolent Association, individuals on farms or in unorganized centres who joined the UWAC, the UWOC, or the Women's Section of the ULFTA as 'free members,' and Catholic women in parish sisterhoods. These sisterhoods are crucial, given that after 1944 the UCWL grew rapidly to challenge its rivals on all fronts. Yet only a fraction of Ukrainian-Canadian women actually joined the organizations created for them. Membership was not necessarily an accurate measure of participation in organizations' programs; only half their members, the Calgary and East Kildonan branches of the Women's Section of the ULFTA reported in 1937, took part in their meetings and activities.[46]

Certain factors affecting women's ability and proclivity to organize lay beyond the control of a leadership elite and were independent of community politics. For example, an exodus of workers after a mine disaster sent the Coalhurst (Alberta) women's branch of the ULFTA into a downward spiral until it finally lost its status when too few remained in the town to elect a competent executive.[47] More fundamentally, large-scale organization (among both sexes) depended on a population sufficiently mature and prosperous to invest its energies and resources in improving the quality of social and spiritual life. Even the progressives, whose reason for mobilization was Ukrainians' economic poverty and exploitation, relied on contributions from supporters to build and equip their network of labour-temples. The degree to which farm women could and would join the new women's organizations hinged on progress in Ukrainian agriculture. The first significant step out of subsistence farming had occurred during the Great War with the Allied demand for wheat, and although the Depression halted and reversed much of the expansion of the 1920s, greater affluence, mechanization of the farming operation, and the purchase of labour-saving devices for the home relieved some women's workload to free them for other pursuits. Improvements in transportation, including the automobile, also let farm folk meet more easily and frequently, although problems persisted. When the Ranfurly ULFTA branch in rural Alberta celebrated International Women's Day and the fifteenth anniversary of the Women's Section in March 1937, muddy spring roads kept the country women who were its members from attending.[48] In addition to male prejudice, a UWAC activist cited the weather, the farm wife's summer workload, and the fact that it was easier for men than women to walk the long miles often necessary to get to a meeting place as obstacles to organization among rural women; children, however, could be left with their fathers.[49] In urban areas, too, women's participation in community life depended on available leisure time. The East Toronto branch of the Women's Section of the ULFTA was small, it apologized in 1937: many members worked, others had small children, and they could not do much.[50]

Other factors in women's decision to organize comment on the relationship between a leadership elite and the grassroots, and suggest that the two often had different priorities and perspectives. Local women were not necessarily motivated by the streamlined and centralized propaganda and programs of progressive and nationalist elites, or by 'professional' agitators dispatched by the national executives of the ULFTA, UWAC, UWOC, or (after 1944) the UCWL. The history of the branches of the Women's Section of the ULFTA showed a centralist and derivative hand: they invariably appeared after the establishment of the main ULFTA branch in an area, did not exist without it, and often removed women from the main body in the promotion of separate organization. Nationalist women, in contrast, frequently joined one of the new national organizations as an already existing group with local roots, its world defined by the neighbourhood church or hall. If this perhaps points to more spontaneous grassroots support for the nationalist orientation, it most certainly points to organization from the bottom up rather than from the top down. This acceptance of the need for separate women's organizations resulted in mobilization independently of pressure from outside.

Did this 'spontaneous' grassroots organization come from the people or from a local elite? The interwar experience of the new national women's organizations suggests a leadership elite. A profile of the first presidents of UWAC branches established in Alberta through the Second World War reveals, for example, a preponderance of teachers and wives of men (teachers, businessmen, one doctor) active in local politics and/or Ukrainian community affairs.[51] How much the UWAC relied on the initiative and leadership of such individuals can be seen from letters and reports that attributed a downturn in the activity of rural branches on the prairies to the departure of a particular teacher or priest's wife, or that chastized other teachers and priests' wives for doing too little.[52] Evidence from the other side of the country, however, modifies this picture while attesting to the pervasive influence of community divisions and affairs. A sociologist researching Ukrainian immigrant life in interwar Montreal found that whether women were organized or not, community considerations dominated their informal and formal social lives: instead of a private female world centred on the kitchen and on kin, religious divisions and Ukrainian politics dictated their friendships, and public events occupied much of their leisure time.[53]

The grassroots did not necessarily share the ideological inflexibility or sophistication of the organizational elite. Some local groups played a brand of musical chairs. For example, the Olha Basarab Women's Society formed at Fedorah, Alberta, in 1924 severed its early ties with the Women's Section of the ULFTA to affiliate with the UWAC; another UWAC branch, in Winnipeg, owed its origins to a future UWOC activist.[54] The women who joined such clubs also had their own ideas about what they wanted. A 1929 ULFTA questionnaire found that branches of the Women's Section preferred lectures on health and hygiene, morals and childrearing to lectures on current affairs, social-political questions, and the class struggle. And unlike the teacher who brought them under the UWAC banner, farm women at Smoky Lake in the Vegreville bloc were more interested in organization to improve their homemaking and childcare than to become involved in community life.[55] There is also evidence that local groups were quite happy with their local profiles, national affiliation being neither an immediate nor a pressing objective. Several years frequently separated the establishment of a local club and its affiliation with the UWAC or UCWL, whether the decision was taken independently, at the urging of UCWL or UWAC spokespersons, or after consultation with the parish priest. Then, too, the grip of the central organization could be precarious; in postwar Ontario, various UCWL branches chafed against the eparchial executive or, on the loss of a priest encouraging wider horizons, turned solely to parish work.[56] These few examples indicate that the grassroots often understood its Ukrainianness first in terms of the immediate and concrete, and not in terms of a remote international community, difficult to visualize and outside the parameters of daily life.

That affiliation with one of the major women's organizations drew local groups into a wider orbit is incontestable. Many UWAC branches, for example, credited national affiliation and exposure to UWAC directives with an upsurge in cultural-educational work and an enhanced sense of belonging to a larger Ukrainian community, particularly through integration into its formal rituals.[57] But the national or international scene never replaced the local community as women's primary focus, and material concerns always absorbed a great deal of their attention and energy.

When in 1930 the ULFTA declared that a building – for meetings, rehearsals, and performances – guaranteed the existence of an organization,[58] it was acknowledging two realities. One was the public, organized, and mass nature of Ukrainian-Canadian community life. The other was that Ukrainians, for psychological as well as practical reasons, needed physical surroundings where their symbols prevailed and they dictated the atmosphere. The local Legion Hall or United Church basement with its assimilationist associations would not do. Women specifically viewed the absence of a building as a severe limitation to organizational effectiveness. Particularly in rural areas, they complained of the difficulties of having to meet in private homes, of having to organize and hold functions in rented premises with dishes and food brought from their kitchens, of not having a permanent place to centralize their operations to improve the quality and quantity of community services they could offer. Conversely, the acquisition of a building acted as a stimulus to broadened activity.[59] That many women's groups formed right before or after the decision to construct a hall, church, or labour temple (and increased their tempo of activity during renovation and modernization projects) was significant.[60] It revealed a practical understanding within the larger Ukrainian-Canadian community that women's cooperation was crucial to paying its debts and running its programs. Without women's work, the Ukrainian-Canadian community would have been hard-pressed to create the physical environment that became its foundation and visible manifestation and the source of its effectiveness.

Women's organizations have always been responsible for much of community fund-raising – through concerts, dances, bazaars, teas, picnics, bake sales, smorgasbords, and suppers; catering for weddings, funerals, farm auctions, and community banquets; and preparing Ukrainian cookbooks, foods, Easter eggs, and embroidered items for sale. These activities represented the transfer of women's traditional

Women have always done the cooking for community functions. Church picnic, Downing, Alberta, 1933

'female' functions from the home into the community. There they underwent Canadianization. UWAC chicken suppers and pie socials, for example, came from rural prairie pioneer culture and not the Galician village; teas were unknown to Ukrainian peasant sisterhoods in Galicia but became the stock-in-trade of women's church groups in Canada. Ukrainian-Canadian women's organizations, in turn, Ukrainized these activities. They served their teas on cross-stitched tablecloths, sold Ukrainian handicrafts instead of crocheted potholders at their bazaars, and replaced the chicken supper with the *pyrohy* supper. In 1928 the Canora (Saskatchewan) branch of the UWAC held a 'tie' social, substituting traditionally embroidered men's neckties for the customary pie.[61] The postwar years also saw imaginative adaptation of their heritage to appeal to a mainstream market. The UCWL at St Josaphat's Church in Winnipeg boasted about the popularity of its 'Uke-a-bobs' (*pyrohy* and garlic sausage on a stick) at the Red River Exhibition, making the venture financially rewarding despite the intensive labour.[62] In the 1980s the Ukraine booth at Edmonton's Heritage Days sold 'mug-rugs' or miniature *kylymy* as coasters. Ukrainian foods and handicrafts, symbols of Ukrainianness simultaneously identified with women's work and finding favour outside the group, have been major money-makers

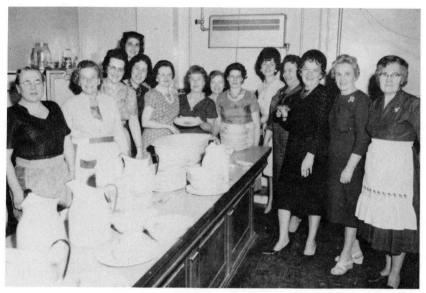

Dinner for Professor Paul Yuzyk, UNF hall, Winnipeg, Manitoba, 1963

for the Ukrainian-Canadian community in every region of the country and among every immigration and generation.

The primary recipient of the money realized by Ukrainian-Canadian women's organizations was the local Ukrainian-Canadian community. Women's work built, maintained, and renovated churches and rectories, *narodni domy*, Ukrainian National Federation (UNF) halls, and labour temples. It paid taxes. It bought rectory furniture, church vestments, pews, iconostases, pianos, theatrical wardrobes, kitchen equipment, auditorium chairs, furnaces, gestetners, and sewer systems. Although organized women jealously guarded their financial independence, this disposal of their money – indeed, that raising money for such purposes was their job – was accepted both by them and by the beneficiaries of their labour. During the Depression, when fundraising was said to hurt youth and educational work and the Central Executive tried to prevent UWAC branches from becoming simply 'housekeepers,' local communities were suspicious of women whose allegiance and membership dues went to an organization with 'its headquarters somewhere "out there."' Nevertheless, they 'continued to praise these women for their financial assistance and to compliment

Fund-raising. UCWL tea marking the silver anniversary of St Mary's
Ukrainian Catholic Church. Sudbury, Ontario, 1953

them for the delicious public meals which they prepared.'[63] Half a
century later, the outgoing UCWL president in the archeparchy of
Winnipeg would remark that many parishes depended on the UCWL
for their upkeep 'in its entirety.'[64] In 1990 a wide-ranging survey
conducted in St Andrew's Ukrainian Orthodox parish in Edmonton
confirmed the depth of the belief that such were women's roles; 93
per cent of respondents found 'bazaars/bake sales/art shows' to be
the most acceptable method of fund-raising.[65]

Reflecting the extension of women's maternal role into the public
sphere, much of their money also supported youth activities – paying
teachers, financing program materials, and providing facilities for youth
affiliates, *ridni shkoly*, Sunday schools, catechism classes, and, eventually, summer camps, kindergartens, and daycare. The close ties between organized women and the formal socialization of Ukrainian-
Canadian children were most noticeable in the nationalist community,
where the establishment and operation of youth groups often depended on the existence, initiative, and leadership of local branches
of the national associations.[66] Nor should focus on the secular community obscure the pioneering work of the Sisters Servants of Mary
Immaculate (SSMI), particularly in remote or unorganized communities; between 1930 and 1940 the sisters at Mundare taught Ukrainian

Ukrainian women's Easter eggs. Long popular with Ukrainians, now sold commercially in fashionable mainstream gift shops. 1949

language and catechism classes during summer vacations to 5147 children in eighty-seven colonies.[67] The organization of progressive youth occurred independently of the Women's Section of the ULFTA and instruction was male dominated, denying women the same ideological role in moulding the next generation. Branch histories in the ULFTA's tenth anniversary almanac indicate no connection between the establishment of local women's and youth affiliates, nor were youth activities described as dependent on women's involvement.[68]

Besides funding community work in Canada, women's organizations also extended material aid to Ukraine. Calls for such aid on behalf of famine-striken comrades in the Soviet Union had justified the creation of the Women's Section of the ULFTA, and between the wars it shifted attention to the victims of various natural disasters in Western Ukraine.[69] In preparation for the expected military campaign to liberate the homeland, and stressing the need for Ukrainian women in Canada to be ready to answer their nation's call, the interwar UWOC actively supported the émigré Ukrainian First Aid and Ukrainian Gold Cross.[70] While raising money for all-community concerns in Galicia – cultural-educational institutions, war invalids, flood victims – the UWAC

Ukrainian women's embroidery, admired and encouraged by outsiders since early in the century. Community Progress Competition for New Canadians sponsored by Canadian National Railways. Hafford, Saskatchewan, 1930

also supported specifically female projects at the behest of organized Ukrainian women in Europe. It took collections for Olha Petliura, widow of the assassinated ex-president of the Ukrainian People's Republic, the writer Olha Kobylianska, the women's press in Galicia, and delegates to represent Ukrainian women and their cause before world forums.[71] One of the first acts of the Pine River (Manitoba) branch of the UWAC when it formed in 1932, for example, was to raise funds to help the Women's Union in Galicia send a delegate to the International Council of Women (ICW) congress in Marseille.[72]

Three examples, all from Saskatchewan, illustrate the extent to which local concerns overshadowed Ukraine, and Ukrainian community or factional concerns those of general Canadian society, as the object of women's fund-raising. By the time of its golden jubilee in 1976, the UWAC in Canora had raised almost $100,000: 76.8 per cent of this money had gone to the local church, manse, and hall; 11.7 per cent to various local youth programs sponsored by the Ukrainian Self-Reliance League and Orthodox church; 6.4 per cent to the UWAC; and 1.5 per cent to the Canadian war effort and various public institutions

Handicrafts display by women in folk costume, Women's Section of the
ULFTA. Hamilton, Ontario, 1938

in Canora.[73] Between 1952 and 1975 the UCWL at St Basil the Great
Church in Regina raised approximately $47,500, of which 85.6 per
cent went towards building and furnishing the local church, rectory,
and church auditorium kitchen; another 4.6 per cent went to miscellaneous Ukrainian community causes (a second Regina parish, the SSMI,
scholarships for the study of Ukrainian, the Sheptytsky Institute in
Saskatoon), and 2.8 per cent to the parish altar boys and the Ukrainian
school.[74] Reflecting its émigré roots and mindset, the UWOC in Saskatoon broke the UWAC–UCWL pattern in that a greater proportion
of money raised left the local community. In its first quarter century,
the UWOC gave 32.3 per cent of its financial donations to overseas
Ukrainian causes (the Ukrainian Gold Cross, the Liberation Fund,
Zhinocha dolia, refugees and veterans); 32.1 per cent to the local UNF
and hall; 14.4 per cent to UWOC headquarters; 12.8 per cent to *Novyi
shliakh* and the UNF cultural centre in Winnipeg; 4.8 per cent to *ridna
shkola* and a kindergarten for local youth; 2.5 per cent to Ukrainians
in the Canadian army; and 1.1 per cent to the Ukrainian Canadian
Women's Committee (UCWC). St Catharines, Ontario, where only 12.6

per cent of funds went to Ukrainian causes overseas and 75.3 per cent to the local UNF hall, is more typical of the UWOC, and conforms to the UWAC–UCWL samples.[75]

If women subordinated material aid to Ukraine to the material needs of the Ukrainian community in Canada, Ukraine was not neglected. The relationship between organized Ukrainian-Canadian women and their homeland constitutes an important theme to be explored under the public sphere and comments on a significant dimension of their activities. Ukraine provided women's organizations with a *raison d'être*, at least in nationalist circles, and a focus. It also bound them together on the basis of common interests dictated by common ethnic origins, while introducing ideological differences that destroyed any possibility of unity among their sex. Representing a minority view anathema to the majority, interwar progressive women were motivated by non-Ukrainian class concerns as much as by Ukrainian ethnic issues. In addition, they defined ethnic issues in class terms – a Soviet order in Eastern Ukraine, peasants and workers struggling against a bourgeois nationalist elite in Western Ukraine. Progressive women were still included in the picture, however. For their part, while interwar nationalist women's organizations worked separately on behalf of a beleaguered homeland, they responded to the same events, employed similar tactics, and offered similar justifications and arguments.

Besides objecting in general to foreign régimes on Ukrainian soil, interwar Ukrainian nationalists in Canada were provoked by several specific events: intellectual purges and artificial famine in Soviet Ukraine, Polish 'pacification' in Galicia, and repression of Ukrainian institutions to strike at the heart of national-cultural life. Alone and with their community at large, organized women took advantage of rights denied their compatriots and used Canada's guarantees of freedom of speech and assembly to publicize conditions in the homeland. In 1928 and again in 1930, for example, mass meetings in Winnipeg protested anti-Ukrainian 'pogroms' in Galicia; and at its annual convention in 1931, the UWAC passed resolutions against both the Polish pacification and Soviet purges.[76] Nationalist women's organizations also acknowledged their ties with their sex, and spoke out on behalf of organized Ukrainian women in Europe – both their efforts to use international women's forums to incline world opinion towards Ukraine, and their struggle for recognition and survival. The UWOC, for example, condemned as 'chauvinistic barbarism' Poland's refusal to permit Women's Union delegates to go to Istanbul in 1935. When

Poland dissolved the Women's Union in 1938, the UWAC directed its branches to organize public protest meetings and sent letters to the governments of Canada, Britain, and Poland as well as to the League of Nations.[77]

A major event in interwar Ukrainian-Canadian community life was the 1929 tour of fifty-year-old Olena Kysilewska, who had been the youngest participant in the historical gathering of Ukrainian women under Kobrynska in 1884. In 1929 she was a well-known activist in the Women's Union, editor of the Galician women's journal *Zhinocha dolia* (Woman's fate), and a member of the Polish senate. Her Canadian contacts went beyond the formal Ukrainian community to include figures in the mainstream women's movement. Moreover, her son had emigrated in 1925 and was editor of the newspaper *Zakhidni visty* (Western news) in Edmonton; Vladimir Kaye-Kysilewsky would have a significant impact on Ukrainian-Canadian life, as a civil servant in Ottawa and as a historian. Organized progressive women denounced Kysilewska's visit, calling her a servant of the Polish bourgeoisie and of international capital.[78] At meetings across Canada, nationalist women extolled this 'great Daughter of Ukraine' as an inspiration and living link to their European sisters and the cause they championed.[79] Kysilewska appealed especially to women within the UWAC, which perceived itself and was perceived in turn as the Women's Union Canadian arm.[80] Physical contact between the two groups had been established the year previously when Savella Stechishin visited Europe, meeting prominent women like Kysilewska and the writer Olha Kobylianska, after whom the UWAC mother branch in Saskatoon was named. The UWAC's ties with the Ukrainian women's movement were strengthened by personal links with Kharytia Kononenko, who on her return to Europe had become involved in the organization of village women in Galicia, and by the attendance of Hanna Romanchych at the first Ukrainian Women's Congress held under the auspices of the Women's Union in Stanislaviv in 1934.[81] The decision at Stanislaviv to organize Ukrainian women internationally led to the formation of the World Union of Ukrainian Women in Lviv in 1937, and the UWAC accepted its invitation to represent Ukrainian women in Canada.

Protest meetings and resolutions confined to the group served little practical purpose. In order to act as ambassadors for an enslaved Ukrainian nation, nationalist women had to acquaint others with its predicament and enlist them in its interests. Thus, the peculiar Ukrainian needs responsible for their organization outside mainstream wom-

Bazaar activities (fish pond and bingo) reflecting the influence of the
mainstream culture. Smoky Lake, Alberta, 1956

en's circles made the courting of these circles equally necessary. In
1935 and again in 1937, the national convention of the UWOC rec-
ommended forging ties with the leaders of non-Ukrainian women's
organizations, the better to educate them in Ukrainian affairs and
aspirations. The UWAC issued a general appeal to the women of Canada, 'who cherish peace, and who are naturally gifted to feel the suf-
ferings of others,' to protest the atrocities of the Polish régime in
Galicia.[82] The undisputed pioneer in exploiting mainstream links came
from outside the new national women's organizations. Anna Hume-
nilovych had been active in Ukrainian community life before the war.
A failed marriage left her with two small children to support, but her
fortunes changed dramatically in 1918 when she married Henry Yonker, a wealthy Dutch-American doctor practising in Winnipeg, in a
quiet ceremony in Chicago. Following the couple's return to Winnipeg, and with her husband's full approval, Anna Yonker contributed
handsomely to Ukrainian community projects in Canada and overseas.
She also used her new status and connections to publicize the Ukrain-

Both a traditional *kolach* (circular braided bread) and Canadian-style
wedding cake to celebrate the silver jubilee of the local UWAC. Smoky
Lake, Alberta, 1954

ian question, forging personal and formal ties with members of the
National Council of Women of Canada (NCWC) and the ICW, including
Cairine Wilson and Lady Aberdeen. The passage of pro-Ukrainian
resolutions by the NCWC and participation by the Winnipeg Local
Council of Women in the mass protest meetings sponsored by Yonker's
Association of Ukrainian Canadian Women showed that such ties bore
fruit.[83]

In their use of protests, resolutions, letters to world leaders, and
appeals to other women, nationalist women's organizations were em-
ploying the tactics of women everywhere outside the male-dominated
power structures of their societies and obliged to pursue their goals
by indirect means. In a world where men interacted on the basis of
the authority statehood conferred, emigration and statelessness hurt
Ukrainian men more than Ukrainian women. Unable to play the game
as equals, Ukrainian men were left with only the options traditionally
available to women to press their cause. But the nature of female
organizational life and political activity that resulted from exclusion
from male politics and institutional structures gave Ukrainian women

Hanna Romanchych, UWAC delegate to the Ukrainian Women's Congress, with Senator Olena Kysilewska and Kharytia Kononenko. Stanislaviv, Galicia, 1934

access to a platform in mainstream women's circles, using means familiar to and recognized as valid by their sex, from which to publicize and court sympathy for Ukraine. The problem, of course, was that this influence was confined to women, who could petition and lobby and try otherwise to sway world leaders but who lacked decision-making power themselves. Then, too, non-Ukrainian women shared the biases of their menfolk. In this regard, Ukrainian-Canadian women fared better from minority status than Ukrainian women in interwar Galicia, hampered at home and abroad by the anti-Ukrainian prejudice and policies of organized Polish women acting in tandem with the Polish state. In Canada – despite Ukrainians' low status and poor reputation, and despite Anglo-Canadian nativism – the possibility of building bridges existed. Ukrainian-Canadian women might be rebuffed in the process, but they were free to make their pitch. When the ICW moved to exclude women's organizations not representing sovereign states, the value of having organized Ukrainian women in countries like Canada, outside Poland, where they could campaign to influence their national councils, increased.[84]

An important tool in gaining access to mainstream Canadian women and their organizations, nationalist women believed, was their handicrafts. Since early in the century, Anglo-Canadian women had admired the beauty and workmanship of Ukrainian embroidery and Easter eggs in particular, supporting exhibitions, making purchases, and enlivening mission life by dressing up in national costume for pictures to be sent back East. During the Depression, Hanna Romanchych exploited this admiration, helping interested women in Alberta produce crafts for sale; Gimble's and Macy's in New York offered two dollars for twelve decorated eggs when an ordinary dozen sold for five cents.[85] To community activists, the political significance of women's handicrafts (and the importance of embroidered cloths in church) outstripped the economic benefits. Criticizing Ukrainian-Canadian women for forgetting their arts, they lamented the loss for the national indifference it showed, when Ukrainian women had a 'sacred duty' to preserve their people's culture, and for its blow to their programs. Women's handicrafts were prized for at least four reasons. First, they were a means of cultivating national pride and raising the self-esteem of their creators. Second, they proved that Ukrainians possessed artistic talents and aesthetic values – that they too were a 'cultured' people. Third, they won Ukrainian-Canadian women prestige in English eyes. And, lastly, because non-Ukrainians liked them, they could be used as lures to provide audiences for propagandization in Ukrainian culture and national aspirations.[86] While the UWAC made handicrafts skills one of its goals from the beginning, the interwar UWOC insisted that the cultivation of Ukrainian domestic arts and national traditions did not create the necessary 'militant, self-sacrificing nationalist spirit.'[87] But all organized nationalist women proudly wore their embroidered blouses as political statements, and viewed their handicrafts as simultaneously useful tactical weapons and an integral expression of their Ukrainianness. It was at a concert and Ukrainian crafts display organized by the Mohylianky for NCWC delegates meeting in Saskatoon in 1929 that the UWAC first made contact with the prestigious mainstream 'women's parliament.'

Embroidery, songs, and dances were at best drawing cards to arouse general interest in things Ukrainian. The next and necessary step was participation in mainstream women's organizations and projects. In this way, it was believed, Ukrainian-Canadian women could earn the reputation as good Canadian citizens that alone would garner widespread support and sympathy for their cause. The UWAC applied to join the NCWC in 1933, seeing it as a platform from which to publicize Ukraine, but was not accepted (ostensibly because its constitution had not been translated into English). Membership was granted in 1939.[88] Reminiscing about the UWAC's early years in the NCWC, especially during the Second World War, a long-time activist recalled a feeling of insecurity in an unfamiliar environment. She also recalled how Anglo-Canadian women found socializing difficult, many reacting to an introduction with the comment, 'Oh, I had a Ukrainian maid once.'[89]

While nationalist women came to see formal participation in mainstream women's organizations as essential to the Ukrainian cause, progressive women had from the beginning been urged to step outside narrow ethnic boundaries. Women's branches of the ULFTA, their individual members, and Ukrainian farm and working women at large were constantly pressed to establish bonds with other class-conscious women and were criticized for not doing so. Press editorials and discussion articles, together with resolutions passed by the Women's Section at its national conferences, exhorted them to join Canadian unions, support the Farmers' and Workers' Unity Leagues, and take part in International Women's Day and May Day celebrations. This agitation, particularly as the Depression worsened, cannot be dismissed as simply part of the campaign by the Communist Party of Canada, through the Popular Front, to mobilize members and sympathizers of its largest mass organization. ULFTA leaders were also Ukrainians consciously addressing other Ukrainians, women inhibited from joining the mainstream of their movement because of language and cultural barriers and uncertainty as to their reception. Integration into the Canadian mainstream for organized progressive women, as for their nationalist counterparts, would not be realized between the wars.

Ukrainianness in the nationalist sense was not a factor in the organization or activities of interwar progressive women. But neither the primacy and internationalism of the class struggle, nor the identification of Ukrainian religious and cultural traditions with self-serving priests and nationalists, ever made 'being Ukrainian' irrelevant. For one thing, their Ukrainian heritage gave Ukrainian progressives an intimacy with events in the Soviet Union that non-Ukrainians in the workers' movement lacked. Progressive mothers were reminded, for example, of the importance of teaching their children Ukrainian as one of the languages of the Great Revolution and a new proletarian literature and culture.[90] Interwar labour temples also sponsored drama and music/dance groups, including Winnipeg's famous All Girls' Mandolin Orchestra, which toured Canada in the 1930s.[91] The purpose of such groups was as much propagandistic as cultural or recreational, and instructors tended to be male. Women's branches of the ULFTA did teach embroidery to young girls, but handicrafts never acquired prominence as a political symbol of Ukrainianness as they did among nationalist women. Progressive women mounted their first handicrafts exhibits – in Winnipeg and Saskatoon – only in 1937. Some of the items were made by women with nationalist associations; others, like the runner embroidered with 'Workers of all countries – unite!' – attested to a non-Ukrainian politicization of women's traditional handicrafts.[92]

Although class-conscious members of a Canadian and worldwide proletariat, women within ULFTA ranks were also class-conscious Ukrainians. As members of the Ukrainian-Canadian community, their first target was the great mass of Ukrainian working and farm women outside their organization. Their second was their political opponents competing for the same audience and speaking on behalf of the same people overseas. The ideological rift that divided progressives and nationalists between the wars extended from Soviet to Western Ukraine, precluding cooperation on even that front. The 'captive brothers and sisters' in Galicia to whom the progressive woman's attention was directed were specifically those struggling against not only foreign tyranny (in anticipation of unification with Soviet Ukraine) but also Ukrainian bourgeois nationalist influences in their midst. The Women's Union was perceived as one of these influences, said to camouflage the selfish ambitions of its leaders under patriotic slogans designed to distract Ukrainian working and peasant women from their class interests. To progressives, the 1934 Stanislaviv congress epitomized the elitism and warped priorities of bourgeois nationalists, especially Peasant Woman's Day when village women paraded in their national costumes in front of 'ladies' (*pani*) who cared nothing for the marchers themselves, only for their clothes.[93] As the Women's Union Canadian arm, the UWAC was also accused of superficiality and narrow, selfish Ukrainianism. With deepening domestic and international crises in the 1930s, organized progressive women moderated their stance. Calling on the UWAC to address the real plight of Ukrainian working and farm women in Canada, they broached the idea of cooperation on

Ukrainian issues whose importance transcended political differences: economic survival in depression Canada, oppression and the menace of war in Western Ukraine, fascist designs on Soviet Ukraine.[94] Progressive women were in for a shock when war came, however. Hitler and Stalin's surprise agreement, the Nazi-Soviet Non-Aggression Pact, put them on the side of the fascists.

Marking the end of one era and the beginning of another, the Second World War had a major impact on Ukrainian-Canadian women's organizations. It forced some to clarify their position and revise their priorities (publicly at least), put others on the defensive, and increased the scope of activity for all. It also encouraged a Canadianism that had seen limited expression in the preceeding two decades, and acted as a catalyst to outreach beyond the Ukrainian-Canadian community. Organizational structures themselves were revolutionized. The war stimulated growth among nationalists, culminating in the creation of the Ukrainian Canadian Women's Committee (UCWC) as a permanent coordinating superstructure, and struck a blow to the progressives, forcing them to adopt a new face.

Banned by the Canadian government in June 1940 and stripped of its property, the ULFTA paid heavily for its support of Moscow. After Germany attacked the Soviet Union in mid-1941 and Stalin became Canada's ally, the progressives regrouped and found a sympathetic ear in the Canadian establishment. Activity by women in the new Association of Ukrainian Canadians on behalf of the Canadian war effort expressed their solidarity with mainstream goals, a solidarity that they, as Ukrainians, felt more comfortable with than the nationalists. Unlike nationalist women, forced temporarily to suppress their anti-Soviet bias and agitation, progressive women could knit mittens for Soviet children and socks for Canadian soldiers without compromising their principles.

In nationalist women's circles, the war became a test of loyalty. Having openly admired Hitler's Germany and Mussolini's Italy, and just as openly damned Poland and the Soviet Union, the UWOC felt the test keenly. Both it and the UNF laboured under accusations of fascism, and some UWOC branches lost members.[95] Before the war, the UWOC had told Ukrainian mothers to teach their children that Canada was not their Fatherland, that they had a higher responsibility to work for a free homeland to which they might return.[96] Such rhetoric complemented the UNF's radio-telegraphy and flying schools established in 1935 and 1938 to train Ukrainian-Canadian youth for the

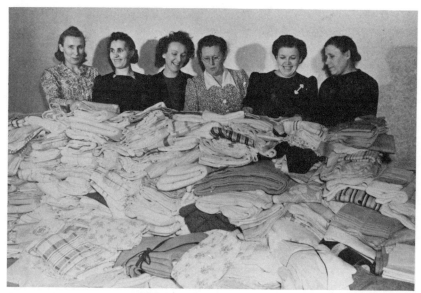

Progressive women's war effort in Ontario. Preparations for a 'Stalingrad linen shower' to help refugees in the Soviet Union, c.1944

Ukrainian campaign in the anticipated European war. When war broke out, and Canada joined, UWOC propaganda began to stress the Ukrainian woman's Canadian responsibilities as well. Mothers were not only to raise nationalist warriors for Ukraine; following the example of the pioneer generation, whose sons now proved their great love for Canada by 'spontaneous voluntary enlistment' and death on the battlefield, they were also to raise good and grateful Canadian citizens ready to defend their country.[97] The psychological atmosphere of crisis, patriotic fervour, and sacrifice that war created struck a responsive chord in an organization with the UWOC's values and eased accommodation of the new fatherland with the old. Yet Ukraine was not abandoned: Ukrainian girls who joined the Canadian armed forces after completing high school, one article implied, aided Canada while acquiring useful experience for the homeland.[98]

For nationalist women's organizations with their origins in the pioneer immigration, the transition to Canadian wartime rhetoric and the sentiments it expressed was less traumatic and could build on a more deeply rooted and indigenous sense of Canadianness. On occasion, however, the UWAC seemed to endorse the totality of commitment in the UWOC message. In 1936 both organizations had reprinted an article from the Galician *Zhinocha dolia* stating that Ukrainian mothers, like German mothers, must teach their children not only to love their country but also to die for it.[99] But in Catholic and Orthodox circles with two or three generations in Canada, the Ukrainian woman's Canadian responsibilities triumphed. Most notably, they were the stimulus behind the formation of the UCWL. Elsewhere, a number of existing local women's clubs, at the urging of the UWAC and in response to government propaganda directed at Canadian women, affiliated with the UWAC in order to contribute more effectively to the war effort; new UWAC branches were established for the same reason.[100]

That the war changed Ukrainian-Canadian women's organizations can be demonstrated by their fund-raising activities. The internationalism of their movement had always ensured progressives a broad mandate, as their assistance to Franco's victims in the Spanish Civil War testified. But it was between 1939 and 1945 that Ukrainian-Canadian women of all political stripes first targeted money for other than Ukrainian causes in a significant way. In an identification with Canadian priorities, it went to the Canadian Red Cross and other mainstream initiatives as their contribution to the common war effort. Women frequently expressed their Canadian citizenship, however, in Ukrainian terms confined to their particular ideological faction. They wrote letters, knit socks, and sent parcels overseas not in concert with other Canadian women, although complementing their activities, but as part of a Ukrainian-Canadian community whose concern was the mental and physical well-being of Ukrainian-Canadian servicemen; after the war, they transferred this attention to their own veterans. The UWAC again exploited the mainstream's liking of Ukrainian handicrafts and produced six hundred embroidered items for sale as part of a dominion-wide project; proceeds went to the Canadian Red Cross.[101] Canada's war was also used to help old friends and causes. Fifty-three local progressive women's committees sent parcels to soldiers valued at nearly $12,000, but the progressive community as a whole raised an impressive $723,167.86 for the Red Army and Soviet civilians.[102] Nationalists told women that if they assisted the Canadian Red Cross, and stressed a common love for freedom and democracy, they would dispose mainstream women more favourably towards them. Shortly after the war, the UCWC president reiterated the necessity of involvement in mainstream women's organizations, arguing that it enabled Ukrainian women to meet the wives of influential men and, through them, to influence Ukrainian affairs.[103]

In the war's aftermath, nationalist women turned shared 'Canadian' wartime experiences and ideals to advantage. They used their labour on the home front, their sons' military record to preserve freedom and democracy in the world, and their personal sacrifices as the mothers of those sons to press for Ukrainian goals. Their argument was two pronged. First, through the deaths of their Canadian sons for ideals held jointly with other Canadians, and as Canadian mothers who gave their sons for those ideals, Ukrainian-Canadian women had earned the right to make demands of all Canadians on their people's behalf. Second, in their historical struggle for survival, Ukrainians in Ukraine had long proven their commitment to freedom and democracy. If Canadians truly prized the values for which they had gone to war, they had no choice but to open their doors to the war's victims, Ukrainian refugees who had been forcibly taken from their homes as 'slave labour' for German agriculture and war industry and now refused to be repatriated to the Soviet Union.[104] Behind this appeal to Canadians' higher conscience and humanity lay continued commitment to the plight of Ukraine and Ukrainians abroad.

But Ukrainian Canadians' war record was also used to confirm and legitimize Ukrainian goals in the Canadian context. Ukrainian-Canadian women, nationalists argued, acknowledged their debt to the dead by raising their children to love all that was good and beautiful, including their own culture, traditions, and faith. 'In this manner,' stated UCWC president, Mary Dyma, in 1946, 'we raise conscious citizens and add our flavour to the cultural wreath of our adopted homeland.'[105] This echo of Lord Tweedsmuir became the essence of organized women's understanding of Canadianness in the postwar period. Young Ukrainian Canadians proud of their heritage, acquainted with Ukrainian heroes, and identifying with Ukraine's struggles possessed a self-esteem absent in assimilated youth, enjoyed greater respect, and produced the sturdy, self-confident citizens on whom Canada's future rested. But a postwar generation of female activists took the benefits of a Ukrainian consciousness beyond the group exclusiveness contained in the national-cultural traditions of a Ukrainian political identity. Children raised to value the ideals for which Ukrainians throughout history had fought brought their dedication to human dignity, freedom, democracy, and justice to the Canadian mosaic.

Moreover, a Ukrainian consciousness tied the Ukrainian-Canadian child to his or her Canadian roots, through the peasant pioneers whose 'superhuman endeavours and maintenance of morals created Canada's historical beginnings and have entered there honestly and deservingly.'[106]

Canadianization in organized women's propaganda and programs would be a major feature of the postwar era. In part it built on the Canadianism evoked by the war. For the first time, Ukrainian-Canadian women had been called upon by their community to work for something other than 'the cause,' and encouraged to prove themselves as loyal citizens of Canada. For the first time, too, they had been asked by mainstream society to cooperate with and work beside other Canadian women as their equals. Canadianization also reflected ever deepening roots in Canada and a Ukrainian-Canadian identity erected on the group's Canadian experience.

5

Canadianizing a Legacy: Women's Organizations after the Second World War

The immediate preoccupation of organized Ukrainian-Canadian women at the conclusion of hostilities in 1945 had little to do with the Ukrainian fact in Canada. The absorption of Western Ukrainian territories into the Ukrainian Soviet Socialist Republic eliminated the need for activity by progressive women on behalf of compatriots under foreign and bourgeois rule, and they, like mainstream Canadian women, geared down at the war's end. But nationalist women's organizations could not. Although any hopes during the war to further Ukrainian independence by direct and concrete means had been thwarted by events in Eastern Europe that placed Ukraine outside their reach, the war's end pushed practical assistance to the thousands of Ukrainians stranded in displaced person camps in Western Europe to the forefront. Nationalist women's organizations contributed to the Ukrainian Canadian Relief Fund, sponsored camp kindergartens, and collected and shipped bundles of food, clothing, and medicine. They added their voice to Ukrainian-Canadian protests against forced repatriation to the Soviet Union and to the lobby to bring refugees to Canada. Special attention was paid to single mothers, widows, and orphans, with help in the camps and in finding sponsors in Canada. Women's organizations also welcomed the new arrivals, especially women, and sought to ease adjustment with English classes, advice, and general information about the country.[1]

Approximately one-third of Ukrainian displaced persons who ended up in Canada as adults were women; most came as wives, although a quarter came alone classified as domestic servants. Almost half of the refugees gave Ontario as their destination; another 20 per cent went to Quebec; the prairies attracted less than one-third.[2] The arrival, settlement pattern, and anti-communist bias of female displaced persons inevitably affected the contours of postwar women's organizational life, although many immigrants, partly because of age, brought no interwar experience with them. Indicative of their impact was the appearance of another major (and vigorous) player, with the establishment of the Women's Association of the nationalistic and right-wing Canadian League for the Liberation of Ukraine. In keeping with the urban and central Canadian orientation of the third immigration, fourteen of twenty-one branches (and most of the one thousand members in the late 1980s) were to be found in Ontario cities.[3] As far as the 'old' interwar women's organizations were concerned, the impact of the displaced persons was uneven, with the 'Canadian' Ukrainian Women's Association of Canada (UWAC) arguably less affected than either the 'émigré' Ukrainian Women's Organization of Canada (UWOC) or the recently formed Ukrainian Catholic Women's League (UCWL).

The war did give the UWAC its personal martyr: shot by the Germans in 1943, Kharytia Kononenko joined the calendar of Great Ukrainian Women honoured annually. A UWAC pioneer claimed that the patriot had prophetically exclaimed at the Mohyla Institute in the early 1920s, 'I want to die for Ukraine.'[4] The official history of the UWAC suggests, however, a less easy relationship with the flesh-and-blood victims of Hitler's eastern policy who resumed their interrupted lives in Canada. It recalls emerging tensions as the 'political' newcomers criticized the cultural-educational orientation of the earlier 'economic' immigration that the UWAC in particular represented. Emphasizing in response 'the country we freely chose to settle,' the UWAC reflected its members' psychological identification with Canadian nation building.[5] An entirely different context confirmed this emotional attachment to Canada, via the peasant pioneers, in UWAC circles. Savella Stechishin dedicated her *Traditional Ukrainian Cookery* (1957), into its seventeenth edition by 1991, to Ukrainian-Canadian women on the sixty-fifth anniversary of Ukrainian settlement in Canada: women who had 'treasured and practised the rich traditions of their homeland and thereby preserved them for posterity in this fair and free land of their choice.' With one or two exceptions from the interwar immigration, all UWAC presidents to 1976, the organization's golden jubilee, represented the first pioneer immigration or were Canadian born.[6] That year the UWAC claimed five thousand members and included reports from 117 branches in its official jubilee history: British Columbia 10, Alberta 23, Saskatchewan 39, Manitoba 22, Ontario 19, Quebec 4.[7] Unlike the interwar years, when UWAC branches sprang from secular as much as religious backgrounds, often with origins in the local *narodnyi dim*, new postwar branches appeared almost exclusively in conjunction with the establishment of Orthodox congregations; many older branches narrowed their field of vision to the parish, others folded.

The other nationalist women's organization with pioneer roots was the UCWL. The religious identity of organized Catholic women had always been strong, and by the mid 1960s the UCWL had grown to some 180 branches, concentrated in Alberta (54), Ontario (47), Manitoba (38), and Saskatchewan.[8] This rapid expansion and distribution pattern attested to a pre-existing solid base in interwar sisterhoods, particularly on the prairies, but also to the presence of Catholic displaced persons behind many new branches in Ontario.[9] The UCWL did not, however, sustain the promise of its early growth. In 1983 it officially claimed 159 branches and 6300 members, although eparchial reports to the national convention produced somewhat smaller totals. A more aggressive Ukrainianism among organized Catholic women after the Second World War owed much to the displaced persons. One prominent activist, uneasy with the exploitation of religious symbols for political purposes, attributed the Ukrainization of the Mother of God in UCWL mythology to their influence.[10] The displaced persons would also seem to be responsible for a backward projection of aggressive Ukrainianness onto turn-of-the-century peasant immigrants, transforming these women into unsung community pillars and patriotic daughters of their people. The official histories of UCWL branches in Montreal and Toronto, for example (and of certain UWAC branches), all show evidence of 'Ukrainizing' by the displaced persons who wrote them.[11]

Unlike the UWAC and UCWL, the UWOC did not see a postwar increase in local affiliates. In fact, by the time of its silver jubilee in 1955, it had suffered a net loss, despite the boost the displaced persons gave to its membership figures. This is not as contradictory as might seem at first glance. The greatest losses occurred in Saskatchewan, where the UWOC presence had always been something of an anomaly; elsewhere, the displaced persons settled in urban areas or on resource frontiers where the UWOC already enjoyed its greatest strength. Both Toronto and Val d'Or, for example, reported a rise in membership as a result of the third immigration, although Val d'Or's increase turned out to be temporary when the majority of the refugees deserted the remote Quebec mining town for southern Ontario.[12] Then too, the militant stance of the UWOC had always had limited appeal: in twenty-five years, for example, the active Saskatoon branch had attracted only ninety-four members. After 1945 the UWOC faced the additional problem of sustaining support among the Canadian-born children of its émigré founders: by 1955 Saskatoon's membership had dropped from thirty-eight at the branch's founding to fewer than twenty, as women died, moved, or left the organization when their 'own concerns became more important than national work.'[13] The UWOC also relaxed its membership criteria to permit non-Ukrainians (married to Ukrainians) to join.[14] By 1980, when the UWOC celebrated its fiftieth anniversary, only fourteen functioning branches, all from large Canadian cities, sent reports to the official jubilee history: British Columbia 1, Alberta 1, Saskatchewan 2, Manitoba 1, Ontario 8, Quebec 1. They represented several hundred members.[15]

If the repercussions of the Second World War affected nationalist women on the domestic front, they also had implications in the international arena. Soviet occupation of Western Ukraine in 1939 had suppressed the organized women's movement in Galicia, ending the contacts of Ukrainian-Canadian women with it. But the presence of interwar female activists among the displaced persons stimulated the large-scale organization of women in the diaspora. It also occasioned a split in their ranks that pushed the more moderate and feminist wing represented by Milena Rudnytska to the background and altered the nature of Ukrainian-Canadian women's foreign ties. In 1948 the World Federation of Ukrainian Women's Organizations (WFUWO), with headquarters in North America, was formed to strengthen and coordinate the political, cultural-educational, and social work of Ukrainian women outside the Soviet bloc.[16] Both the UCWL and the UWOC were charter members, but the UWAC, its sympathies with Rudnytska, retreated from its close interwar involvement with the international Ukrainian women's movement and did not join.[17] The president of the WFUWO until her death in 1956 was Olena Kysilewska, who immigrated to Canada in 1948.

Unlike nationalist women, postwar progressive women continued to enjoy ideological convictions and unfettered ties with the homeland. A sketch of women's branches of the Association of United Ukrainian Canadians (AUUC), which succeeded the Ukrainian Labour-Farmer Temple Association (ULFTA) in representing pro-Soviet, pro-communist Ukrainian Canadians, is hampered by incomplete membership data and no breakdown by sex for the statistics that do exist. Certain facts and trends, however, are clear. First, the movement obviously received little new blood or boost from the anti-communist displaced persons immigration. Second, before the Cold War and increasing prosperity sent the AUUC into decline, it was able to profit from its wartime record and reputation and showed healthy growth. Women's branches, for example, doubled from fourteen to twenty-nine between 1945 and 1947. By 1954, however, the total number of AUUC branches had fallen from a high of 315 in 1945 to 152, and only sixteen of thirty-two postwar English-speaking branches remained; in 1969, the last year for published statistics, there were only forty-eight recruits (compared with 2579 in 1945), and new members no longer replaced losses through death or drifting away. In 1968 Mary Prokop told the national convention that the women's branches specifically were not being renewed by younger members.[18] When the Women's Section celebrated its golden jubilee in 1972, special ceremonies marking the event were held by eighteen AUUC branches (not all of them women's): British Columbia 2, Alberta 3, Saskatchewan 2, Manitoba 2, Ontario 8, Quebec 1.[19] In contrast to the nationalist community, where the traditional 'male' organizations remained male bastions, progressives welcomed women into the main body of the AUUC, so the existence of separate women's branches did not necessarily gauge the extent of women's involvement in the movement.

Canadian factors, as well as Ukrainian or political factors, also had an impact on Ukrainian-Canadian women's organizations in the years after the Second World War. Foremost among them were demographic changes within the Ukrainian-Canadian population, responding to general trends within Canadian society, that affected postwar developments and decisions among Ukrainian-Canadian women's organizations. In other words, ideology rooted in differences among the immigrations and the generations did not act alone to dictate the course of organized women's life. Apolitical and impersonal forces, reflecting but often transcending immigration and generation, introduced a second set of variables. The postwar fortunes of the UWAC and the UCWL best illustrate the operation of these other forces. After 1945 interregional and intraprovincial redistribution of both UCWL and UWAC branches followed Ukrainian-Canadian migration patterns – from the prairies to British Columbia and central Canada; to new localities (both urban and rural) in each of Alberta, Saskatchewan, and

Manitoba, in sufficient numbers to sustain community institutions; and to new suburbs in cities where the UCWL and UWAC had long been present.

In Manitoba, for example, almost half of UCWL branches functioning in 1983 existed in the Greater Winnipeg area. In the two preceding decades, Alberta lost twenty-six of fifty-five branches, the casualties being those in rural areas of the large, once populous, Vegreville bloc. They either became defunct or amalgamated with branches in neighbouring towns or villages as crossroads communities ceased to be the focus of Ukrainian organizational life, as young women and families left the area, as members grew old and inactive (or retired to Vegreville or Edmonton), and as deaths depleted their rosters. UCWL membership figures in the province fell by four hundred over the same period; in 1980–3 alone, losses totalled 150 members as recruiting failed to keep pace with attrition through aging and death.[20] The experience of the UWAC in the prairie provinces was similar, particularly in rural Saskatchewan where so much of its organizational energies had been concentrated. What happened to the UWAC and UCWL mirrored in dramatic fashion perhaps irreversible trends in the original heartland of Ukrainian-Canadian life – the bloc settlements of western Canada. But while marking the passage of an era, the demise of once vibrant crossroads communities did not always evoke regret or nostalgia; when the rural *narodnyi dim* that was its focus of activity relocated to a nearby village, the Meacham branch of the UWAC greeted the move as a sign of welcome economic prosperity.[21] Retrenchment on the prairies, for both the UCWL and the UWAC, was accompanied by expansion in British Columbia and Ontario. British Columbia was particularly attractive to prairie retirees, Ontario to an increasingly mobile labour force already affected by the Depression. In the 1930s, for example, the UWOC branch in Winnipeg reported a loss of members as families went east in search of jobs.[22] Ontario emerged in the post-1945 era as the most populous Ukrainian-Canadian province and issued a challenge to prairie dominance in community affairs.

These declining and aging memberships reflect the limited appeal of the Ukrainian or class message of organized nationalists and progressives for the postwar as well as the interwar period. Whether because of conscious indifference or hostility towards the group goals defined by community leaders, or because of alienating forces in the Canadian environment, an activist elite never succeeded in mobilizing the great mass of Ukrainian-Canadian women behind its agenda.

Adapting tradition for the modern world. Red-and-black embroidery
Ukrainizing otherwise generic ceramic pottery, church bazaar. Sudbury,
Ontario, 1970s

Moreover, the national profile of Ukrainian-Canadian women's organizations – each with its own audience in different segments of the
population – reflected Ukrainian-Canadian settlement patterns rooted
in class, immigrational, and generational differences. As a 'Canadian'
phenomenon, the postwar evolution of Ukrainian-Canadian women's
organizations followed a logic dictated by circumstances beyond their
control: urbanization among Ukrainian Canadians, movement from
the prairies to the West Coast and central Canada, and relocation from
immigrant reception areas in Canadian cities to more affluent suburbs.
Regardless of the appeal of their specific messages, the fortunes of
Ukrainian-Canadian women's organizations were tied to the push and
pull of forces in Canadian society that affected Ukrainian Canadians
both individually and as a whole.

Unlike populations in motion, women's organizations could try to
do something about another effect of Canadianization – assimilation.
By the 1950s the AUUC was organizing special branches for a Canadian-

born, English-speaking generation of women and young mothers.[23]
Three of five UWOC branches founded between 1945 and 1955 were
junior branches of existing clubs in Winnipeg, Edmonton, and Sudbury, intended to attract a second (non-immigrant) generation. Yet
such were the advantages befalling the Canadian born that liaison with
the Canadian Red Cross and other mainstream women's organizations
was slated as one of their major responsibilities.[24] Junior branches or
new branches became the answer for all Ukrainian-Canadian women's
groups faced with problems and strains created by both generational
and immigrational differences. Some, like 'Dobra volia' organized at
St Josaphat's in Edmonton in 1941 by young Catholic women anxious
to extend their work beyond the parish into the wider Ukrainian-
Canadian and Canadian communities, addressed the concerns and
priorities of a Canadian-born generation.[25] Some, like the second UCWL
branch established in Yorkton, Saskatchewan, in 1952, accommodated
younger and English-speaking women, including non-Ukrainians from
mixed marriages.[26] The initiative for other branches came from women
busy raising families or from a new immigration: a second 'Dobra volia'
branch of the UCWL was organized in Edmonton in 1958 by young
mothers from displaced persons circles.[27] In 1989 yet another UCWL
branch was proposed for St Josaphat's to answer the needs of yet
another generation of 'younger' women, English-speaking professionals and homemakers, often non-Ukrainians. While in one sense an
adaptive response to new conditions, a recurring pattern of junior or
new branches also suggested a certain inflexibility in organizations'
programs, in which the failure to adjust to changing realities prevented
existing groups from renewing themselves.

Structural changes, whether consciously initiated or set in motion
by forces outside women's control, were only one area where the postwar environment had an impact on the profile of Ukrainian-Canadian
women's organizations. Continuity and change in their propaganda
and programs also expressed organized women's response to a vastly
altered world. Two aspects warrant particular attention. One concerns
the actual activities of women's organizations as an inheritance and a
departure from the interwar years. The other concerns the extent to
which women's organizations with interwar roots developed a mythology around their organizations and selected members, reflecting
growing identification with their history and the Ukrainian experience
in Canada, to claim a niche in both Ukrainian-Canadian community
life and Canadian society.

Ukrainian work proper, on behalf of the nation in Europe, pro-

ceeded along the lines established between the wars, with one important difference. In the earlier period, nationalists had kept in close
contact with Western Ukraine and had been able to extend material
as well as moral support; their postwar role became primarily one of
propaganda in the West (although the UWOC, for example, through
the Ukrainian Gold Cross, assisted prisoners of conscience in Soviet
Ukraine). From ever broader platforms, nationalist women's organizations continued to protest conditions in the homeland and to court
mainstream support and exploit mainstream forums for the Ukrainian
cause. In 1974, for example, the UCWL presented a resolution protesting persecution of the Ukrainian Catholic church, denial of civil
rights, and intolerance of dissent in Soviet Ukraine to the World Union
of Catholic Women's Organizations, which it had joined in 1957. When
the union held its assembly in Canada in 1983, the UCWL used the
opportunity again to publicize religious persecution and to introduce
delegates to the Ukrainian rite, religious traditions, and arts and crafts,
with gifts of embroidered bookmarks for everyone.[28] As a host organization asked to describe its activities when the International Council of Women (ICW) met in Vancouver in 1976, the UWAC chose
Ukrainian culture, Russification, and political oppression in Soviet
Ukraine. It also formally presented its resolution from International
Women's Year (1975), appealing to the conscience of Western women
on behalf of Soviet Ukrainian female dissidents.[29] The authors of such
statements focused on the oppression of Soviet Ukrainian women as
Ukrainians, to the neglect of their oppression as women, a decision
that affirmed the persisting dominance of national over gender issues
in nationalist thinking. 'In particular,' read one UWAC resolution,

> we sympathize with the fate of Ukrainian women and mothers living
> in Ukraine, who contrary to the laws of God and man, must suffer
> the indignity of being deprived of their religion, church, historical
> traditions, customs and of the opportunity to mold their children's
> souls ... [The UWAC] appeals in this era of human rights to all
> women in the free world to stand up in defence of those who have
> been wronged and asserts that in the interests of world peace, every
> nation should have the right to cultural and creative self-expression
> and the opportunity to develop its national life in an independent
> state of its own.[30]

The participation of organized Ukrainian-Canadian women in mainstream projects and charitable fund drives also expanded from its

Ukrainian Catholic women helping with bingo at Holy Trinity Senior Citizens' Home. Winnipeg, Manitoba, 1963

wartime base to become a fixed feature of their agenda. The UCWL's broad social conscience, for example, took it well beyond the Canadian and Ukrainian-Canadian communities. In 1983 what began as a 'fasting lunch' to commemorate the fiftieth anniversary of the 1933 artificial famine that accompanied collectivization in Soviet Ukraine became a hand extended to the hungry and oppressed throughout the world, with much of the money collected going to Mother Teresa in India.[31] Nationalist women also continued to help Ukrainians in the diaspora. UCWL monetary support of the Sisters Servants of Mary Immaculate, for example, expanded from orphanages, schools, and hospitals in Canada to include the order's mother house, relocated after the war from Galicia to Rome, and its work among impoverished Ukrainians in Argentina and Brazil.[32] As in the interwar years, however, the bulk of funds raised remained in Canada, although the March of Dimes, the public library, and the municipal hospital could expect to benefit alongside the Ukrainian community.

At their postwar conventions, nationalist women's organizations annually rededicated themselves to what remained fundamental respon-

Progressive women in Ontario working for peace. Nd

sibilities: raising good Ukrainian children, furthering their members' spiritual growth and Ukrainian consciousness, preserving the Ukrainian language, culture, and religion in Canada, and socializing their youth. As a sign of assimilation, but also of the growing popularity of Ukrainian culture in the mainstream, they introduced courses to improve members' language skills and to instruct them and other women (Ukrainian and non-Ukrainian) in Ukrainian cooking and handicrafts. Museums became another focus. Although initially intended to preserve 'authentic' folk art and other artifacts from Ukraine, they evolved towards depicting the history of Ukrainian settlement in Canada as well. The most ambitious undertaking as women attempted to rescue what had otherwise disappeared from daily life was the UWAC's Ukrainian Museum of Canada in Saskatoon, officially opened in 1941, although collecting had begun earlier.[33] The tangible fruits of changing Canadian attitudes towards the country's multicultural reality, particularly the Ukrainian community's successful lobby on behalf of language and education rights, also had an effect on nationalist women, shifting some responsibility for raising Ukrainian-Canadian youth from their shoulders onto the Canadian state. A number of local branches of women's organizations in the prairie provinces withdrew from *ridna shkola* or curtailed their involvement with the introduction of Ukrainian language courses in the 1950s and 1960s, and bilingual programs in the 1970s and 1980s, into the public schools. Even as they retrenched, however, they pointed out that the public school could and would not provide the emotional atmosphere to create the necessary patriotic Ukrainian consciousness in its pupils.[34]

How women in the progressive movement, through the AUUC as the ULFTA's successor, interpreted their role and responsibilities after 1945 also represented both continuity and change. Building on the interwar fight against fascism, the peace movement joined the workers' and women's movements as one of three major foci.[35] Involvement in these activities through mass meetings, petitions, and the like was defined in terms of the dedication of organized progressive women to world peace (with averting nuclear war the chief goal), and to equality, progress, democracy, and human dignity. These values corresponded to what postwar progressives defined as their contribution to the Canadian mosaic and, when stripped of their specific ideological nuances, possessed a universality with which no one could quarrel. They also contained the progressive woman's understanding of good citizenship, both as a Canadian and as a member of the world community. On the fiftieth anniversary of the organized progressive women's movement, Mary Prokop looked back:

> Together in organized fashion, we acquainted ourselves with the freedom-loving traditions and cultural heritage of the Ukrainian people, acquired ideological, national and social consciousness, an understanding of the mutual interests of all who labour. We learned to live and to struggle for our dignity as human beings, for equality in the general struggle for human rights, for democracy, peace and progress. While on this path we cultivated our cultural heritage, our love for the people from which we came and respect for other people. In this spirit we brought up and continue to bring up our children.[36]

Emphasis in progressive propaganda and programs on women as transmitters and preservers of Ukrainian culture was a postwar phenomenon. The shift to a more cultural focus reflected perhaps declining politicization and ideological fervour by an aging membership

Statue of Lesia Ukrainka, High Park, Toronto. Erected by the UCWC (Toronto Branch) in International Women's Year, 1975, to honour the centenary of the poet's birth. Sculptor Mykhailo Chereshniovsky

labouring in the difficult atmosphere of the Cold War, coupled with a less committed younger generation curious about its roots. In their attention to the visible symbols of Ukrainianness, particularly handicrafts, progressive women moved closer to their nationalist counterparts. A competition to embroider towels for the Ivan Franko Museum, the preparation of a Ukrainian cookbook, and a project to outfit dolls in Ukrainian folk costumes were just three postwar cultural activities undertaken by younger AUUC members in English-speaking branches during the 1950s.[37]

Statue of Lesia Ukrainka, campus of the University of Saskatchewan, Saskatoon, unveiled 1976. A gift from the people of Soviet Ukraine to honour the Ukrainian builders of Canada. Sculptor Halyna Kalchenko

After 1945 organized progressive women continued to acknowledge the role of the home in rearing progressive youth, and they stressed the necessity of formal work with the AUUC's youth wing. They also continued to agitate for the intensification and expansion of organizational activity, cultural-educational work among their members, and the training of quality leadership cadres. Like their nationalist counterparts, they became increasingly active in non-Ukrainian organizations, such as the Canadian Congress of Women and the Women's International Democratic Federation (WIDF), and they voiced their

Lesia welcome statue, Canora, Saskatchewan, bearing the traditional gifts of bread and salt. Unveiled 1980 by Governor General Edward Schreyer. Artists Nick and Orest Lewchuk

pride in their representatives and the coming-of-age this mainstreaming demonstrated. The ULFTA had begun to train functionaries from among the Canadian born and/or raised in the 1930s; their ranks included three women – Mary Kardash, Helen Weir, Mary Skrypnyk – who subsequently played prominent roles in the AUUC, although none of the three confined herself to women's branches and their activities. Both Skrypnyk, the daughter of a Timmins-area farmer, and Weir, the daughter of a Lethbridge coal miner, were active in the trade union movement in Ontario. Skrypnyk served as shop steward and executive member of her United Electrical Workers (CIO) local; Weir organized a local of the Cafeteria and Restaurant Employees Union (AFL) in Toronto. In 1949 Kardash, then a mother of two active in the English-speaking Young Women's Club in Winnipeg, was chosen (along with Dorise Neilsen, former CCF member of parliament for Saskatchewan) to represent the Canadian Women's Peace Action Committee at the World Council of the WIDF meeting in Moscow. 'We are very proud,' Skrypnyk wrote, noting that Kardash was the 'first Ukrainian-Canadian woman to be honoured with such a job.' Kardash herself said her selection showed the 'long way' Ukrainian women in the progressive movement had come.[38] Mainstreaming for progressive women, however, meant integration into a larger pro-Soviet, pro-communist network that the Cold War relegated to the margins of Canadian society.

Organized nationalist women did not face this problem and, for them, mainstreaming meant entry into establishment institutions. Increased participation in both Canadian and international women's organizations after the Second World War was a measure of integration and reflected acceptance by the outside, but it also depended on a maturity and self-confidence among Ukrainian-Canadian women that made such participation possible. For the UWOC, which joined the National Council of Women of Canada (NCWC) in 1949, it represented a new Canadianism.[39] Reversing earlier priorities, the UWOC described itself in the next NCWC yearbook as 'non-sectarian, non-denominational and non-partisan ... stressing Ukrainian loyalty to Canadian interests, Ukrainian culture in the Canadian ethnic mosaic, and advocating Ukrainian independence and national reinstatement in the homeland of our forefathers.'[40] Its actual application to join the NCWC had made no mention of things Ukrainian, listing as its aims Canadian citizenship (for both members and their children), cooperation with Canadian women for the good of Canada, and humanitarian work, specifically the Red Cross.

Both women's organizations and the nationalist community in general regarded mainstream involvement, particularly in prestigious executive positions, as a positive reflection on all Ukrainian-Canadian women and on the entire Ukrainian-Canadian group. A Ukrainian Canadian Committee (UCC) spokesman set the tone in 1943 when he singled out the women who represented their organizations on Red Cross executives, praising the performance that won the respect of their non-Ukrainian co-workers.[41] As its mainstream involvement increased after 1945, the UWAC was particularly profusive concerning its members' performance on the NCWC and the ICW. In 1960 it noted 'with pride' that Helen Hnatyshyn, vice-president of the NCWC, was a delegate to the ICW congress in Istanbul, 'indeed ... a great step forward for Ukrainian women from their pioneering days.'[42] The Canadian-born wife of a Conservative senator (and mother of a future Conservative cabinet minister and governor general), she herself a former teacher, Hnatyshyn's credentials to represent Canadian establishment women were impeccable. Individuals like her, extolled as proof of Ukrainians' abilities and as recognition by the larger society of their worth, became fixtures in a new pantheon of Ukrainian heroines – one that was rooted in Canada.

Moreover, the presence among the displaced persons of prominent figures from the interwar Ukrainian women's movement in Galicia brought the Great Women of Ukraine to Canadian soil. With their entry into organized women's life they became living links to the struggles in the homeland and catalysts to renewed activity by Ukrainian-Canadian women. Irene Pawlikowska, who had spearheaded the split in the diaspora with Milena Rudnytska, joined the UCWL and served as its national president from 1964 to 1968; Olena Zalizniak, a president of the WFUWO after Kysilewska, joined the UWOC.[43] But Olena Kysilewska, then in her late seventies, was by far the most important Ukrainian woman to come to Canada in the wake of the Second World War. Acknowledging her importance as a figurehead and symbol to organized Ukrainian women in the diaspora, the umbrella Ukrainian Canadian Women's Committee (UCWC) and the WFUWO jointly erected a monument at her grave in Ottawa in 1957 to pay homage to this 'servant of her people.'[44] Named an honorary citizen of Canada in 1954, Kysilewska also played a role in the self-legitimization of Ukrainian Canadians in the Canadian context, as the esteem in which the former member of the Polish senate was held in mainstream circles brought reflected glory. With more than a little licence, the Catholic Church Extension Society acclaimed her as one of the 'builders of Canada.'[45]

The group function that Kysilewska served in bolstering Ukrainian Canadians' self-esteem in Canada was performed by other women as well. They appeared in the organizational press as evidence of 'success,' upward mobility and integration, and as examples for their sex to follow. Postwar women were, in effect, building on an earlier foundation. In 1923, three years after the gymnasium graduate and future inaugural president of both the UCWL and the UCWC arrived in Canada, Mary Savchak (Dyma) had become the first Ukrainian-Canadian woman to receive a university degree. Her accomplishment was proclaimed at the time as a turning-point for Ukrainian-Canadian womanhood on its road to enlightenment, progress, and equality with others.[46] When awarded her BA in 1930, Savella Stechishin was acclaimed not only for her academic achievement but also for her example in successfully combining studies with motherhood and community work.[47] The mother of a 1956 recipient of a university scholarship received as much praise and publicity as a model for her peers as the student herself – for having raised good Ukrainian daughters who were 'living proof that those who are interested in Ukrainian matters, speak Ukrainian, and go to their church are not hindered in their education and success.'[48] Indicative of the status that academic success acquired in the thinking of nationalist women's organizations, good mothers increasingly raised not only good Ukrainians but also university graduates who embraced professional careers. As a result, a woman's worth came to be measured as much by the Canadian socioeconomic success of her children and grandchildren as by their Ukrainian consciousness and commitment.[49]

Bridging the Ukrainian and mainstream worlds, Mary Dyma was the first woman of Ukrainian origin to serve as a school trustee (Winnipeg) and to contest a provincial or federal election. She was also active in the local Canadian Women's Club, and in 1950 received perhaps the ultimate gesture of acceptance when a branch of the Imperial Order Daughters of the Empire was named after her.[50] Because of her performance on the all-Canadian as well as the community stage, Dyma introduces an important phenomenon within the postwar nationalist community as a whole: the adoption, in its literature and mythology, of individuals of Ukrainian origin whose mainstream prominence earned them a niche in the nation's collective consciousness as 'great' Canadians. The progressive community failed to develop a parallel tradition, partly because socioeconomic success contradicted its social philosophy, partly because the individuals involved did not share its political bias. One exception was William Kardash (husband of Mary), elected to the Manitoba legislature for the Labour Progressive party in 1941, 1945, 1949, and 1953.

Members of the nationalist pantheon ranged from the artist William Kurelek, whose paintings received nationwide recognition for capturing the essence of the Canadian experience, to Governor General Ramon Hnatyshyn, son of the UWAC activist said to represent her organization effectively in mainstream women's circles. The debate in the 1980s over whether hockey superstar, Wayne Gretzky, was of Ukrainian ancestry illustrated the importance of such persons. 'Successful' Ukrainian Canadians belied the group's traditional lowly status and negative stereotype, and bolstered members' self-image as Canadians more than able to hold their own. Although these examples were all male, group function and not sex or gender constituted the community's criterion for inclusion. Just like women whose work made a statement of Ukrainian consciousness and identity, women prominent in mainstream society were as important as their male colleagues.

As notable Ukrainian Canadians, women lagged behind men, showing better in the arts and letters than in the traditional male preserves of business, industry, the professions, and politics.[51] Heading the exceptions, Sylvia Fedoruk of Saskatoon was acclaimed in one community history as 'the first woman physicist actively engaged in cancer research in Canada' and 'undoubtedly one of Canada's most brilliant women.'[52] In 1988 Fedoruk marked another milestone as the first Ukrainian-Canadian woman to be appointed a lieutenant-governor (Saskatchewan). In the arts, 'child prodigy' violinist Donna Grescoe symbolized Ukrainian talent and success for more than forty years; cutting her teeth in Ukrainian halls in North End Winnipeg, she was discovered by the larger society in the mid 1940s.[53] The 1960s singer 'Juliette' Sysak not only represented talent and success but also legitimized Ukrainian ethnicity with special Ukrainian song and dance numbers on her CBC television show.[54] In the 1980s the Montreal rock singer, 'Luba,' inherited their mantle; an invitation to perform at the National Opening Ceremonies of the Ukrainian Canadian Centennial in 1991 confirmed her role as a group symbol.

Individuals recognized for achievements in the all-Canadian context did not perform the same function, either within the nationalist community as a whole or among organized nationalist women, as individuals recognized for their activities within the ethnic group alone. The latter were symbols and models of Ukrainian consciousness and service, whose identification with the Ukrainian-Canadian community was voluntary. The former were symbols and models of success and integration, in which Ukrainianness as a quality was secondary and the dominant society (traditionally Anglo-Canadian and male) set the standards. They were arbitrarily claimed by the group regardless of their own preference, and regardless of any active and positive sense of themselves as Ukrainian Canadians.

Nationalist women's organizations also brought a distinctive perspective to the community cultivation of prominent Ukrainian Canadians. The individuals featured in their postwar magazines for non-Ukrainian activities came from their own organizational ranks. For example, the UCWL boasted of 'its' Catherine Chichak, Progressive Conservative MLA in Alberta, and of 'its' Mary Wawrykow, family court judge in Manitoba. The political and career accomplishments of the two women produced in their admirers vicarious feelings of self-worth, belonging, and contribution as Canadians, and also enhanced the status of the UCWL.[55] Such feelings were not only vicarious. Organizational publications suggest that UCWL and UWAC memberships on the prairies in particular identified strongly with the surrounding society, reflecting their roots in the turn-of-the-century peasant pioneers and the fact that, on the prairies, unlike British Columbia or the East, Ukrainians' numbers and concentration often made *them* the dominant group in their locality and thus its Canadian expression. The resulting grassroots sense of belonging was reinforced when the prairie mainstream acknowledged nationalist organizational figures as builders of their common society. In 1980, on the seventy-fifth anniversary of the creation of the province of Saskatchewan, Savella Stechishin was one of seventy-five 'notable' Saskatchewan women profiled in a special anniversary publication. Five years earlier, on the nomination of the UCWC, the Saskatchewan Council of Women had named her Woman of the Year.[56] Regional recognition of outstanding individuals – as well as the national recognition accorded by Canadian Centennial medals and the Order of Canada[57] – represented to organized Ukrainian-Canadian women mainstream acceptance of Ukrainian partnership in nation building. In the process, because these women were Ukrainian-Canadian community activists as well as all-Canadian figures, they also represented the legitimization of the Ukrainian particularity.

Postwar Canadianization among the old nationalist women's organizations came not only from looking inward and at themselves but also from looking outward and beyond themselves. Central to the latter was retrospective identification with mainstream Canadian women and the mainstream women's movement. Until the Second World War, when the government used ethnic as well as mainstream newspapers to exploit 'war heroines' to mobilize Canadian women for war work, it was unusual to find heroines of Canadian history in the women's pages of the nationalist press. It was not unusual in the years that followed. To the surprise of some, perhaps, a 1980 UWAC Mothers' Day editorial described Prime Minister Mackenzie King's mother as 'the great mother of a great man,' a worthy model and source of inspiration for Ukrainian-Canadian women. The UWAC magazine, *Promin* (Sunbeam), carried articles on several traditional Canadian heroines, including Marie (Rollet) Hébert, the first European woman to settle permanently in New France; social reformers Adelaide Hoodless and Lady Aberdeen, founders of the Women's Institutes and the NCWC, respectively; the 'Famous Five' of the 1929 Persons Case; Agnes Macphail, the first female member of parliament; and Cairine Wilson, the first woman appointed to the Canadian Senate.[58]

These women and others like them could not possibly and were not intended to perform the function of the Great Women of Ukrainian history, but they signaled something equally significant – the internalization, by Ukrainian-Canadian women, of the Canadian women's movement (including its ideals, struggles, and achievements) as part of their history as Canadian women. In other words, an unhyphenated Canadianness had permitted gender to triumph over both the Ukrainianness that kept Ukrainian-Canadian women in ethnically exclusive organizations and the sense of British superiority that had characterized the early twentieth-century mainstream women's movement.

At the same time, the Ukrainian-Canadian women's movement was so defined as to become part of the larger mainstream phenomenon. In 1966 organized nationalist women celebrated, as their legacy, the fiftieth anniversary of the granting of female suffrage in Manitoba, with the Ukrainian Women's Enlightenment Association established in Winnipeg in 1916 representing their contribution. To do this they had to turn a blind eye to history, specifically the nativism of the suffrage crusade's Anglo-Canadian leaders that had branded Ukrainian women as 'foreigners' and precluded their participation. A longtime UWAC activist who admitted that Ukrainian women had taken no part in the struggle for women's emancipation in Canada attributed it not to mainstream prejudice, or to Ukrainian 'backwardness,' but to the demands that pioneering made on the time of new settlers.[59] Even symbolic integration of the Ukrainian and mainstream women's movements, however, proved to be a one-way street. When six prominent women's historians wrote the first general history of Canadian women in 1988, the Ukrainian Women's Enlightenment Association, whether as an ethnic organization or as one of many Canadian responses to women's enfranchisement, was not mentioned.[60] Illustrating the degree to which nationalist Ukrainian-Canadian women's organizations saw themselves as part of a common Canadian women's movement was an article published in the UWOC journal, *Zhinochyi svit* (Women's world), for Canada's Centennial in 1967. It began with the nineteenth-century women's rights activist, Emily Stowe, the first woman to practise medicine in Canada, and ended with the Ukrainian women's organizations established by the displaced persons. Yet, significantly, women's Canadianness and not gender dictated the form of the relationship, as the bond between Ukrainian-Canadian and other Canadian women was expressed not in terms of women working for women but in terms of women working for their nation: Ukrainian-Canadian womanhood, the author asserted, should be proud of its role in building together with other Canadian women a free and democratic country.[61] While the UWOC had Canadianized its message, the nation remained dominant.

NCWC vice-presidents, rock singers, scientists, lieutenant-governors, lawyers, politicians, Lady Aberdeen as a Ukrainian-Canadian heroine, Ukrainian-Canadian women's organizations as part of a pan-Canadian women's movement all testify to actual and psychological integration into Canadian society. Ukrainians' acceptance and full participation in Canadian life as equals had been desired by community activists and spokespersons since the pioneer immigrant intelligentsia launched its campaign on behalf of enlightenment and progress. Women like Helen Hnatyshyn and 'Luba' vindicated their efforts and pointed to realization of the nationalist agenda.

Women claiming their place on the mainstream stage also exposed the internal weaknesses in that agenda, weaknesses that jeopardized its fundamental goal. Female educational and career successes offered as proof of integration and progress, as examples for their sex, and as sources of collective pride contained inherent tensions and contradictions that jeopardized the *raison d'être* of nationalist women's organizations – group survival. The university graduate did not necessarily follow her mother's footsteps into traditional Ukrainian-Canadian women's organizations. Myrna Kostash, featured in *Promin* for her university accomplishments,[62] rejected the establishment community and wrote *All of Baba's Children* (1977), a provocative challenge to Ukrainian Canadians' complacent view of the past as a parade of 'firsts' and success stories. Moreover, a university degree implied a career, and it was for their careers as much as for their community activity that women like Mary Wawrykow received recognition. To promote women who worked outside the home as models and sources of inspiration countermanded what nationalist women's organizations, in the name of Ukrainianness, had insisted was the primary responsibility of Ukrainian-Canadian women – homemaking and motherhood.

Education struck at the heart of Ukrainian-Canadian society, the family, in yet another way. The spectre of intermarriage had once been an argument for female education – to provide satisfactory Ukrainian wives for upwardly mobile Ukrainian males – but education inevitably raised the spectre of assimilation. By 1961, for example, Ukrainian professional and managerial males in Saskatchewan married Ukrainian brides only 43.6 per cent of the time (the percentage was higher among farmers). A contemporary survey of attitudes among Ukrainians in Alberta showed a direct relationship between North American material or career success and alienation from things Ukrainian, including the idea that marriage to a wealthy non-Ukrainian constituted a 'good' marriage. The survey also found women to be less alienated than men (reflecting greater conservatism, powerlessness, and perhaps social isolation) and rural residents to be less alienated than urban.[63]

Community concern for intermarriage – among both sexes, and for all educational levels – never abated. That the subject was a sensitive one was aptly demonstrated in 1973, when the CBC produced 'The Ninth Summer' by Ukrainian-Canadian playwright George Ryga; many were upset at its suggestion that Ukrainians 'use intermarriage as a means for social advancement.'[64] In the 1980s nationalist leaders informed young people that there was a 'higher law' and purpose to being born Ukrainian, and warned of the community's right to criticize and dictate, even in their private lives, when survival was at stake. Some went so far as to endorse a Ukrainian marriage bureau (with headquarters in Philadelphia) to guarantee conscious Ukrainian spouses for conscious Ukrainian-Canadian youth.[65] Proclaimed the decade of the Ukrainian family by the World Congress of Free Ukrainians, the 1980s were dedicated to the preservation of the Ukrainian nation and identity by strengthening and safeguarding them at their core. While the primary evil in Ukraine was seen as Russification, in the West it was the alienation of youth from organized community life and what one commentator termed 'the mass epidemic of national and religious suicide' among Ukrainian youth 'drowning in the cauldron of mixed marriages, ... effecting a total demise of our nation in the diaspora.'[66]

After one hundred years, assimilation had become a fact of Ukrainian life in Canada, with far-reaching implications for the nationalist agenda. Influenced by Canada's nineteenth-century political debate over 'representation by population,' and the notion that in a democracy numbers count, French Canadians traditionally stressed fecundity in the interests of *la survivance*. But in their struggle for group survival, Ukrainian Canadians lacked French Canada's advantages of constitutional recognition as one of two 'charter peoples,' a legally defined territorial base, and geographical concentration (except to some extent on the prairies). One result was the nationalist community's emphasis on quality, not quantity, in its propaganda and programs: women were told not so much to bear Ukrainian children as to rear Ukrainian children. *Building the Future* (1986), the UCC's blueprint for the twenty-first century, greeted with alarm a group fertility rate below minimum replacement levels as revealed in the 1981 Canadian census.[67] Traditionally, however, women's reproductive role was less important than their socially prescribed roles as mothers and homemakers. Emphasis on quality, not quantity, also made possible, and even encouraged, an elite survival. Although Ukrainian-Canadian numbers could be employed to exert political pressure for community goals, the community could survive without the numbers; ultimately, Ukrainian consciousness was what mattered, and without it the numbers were meaningless.

In 1981 slightly fewer than half of all Ukrainian Canadians reported Ukrainian as their mother tongue. Especially disquieting for a community that stressed language as the cornerstone of survival, only 9.4 per cent of that number were under the age of twenty-five, while 49.9 per cent were fifty-five or older, and only 31.0 per cent actually spoke Ukrainian at home. Two-thirds of those who reported Ukrainian as their home language were fifty-five or older. Nor did these figures correspond to the group's age profile: 29.4 per cent under twenty-five, 27.9 per cent over fifty-five.[68] Slightly fewer than half of all Ukrainian Canadians belonged to the Ukrainian Catholic (30.0 per cent) and Orthodox (18.6 per cent) churches; over a third of members in both cases exceeded the age of fifty-five.[69] In 1967–8 a survey of ethnic identification and attitudes conducted among students of Ukrainian descent at the University of Alberta had probed more deeply into Ukrainian consciousness and knowledgability about Ukrainian affairs. Significantly, attachment to things Ukrainian was found to be stronger among females than males; a majority of respondents also favoured a hyphenated identity and independence for Ukraine. Other findings were less comforting: over 90 per cent neither subscribed to Ukrainian periodicals nor read Ukrainian books (half, in fact, had never looked at any), few could identify Ukrainian historical figures, and less than 9 per cent could correctly name at least one Ukrainian-Canadian organization.[70] In 1991 the young men and women interviewed for the survey were in their late forties, the parents of children embarking on their own parenthood careers, with whatever sense of Ukrainianness the older generation imparted.

One purpose of the charge to mothers to rear conscious Ukrainians was aid to Ukraine, rising from a continuing sense of duty to the homeland. The other was group survival in Canada – so that youth as adults married to like-thinking Ukrainians would perpetuate their language, culture, and values in their own children and maintain community institutions. Yet ghettoization was to be avoided – good Ukrainian mothers encouraged the higher education necessary for full integration into Canadian life in all areas. Language loss, religious assimilation, intermarriage, and alienation from community political institutions (despite interest in nonlinguistic cultural activities) attested to a contracting base of committed Ukrainian Canadians. Either Ukrainian-Canadian mothers had failed in their duty, or they had proved powerless against both the tensions in the community blueprint and the attractions and pervasiveness of Canadian society.

The effects of assimilation can be observed in women's organizations themselves. In 1984, for example, sixty of one hundred members in an unidentified UCWL branch had children in mixed marriages, and of those sixty mixed marriages only twenty families attended the Ukrainian Catholic church.[71] As a quiet admission of the impact of intermarriage, nationalist women's organizations increasingly advised their memberships not only of a mother's responsibility to rear her children so as to forestall marriage outside the group, but also of the proper attitude towards the non-Ukrainian son- or daughter-in-law and the grandmother's role in the Ukrainization of the children. They paid attention as well to the problem of alienation, by discussing ways in which to attract younger and working (including professional) women, whose interests and needs differed from those of current memberships. One response, no longer new, was to create English-speaking branches that catered both to members' non-Ukrainian-speaking daughters and to the non-Ukrainian wives of their sons. Another suggestion was to use the popularity of Ukrainian foods and handicrafts, through cooking and embroidery classes, to solicit and proselytize new recruits. Other proposals included updating their buildings, revamping their programs to focus less on women's national responsibilities and more on daycare facilities, and examining their kitchen image.[72]

In the 1970s and 1980s this kitchen image, together with the interrelated issues of community expectations and women's freedom of choice, were addressed in other quarters as well, by Ukrainian-Canadian feminists seeking to reconcile their ethnicity with their feminism. The most vocal among them, Myrna Kostash, explained her wholehearted adoption of Anglo-American culture at the age of fifteen:

> I intuitively figured out that at the heart of ... the concerned attempt [in the Ukrainian-Canadian community] to preserve identity and resist assimilation, of the revivalism that is ethnic pride, lay the oppression of women ... To serve 'my people' in their struggle for cultural specificity I would have to maintain the so-called tradition of the Ukrainian woman: she goes straight from her father's house to her husband's, she devotes her time to the rearing of Ukrainian children (for this the mother must be constantly in their attendance, or they will be socialized by the anglo world) and the keeping of a Ukrainian home (needlework, bread-making, ritual observation), she provides her Ukrainian husband with an oasis of serenity, deference and loyalty, and she goes to church, there to be reconfirmed in her chaste, selfless and complacent Ukrainian identity.
>
> I turned and ran ... I had to choose between ethnicity and personhood.[73]

Choosing between ethnicity and personhood was a dilemma faced by all Canadian feminists who belonged to minorities that assigned women inferior status and/or imposed specific roles and responsibilities in the name of the group and its preservation.[74] The Anglo-Canadian women who dominated the mainstream women's movement could afford to be single minded, but for many ethnic women the problem was not simply to improve women's position in society. It was to improve their position in Anglo-dominated society (as women and as non-Anglo-Canadians) while simultaneously improving their position (as women) within their group. The group's status and interest in survival, as well as their own feelings towards the preservation of all or part of their heritage, complicated their options.

In re-evaluating women's relationship to the Ukrainian community, Ukrainian-Canadian feminists were joined by women elsewhere in the diaspora. Daughters of displaced persons in the United States, for example, also complained of personal suffocation. The sole purpose of a girl's upbringing, one rebel charged, was marriage to a Ukrainian professional who provided the North American materialistic symbols of success and did the decision making for the Ukrainian community while she 'produc[ed] more children for freeing Ukraine' and 'embroider[ed] millions of yards of useless garments.'[75] Women dissatisfied with the status quo but sympathetic to the Ukrainian cause sought a positive redefinition of their role, in a community that acknowledged women's right to personal fulfilment and full partnership and that accommodated the realities of late twentieth-century North America. In 1985 Ukrainian-Canadian feminists outside establishment circles organized a conference in Edmonton to mark the centenary of the Ukrainian women's movement. This first 'Second Wreath' (a second was held in Toronto in 1988) was named after the woman's almanac *Pershyi vinok* (First wreath) that Natalia Kobrynska and Olena Pchilka had published in 1887. Participants examined women's position in Ukrainian society and formal community structures, past and present, and explored issues pertinent to the ethnic identity, roles, and expectations of contemporary Ukrainian-Canadian women. The conference also addressed the need to promote ethnic issues among mainstream feminists and feminist ideas in ethnic communities. Despite involvement by other ethnic women, particularly Jewish feminists, dialogue with and participation by women from traditionalist Ukrainian-Canadian women's organizations was limited and strained.[76]

The authors of the UCC blueprint, *Building the Future*, identified 'the very limited impact of the women's movement in mainstream society ... on our organizations and their members' as a major reason for women's historical and current subordinate role in community life. Its recommendations for community renewal in the face of 'critical' assimilation, low fertility, increasing intermarriage, and high divorce included making women equal partners. 'By excluding women from decision-making structures,' it stated, 'we fail to recognize issues that are of particular concern to women. This limits the involvement of women in our community's development, since many women choose to work in the mainstream women's movement where their specific concerns are addressed. Nor, moreover, should women's issues be of concern only to women. They must be addressed by all of us to ensure the full development of our community. Accordingly, specific initiatives that include a broad educational programme need to be implemented to deal with the central issue of equal opportunity for women.'[77] Whether such recommendations, largely the work of a small number of intellectuals and professionals,[78] would be embraced by the male-dominated organizations making up the UCC or by the existing women's organizations remained to be seen. Whether their implementation would attract the great majority of women outside formal Ukrainian networks was uncertain. Regardless of these unresolved questions, a major community document had proclaimed a redefinition of the nature of women's relationship with the Ukrainian-Canadian community, taking into account their changing profile and needs, as crucial to its future.

Moreover, women within the establishment began to query their subordinate role. In 1983 a delegate to the WFUWO demanded the integration of women into Ukrainian-Canadian community power structures. She criticized the existing situation – where women worked and men played politics, and where male 'maternal' organizations, through the UCC, spoke for everyone. She criticized, too, the compartmentalization of roles and contributions that made Taras Shevchenko an all-Ukrainian hero while Olha Basarab (who died for all Ukrainians, not just women) had to be a female heroine. Finally, she criticized women's stereotyped image and activities, particularly the fund-raising that enabled the male organizations to function but that provided no mental stimulation.[79]

In advocating change, the above critic implied that the status quo served a passing generation. This raised the possibility that as younger, better-educated (often professional) women demanded more equal participation in the formal life of their community and its power structures, the older, less-educated woman and housewife would be left behind, probably in the kitchen, whether in separate women's organizations or the general community. Similar strains had surfaced within the pioneer Ukrainian Catholic religious order, the Sisters Servants of Mary Immaculate, in the 1920s: between an emerging professional class of nursing and teaching sisters, feeling that their special needs went unappreciated, and other nuns, who objected to the formers' liberties and lesser contribution to their communal work. The division between 'academic' nuns and 'nonacademic' nuns in the convents, who increasingly withdrew from an active apostolate, persisted.[80] 'Class' divisions had always existed within secular women's organizations in the distinction between a leadership elite and the rank and file, between those who made *pyrohy* and those who took minutes; and generational and immigrational differences had sparked the establishment of more than one new club. But women had not been divided by fundamentally different interpretations of their 'proper sphere.' The tensions that the identity crisis of the 1970s and 1980s generated manifested themselves in organized women's attitudes towards their place in history.

Mythmaking, as a phenomenon of the postwar Canadianization of women's organizations, involved not only the legitimizing function of successful and prominent members, who acted on behalf of Ukrainian Canadians outside as well as inside organized women's circles. It also involved, and validated, women's organizations as such. The jab that without decades of fund-raising by women, the male 'maternal' organizations in the Ukrainian community would have had no finances is significant. In their jubilee histories and frequent assessments of their achievements and goals, Ukrainian-Canadian women's organizations compensated for their lack of real power by extolling their role as builders, in a very concrete sense, of the Ukrainian-Canadian community and thus of Canada. Rejecting the image of the UCWL as a 'cooking' organization, one article in *Nasha doroha* (Our path) could not resist adding that the Ukrainian woman who cooked had built more than one church or hall in Canada in the past and now (1984) was helping to keep them in the black.[81] Such a view was not restricted to women alone. In 1968 the official fiftieth-anniversary history of the Ukrainian Greek Orthodox church time and again stressed how the local UWAC was the most active and valuable body in the parish.[82] In his introduction to the silver jubilee history of the UCWL in the archeparchy of Winnipeg, a Catholic priest was more effusive, praising the women, wives, and mothers in the UCWL who had not only given of their time, advice, and money but had also, by their labours, made Canada stronger, more beautiful, and richer. Theirs, he said, was the type of work of which any state and nation could be proud.[83]

Organized women's self-image as builders voiced a genuine feeling of accomplishment and a sense of their place in history that was less evident in their male counterparts. Perhaps because their largely political activity did not have the same concrete ends and visible results as women's work, men's organizations felt less compelled to record their deeds and accomplishments, in either the creation or the expression of collective memory.[84] Women's organizations themselves exhibited a stronger collective memory on the prairies than elsewhere in Canada, if their branch histories, more detailed and precise as to their origins and past, were any indication. Longevity, together with greater stability and continuity in membership, particularly in rural areas, partly accounted for the difference. It also reflected the fact that the West, and not Ontario, was long the undisputed centre of community life.[85]

Women were their own best defenders and apologists for the 'women's work' that represented their contribution to the Ukrainian-Canadian community. Their labour, they insisted, built and supported its institutions, paid its debts, and funded its projects. Regardless of any subsequent movement to malign and escape their traditional kitchen function, and regardless of criticisms that things of the mind and spirit got lost in the flurry of money-raising projects, organized nationalist women remained convinced that that kitchen function had made the Ukrainian-Canadian community what it was. 'It is the U.C.W.L.C. that has kept the Ukrainian Catholic Church of Canada, the strong and unified institution that it is today,' said a delegate to the UCWL national convention in 1983: 'The Bishops have their role to play, but we, the faithful, have done even more than they to make the Ukrainian Catholic people of Canada feel and know that they are one.'[86] On the fortieth anniversary of their national organization in 1984, Ukrainian Catholic women commended themselves for their 'vital role' in the religious, cultural, educational, and social life of Ukrainians in Canada and in the growth of the Ukrainian Catholic church.[87] The UWAC was not to be outdone. On its thirty-fifth anniversary in 1961 an article had paid tribute to the organizational activities that had 'definitely been great contributing factors to the tremendous gains the Ukrainian people made in Canada in every phase of life, raising their social, cultural and economic standards to a high level.'[88]

A sense of organized women's centrality to community growth and progress, on which their contribution to Canadian life hinged, developed in the progressive tradition as well. How could an important anniversary of the progressive women's movement slip by unnoticed, AUUC activist Mary Skrypnyk asked in 1957: 'It should have been shouted from the housetops, considering that the women in the ranks

of the AUUC have been its heart and soul for the past thirty-five years.'[89]
On their fortieth anniversary, Mary Kardash wrote:

> The history of the Women's Branches of the AUUC constitutes an in-
> tegral part of the history of the development of Canada in this cen-
> tury ... The economic development of Canada took place with the
> greatest acceleration in this century, and the Women's Branches of
> the AUUC have existed 40 of the 62 years of this period.
>
> The history of the Women's Branches of the ULFTA–AUUC, as a
> vital section of the progressive Ukrainian community in Canada, at
> the same time constitutes an important chapter in the history of the
> general Canadian labour movement.
>
> Only within such a concept can a proper evaluation of the contri-
> bution of Ukrainian workingwomen to the economic, political, cul-
> tural and social life of the Canadian people be given.[90]

In both nationalist and progressive traditions, organized Ukrainian-
Canadian women validated themselves and their work, within the
framework of the missions of their respective communities, by creating
a mythology that legitimized traditional 'female' activities and traditional 'female' roles performed through separate women's organizations. A genuine and positive expression of self-worth and value, by
women who perceived themselves as full members of their community,
it was also a rationalization of political powerlessness.

As Ukrainian-Canadian community figures and 'successes' in the larger
Canadian society came to supplement the Great Women of Ukraine
as models and sources of inspiration for Ukrainian-Canadian women,
they bore witness to a process of Canadianization in organized women's
propaganda and programs. They also exposed the special tensions and
contradictions that had existed from the beginning in the community
blueprint for their sex, in the command that women be simultaneously
Ukrainians and full citizens of Canada. The participation in Canadian
society that was expected of women as Canadians had proved to jeopardize their ability and willingness to perform what was expected of
them as Ukrainians, both in the public sphere as community activists
and in the more important private sphere as mothers and homemakers.
The displaced persons who brought the Great Women of Ukraine to
Canadian soil in the form of activists from the interwar women's move-

ment did not present such problems as models and sources of inspiration. But their nineteenth-century predecessors were also brought to Canada, there to play new symbolic roles that reflected Ukrainians' Canadian experience as well as their old-country ties.

Statues of Lesia Ukrainka stand in High Park, Toronto, and on the campus of the University of Saskatchewan in Saskatoon. The first, the work of the Ukrainian-American sculptor, Mykhailo Chereshniovsky, was erected by the UCWC in International Women's Year to honour the centenary of the birth of the poet who symbolized 'the humanitarian and freedom loving spirit of Ukrainians.'[91] The second, a gift from the people of Soviet Ukraine in tribute to the Ukrainian pioneers and builders of Canada, was erected in 1976 through the efforts of the AUUC. The University of Saskatchewan was chosen as an 'impartial' home for Ukrainka after the City of Saskatoon bowed to pressure from the UCC and rescinded its decision to put the statue (by the Soviet sculptor, Halyna Kalchenko) on city property. An outraged UCC labelled the Soviet gesture a mockery when Ukrainka's words were censored by a régime that promoted 'tyranny, oppression and cultural genocide.'[92] In the process of transplantation, Ukrainka's function as a mentor for Ukrainian-Canadian women was overshadowed by her role as a model and source of inspiration for all women, by the universality of her poetic message, by her all-Ukrainian significance, by her use as a pawn in nationalist-progressive quarrels, and by the mainstream legitimization of Ukrainian community politics and bonds with Ukraine that her public resting places represented.

But transplantation was also accompanied by transformation, at the hands of descendants of the first immigrants, who identified Ukrainka with their peasant pioneer heritage in western Canada. As *Lesia*, a giant fibreglass statue of a Ukrainian girl in national folk costume, she has welcomed visitors to Canora, Saskatchewan, with the traditional gift of bread and salt since 1980. By local artists Nick and Orest Lewchuk, and unveiled by Governor General Edward Schreyer, *Lesia* was a project of the Canora and District Chamber of Commerce.[93] This popular Canadianization of Great Ukrainian Women at the grassroots level bore little resemblance to their political Canadianization by the upper echelons of the organized community. The differences between the two became even more apparent with the replacement of traditional heroines from Ukraine with female symbols rooted entirely in the Ukrainian-Canadian experience, exalting the peasant pioneer to unanticipated heights.

6

Rehabilitating the Peasant Immigrant: Baba and the Canadianized Heroine

As she lay dying, Gabrielle Roy's Marta Yaramko wondered if ordinary souls survived. 'Perhaps it was possible for certain ones,' she decided, 'the great souls, the noble and profound minds, whose loss people would never cease to mourn. But Marta! An ignorant old woman who lagged so far behind even her own children – how could she deserve to be rescued somewhere beyond this world? No, she could not imagine herself living forever, surviving herself.'[1] But Marta was mistaken. If Ukrainian Canadians possess a Great Woman, or indeed boast a general mythic figure, she is the peasant immigrant pioneer in western Canada in the opening decades of the twentieth century. The genesis of her myth lay in the period of immigration and settlement itself, but its flowering belonged to a later era, especially the coincidence of the seventy-fifth anniversary of Ukrainian settlement in Canada in 1966 and the Canadian Centennial in 1967. With the rehabilitation of the peasant immigrant, the discussion of the relationship between gender and ethnicity in Ukrainian-Canadian history comes full circle. The focus has moved from the peasant immigrant pioneer woman and her contemporaries, however, to her legacy at the hands of two subsequent immigrations and several Canadian-born generations often far removed in time and place from her specific experience. To Ukrainian Canadians, history was not something past but an important part of the present; and in the cultivation and expression of their self-image, the peasant immigrant pioneer woman came to play a central role.

The myth of the Ukrainian peasant immigrant pioneer woman draws together three distinct yet interrelated threads from the preceding chapters. The first is the Canadianization of Princess Olha and the Cossack Mother, particularly in the propaganda and programs of the national women's organizations that emerged between the wars. Now a figure of veneration, the peasant immigrant pioneer woman was portrayed as having slaved with superhuman strength and great sacrifice for the spiritual and physical welfare of her family, consciously raising her children to remain true to their people and traditions and to their faith or class, and joining with like-minded women to broaden her horizons and serve her community. A model and source of inspiration for her female successors, her appeal transcended region, immigration, and generation. Beginning with their prototype in the peasant immigrant pioneer, Princess Olha and the Cossack Mother in their Canadian incarnation were presumed by a women's organizational elite to be self-perpetuating. As community activists and the mothers of consciously Ukrainian daughters who became community activists and mothers in turn, they guaranteed the physical survival of their group and its commitment to things Ukrainian. In this official community perspective, the Ukrainian peasant immigrant pioneer woman played a symbolic role similar to that of the French-Canadian mother figure in *la survivance* and shared also in her timelessness.

But the popular image was not of the mother and community servant recreated with each generation and ultimately identified with group survival and Ukraine. It was of the peasant immigrant pioneer as baba, the old woman or grandmother, who outstripped her rival in popularity. The replacement of the eternally young woman with the old marked the passage of the peasant immigrant pioneer from a functional model of Ukrainianness for her sex. She became instead an intensely personal but essentially passive symbol for her direct descendants of both sexes. For third-, fourth-, and even fifth-generation Ukrainian Canadians, baba was the spiritual and physical link to their peasant pioneer heritage, the medium through which they understood themselves as both Canadians and Ukrainians. Here are to be found the two remaining themes the peasant immigrant pioneer woman's myth embraces.

Baba, the old woman who could not be recreated, personified the specific unrepeatable experience of her people – the immigration of Ukrainian peasants to the virgin lands of western Canada at the turn of the century and their invaluable contribution to Canadian nation building. As such, she functioned as part of a 'founding fathers' or 'peasant pioneer' myth to confirm her descendants in their Canadian birthright and to legitimize the Ukrainian group within Confederation. This feminization of an otherwise male-dominated story would have been unimaginable, however, were it not for the third thread on which baba's identification with the Ukrainian-Canadian peasant pioneer heritage drew. As a popular group symbol, she illustrated how the peasant cultural baggage of the first immigration, and not the political propaganda and programs of the community elite, dictated Ukrainian Canadians' sense of themselves as Ukrainians. The most pervasive and enduring expressions of Ukrainianness in Canada have been shown to come from Ukrainian peasant culture; they also represented activities associated with women, making baba the custodian of traditions and arts that defined the Ukrainian identity of her descendants. But immortalization as the old woman simultaneously attested to the success of the Ukrainian emphasis on progress, which pronounced the death sentence on a peasant lifestyle. It forced the peasant immigrant pioneer into a nostalgic and frozen figure representing roots, but with limited potential as an active model and source of inspiration for either her group or her sex.

In *The Last Best West*, her account of women on the Alberta frontier between 1880 and 1930, Eliane Silverman contends that the sheer necessity and overwhelming nature of work, as the means to survival, left women with neither the time nor the inclination to create mythic heroines, express themselves in poetry, or elevate their labour to nation building. Work was something 'you just had to do.'[2] A celebration of that work and of the women who performed it, Silverman's book obscures prejudices of the period like the Anglo-Canadian nativism that condemned the workload of Ukrainian pioneer women as crushing, desexing, and barbarous. But Ukrainians at the time were neither ignorant of nor indifferent to such attitudes. Although themselves critical of their womenfolk for obstructing progress and hurting their group's image and status, they also admired the peasant immigrant and defended her against outside attack. Contrary to Silverman's contention, Ukrainians fashioned mythic heroines of their pioneer women and ennobled their work by equating it with nation building. Contrary to the Ukrainian peasant woman's general negative image among outsiders, the occasional Anglo-Canadian, too, overlooked her faults to commend the labour on the land that did its bit towards building the country.[3]

The Ukrainian immigrant folksong, the best measure of the popular ethos, seldom concerned women's work. Immigrant female *memorat* (reminiscences) also have not possessed the sense of personal mission and sweeping perspective that characterize immigrant male *memorat*.[4] But the presence of women as creators of both folksong and folklore belies the notion that work left women incapable of poetry or imagination. Both as emigrants and as wives left in Galicia, turn-of-the-century Ukrainian peasant women found an outlet for their emotions in poetry. Perhaps most of these poems remained part of an oral tradition, but some appeared in the pioneer press, transcribed by others if their composers were illiterate.[5] Ukrainian-Canadian folklorist Robert Klymasz includes Ukrainian immigrant women among his informants, although he identifies the telling of tales as an essentially male occupation. Moreover, women's storytelling performed a specific female function. Klymasz argues that while the predominance of male storytellers resulted in an often derogatory portrayal of women, female folksongs and poetic narratives functioned as an outlet for repressed emotions and increasingly expressed women's rebellion against their oppression in Ukrainian peasant and immigrant life. One example illustrates the impact of Canadian ideas: the poem's author announces that in Canada, unlike Galicia, her husband must treat her as a 'lady' (this word in English) or expect the jail sentence he received for mistreating her.[6]

Nor was work simply something 'you just had to do.' In its periodic defence of the peasant immigrant woman homesteading in western Canada, the Ukrainian intelligentsia applauded her toil and unselfishness, tying both to nation building. Unlike her weak and fastidious Anglo-Canadian detractors, one commentator claimed, the Ukrainian pioneer contributed significantly not only to the well-being of her family and people but also to the development of her country.[7] It is impossible to measure the existence or depth of a corroborating sentiment among the mass of illiterate and inarticulate peasant immigrant women. Some, at least, shared the prejudices of their elite and derived a sense of satisfaction and value from their work, as indicated by this peasant woman interviewed for Woodsworth's 1917 survey of Ukrainian rural communities. 'I think the English do not like ... our women,' she told the fieldworkers, 'because our women help their men in farming. The English women are very lazy. They sleep too long – their husbands prepare breakfast for them. Our women like to help their men because they know that they work for themselves.'[8] Feminist Helen Potrebenko, who grew up in northern Alberta in the 1940s and 1950s, testified to the endurance and deep-rootedness of popular Anglo-Canadian and Ukrainian stereotypes. Ukrainians in her community questioned the useless femininity of the 'English,' and their English neighbours bemoaned the dearth of feminine qualities in the Ukrainian farm wife.[9]

The Ukrainian experience also questions the claim that pioneer women failed to fashion mythic heroines. Romanticization and veneration of the Ukrainian peasant immigrant pioneer woman began not with her descendants on a quest for roots, but with her female contemporaries among the intelligentsia in the period of initial immigration and settlement. In 1920 the *Grain Growers' Guide* published a somewhat maudlin article on the Ukrainian pioneering experience. Written by Anna Bychinska, whose status as the wife of a Ukrainian Protestant clergyman gave her Anglo-Canadian contacts, it evoked the ingredients of the subsequent myth: the Ukrainian peasant pioneer woman's courage and perseverance; her self-denial for her family's sake; her material hardship and poverty; her emotional trauma at the death of a child, when emigration and pioneering exacted woman's supreme sacrifice; her loneliness and disorientation in the great void of prairie and bush; her responsibility for basic survival during her husband's absence; her labour on the land; and the progress and reward the purchase of the first cow promised. Not only were women placed on a pedestal but they were also, even upstaging their men, tied to nation building. Bychinska concluded:

> The Ukrainians are truly pioneers of Western Canada. When they came here their greatest possessions were good health, strong arms and great perseverance. Their hardships were great but it taught them to love the land into which culture the best years of their lives were given. The men profited by having to go out in search of work, for they became aquainted with more modern ways of farming and learned to speak a little English.
>
> In the first years of extreme struggle the Ukrainian women have proved themselves to possess dauntless courage and perseverance, and we may truly say of them that they have been an inspiration that has carried the men through.[10]

Such sentiments had little in common with the dominant contemporary images of Ukrainian women. They lay in stark contrast to the ignorant peasant and farm girl, the indifferent housewife and mother, and the frivolous working girl that the nationalists decried, and to the oppressed woman and exploited wage-slave that the progressives championed. These sentiments show that condemnation of the attitudes and behaviour of Ukrainian women by those most sensitive to their group's position in Canadian society and to Ukrainians' national-cultural responsibilities was by no means universal and unrelieved. Genuine support and praise of Ukrainian pioneer women was in part a defensive reaction to Anglo-Canadian prejudice, in part a practical acknowledgment of women's vital role on the Ukrainian homestead within the family farming unit, and in part a reflection of Ukrainians' pride in their people's contribution to its new homeland.

The peasants' sense of belonging was undoubtedly influenced by the right to ownership of the soil, the fact that the new society in the West prized the same agrarian way of life and rural values, and the fact that their leaders defined their role in nation building not in abstract terms but in more easily understood terms of the land itself. Writing in a Galician newspaper in the 1920s after a sojourn in Canada, a Greek Catholic priest described how Ukrainian immigrants had felled the forest, tamed the land, brought 'civilization and culture to the Canadian wilderness,' fed the country with their wheat, given their lives for its railways, and extracted the resources that would make it wealthy. History, he concluded, 'will not be able to deny the Ukrainians recognition.'[11] The priest also extolled the virtues of the Ukrainian pioneer woman, to the detriment of women from other nationalities, and tied her to Canadian nation building beyond a childbearing and childrearing role. The curses and blows from her husband that he maintained were often a wife's sole reward, however, would have no place in the romanticization of Ukrainian peasant family life and pioneering undertaken by subsequent Ukrainian-Canadian mythologizers.

In a companion piece to her homesteading article, describing Ukrainian women in their homeland for *Grain Growers' Guide* readers, Anna Bychinska unwittingly illustrated the problems that would be encountered in juggling myth with reality. Her attempt to tackle the issue of women's position in Ukrainian peasant society had curious results, as an idyllic picture of village life sat incongruously with poverty, oppression, and female drudgery. More to the point, the effort to demonstrate a strict community morality that spoke in Ukrainians' favour only exposed (and condoned) a double standard for men and women. 'If perchance a girl has fallen,' Bychinksa wrote, 'she is publicly exposed, her hair is cut off and she is shunned by the whole community. If a husband beats his wife when she is contrary, then the whole village approves of it, but should he beat her out of spite, then the whole village reproves him.'[12] The myth as it blossomed would find wife-beating, whether 'justified' or not, and other signs of women's oppression in Ukrainian peasant and immigrant life, less easy to accommodate.

Unlike the pioneer intelligentsia, whose desire to change the present often forced it to focus on the negative and unpleasant, myth makers were driven by the desire for a tidy and satisfying picture of the past that promoted the goal of recognition for their group as a legitimate and valuable actor on the Canadian stage. The result was a founding fathers myth erected on the peasant pioneers: in their backbreaking toil and sacrifice to introduce the prairie and parkland to the plough and to exploit mining and forest frontiers so that Canada could be great, lay Ukrainians' right to full partnership in Confederation.[13] This tradition, with its corollary of progress and success extended to all walks of Canadian life, embraced the grassroots as well as the community elite, those outside the nationalist circles most closely associated with it, all immigrations, and all generations.[14] It brooked no failures, no probing questions, no imperfections. The myth's impact on the peasant immigrant pioneer woman was twofold. On the one hand, her experience was accepted and incorporated as part of the story; on the other hand, acceptance and incorporation had conditions attached.

Women figured little in traditional Ukrainian-Canadian histories, confirming the dominance of the male perspective in ethnic as well as mainstream historiography. To identify the father but not the mother of the 'first-Canadian-born Ukrainian,' for example, was symptomatic of an attitude relegating the female experience and perspective to the background.[15] Both settlement and community development were typically explained through the male members of a family and the group, with their activities the focus. It was men who emigrated and immigrated (women accompanied them as wives, mothers, and daughters); and it was men who took homesteads, found work, earned money, made decisions, erected schools and churches, and gave their society shape.[16] Intellectual and community life itself was defined in male terms that reflected the actual distribution of power: men's organizations represented the various ideological camps, women's and youth groups acted as their appendages.

Yet the important place Ukrainian Canadians' role in settling the West occupied in the group consciousness led both nationalists and progressives to acknowledge the peasant immigrant woman home-steading in the prairie provinces. Her hard work and physical labour on the land that contemporary Anglo-Canadians decried became virtues, part of the courageous, self-sacrificing, and toiling image of the peasant pioneer myth and contributing to growth and progress. The major figure from the displaced persons immigration to write about the Ukrainian-Canadian experience both absorbed and feminized the founding fathers myth. Ukrainian pioneer women, said Michael Marunchak, 'took care of the farms ... cut and uprooted the trees, picked roots and stones, plowed, dug and hoed – in one word, they transformed the brushwood and the prairie into a fertile grain-growing soil. Thousands of acres were prepared for planting, by these steadfast and heroic women.'[17] However, accompanying this admiration of the qualities and accomplishments of Ukrainian pioneer women was a romanticization of their struggles and hardships that precluded critical appraisal of conditions under which they lived.

Salt and Braided Bread (1984), Jars Balan's popular history of Ukrainian life in Canada, accepted as fact features of Ukrainian pioneer life that had fostered the negative Anglo-Canadian stereotype of the early twentieth century: drunken weddings, wife-beating, child abuse, arranged marriages, and child brides. Writing a few years earlier, Zonia Keywan identified poor nutrition, overcrowding, peasant fatalism, arranged marriages, and high infant mortality rates due to overworked women and unsanitary conditions as unpleasant realities of Ukrainian homesteading in western Canada.[18] The two books were unusual in that the nationalist community, in looking at the past, had been loathe to criticize or to scrutinize too deeply. It was entirely possible, for example, to admit that the primitive burdei (hut) with its dirt floor was a 'mud-hole' when it rained, yet refuse to pursue the implications for health and living standards, or to make the connection with the unfavourable Anglo-Canadian stereotype condemned as unwarranted.[19] Nor were women necessarily the focus of 'female' issues. For example, the community historian who recounted how a Stuartburn-area homesteader killed his wife after finding her wounded at the bottom of a ladder was unmoved by the human drama and personal tragedy. Instead, he focused on the settlers' fear that such incidents would prejudice Anglo-Canadian opinion against them.[20] The fate of the woman, and what her story said about the precariousness of homestead life, were secondary to the image and status of the Ukrainian group.

In making virtues of what Anglo-Canadians condemned and exalting as heroic the ordinary deeds of ordinary women, Ukrainian-Canadian mythologizers had to exert caution. They could ennoble sacrifice and suffering, courage, industry, and poverty in the abstract, but to relate such qualities to Ukrainian peasant practices and standards of living, or to notions and treatment of women as subordinate and inferior, was impossible. Not only would it have robbed the Ukrainian peasant immigrant pioneer woman of dignity and stature; it would also have blackened the 'progressive' and successful group image Ukrainian Canadians tried so hard to cultivate. Rather than take that risk and put the peasant immigrants' cultural baggage under the microscope, a selective and carefully constructed vision of the past either ignored potentially embarrassing problem areas or blamed repression under foreign masters, pioneering conditions, and nativisitic attitudes for Ukrainians' shortcomings. The resulting idealized image of the Ukrainian peasant immigrant woman, her status and role, touched the realities of her environment both before and after immigration only at points.

Although highly anecdotal, superficial, and selective, the family biography sections of local histories from Ukrainian blocs in the prairie provinces revealed how the direct descendants of the pioneers perceived the past. A majority of the biographies reflected the perspective of the male and family 'head,' but others were written by women themselves or from their viewpoint. Their themes were those of the peasant pioneer and progress myths: woman's toil and sacrifice for the future of her children, the building of her new homeland, and the welfare of her people.[21] In reminiscences closer to the period, however, progress was not the automatically understood reward or end. Much of the romanticized hardship and exaggerated image that the passage of time or a later generation encouraged was absent, and more of the ugliness and blemishes in evidence. The 1930s' memoirs of Maria Adamowska, for example, described her mother's bitter disillusionment when the meanness of homestead life belied the propaganda of earlier immigrants, and disputed a generalization of pioneer sharing and sisterhood on the frontier. Adamowska's account of how a Ukrainian neighbour woman threatened to club her for stealing a turnip because she was hungry had little in common with the picture painted by Zonia Keywan in her 1975 article on the Ukrainian pioneer woman, significantly entitled 'Women Who Won the West.' A 'tremendous sense of community,' Keywan claimed, 'kept pioneer women going,' and hospitality was 'a vital part of pioneer life.'[22]

Postwar romanticization of the Ukrainian immigrant pioneer woman revolved around a larger-than-life figure who coped with everything – housework, fieldwork, childbearing and rearing, culture preservation – amid great isolation and poverty in a strange land. A 1980 study of women in Ukrainian-Canadian folklore and reminiscences, including oral and written pioneer memoirs, illustrates the attraction and popular institutionalization of the heroic Ukrainian pioneer woman. The author chose her subject because 'the Ukrainian pioneer woman in Canada has made such a tremendous contribution to the development of this country.'[23] A predetermined commitment to progress and heroic stature, and the resulting emphasis on women's fine attributes, service, and vision, blurred the distinction between the Ukrainian woman's image in folklore and reminiscences, particularly the latter, and this image as a reflection of reality. As the image became the reality, the Ukrainian pioneer woman's qualities of beauty and charm, commonsense and ingenuity, courage and determination, diligence and perseverance, generosity and hospitality, humility, religiosity, confidence in her own ability, eagerness and determination to get ahead, faithfulness as a wife and dedication as a mother, intelligence, and sense of responsibility to Ukrainian community needs and her cultural heritage emerged as the facts for which folklore and reminiscences were the proof. The fact, for example, was the Ukrainian pioneer woman's 'good common sense and ingenuity,' the rather dubious proof the young girl who fashioned a twig cross to stave off evil when lost in the bush.[24]

Looking at the impact of Ukrainian ethnicity on women instead of tying women to Ukrainian group myths, Ukrainian-Canadian feminists angrily challenged such sanitized history. While equally admiring the peasant immigrant pioneer woman, they censured her oppression and exploitation and noted both the costs and limitations of progress. Not only the constraints of capitalist, male-dominated Anglo-Canadian society but also traditional sex roles in Ukrainian peasant culture, together with persisting inequalities in Ukrainian-Canadian family and community life, were targets of criticism. Helen Potrebenko's *No Streets of Gold* (1977), a social history of the Ukrainian experience in Alberta, was the most stinging indictment of the role and status accorded Ukrainian-Canadian women. Highly personal, with a feminist and Marxist perspective that yielded uncompromising black-and-white analysis, the book was refreshing in its focus on the Ukrainian working class as well as farm life, and in its sensitivity and attention to women.[25]

Rejecting a steady march towards prosperity and integration as the inevitable rewards of Ukrainian toil and sacrifice, Potrebenko presented another side of the Ukrainian-Canadian experience: unglorified poverty, endless drudgery by pioneer women that 'never resulted in anything observable except survival,' callousness and fatalism encouraged by stark and precarious homestead life, and socioeconomic discrimination in mainstream circles because of ethnicity or ethnicity compounded by sex.[26] Potrebenko's discussion of male/female relationships, gender roles in peasant society, and her own parents was frequently angry and bitter. 'When the land was plowed for sowing,' she wrote, 'whatever manure was available was scattered on the field by women ... My father says you wouldn't expect men to get shit on their hands.'[27] As a denunciation of the peasant pioneer and progress myths, *No Streets of Gold* was damning.

The Ukrainian peasant immigrant pioneer woman as a romanticized and heroic figure and the Ukrainian peasant pioneer myth of which she was an integral part were inseparable from the broader western Canadian social context in which both were rooted. The decades after 1945 witnessed a large-scale popular romanticization of the homesteading era in the prairie provinces and of the men and women called to superhuman feats. It represented a nostalgic escape from an increasingly complex world, which saw the significance of rural prairie communities and their residents eroded, to a simpler time when the West figured prominently in the larger scheme of things and westerners were perceived to be in command of their fates. The proliferating local histories that were a product of this phenomenon transcended the pioneer generation to embrace the newest babe in arms, testifying to the need for the descendants of the pioneers to establish a sense of continuity and place, and for westerners to reaffirm themselves in the present. Ukrainian Canadians' participation in these processes reflected experiences and convictions shared as westerners with other nationalities.

Nor were whitewashing and selective memory, or exaggeration and idealization, unique to Ukrainians. Rape, bastardy, mental illness, suicide, battered women, social marginality, economic failure, and community feuding had no place in prairie local histories. Their universal purpose was to record how the expectations and struggles of their authors' forebears (regardless of nationality) yielded fruit to leave an enduring legacy. They admitted this bias by their titles: from sods to silver, homesteads and happiness, pioneers and progress, forests to grainfields, dreams and destinies (Ukrainian), we came and we stayed, this is our land, wagon trails to hardtop, our priceless heritage, great pioneers who cleared and broke the virgin land, children of the pioneers, to the future – your heritage, century of progress (Ukrainian), and golden memories.[28]

Following the lead of conventional western Canadian historiography, local histories tended to frame the past as a male experience. When they dealt with women – for the contribution and role of the female pioneer was acknowledged – they depicted a figure not unlike the Ukrainian peasant pioneer in her emotional strength, resourcefulness, and commitment to hard work. In fact, uncomplaining toil and sacrifice, suffering, patience, endurance, familial devotion, and quiet courage constituted basic elements of the pioneer woman's image whatever her ethnic origins, and they corresponded to traditional ideas concerning female roles and the female character.[29] What is interesting in the Ukrainian case is that the virtues of the Ukrainian immigrant enshrined in the peasant pioneer myth – courage, perseverance, industry, thrift, uncomplaining toil, silent suffering and sacrifice – were not particularly 'manly' virtues and corresponded more to the female than to the male pioneer stereotype. That this was so no doubt reflected similarities in status between women in general and ethnic groups like the Ukrainians.

Other female attributes were not reflected evenly across the prairies. As has been demonstrated, Ukrainians regarded their pioneer woman's labour on the land with pride, linking Ukrainian-Canadian women directly with their group's claim to nation building and its socioeconomic progress. Not all groups or communities, however, considered the pioneer woman's work outside her responsibilities for the house and children as an integral component of her image and legacy. The Finnish pioneer woman in Saskatchewan, for example, was commemorated as a homemaker – baking, cooking, ironing, cleaning, bearing and rearing children.[30] Compare this image with the farm woman's life told in pictures in a local history from the Ukrainian bloc in east-central Alberta. The women were shown at a feathering bee, tending poultry, picking mushrooms, gardening, milking, stooking, shovelling grain, preparing clay plaster, and applying the plaster to the building itself.[31] Norwegians also commemorated an essentially domestic and maternal figure; one local history was 'lovingly and respectfully' dedicated to pioneer mothers, self-denying women of strong faith 'who faced great hardships with courage and cheerfulness, who never spared themselves, nor asked for any reward.'[32] Such different mythic images did not necessarily mean that pioneer women from different ethnic groups performed different types of work – that labour on the land was indeed unique to Ukrainians. What they do indicate is that different historical experiences and needs affected how ethnic groups perceived both themselves and their women. For Ukrainians, the demands of legitimization and a 'progressive' self-image made gender irrelevant: women's contribution and role, in whatever form, was as significant and as exploitable as men's.

National-cultural function also varied. The Norwegian pioneer woman was not associated with passing on 'Norwegianness'; and although her Finnish counterpart was credited with teaching her children the Finnish language and Finnish history and songs, there was no sense that this role represented a specific responsibility or had an ulterior goal and special urgency. But the Ukrainian peasant immigrant pioneer woman was neither a female heroine unqualified nor a Canadian heroine unhyphenated. Whether as a community or a popular figure, she served her group's interests and needs in ways that went beyond affirming Ukrainian Canadians' birthright as westerners and Canadians. She also expressed two very different kinds of Ukrainianness in Canada: at the elite level, a politicized Ukrainian consciousness that was pan-Canadian in its message; at the grassroots level, a cultural ethnic consciousness that drew on the Ukrainian peasant heritage in western Canada. The interplay within the peasant immigrant pioneer woman of elite and popular definitions of the Ukrainian-Canadian identity revealed major tensions and divisions within her group. They in turn reflected, although imperfectly, the differences in composition and politicization that characterized the three waves of Ukrainian immigration to Canada, producing often antagonistic interpretations of group goals. How the peasant immigrant pioneer woman was used in the process to express Ukrainianness not only illuminated two incompatible perceptions of the Ukrainian-Canadian experience and identity. It also made two quite distinct statements concerning women's roles and responsibilities as Ukrainians.

The peasant immigrant pioneer as the official community heroine came to life in *Madonna of the Wheat*, one of two statues financed by the Ukrainian-Canadian community to be erected in front of the city hall in Edmonton. Such a prominent site acknowledged local Ukrainian political influence but sparked controversy about recognition for ethnic causes, and the statues' temporary removal in the spring of

Madonna of the Wheat, unveiled 1981. Presented to the city of Edmonton by the UWAC on Alberta's seventy-fifth anniversary, dedicated to all pioneer women of the province. Sculptor John Weaver

1990 during construction of a new city hall precipitated calls for relocation to an area reserved for things 'multicultural.' The second statue, sponsored by the Ukrainian Canadian Committee (UCC) to commemorate the fiftieth anniversary of the artificial famine of 1932–3 in Soviet Ukraine, attached Ukrainian Canadians firmly to the homeland. *Madonna of the Wheat* attached them just as firmly to Canada. Commissioned by the Ukrainian Women's Association of Canada (UWAC) and executed by John Weaver, she was dedicated to all pioneer women of Alberta on the occasion of the province's seventy-fifth anniversary in 1980 – to honour their labour, determination, sacrifices, and achievements.[33] In unveiling the statue, Martha Bielish (herself a member of the Ukrainian-Canadian pantheon of heroines as the first woman senator of Ukrainian origin) applauded its dedication to all pioneering women as a pioneering step itself – a deliberate attempt to transcend the self-imposed ghettoization often characterizing the Ukrainian community.[34] *Madonna of the Wheat* most obviously identified Ukrainian Canadians with their pioneer heritage in western Canada. But she also, it could be argued, identified the pioneer heritage of western Canadians generally with the specific Ukrainian experience.

It would be unwise to overstress the universality of *Madonna of the Wheat.* Young, slender, beautiful, her hair neatly coiled in braids, her eyes contemplating the distant horizon, she wore her 'Sunday best,' a Ukrainian embroidered blouse, and carried in her arms a sheaf of wheat, time-honoured Ukrainian symbol of life and unity with one's ancestors. She reflected the instructions of the women who financed her, unhappy with the portrayal of the Ukrainian pioneer woman by the noted Ukrainian-Canadian sculptor, Leo Mol, at the Alberta government's Ukrainian Cultural Heritage Village east of Edmonton.[35] Mol's figure was an unmistakable peasant – seated beside her man, eyes downcast, a swaddled child in her lap, her hair covered with the ubiquitous headshawl. *Madonna of the Wheat,* the Ukrainian-Canadian pioneer, was the idealized Ukrainian maiden, evoking the nation, who adorned the banknotes of the Ukrainian People's Republic of 1917–20 or symbolized the great heroines of Ukrainian history. She had, in fact, a predecessor, in Myron Levytsky's pioneer couple on the UCC plaque commemorating the sixtieth anniversary of Ukrainian settlement in Canada in 1951 unveiled in the Manitoba legislature building. Both man and woman were very much in the heroic mould, both were young, and the woman again cradled a sheaf of wheat.

It is unlikely such resemblances were accidental. Ukrainian-Canadian women had publicly tied the Ukrainian pioneer woman in Canada to the Great Women of Ukraine at the first national congress of the UCC in 1943. A spokesperson for the Ukrainian Women's Organization of Canada (UWOC), anxious to stress her association's Canadian loyalty in wartime, expanded its traditional list of models and inspirational figures to include the pioneer who had been 'greatly instrumental in the development of Canada' and 'reared her children to be good, respectable Canadian citizens.'[36] In 1945 the UWOC added 'those self-denying Ukrainian mothers-pioneers labouring painfully to secure a better life for the present generation' to its list of heroic Ukrainian women to be honoured on Mothers' Day. The next step came when

Pioneer Family, unveiled 1980, at the Ukrainian Cultural Heritage Village east of Edmonton. Sculptor Leo Mol

Olha Basarab was asked to share the spotlight with the pioneer woman in Canada during the annual February commemoration of Ukrainian heroines.[37] The war constituted a major turning-point in the UWOC's Canadianization – and a departure from its traditional emphasis on Ukraine, Ukrainianness, and the Ukrainian role of Ukrainian women in Canada. But too much should not be read into the Canadianism in its wartime utterances. The identification, by Ukrainian-Canadian women's organizations, of the pioneer woman in Canada with the Great Women of Ukraine was above all a Ukrainian statement.

Taking part in community celebrations marking the Ukrainian-Canadian diamond jubilee in 1951, the new immigrant, Olena Kysilewska, set the tone for the postwar flowering of this idea. Rather than

DEDICATED TO THE PIONEER UKRAINIAN SETTLERS
ON THE OCCASION OF THEIR SIXTIETH ANNIVERSARY
IN RECOGNITION OF THEIR CONTRIBUTION TO THE
DEVELOPMENT OF CANADA
SEPTEMBER, 1951   UKRAINIAN CANADIAN COMMITTEE

Plaque commemorating the sixtieth anniversary of Ukrainian settlement in Canada, Manitoba Legislative Building. Designer Myron Levytsky

tie the peasant pioneer to Canadian nation building, she praised her for her commitment to her language, faith, and cultural traditions.[38] That the UWOC, the UWAC, and the Ukrainian Catholic Women's

Woman in folk costume, carrying a sheaf of wheat, on banknote issued by the short-lived Ukrainian People's Republic, 1917–20

League (UCWL) all tied the pioneer woman to her Ukrainian forebears underscored the pervasiveness and persistence of the link as an important community image and point of identification for organized women. Their various spokespersons also made clear the ultimate Ukrainianness of its function. As the equal and legitimate successor of Princess Olha and her heirs, the Ukrainian-Canadian pioneer woman was part of the Ukrainian nation, serving its interests, defending its rights, and acting for the good of her people.

A few examples will illustrate. In 1981 the UWAC published a Mothers' Day article acknowledging 'the many Ukrainian mothers deserving deep love and respect.' In significant contrast to the interwar years, when only the homeland produced such women, it began with Princess Olha telling her warrior son to return victorious or die fighting for Ukraine and ended with the pioneer immigrant woman who had preserved the Ukrainian language and culture in Canada.[39] A contemporary UCWL editorial established a similar bond – between the mothers of captive Ukraine, struggling and suffering for their children, and Ukrainian pioneer mothers in Canada, whose strong faith and attachment to their homeland and traditions had laid the foundations of Ukrainian life and prosperity in emigration.[40] A second UWAC article left no doubt as to the implications of the connection for the Ukrainian mother in Canada. The 'living link between the dead and the unborn,' she was part of an unending continuum: 'She is the Ukrainian mother whose faith is stronger than death. She kept the torch of national life burning through the darkest hours of Ukrainian history. It is due to her love and devotion that the toil which already has been put into our Canadian life will not perish but continue to live as a vital contribution from the beautiful rich land of Ukraine.'[41] More specifically, through her pioneer grandmothers labouring to establish Ukrainian life in this country, the Ukrainian mother in Canada inherited centuries-old standards to uphold. She had to keep alive in her children, and through them her grandchildren, the Ukrainian consciousness and 'spark of freedom' which one day would unite with freedom-loving Ukrainians everywhere 'in the struggle for liberty and Ukraine's independence.'[42] Others inverted the obligations arising from the sisterhood of women in Ukraine and Canada: drawing on the recent as opposed to the distant past, a UCWL article asked its members to emulate the courage of the five hundred women martyred by Soviet tanks and protect the Ukrainian life their predecessors had built in their adopted homeland.[43] Still others used the Canadian experience as a metaphor, arguing that the idea of the prairie frontier, where the immigrant pioneer woman toiled, must be expanded by her successors to make the world the frontier of pioneering work on behalf of Ukraine.[44]

The role of the pioneer woman in the official mythology of nationalist women's organizations helps to explain the symbolic significance of her visual commemoration as the young woman. Dynamic and idealized, dressed in her 'Sunday best' and obvious Ukrainian costume, the pioneer woman was transformed into a timeless and unassailable Ukrainian patriot, deliberately preserving her language and culture in Canada and dedicating herself to Ukrainian causes. The physical link with Ukraine through immigration, the spiritual link with Ukraine through her sisterhood with the Great Women of Ukrainian history, she acted as a functional myth for her female successors. The pioneer woman was the source of values, principles, and guidelines for present and future generations of Ukrainian women in Canada; she defined them as Ukrainians; and she imposed on them an obligation as her Ukrainian heirs, both on behalf of the group and community in Canada and on behalf of the nation in Ukraine. By becoming herself one of the Great Women of Ukraine, 'domesticating' their legacy for

Ukrainian-Canadian women, the peasant pioneer also provided her successors with a more realistic model and source of inspiration than the likes of Zavisna, Ukrainka, or Basarab. She showed that ordinary women in the course of daily life could be heroic too.

Progressives' definition of the nation's rights and interests and the good of the people differed from that of the nationalists. So did their interpretation of the inspirational role of the Great Women of Ukraine, combining class with Ukrainian consciousness. It should therefore not be surprising that as organized progressive women developed a parallel mythology around the pioneer woman, important distinctions as well as similarities emerged. The woman in the official portrait commemorating the fiftieth anniversary of the women's branches of the Ukrainian Labour-Farmer Temple Association and the Association of United Ukrainian Canadians (AUUC) best symbolized the differences. She was not the Ukrainian of the nationalists, but neither was she the stereotypic revolutionary. Instead, a simply dressed but beautiful young peasant woman in profile sat at a table; her head was covered, her hands rested in her lap, and her eyes gazed serenely ahead.[45] Except for the absence of visible Ukrainization, it is difficult to read any political message in this gentle and idealized figure.

The most conspicuous progressive symbol of the relationship between the pioneer woman in Canada and her predecessors in Ukraine, although transcending gender in its tribute to all Ukrainian pioneers and builders of Canada, was the Lesia Ukrainka statue at the University of Saskatchewan in Saskatoon. Yet there were more direct expressions of the symbolic role the pioneer woman came to play in AUUC mythology as she tied her Ukrainian-Canadian successors to their forebears in Ukraine. The progressive historian, Peter Krawchuk, made explicit the first half of the continuum having the peasant pioneer as its pivot when he attributed the political consciousness and activities of Ukrainian pioneer women in Canada to the ideological influence of female socialist activists in Ukraine, especially Natalia Kobrynska.[46]

Others articulated the Canadian end of the continuum and pursued the implications for the peasant pioneers' female descendants. As among nationalists, Mothers' Day in AUUC circles evolved to pay homage to the pioneer, 'the Grannies ... who gave their youth away in toil and drudgery in order to make homes in Canada and to raise us': these women, too, were nation builders, breaking the land, rearing children, and making sacrifices for a better future.[47] Such an image was conclusive proof of the power of the peasant pioneer myth to cross

Official fiftieth-anniversary poster for women's branches of the ULFTA–AUUC, featuring commissioned painting by Jeanette Lodoen (1971)

ideological boundaries. Although prepared to question the politicized Ukrainianness of the peasant immigrant pioneer (contending that what she practised and passed on was natural and normal), progressives also credited her with maintaining Ukrainian identity among her children.[48] And AUUC women, like their nationalist counterparts, were urged to follow the footsteps of their pioneer mothers and themselves sought inspiration and guidance from their example. One woman remembered her mother's 'strong fervour and courage' in teaching her to read Ukrainian progressive literature, and the 'understanding and abiding faith' the older woman had found within the AUUC. The daughter hoped the memory would spur her to reach out to her own children so they would continue the tradition, 'working within the AUUC for the betterment of themselves and all Ukrainian Canadians.'[49] This image, in contrast to the all-inclusive peasant pioneer myth, identified the legacy of the pioneer woman with a single political camp.

The dual ideological role that the pioneer woman played for organized women reflected the fundamental and acrimonious division within the Ukrainian-Canadian community between supporters and opponents of the Soviet Ukrainian state. Her role was further splintered in that she was simultaneously the instrument and exclusive property, narrowly defined, of each of the women's organizations making up the two camps. The propaganda and programs of competing political and religious factions defined the precise content of the traditions and values the pioneer women was held to have practised and perpetuated in her children. Her exclusivity was apparent in the literature extolling her virtues as a mother and homemaker, both in the form her Ukrainianness took and in her supplementary attributes (Catholicism or class consciousness, for example). Her exclusivity became even more apparent in her image as successor to Princess Olha, the public figure. For the pioneer woman participated in and contributed to Ukrainian community life through her organizational affiliation. The official AUUC eulogy to the pioneer woman on the occasion of the seventy-fifth anniversary of Ukrainian settlement in Canada in 1966, for example, ultimately saw her as a progressive activist, helping her husband 'to build an articulate Ukrainian-Canadian community that has become a force for peace and progress in Canada.'[50] Being tied to a specific organization meant that the pioneer woman's role as a generalized figure representing a particular ideological or religious camp was to a large extent pre-empted by her identification with individual 'Great Women' who founded, led, and built their organizations locally and across Canada. The naming of the Kelowna branch of the UWAC after Savella Stechishin symbolized the official equality of these women with Princess Olha, Olha Basarab, Olena Kysilewska, and other Ukrainian heroines chosen as local patronesses.[51]

Examples of individualization are found at a humble level in newspaper obituary columns and the family biography sections of local histories. The 1937 obituary of Comrade Kalyna Humen, an Alberta homesteader, paid tribute to the progressive mother: although the seventy-three-year-old had not herself been active in the ULFTA, she had both witnessed and experienced capitalist exploitation, and her children were members.[52] When she died in 1935, seventy-eight-year-old Maria Svarich of Edmonton was remembered in what would become a familiar formula in nationalist circles as 'an exemplary mother and homemaker, a member of her community, an active patriot and a generous donor.'[53] While ordinary women received their moments of glory, greater things awaited the high-profile Anna Yonker, who died in 1936 at the young age of forty-five. Eulogized at her funeral as a 'builder of this new Canadian nation' rich in its variety of peoples and cultures, and acclaimed as 'an exemplary Canadian citizen and an incomparable Ukrainian patriot,'[54] she came to symbolize to nationalist women the ideal community servant. In later years, regardless of the prominence of their subjects, obituaries would add the professional status and community activities of a deceased's children to the list of accomplishments that bespoke the woman's worthiness as both a Ukrainian and a mother.

At the more structured level, examples of individualization appear in anniversary collections of female biography like *Zhinochi doli* (Women's fates), honouring women in the progressive movement on the occasion of their golden jubilee in 1972. Subsequently republished in English translation, the book included humble workers and organizational cadres, the unsung heroines of the kitchen and fund drives, as well as more high-profile activists.[55] Examples also appear in jubilee books where organizations specifically acknowledged their 'Great Women,'[56] and in feature articles on prominent women that dotted the pages of the women's press.[57] These individuals changed the meaning of 'pioneers' from its original association with prairie settlement and peasant immigrants. Not only were they primarily organizational figures, but they represented the first Canadian-born or -raised as well as the immigrant generation. The extent to which such women will continue to be recognizable names, in order to be meaningful models and sources of inspiration for an organization's members or the women it hopes to attract, is uncertain. Trends in the 1970s and 1980s, with aging and declining memberships, suggest that as a functional myth embodying politicized Ukrainianness the pioneer woman appealed to a limited and shrinking audience.

With one partial but significant exception, the peasant was lost in official community myth and commemoration. The exception was William Kurelek's series of paintings, unveiled in 1968, depicting the experience of Ukrainian pioneer women in western Canada. The series was originally commissioned by the executive of the UWAC for Canada's Centennial in 1967, but the executive, in Kurelek's words, 'unfortunately ... failed to communicate their vision and enthusiasm to the rank-and-file members of their group.'[58] The twelve paintings the UWAC eventually bought, forming part of its collection at the Ukrainian Museum of Canada in Saskatoon, were mostly those with distinctly Ukrainian national-cultural themes and related to women's organizational work.[59] Inspired by the virtues of Kurelek's own mother, the twenty-piece exhibit opened with scenes of Ukrainian women on the Cossack settlement frontier and concluded with baba surrounded by her grandchildren in a prosperous modern home. The intervening panels showed the pioneer woman in her various guises: at work on the homestead, at leisure at a rural Sunday picnic, as a member of her community at a UWAC organizational meeting, as a mother teaching her son to read Ukrainian and her daughter to do Ukrainian embroidery. Commenting on *The First Meeting of the Ukrainian Women's Association in Saskatchewan*, Canadian historian Ramsay Cook contended that it 'reveal[ed] a great deal about prairie history,' specifically 'the country school with its inadequate stove, and the women gathered to form an organization to break down the isolation around them and to protect the community from powers outside.'[60] What this analysis missed is that the pictures were as Ukrainian in their Canadian content as they were Canadian in their Ukrainian content. The Ukrainian hall and not the alien school was the women's gathering place, the portraits on the wall were of Lesia Ukrainka and Olha Kobylianska not King George V, and the sense of Ukrainian community that lay behind the founding of the UWAC insisted on contact with outside groups.

The optimism and fulfilment of Kurelek's final panel, *Material Success*, was tempered by an unnoticed atomic blast visible through the

Mother Teaching Her Son to Read Ukrainian (1973), by William Kurelek. A
similar painting from Kurelek's 1968 series on the Ukrainian-Canadian
pioneer woman forms part of the collection of the Ukrainian Museum of
Canada in Saskatoon.

window, an ultimate challenge to the progress theme dear to the UWAC.
Nor was Kurelek's pioneer woman – sturdy and kerchiefed, although
without the submissiveness of Mol's figure in the *Pioneer Family* group
– a *Madonna of the Wheat*. While faulting Kurelek for not showing
Ukrainian-Canadian women involved in social struggles, the AUUC in
the only review of opening night in the community press gave the
exhibit grudging approval:

The artist told his audience of a brief period of his youth in Winnipeg when he had been a devoted nationalist. At that time he pictured Ukrainian womanhood as richly dressed in costume, standing on the ramparts, urging the liberators of his homeland on to battle.

That conception he has abandoned it seems, in favour of a more realistic picture. He shows us instead a plain, almost ugly woman, hardened by hardships and life itself.[61]

The peasant that Kurelek commemorated during her prime – both as a repository of Ukrainian culture and as a homesteader on the land – was fully resurrected at the popular level. In this transition from the Ukrainized patriot of community propaganda to the peasant of the grassroots, the turn-of-the-century pioneer woman underwent a significant aging process. Moreover, as baba or the old woman, she was able, unlike her politicized double, to transcend ideological and religious cleavages and act as a common group symbol.

To Ukrainian Canadians with western peasant pioneer roots, baba served both a private and a public function. She evoked an intensely personal image, of their immigrant grandmothers in the days of prairie settlement; she also expressed a collective ethnic consciousness that drew on their peasant pioneer cultural heritage. She was important to her descendants because she defined who they were and where they came from, as individuals and as members of a larger group. In the process, the popular meaning of the word 'baba' itself changed. Although the revered pioneer grandmother embodied traits identified with peasantness, all negative connotations from the peasant's own use of 'baba' to belittle and express contempt for women were gone completely. Baba might still be a peasant but she was equally a beloved figure. This is most easily demonstrated by the contemporary folk artists, predominantly women, who gave her physical form. Whether a Christmas tree ornament marketed as a 'Baba bell,' a figurine made of *papier maché*, or a Raggedy Ann-type doll, baba was recognizable by her plumpness, her voluminous skirts, and her trademark headscarf.[62] The contrast she made with the North American stereotype of the grandmother as feminine and homey was all the more marked for the exception to the popular consensus. The exception was baba's 'Canadianization' on mass-produced ceramic cookie jars, although the bespectacled, aproned, and cherubic grandmother had been Ukrainized (like the Mother of God) with red-and-black embroidery.

Baba did not conform to the stereotype of the Ukrainian peasant

Christmas tree ornament. The accompanying card reads: 'Baba bell – a little lady reminiscent of a Ukrainian grandmother.' Creator Sandi Skakun

woman as submissive and downtrodden. She was more in the tradition of Nasha Meri and Katie. A strong personality, highly individualistic, and with a touch of the eccentric, baba displayed the wit and character of the old peasant woman of Ukrainian folktales.[63] As 'Baba Podkova,' the creation of writer Maara Haas, she kept her dead husband's gall stones in a pickle jar in the kitchen; she felt mildly superior to the people of River Heights, Winnipeg, who grew grass simply to cut it and watch it grow again; and she used the onion skins in their first

Baba figurine (*papier maché*) extending the traditional welcome of bread and salt

editions to roll her cigarettes.[64] Baba drank beer and raised chickens in downtown Winnipeg.[65] She also dwarfed her social-climbing daughter, ashamed of the green-roses kerchief and black felt boots worn to tea in the River Heights mansion.[66] In this respect, Haas's tale was as much about the attitude of a status-conscious and assimilationist second generation as it was about Baba Podkova and her irrepressibility despite external demands for change. Although her peasant attributes and habits aroused disfavour in Canadian society and rankled the ambitious among her own people, baba possessed an inviolable dignity and sense of herself. As one of 'Hell's Babushkas,' madly pedalling her tricycle, her kerchief flying in the wind, she could adorn a mass-

Ceramic cookie jar from mass-produced mould, reflecting mainstream consensus of the 'grandmotherly grandmother,' Ukrainized with red-and-black embroidery and named after baba

produced lapel button in a parody of the infamous motorcycle gang without being diminished in any way.[67]

Contrary to the accusations hurled at her in her youth by the pioneer intelligentsia, baba did not cower like a mouse in its hole or hide behind closed doors.[68] If the peasant immigrant woman had been solely the ignorant and apathetic creature the embryonic Ukrainian community leadership sought to take in hand, or the domestic drudge and beast of burden early twentieth-century Anglo-Canadians saw, she could only with great difficulty have blossomed into the self-composed, opinionated, and slightly irreverent baba of later years. The earthy and humourous peasant had little place in official community circles concerned with national heroines, social mobility, and a pleasing view of the past. But as a grassroots phenomenon, in endearing traits once branded as foreign and inferior, even unwomanly, baba testified to a generation sufficiently secure in itself and its Canadianness not to be ashamed of its peasant origins. She also intimated that despite unde-

Baba the eccentric, in a parody of Hell's Angels, on a lapel button.
Designer Gee Bee Buttons of Saskatoon

niable male dominance in the Ukrainian peasant family and community, the peasant immigrant pioneer woman was by no means a passive
bystander in her life. Moreover, she and not her male counterpart
emerged as the dominant figure from their period and generation.
When he chose *Was That Your Baba's Coat?* as the title for his 1978
painting of the peasants' once-despised and now discarded sheepskin,
artist Peter Shostak was making a political statement in more ways
than one. Deliberately repudiating the prevailing imagery of '*men* in
sheepskin coats,' he defined the Ukrainian immigrant experience in
female terms.

'In Search of Multicultural Woman,' Maara Haas's guest editorial
in a special issue of *Canadian Woman Studies* devoted to questions of
ethnicity, illustrates the power of baba's appeal at the personal level.
Haas rejected an each-to-her-own definition of multiculturalism, while
criticizing Canada's propensity for labels and the inequalities and assimilatory pressures it represented. She also returned to the Baba
Podkova theme, with a possessiveness that belied the generous sharing
of cultures her definition of multiculturalism implied. Woven into the

discussion of her own confusion growing up in the 1930s with a hyphenated identity was a restaurant scene in the 1980s as Haas and her friend, Rochelle La Roche, met for dinner. Rochelle came dressed as Baba Podkova. As they relaxed, Haas involuntarily exclaimed, 'What I can't explain is why I'm so furious with Rochelle La Roche in her Paris version of a Ukrainian immigrant.'[69] Baba, in other words, was not for outsiders to share or adopt or alter.

As both a private and a public symbol, baba represented to her descendants not only their Canadian birthright and western Canadian pioneer heritage, for in this the male easily equalled her. She also expressed their heritage as Ukrainians. Research into the meaning of 'Ukrainianness' in late twentieth-century Canada highlighted the unimportance of formal institutions and language, long hailed by community spokespersons as the key to meaningful group survival. Rather, selected primary synoptic symbols from the peasants' world constituted the essence of Ukrainian Canadians' Ukrainian identity. Enjoying the greatest staying power as best reflecting the unique shared experience of the group and most successfully bridging past and present were things like food, embroidery, and Easter eggs – things visible and tangible. So closely identified with the family while uniting its members in a larger communion, food formed a particularly significant bond and aspect of Ukrainianness.[70] Another popular expression of Ukrainian-Canadian identity, folk dance (now taught by professional instructors) was similarly nonverbal and recreational; but while foods and handicrafts were often private and personal in their execution and enjoyment, dance was a public and social activity.[71] All such symbols, however, were politically innocuous and in themselves largely valueless, compatible with an apparently satisfactory definition of multiculturalism as a showcase of Canadians' cultural heritages. In the dominance of a cultural ethnicity over a politicized national consciousness as the core of Ukrainian-Canadian identity, baba's role went beyond playing the peasant.

Although she was not portrayed as particularly feminine, baba overshadowed *dido*, the old man or grandfather, as an ethnocultural symbol because of the 'female' tasks she performed and the 'female' attributes she possessed. The major postwar symbols of Ukrainian-Canadian identity represented work historically done by women. This was true of the gigantic metal *pysanka* or Easter egg erected in Vegreville, Alberta, to mark that quintessential Canadian event, the one hundredth anniversary of the Royal Canadian Mounted Police. It was true of the

The mainstream view. Photograph accompanying a feature article on Ukrainian Christmas in the *Edmonton Journal* (31 December 1986), with women from the UWAC displaying the traditional twelve meatless dishes

controversial giant fibre-glass-and-steel 'perogy' and fork erected as a tourist attraction by the northern Alberta town of Glendon in tribute to the Ukrainian Canadian Centennial in 1991. It was true of the Christmas Eve supper of twelve dishes eaten by Ukrainian Canadians as much as an ethnic as a religious statement and acknowledged as such in the mainstream press.[72] In other words, baba's prominence rested on traditional socially prescribed female functions that bore directly on popular conceptions and expressions of Ukrainian-Canadian identity.

But if gender dictated baba's role as a group symbol, that role meant rejection of narrow identification with her sex – despite her potential to be a model of female strength and individualism for late twentieth-century Ukrainian-Canadian feminists. Without being able to measure the extent to which such a legacy consciously or unconsciously influenced baba's evolution as a popular symbol, it would not be amiss to suggest that it had an impact. American studies have shown how ethnic

Pencil drawing by Julian Sadlowski, *A Tribute to Baba* (1979), in the
Ukrainian Senior Citizens' Centre in North Battleford, Saskatchewan

feminists in the United States ressurected, as models and sources of
inspiration, the strong women from their immigrant past.[73] There is
little doubt that a similar image of the Ukrainian pioneer woman in
Canada influenced Ukrainian-Canadian feminist and journalist Myrna
Kostash in her 1976 article, 'Baba Was a Bohunk,' and her subsequent
book, *All of Baba's Children* – both in the choice of imagery and portrayal of the pioneer woman, and in the decision to frame the Ukrainian-Canadian experience in female terms. Regardless of baba's
identification with her sex through feminist politics, and in contrast
to the official community heroine, any Ukrainian obligation her female function imposed on her female heirs was strictly implicit, voluntary, and incidental.

   Just as baba and the official community pioneer shared participation
in Canadian nation building, so they shared traits as the guardians of

customs and creators of cultural artifacts identified with Ukrainian-ness, especially food preparation and handicrafts, both activities traditionally associated with their sex. In an interwar play, for example, the old woman was the source of collective memory, the transmitter of Ukrainianness expressed through time-honoured ritual and custom, as she described Ukrainian Christmas traditions to her grandchildren on a Canadian farm.[74] Unlike baba, the community heroine was portrayed as a paragon of Ukrainian national consciousness in the aggressive preservation and execution of her tradition and art. At Easter, her female successors decorated elaborate eggs while wearing fancy, intricately embroidered Ukrainian costumes; at Christmas, they tied blue-and-yellow ribbons, the colours of the defeated Ukrainian People's Republic, around the sprig of wheat that replaced the traditional *didukh* with its pagan agricultural roots and ancestral associations.[75] Their actions were deliberate, formalized, ritualistic, and political. Baba's tradition and art were also used to make a definite Ukrainian statement. Julian Sadlowski's drawing, *Painting Easter Eggs* (1987), featured a gnarled old woman in her kerchief and Ukrainian blouse in front of a *rushnyk*-draped icon of the Madonna and Child. In a second drawing, *A Tribute to Baba* (1979), hanging in the Ukrainian senior citizens' hall in North Battleford, Saskatchewan, baba became herself an icon. Again kerchiefed and in her Ukrainian blouse, she was surrounded by the visible symbols of Ukrainianness (a loaf of braided bread and an Easter egg) and wore a halo. In Mary Nagy's painting, *What Baba Taught Me*, housed in the Ukrainian Museum of Canada in Saskatoon, the ordinary old woman dressed in black and working on an Easter egg was not the overtly Ukrainized woman of Sadlowski's drawings, but the underlying message was the same.

However, baba's mandate was ultimately more modest and her Ukrainianness more humble. Her descendants associated her above all with food, and she in turn was the figure most associated with food. A pioneer in the large-scale production and marketing of Ukrainian dumplings or *pyrohy*, their products sold to mainstream consumers in the 'perogies' section of the frozen food departments of western Canadian supermarkets, the Edmonton-based Cheemos Perogies[76] was a business venture of the progressive community. Its packaging showed a young woman in Ukrainian costume extending a plate of dumplings on an embroidered *rushnyk* in imitation of the traditional Ukrainian welcome greeting of bread and salt. It was much more usual to find baba in such a context. Baba, too, was used to market *pyrohy*; she was put on mass-produced teeshirts to advertise 'Baba's Borscht Soup'; she had *Baba's Cook Book*, a national best seller, attributed to her genius;[77] and she served as the inspiration for restaurants and fast-food outlets. In the 1970s and 1980s Edmonton alone was home to Baba's Village, Baba's Ukrainian Food, Baba's Best Ukrainian Food, and Granny's Perogies; in the l980s residents of the rural community of Buchanan, Saskatchewan, bought their bread at Baba's Bakery. Only one restaurant, in Regina, was named after *dido*.

Such gestures acknowledged women's central role in food's creation and ritual and baba's function as an ethnic group symbol. They also reinforced food's enduring centrality to popular Ukrainian-Canadian identity. During the Second World War, visitors to the Ukrainian Canadian Servicemen's Association club in London, England, saw the food as the highlight of their stay. 'Was in my glory last night,' wrote one man on leave, 'when I enjoyed my first plate of "perohe" since leaving Canada last year.' His buddy was equally appreciative: 'Just like mother used to make 'em long ago.'[78] Ukrainian peasant food, especially in western Canada, shed its turn-of-the-century reputation as unappetizing and unwholesome and moved outside the group, to be enjoyed by the mainstream and dominating its popular image of 'Ukrainian.' Eating is at once an ethnic, a family, and a social activity. It draws attention to the kitchen with the woman as its pivot, and from there again to the larger question of women's position in Ukrainian peasant immigrant pioneer society and family life.

'When I paraphrase a tough Ukrainian *baba* I've heard back home,' Ukrainian-Canadian poet Andrew Suknaski replied when asked if ethnic groups risked fossilizing or caricaturing their heritage and group experience, 'she speaks in a dialect':

> Maybe she's a bit monstrous in some way, but I don't feel that I am detracting from her dignity in doing this. I'm being true to the reality and I'm pointing something out, that is, that *baba* demythologizes our long-standing belief that the man is the head of the household in those days. In fact, *baba* was the god and the head of the household.[79]

Suknaski's comment should not be lightly dismissed. The role baba played in the popular consciousness, both as the group figure through which Ukrainian Canadians perceived and interpreted their heritage and as an intensely personal image, suggested that in important ways

The *Edmonton Journal* (3 April 1985) celebrates Ukrainian Easter with baba and her freshly baked *paska*.

he was right. Baba (and not *dido*) was the god and head of the household – perhaps not in the absolute distribution of power or authority or wealth, but as the emotional mainstay and focus of the family, dominant in the domestic circle, and the individual most associated with stability, continuity and human warmth. With a novelist's licence

Teeshirt playing on the familiar Campbell soup label attests to baba's popular association with food.

and an outsider's perspective, Gabrielle Roy hinted at this role in her contrasting portraits of old Marta and Stepan, her husband. The one had an inner calm, quiet strength, spiritual richness, and her garden; the other was beaten, bitter, complaining, helplessly furious that despite life's blows his wife should continue to water her flowers.[80]

'Female' nurturing qualities and roles, the product of gender stereotyping and divisions of labour, made Ukrainian peasant immigrant pioneer women major emotive forces and points of identification within the family unit. In the biography sections of local prairie histories they were remembered as the source of emotional life and companionship for their pioneer families, the source of warm memories for their

Baba's Best, a fast-food stand in Kingsway Garden Mall, Edmonton, one of several eating establishments in the city during the 1970s and 1980s to be named after baba

descendants. There were two additional factors in baba's emergence as a figure of dominance and strength: the distinct likelihood that Nasha Meri and Katie's spunk represented not something alien but a trait within the peasant immigrant herself, and the impact of periodic male absence from the Ukrainian homestead as the shortage of cash forced men to seek temporary outside employment. In the southern Italian village of his interwar political exile, Carlo Levi observed female assertiveness in the wake of a mass male exodus to America, coupled with tensions between husbands and wives when the returning sojourners sought to reimpose their authority.[81] While there is no concrete evidence that similar experiences with separation challenged traditional gender roles and authority relationships among Ukrainian immigrants in Canada, the possibility cannot be ignored. The fact that women generally outlive men could also explain why baba overshadowed *dido* in the consciousness of their joint descendants within individual families. As an overall explanation, however, it is unsatisfactory: the preponderance of males in the first two Ukrainian immigrations to Canada left the peasant immigrant pioneer woman a minority both in her youth and in her old age.[82]

There may also be deeper roots for baba's evolution as a mythic figure among Ukrainians in Canada. A recent study of the feminine myth in what its author described as 'Russian' culture (some of her evidence came from Ukraine or Ukrainian sources) suggests interesting parallels. Beginning with the pagan goddess, it explored the persistence, at elite and popular levels, of an earth mother theme – in folklore, literature, the peasant village, and the contemporary Soviet Union, where a literary baba embodying the motherland coexisted with the real peasant baba (or *babushka*) who cared for her grandchildren.[83] Canadian sources from the period of settlement, all the more valuable because their authors were unencumbered by any knowledge of Ukrainian cultural icons or myths and made their observations solely on the basis of what they saw, indicate that the grandmother figure had more than simply symbolic significance for the peasant pioneers' descendants. They suggest that the old woman occupied a special place in Ukrainian peasant immigrant society itself, and that an immigrant baba played an influential role in childrearing.

In fact, baba made her official debut in 1914 when Miriam Elston's 'Baba Petruchevich: The Patriotism of an Adopted Daughter' won first prize in the *Edmonton Journal*'s annual short-story contest. Like many of Elston's vignettes, the tale emphasized the uplifting and saviour role of young Anglo-Canadian women serving in the Ukrainian colony east of Edmonton, as the superior medical knowledge of the new teacher saved baba's grandson from certain death. But it went beyond a confirmation of contemporary prejudices. The teacher's grief at her brother's departure for war 'dwindled into nothingness' and her original cold indifference to baba was transformed into 'an almost reverential esteem' as she realized the woman's 'infinitely greater sacrifice of giving her Canadian son to fight the son who remained in Austria. As baba saw it, she was repaying the country that had blessed her and hers with freedom, security and justice.'[84] Elston's heroine was simultaneously a symbol of assimilation to Anglo-Canadian values, an example (in a reversal of roles) of patriotic courage and sacrifice for her Anglo-Canadian 'better,' and proof of the common humanity and sisterhood under the sheepskin and headshawl.

Baba's appearance at this early date, through the pen of a non-Ukrainian and in a context where a mother figure is more usual, shows that the grandmother's importance to childrearing in Ukrainian peasant immigrant pioneer families was common enough for her to supplant the mother in an outsider's mind. She also reveals the existence, at the time of first settlement, of a popular Ukrainian consensus of a baba image, sufficiently strong to influence an outsider's word choice (without translation) and Ukrainian typecasting. Baba also figured prominently in another Elston story, where again Anglo-Canadian superiority over peasant ignorance and resistance saved a sick child; this time, however, she did not usurp the mother's role, functioning instead as the 'good angel' of the Ukrainian colony, as its do-gooder and healer.[85] Baba, the peasant immigrant who was already an old woman in 1914, did not enter the Anglo-Canadian consciousness or English vocabulary in the wake of Elston's literary efforts; and she was not the same baba, the ethnic group symbol, popularized by subsequent generations of Ukrainian Canadians in the prairie provinces. Nevertheless, the two were related: the role of the grandmother in Ukrainian peasant immigrant culture, especially in childcare as part of an extended family, provided a precedent and rationale for baba.

In Maria Campbell's moving autobiography *Halfbreed* (1973), it was her Cree great-grandmother who reconciled her with her native heritage in a process of self-discovery.[86] That the grandmother-grandchild relationship acted in a similar fashion in making baba the figure with which Ukrainian Canadians identified is illustrated by the 1979 play *After Baba's Funeral*, by Ukrainian-Canadian playwright Ted Galay.[87] It was also a clear statement that baba functioned as an ethnic group symbol, of Ukrainianness transmitted and interpreted through the cultural baggage of the early twentieth-century peasant immigrant. The play featured Ronnie Danischuk, a doctoral student in mathematics in his late twenties, who returned to his home town in rural Manitoba for baba's funeral and, while there, came to terms with his hyphenated identity. Baba and the contents of her immigrant's trunk were the vehicle. When the family pulled out her old *valyanky* (felt boots), Ronnie remembered why as a young boy he had fought with a visiting cousin and refused to stay with his grandmother:

> That's why I wouldn't stay at Baba's. He laughed at her. He said she dressed funny, she talked funny. He even said she smelled funny ... So I wouldn't play with him. But I was ashamed and when Baba tried to hug me, I pushed her away and I wouldn't go to her. Because she did smell funny. And she was wearing *valyanky*. Then I wanted to tell her I was sorry but never did.[88]

In the final moment of the play, Ronnie asked for the boots. *Tsymbaly*, another Galay play, called upon a host of symbols from the Ukrainian peasant immigrant heritage (of which baba's handful of Ukrainian earth and the *pich* or outdoor oven were the most important) as Nickie Stefanyk, the successful professional, came to terms with his roots and himself as part of a continuum. A review of the 1986 Manitoba Theatre Centre production described the 'impossibly old Baba' as a 'granite rock at the centre of Tsymbaly's mythopoeic universe.' While insisting on the universality of the play's message and emotional appeal, the reviewer remarked on the sentimental involvement of the Ukrainian members of the audience, singing with the actors to urge Nickie to acknowledge his people and his past.[89]

The role the peasant immigrant pioneer woman played in collective myth, at both organized and popular levels, most obviously commented on the relationship between Ukrainian-Canadian women and the Ukrainian-Canadian group. The relationship revealed women's centrality to Ukrainian Canadians' self-image and goals, although the involuntary and obligatory legacy of the pioneer woman as the official community heroine was missing in baba.

The official community heroine constructed on the Ukrainian pioneer woman, who acted as a functional model for her female successors as the Ukrainian group constantly renewed itself, was a logical evolution from the Canadianization of Princess Olha and the Cossack Mother. But she was overshadowed by baba, an essentially nostalgic figure mired in her peasant immigrant pioneer origins, who could be neither recreated nor perpetuated. As a grassroots phenomenon, baba marked the victory of a cultural ethnic consciousness (whose symbols the elite nevertheless shared) erected on foods and selected handicrafts as the essence of Ukrainian-Canadian identity. The loser was a politicized national consciousness, in which language and religion were the principal underpinnings of a viable, distinctive, and self-perpetuating Ukrainian-Canadian community that had group survival and aid to Ukraine as its goal. In either case, with the important but only partial exception of food, visible expressions of 'being Ukrainian' were overwhelmingly self-conscious, symbolic, ceremonial, and stylized. They had lost the unconscious spontaneity and universality they enjoyed as an integral and natural part of daily life in the early years of Ukrainian settlement in Canada.

Baba symbolized not her sex or her family but the specific unrepeatable experience of her people. She legitimized, as did the Ukrainian male pioneer, Ukrainian Canadians' sense of their place and role in Canadian nation building, as founding peoples of western Canada; and she embodied the essence of their Ukrainian peasant heritage. She deserved respect and admiration, but she represented what had been, not what was or should be. Her spiritual strength, courage, individuality, and perseverance could be evoked to inspire her Canadian descendants, including Ukrainian-Canadian feminists. Her cruder peasant and 'unprogressive' traits (the *babushka* or headscarf, the eccentricity) had to die with her, and baba suffered accordingly from both fossilization and caricature. Much of the nostalgia in the Ukrainian peasant pioneer myth and in Ukrainian Canadians' attachment to their heritage was for what they no longer wanted, concerned as they were with upward mobility and full participation in Canadian society. Although annually trotted out for display and demonstration at popular summer festivals like those in Vegreville and Dauphin, the agricultural and domestic practices and artifacts of Ukrainian peasant immigrant life had by the 1970s been banished to the museum. Baba the frozen timepiece was the inevitable product of progress and large-scale assimilation, as was the cultural Ukrainianness, apolitical and inoffensive, she symbolized. Early community leaders would have felt themselves vindicated for criticizing the ignorance and apathy of the peasant immigrant and her daughters as obstacles to the national consciousness of subsequent generations of Ukrainian Canadians.

Conclusion:
Baba Meets the Queen

In that being female and Ukrainian long prejudiced the mobility of Ukrainian-Canadian women in Canadian society, ethnicity was not willingly chosen or understood to be a positive aspect of their identity. Although they could and did manoeuvre within its limits, it reflected external factors impinging upon women because of their sex and Ukrainian origins and beyond their control: Ukrainians' immigrant entrance status, the position of women in traditional Ukrainian peasant society, the nativism shared by Anglo-Canadian men and women alike, and Canadian attitudes to women's roles in both public and private spheres. Being female and Ukrainian also resulted in group-imposed behaviour models and obligations that tied Ukrainian-Canadian women to Ukraine and emphasized their membership in the Ukrainian nation. In this instance, although women could chose whether to make it part of their identity, ethnicity was presumed to be involuntary – by a community that insisted that the predicament of twentieth-century Ukraine imposed special obligations on Ukrainian Canadians and gave them special needs. Women's traditional 'female' functions of mothering and homemaking became magnified and carried special Ukrainian nuances; so did the community work, for the most part an extension of their domestic roles, that their group's circumstances were said to require. Women also acquired additional functions as group symbols, in which femaleness was often secondary to Ukrainianness and elite perspectives were divorced from those of the popular consciousness.

Had the starting point for this study been the Ukrainian-Canadian woman's female condition instead of the nation and ethnic group to which she belonged, an entirely different book would have resulted.

How a particular work approaches the subject of ethnic women inclines it more towards 'women's' or 'ethnic' history. Should the primary concern be the impact of ethnicity as a third, often negative variable (the other two being class and gender) affecting women's position in society, the female experience and the reality of women's lives dominate the discussion. When the primary concern is the ethnic group, as a national-cultural collectivity that may or may not occupy an unwanted position in an ethnic socioeconomic hierarchy, its perspective is more important. Female images, roles, and myths as cultivated and defined by the group – at both elite and grassroots levels, by both men and women – constitute the focus. They reflect the group's priorities and concerns, and not women's, although many women identify with the group and therefore either endorse or help to create female images, roles, and myths. While the reality of women's lives, together with the reactions of ordinary women to expectations for their sex, are vital to the success or failure of group agenda, they neither dictate that agenda nor define women's relationship to it.

At issue in the case of Ukrainians in Canada was the effect of statelessness and national oppression in the homeland, coupled with low status and a negative stereotype in the new country, on perceptions of women and thus the place assigned to them in the collective experience and consciousness. Central to the study were the attitudes of spokespersons for the organized nationalist community, united by a common Ukrainianness but divided religiously and ideologically to reflect different approaches to Ukraine and Ukrainian ethnicity in Canada. How a female leadership elite, as part of this Ukrainian community, saw its sex, was crucial, as was the nature of the activities undertaken by women for whom their group and its needs took precedence. A secondary thread drew on the propaganda and programs of the pro-communist, pro-Soviet progressive minority. The primacy of the class struggle and the victory of socialism in their homeland simultaneously attached less importance to women's responsibilities as Ukrainians and provided them with an ethnic identity that incorporated both class exploitation and class consciousness.

Women first mobilized on a large scale between the wars, after more than thirty years in Canada, during which time a new 'Canadian' generation of young women slowly replaced its peasant immigrant mothers and a female leadership elite began to organize its sex within community structures. The interwar years also brought a second immigrant wave politicized by the tumultuous events of the Ukrainian

Revolution, which further stimulated the organization of women and further contributed to their factionalization. Out of this period came a definition of women's roles as Ukrainians, in both public and private spheres, that would persist into the postwar era and often transcend organizational differences. 'Being Ukrainian' meant commitment to the cause of an independent and united Ukrainian state in Europe and to linguistic and cultural survival in Canada. It meant mothers rearing their children in a proper Ukrainian spirit, and homemakers providing their families with the proper Ukrainian atmosphere and physical surroundings. It meant community activists who publicized the plight of their homeland in non-Ukrainian circles, raised funds for community projects, taught Sunday school and *ridna shkola*, suppported their church, and preserved the folk arts and traditions that expressed their people's Ukrainian identity. 'Being Ukrainian' also meant the obligation to follow in the footsteps of the Great Women of Ukraine, who acted as models and sources of inspiration and bound Ukrainian women together in a sisterhood that stretched across the ocean and over the centuries.

The second preoccupation of nationalist activists and spokespersons, beginning with the pioneer intelligentsia, was their group's acceptance and status in Canada. Nationalists' understanding of the Canadian mosaic or multiculturalism did not entail the desire to maintain values counterproductive to upward mobility, or to support a way of life that would preclude or conflict with full participation in Canadian society. As a result, they made virtues of socioeonomic progress and education, encouraging women as well as men to 'become Canadian' and take full advantage of Canada's opportunities to leave a peasant lifestyle behind. Grassroots sentiment endorsed this view; the image of baba the peasant popularized by the descendants of the peasant pioneers marked the end of an era that was to be celebrated but not regretted, even if the cultural ethnic consciousness and Canadian roots she represented defined them in the present. Women who achieved prominence in mainstream society as 'successful' Canadians also became group symbols, albeit more deliberately cultivated, where their sex was irrelevant: their individual achievement reflected positively on Ukrainian Canadians as a whole and was proof of upward mobility and integration. Overlooked were the contradictions between encouraging women to pursue higher education and applauding their career successes and the goal of women's traditional maternal, domestic, and cultural roles on which group survival and Ukrainian identity were presumed to depend. Regardless of the assimilative pressures of Canadian society, both deliberate and unconscious, that alienated many women from Ukrainian community objectives, the nationalist agenda itself would have strained women's ability to fulfil what was declared to be their primary function.

The visible Ukrainianness that baba represented was also built into the nationalist agenda. A group that wished to integrate into a new society of which it perceived itself to be a co-builder, while retaining its national-cultural identity, could not permit the range and extremes of the mother society with respect to its distinctiveness. As 'being Ukrainian' was not to embrace a lifestyle that isolated Ukrainians from other Canadians, the boundaries of legitimate and identifiable Ukrainian behaviour were immediately and automatically narrowed from what they were in Ukraine. There, despite the deliberate cultural and political statements of Ukrainianness that Polonization, Russification, and Sovietization evoked and necessitated, an individual's entire life – walking down the street, choosing a career, having a baby – was part of naturally and unconsciously 'being Ukrainian.' In Canada, outside the framework of the church and Ukrainians' political organizations, 'being Ukrainian' had to become a deliberate statement built around easily recognized, formal, ritualistic, and homogeneous symbols that did not interfere with 'being Canadian.' Whereas the Ukrainian in Ukraine could dislike singing, *pyrohy*, cross-stitch embroidery, or the church and not have his or her Ukrainianness challenged, in Canada, musicality, Ukrainian foods and handicrafts, and Ukrainians' peculiar religious rite became distinguishing Ukrainian traits and hallmarks of Ukrainianness. Language, considered crucial to national-cultural survival by a community elite and at the heart of Russification at home, was the aspect of the Ukrainian heritage most vulnerable to assimilatory pressures.

Visible expressions of Ukrainianness compatible with integration (and with an apolitical definition of multiculturalism) came from the folk arts, traditionally equated with female activities and reinforcing women's domesticity. Imported with the first immigrants, folk arts were politicized by nationalists in Canada and perceived as both a base for and a component of a subjective Ukrainian consciousness. In stressing their obligation to preserve and create Ukrainian handicrafts, and in proudly wearing their embroidered blouses (once heard described as their 'battlegear'), organized women acknowledged both the symbolic importance of handicrafts and their own role in ensuring their survival. Organized women also adapted their traditional handicrafts to appeal to the popular culture of twentieth-century Canada, and they used their popularity to gain access to mainstream women's organizations in order to publicize the Ukrainian cause. Yet the Ukrainian-Canadian woman's cross-stitch and Easter eggs could not have the significance of the embroideries done by Ukrainian female political prisoners in the Soviet Union and smuggled out of the camps to the West. These embroideries not only expressed personal creativity and emotion; as expressions of Ukrainianness, they were also powerful national-political, religious, and cultural symbols.[1] In Canada, where the use of identifiably Ukrainian symbols, whether political or cultural, required no courage and carried no threat of reprisal, this type of 'women's work' could much less easily be translated into a meaningful Ukrainianness.

Another aspect of 'women's work' became the basis of a sense of Canadianness that reflected organized women's domestication of the message of the Great Women of Ukraine. Not only did they honour the interwar pioneers of their organizations as Great Women themselves and find inspiration in their past achievements, but they also saw their organizations as vital components of the Ukrainian-Canadian community. This sentiment, flowering in the postwar years, was predicated upon the conviction that 'women's work' – their so-called kitchen function and their fund-raising – had in a very concrete sense built the Ukrainian-Canadian community and enabled it to function. Regardless of the fact that their appointed role relied upon gender stereotyping and separate spheres for men and women, and represented physical as opposed to intellectual labours, late twentieth-century organized women felt secure about their place in their community and its history.

Bibliographic Note

A study primarily concerned with the attitudes of a community elite towards the members of the group to which it belongs and in whose name it presumes to speak must use the propagandistic publications of that elite as its major source. In this instance they are of two types. The first is the ideological press, an outlet for public opinion in the form of letters to the editor and unsolicited articles, and the medium through which rival religious and political camps reach out to the mass of Ukrainian Canadians. The second is the official volumes posterity-conscious Ukrainian-Canadian women's organizations publish to mark important milestones.

Women's organizations can appear as part of commemorative works, sometimes national but often regional or local in scope, that focus on the larger movement to which the women belong. The value of such histories lies in this context, for otherwise the information is limited and basic. Except for male-authored works in the progressive community, separate books devoted to a single women's organization have invariably been both commissioned and written by their subjects. Also anniversary publications, they too favour factual narrative, grouped around personalities, major events and activities, and branch reports; as celebrations of achievement, they tend to be nonanalytical and self-congratulatory. Women's own organizational histories not only constitute a record of the past; they also package the past, and in the process say a great deal about organized women's understanding of their role within the Ukrainian-Canadian community.

The ideological press is important more as a record of contemporary response to specific situations and changing circumstances, particularly by those anxious to influence their outcome. During the first decade of Ukrainian settlement in Canada, the American-Ukrainian news-paper *Svoboda* (1893–) was the sole forum for the exchange of infor-mation, ideas, and experiences among individuals in widely scattered communities. For the remainder of the period until the end of the First World War, before the creation of women's organizations to speak for and address their sex directly, the newspapers of greatest significance reflected the views of the principal factions in the pioneer immigrant community. They included *Kanadyiskyi rusyn* (1911–19) and its successor *Kanadiiskyi ukrainets* (1919–31), official organs of the Greek Catholic church; *Robochyi narod* (1909–18), organ of the Ukrainian Social Democratic Party; the Presbyterian *Ranok* (1905–20) and Meth-odist *Kanadyiets* (1912–20), which merged to become *Kanadiiskyi ranok* (1920–61); and *Kanadiiskyi farmer* (1903–81) and *Ukrainskyi holos* (1910–), both mouthpieces of the secular nationalists. While the Liberals ini-tially funded *Kanadiiskyi farmer*, *Ukrainskyi holos* was founded by Ukrainian bilingual teachers and came to serve the lay organizations of the Ukrainian Greek Orthodox church; after more than seventy years, declining readerships forced it to absorb *Kanadiiskyi farmer*.

Between the wars, only the Women's Section of the Ukrainian La-bour-Farmer Temple Association could boast its own organ, with the monthly *Holos robitnytsi* (1923–4) quickly superseded by the semi-monthly *Robitnytsia* (1924–37). Men edited both publications. The Ukrainian Women's Association of Canada and the Ukrainian Wom-en's Organization of Canada maintained pages in *Ukrainskyi holos* and *Novyi shliakh*, respectively, the official newspapers of their 'male' af-filiates, the Ukrainian Self-Reliance League and the Ukrainian Na-tional Federation. After *Kanadiiskyi ukrainets* folded, *Ukrainski visti* (1932–) became the major vehicle for reporting the activities of or-ganized Catholic women.

Progressive women had no separate publication after 1937, and the progressive community debated the necessity of even separate wom-en's pages in its postwar publications. *Ukrainske zhyttia* (1941–65), *Ukrainske slovo* (1943–65), *Zhyttia i slovo* (1965–91), and the *Ukrainian Canadian* (1947–91), for a younger English-speaking audience, existed as outlets for the Women's Section of the Association of United Ukrainian Canadians and for reporting female activities. Following the Second World War, the major nationalist women's organizations graduated from women's pages to their own magazines, supported by membership subscriptions and annual fund-raising campaigns. *Zhino-chyi svit* (1950–) of the UWOC and *Promin* (1960–) of the UWAC were monthlies; *Nasha doroha* (1970–), organ of the Ukrainian Catholic Women's League, was a quarterly. Prior to the latter's launching, UCWL pages were carried in the Catholic weeklies, *Nasha meta* (1949–) and *Postup* (1959–). The women's press contains material that is practical and informational as well as inspirational and instructional, with recipes and embroidery patterns alongside articles on Ukrainian heroines, branch activities reports, commentary on current affairs, and items relating specifically to women's responsibilities as Ukrainian Canadians. English-language sections are now also the norm.

To conserve space in this book, citations in the notes have been pared to a minimum: title and date for newspapers; title, date, and page number for monthlies and quarterlies. This decision has sacrificed often illuminating titles and their authors' identity, and the interested reader is directed to the doctoral dissertation on which this study is based for more detail. One final point should be made. Given the ritualistic, repetitive, and enduring nature of community beliefs and observances, references in the notes are selective and include only a fraction of the documentation available. An attempt has been made, however, to include both representative and a variety of pieces as well as to cover different camps and periods.

Notes

INTRODUCTION Queen Elizabeth the Ukrainian

1 Michael Czuboka, *Ukrainian Canadian, Eh? The Ukrainians of Canada and Elsewhere as Perceived by Themselves and Others* (Winnipeg 1983), 1
2 See the frontispiece to Paul Yuzyk, *Ukrainian Canadians: Their Place and Role in Canadian Life* (Toronto 1967), a photograph of Her Majesty accompanied by a statement of her Ukrainian ancestry to open Yuzyk's plea for Ukrainians' right to be considered full partners in Confederation.
3 On conditions among the Ukrainian peasantry in late nineteenth-century Austria-Hungary see John-Paul Himka, 'The Background to Emigration: Ukrainians of Galicia and Bukovyna, 1848–1914,' in *A Heritage in Transition: Essays in the History of Ukrainians in Canada*, ed. Manoly R. Lupul (Toronto 1982), 11–58; Orest Martynowych, *Ukrainian Canadians: The Formative Years, 1891–1924* (Edmonton 1991), 3–33; and Stella Hryniuk, *Peasants with Promise: Ukrainians in Southeastern Galicia, 1880–1900* (Edmonton 1991). On the Ukrainian national movement in Galicia see Jan Kozik, *The Ukrainian National Movement in Galicia, 1815–1849* (Edmonton 1986); Ivan L. Rudnytsky, 'The Ukrainians in Galicia under Austrian Rule,' in *Nationbuilding and the Politics of Nationalism: Essays on Austrian Galicia*, ed. Andrei S. Markovits and Frank E. Sysyn (Cambridge, Mass. 1982), 23–67; and the following works by John-Paul Himka: 'Priests and Peasants: The Greek Catholic Pastor and the Ukrainian National Movement in Austria, 1867–1900,' *Canadian Slavonic Papers* 21, 1 (March 1979): 1–14; *Socialism in Galicia: The Emergence of Polish Democracy and Ukrainian Radicalism (1860–1890)*

(Cambridge, Mass. 1983), 40–60, 106–72; and *Galician Villagers and the Ukrainian National Movement in the Nineteenth Century* (Edmonton 1987).

On conditions in Russian Ukraine see Konstantyn Kononenko, *Ukraine and Russia: A History of the Economic Relations between Ukraine and Russia (1654–1917)* (Milwaukee 1958), 33–100; and H.R. Weinstein, 'Land Hunger and Nationalism in the Ukraine, 1905–1917,' *Journal of Economic History* 11 (May 1942): 24–35. On the Ukrainian national movement in the Russian empire see George S.N. Luckyj, *Between Gogol' and Ševčenko: Polarity in the Literary Ukraine, 1798–1847* (Munich 1971); and Bohdan Krawchenko, *Social Change and National Consciousness in Twentieth-Century Ukraine* (London 1985), 1–45.

4 Immigration figures based on William Darcovich and Paul Yuzyk, eds., *A Statistical Compendium on the Ukrainians in Canada, 1891–1976* (Ottawa 1980), series 50.24–38, 506–7. The literature on the first Ukrainian immigration to Canada is extensive. In contrast, only two full-length studies focus on the two subsequent waves: Myron Gulka-Tiechko, 'Inter-war Ukrainian Immigration to Canada, 1919–1939' (MA thesis, University of Manitoba 1983); and Lubomyr Y. Luciuk, 'Searching for Place: Ukrainian Refugee Migration to Canada after World War II' (PhD dissertation, University of Alberta 1984).

5 See Taras Hunczak, ed., *The Ukraine, 1917–1921: A Study in Revolution* (Cambridge, Mass. 1977).

6 On interwar Galicia and Soviet Ukraine, the Second World War years, and post–1945 Ukraine see Stephan Horak, *Poland and Her National Minorities, 1919–1939* (New York 1961); Krawchenko, *Social Change and National Consciousness in Twentieth-Century Ukraine*, 46–152; George S.N. Luckyj, *Literary Politics in Soviet Ukraine, 1917–1934* (Freeport 1971); James Mace, *Communism and the Dilemmas of National Liberation: National Communism in Soviet Ukraine, 1918–1933* (Cambridge, Mass. 1983); Hryhory Kostiuk, *Stalinist Rule in the Ukraine: A Study of the Decade of Mass Terror (1929–1939)* (New York 1961); John Armstrong, *Ukrainian Nationalism*, 2d ed. (Littleton 1980); Yury Boshyk, ed., *Ukraine during World War II: History and Its Aftermath* (Edmonton 1986); Borys Lewytzkyj, *Politics and Society in Soviet Ukraine, 1953–1980* (Edmonton 1984); and David R. Marples, *Ukraine under Perestroika: Ecology, Economics and the Workers' Revolt* (Edmonton 1991).

7 *Kanadiiskyi farmer*, 14 June 1907, 15 Nov. 1907, 15 Feb. 1911, 27 July 1917, 2 Aug. 1918; *Ukrainskyi holos*, 25 Nov. 1914, 4 Sept. 1918, 26 March 1919, 26 Sept. 1923, 4 and 11 Aug. 1926, 18 May 1927, 20 Aug. 1930; and *Kanadyiskyi rusyn*, 30 Aug. 1916. These ideas concern-

ing the group leadership role automatically accruing to the educated and successful persisted in community thinking: see Stanley Frolick, 'The Future of Ukrainian Youth in Canada,' in Ukrainian Canadian Committee, *First All-Canadian Congress of Ukrainians in Canada* (Winnipeg 1943), 168; and the speech by Basil Kushnir in Komitet ukraintsiv Kanady, *Piatyi i shostyi vse-kanadiiski kongresy ukraintsiv Kanady* (Winnipeg [1959]), 167–8.

8 For an excellent and thorough discussion of the Galician roots and early evolution of the major religious and secular factions in the pioneer Ukrainian-Canadian community see Martynowych, *Ukrainians in Canada*, 155–449.

9 The American Roman Catholic hierarchy had objected to married Greek Catholic priests accompanying the earlier Ukrainian immigration to the United States, and in the early 1890s they successfully pressured Rome to have married clergy excluded from North America; Paul Yuzyk, *The Ukrainian Greek Orthodox Church of Canada, 1918–1951* (Ottawa 1981), 41.

10 For the church's own assessment of its formative years and achievements see *Propamiatna knyha z nahody zolotoho iuvileiu poselennia ukrainskoho narodu v Kanadi, 1891–1941* (Yorkton 1941).

11 On the church's formation and early history see Yuzyk, *Ukrainian Greek Orthodox Church of Canada*, 55–96.

12 On Ukrainian Protestantism's indigenous roots see John Bodrug, *Independent Orthodox Church: Memoirs Pertaining to the History of a Ukrainian Canadian Church in the Years 1903 to 1913*, ed. J.B. Gregorovich (Toronto 1982); and Oleksander Dombrovskyi, *Narys istorii ukrainskoho ievanhelsko-reformovanoho rukhu* (New York and Toronto 1979). Anglo-Canadian missionary activity among the Ukrainians is discussed by Vivian Olender in 'The Reaction of the Canadian Methodist Church towards Ukrainian Immigrants: Rural Missions as Agencies of Assimilation' (MA thesis, University of Toronto 1976), and 'Presbyterian Missions and Ukrainians in Canada, 1900–1925' (PhD dissertation, University of Toronto 1984).

13 Orest T. Martynowych, 'The Ukrainian Socialist Movement in Canada, 1900–1918,' *Journal of Ukrainian Graduate Studies* 1, 1 (autumn 1976): 27–44, and 2, 1 (spring 1977): 22–31, is the best separate analysis of this period. For the progressives on their early history see Peter Krawchuk, *The Ukrainian Socialist Movement in Canada (1907–1918)* (Toronto 1979).

14 For an assessment of the Ukrainian role and the role of individuals like

Senator Paul Yuzyk in creating both an ideology and a policy of multiculturalism, together with positive and negative reaction to it, see Bohdan Bociurkiw, 'The Federal Policy of Multiculturalism and the Ukrainian-Canadian Community,' in *Ukrainian Canadians, Multiculturalism, and Separatism: An Assessment*, ed. Manoly R. Lupul (Edmonton 1978), 98–128.

15 Ukrainian Community Development Committee, Prairie Region, *Building the Future: Ukrainian Canadians in the 21st Century, A Blueprint for Action* (Edmonton 1986), 25

16 In nationalist historiography see Michael H. Marunchak, *The Ukrainian Canadians: A History*, 2d ed. rev. (Winnipeg and Ottawa 1982), 95; and Myron Chorney, 'Obituary,' in *The Ukrainian Pioneers in Alberta, Canada*, ed. Joseph Lazarenko (Edmonton 1970), 31–6. For the progressives see Eugene Dolny's speech in Association of United Ukrainian Canadians and Workers Benevolent Association, *A Tribute to Our Ukrainian Pioneers in Canada's First Century* (Winnipeg 1966), 46–7.

17 Progressives labelled multiculturalism an act of political expediency by Anglo-Canadians to avoid recognizing the French-Canadian nation and sharing real power with ethnic groups; see *Ukrainian Canadian*, 1 May 1968, July–Aug. 1978.

18 Association of United Ukrainian Canadians and Workers Benevolent Association, *Tribute to Our Ukrainian Pioneers*, 27, 48, 54–5, 81–2, 96, 98; Petro Kravchuk, *Na novii zemli: Storinky z zhyttia, borotby i tvorchoi pratsi kanadskykh ukraintsiv* (Toronto 1958), 372–81; Marko Terlytsia [Petro Kravchuk], *Pravnuky pohani: Ukrainski natsionalisty v Kanadi* (Kiev 1960), 294–8; and *Ukrainian Canadian*, 15 May 1955, 7–8; 1 Nov. 1957, 24; May 1978, 6–7; June 1978, 6–9; Dec. 1980, 7

19 Paul Yuzyk describes the pioneer immigrant intelligentsia as 'petty,' and Orest Martynowych calls them 'village' intelligentsia (his *Ukrainians in Canada* is the best attempt at a profile). See also Bohdan Kordan, 'The Intelligentsia and the Development of Ukrainian Ethnic Consciousness in Canada: A Prolegomenon to Research,' *Canadian Ethnic Studies* 17, 1 (1985): 22–33.

20 Nataliia L. Kohuska, *Pivstolittia na hromadskii nyvi: Narys istorii Soiuzu ukrainok Kanady* (Edmonton and Winnipeg 1986), 741; and Michael Luchkovich, *A Ukrainian Canadian in Parliament* (Toronto 1965), 6–13. Two of Luchkovich's sisters were teaching in rural Manitoba before he immigrated in 1907; Olha came later.

21 Claudia Helen Popowich, *To Serve Is To Love: The Canadian Story of the Sisters Servants of Mary Immaculate* (Toronto 1971), 34

22 Discussed in *Kanadyiskyi rusyn* between December 1915 and March
    1916
23 *Robochyi narod*, 20 April 1918; see also ibid., 24 Oct. 1917, 2 Sept.
    1918. The *Edmonton Journal*, 5 Jan. 1915, described the young woman
    who starred in a Ukrainian play staged in the local Empire Theatre as
    an 'actress of much charm and dramatic instinct.'
24 In Semen Kovbel, comp., and Dmytro Doroshenko, ed., *Propamiatna
    knyha Ukrainskoho narodnoho domu u Vynypegu* (Winnipeg 1949), 227
25 *Ukrainskyi holos*, 15 Aug. 1917, describes one such attempt at Malanton
    in the Interlake region of Manitoba.
26 The strength of Martha Bohachevsky-Chomiak's *Feminists Despite Them-
    selves: Women in Ukrainian Community Life, 1884–1939* (Edmonton 1986)
    is its discussion of the Women's Union, particularly the role of the
    leadership elite.
27 *Ukrainskyi holos*, 18 Feb., 18 March, and 1 July 1925
28 For the Mohylianky's own assessment of their influence on early
    Ukrainian-Canadian community life see the articles by Daria Yanda
    and Savella Stechishin in the Petro Mohyla Institute's silver jubilee his-
    tory, *Iuvileina knyha Ukrainskoho instytutu im. Petra Mohyly v Saskatuni,
    1916–1941* (Saskatoon 1945), 297–305, 313–17. On the Olha Kobylian-
    ska Society, the UWAC mother branch, see Savelia Stechyshyn, *Pivrich-
    chia (1923–1973) Zhinochoho tovarystva im. Olhy Kobylianskoi v Saskatuni,
    Saskachevan, pershoho viddilu Soiuzu ukrainok Kanady* (Saskatoon 1975).
29 *Promin*, May 1961, 3–5
30 The breakdown of branches (1936) was as follows: British Columbia 2,
    Alberta 24, Saskatchewan 45, Manitoba 19, Ontario 13, Quebec 1.
    Ukrainskyi holos, 8 March 1939; and Soiuz ukrainok Kanady, *Iuvileina
    knyzhka Soiuzu ukrainok Kanady z nahody 10-litnoho isnovannia, 1926–1936*
    (Np 1937), 89–93.
31 Of the remaining UWOC branches, 2 were located in Alberta, 7 in Sas-
    katchewan, 2 in Manitoba, and 2 in Quebec. *Novyi shliakh*, 6 July 1937
32 On the wartime formation of the UCWL see Iryna Pavlykovska, ed.,
    *Dlia Boha, tserkvy i narodu: Liga ukrainskykh katolytskykh zhinok edmonton-
    skoi ieparkhii v 1944–1966 rokakh, pochatky i diialnist* (Edmonton [1966]),
    16–20, 227–30; Vira Buchynska, ed., *Slidamy dyiakonis: 25 rokiv pratsi
    Ligy ukrainskykh katolytskykh zhinok Kanady u Manitobi* (Winnipeg 1973),
    9–10, 15–16, 146–7; and *Nasha doroha*, Oct.–Dec. 1984, 27–8.
33 Distribution by eparchy was as follows: New Westminster, 12 branches
    (372 members); Edmonton, 26 branches (1217 members); Saskatoon,
    17 branches (1147 members); Toronto, 41 branches (1548 members);

and the archeparchy of Winnipeg, 38 branches (1673 members). E. Iankivska, comp., *Liga ukrainskykh katolytskykh zhinok Kanady: Vira – nadiia – liubov* (Toronto 1985), xix, 165, 266, 272, 280, 288

34 The founding of the Vancouver branch of the Women's Section of the ULFTA is an excellent case of the 'outside' male worker parachuted into a community to organize local women; *Robitnytsia*, 1 April 1925, 21–2.

35 *Ukrainian Canadian*, March 1972, 22–4; see also Vinohradova's autobiography in Petro Kravchuk, comp., *Zhinochi doli* (Toronto 1973), 60–7 [English translation by Michael Ukas, *Reminiscences of Courage and Hope: Stories of Ukrainian Canadian Women Pioneers* (Toronto 1991), 265–72].

36 British Columbia had 6 branches (120 members); Alberta, 21 branches (378 members); Saskatchewan, 4 branches (86 members); Manitoba, 7 branches (400 members); Ontario, 30 branches (749 members); Quebec, 8 branches (169 members); and Nova Scotia, 2 branches (21 members). *Robitnytsia*, 1 March 1937, 3–4; Aug. 1937, 8

37 See, for example, the comments of Stephanie Sawchuk (UWOC) in Ukrainian Canadian Committee, *First All Canadian Congress of Ukrainians in Canada*, 79.

CHAPTER 1   Failing to Measure Up

1 Gabrielle Roy, *Garden in the Wind*, trans. Alan Brown (Toronto 1977), 140–1

2 Based on William Darcovich and Paul Yuzyk, eds., *A Statistical Compendium on the Ukrainians in Canada, 1891–1976* (Ottawa 1980), series 50.94–103, 517. 'Adult' is loosely defined, reflecting the nature of the data. Between 1896 and 1910, immigrants to Canada were recorded as being over or under the age of twelve; during the next four years, the dividing line was fourteen.

3 Based on ibid., series 20.63–80, 41–4

4 Stella Hryniuk, 'The Peasant and Alcohol in Eastern Galicia in the Late Nineteenth Century: A Note,' *Journal of Ukrainian Studies* 11, 1 (summer 1986): 75–86, attempts to demonstrate, albeit inconclusively, that alcoholism was not the problem that contemporaries and historians since have painted.

5 John-Paul Himka, 'The Background to Emigration: Ukrainians of Galicia and Bukovyna, 1848–1914,' in *A Heritage in Transition: Essays in the History of Ukrainians in Canada*, ed. Manoly R. Lupul (Toronto 1982),

17–18. In 1901 men earned .60 crowns, for a thirteen- to sixteen-hour day, women .36 crowns, and children .28 crowns; *Charities*, 3 Dec. 1904.

6 *Svoboda*, 15 Dec. 1898

7 Samuel Koenig, 'Ukrainians of Eastern Galicia: A Study of Their Culture and Institutions' (PhD dissertation, Yale University 1935), 133, 379, 392–462, 369

8 John-Paul Himka, *Galician Villagers and the Ukrainian National Movement in the Nineteenth Century* (Edmonton 1988), 103

9 Koenig, 'Ukrainians of Eastern Galicia,' 493–4; and *Ukrainskyi holos*, 25 Feb. 1931

10 Koenig, 'Ukrainians of Eastern Galicia,' 495, 492, 422–4; and *Robitnytsia*, 1 July 1924, 4–6

11 For the revisionist version see Stella Hryniuk, *Peasants with Promise: Ukrainians in Southeastern Galicia, 1880–1900* (Edmonton 1991). John-Paul Himka (for Galicia) and Orest Martynowych (for Canada), whose works are cited elsewhere in this study (Introduction, n. 3), present a less positive picture. Martynowych's *Ukrainians in Canada: The Formative Years, 1891–1924* (Edmonton 1991), 26–7, convincingly queries Hryniuk's use and interpretation of statistics.

12 *Ukraine: A Concise Encyclopedia* (Toronto 1971), vol. 1, 187; and vol. 2, 1016

13 The point about Ukrainian handicrafts is made by Martha Bohachevsky-Chomiak in her manuscript, 'Feminists Despite Themselves: Women in Ukrainian Community Life, 1884–1939' (Canadian Institute of Ukrainian Studies Archives, University of Alberta), 124.

14 On the Ukrainian women's movement in late nineteenth- and early twentieth-century Galicia see Martha Bohachevsky-Chomiak, *Feminists Despite Themselves: Women in Ukrainian Community Life, 1884–1939* (Edmonton 1988), 47–102; also her 'Natalia Kobryns'ka: A Formulator of Feminism,' in *Nationbuilding and the Politics of Nationalism: Essays on Austrian Galicia*, ed. Andrei S. Markovits and Frank E. Sysyn (Cambridge, Mass. 1982), 196–219.

15 Himka, *Galician Villagers*, 97–104

16 In 'The Stone Cross,' the short story by the late nineteenth-century Galician writer, Vasyl Stefanyk, it is the old woman and not her husband who wants to emigrate to Canada; Vasyl Stefanyk, *The Stone Cross*, trans. Joseph Wiznuk and C.H. Andrusyshen (Toronto 1971), 21–32.

17 Maria Adamowska, 'Beginnings in Canada,' in *Land of Pain, Land of*

Promise: First Person Accounts by Ukrainian Pioneers, 1891–1914, comp. and trans. Harry Piniuta (Saskatoon 1978), 55–6; and *Svoboda*, 28 Jan. 1897 (Cyril Genik), 10 June 1897 (Nestor Dmytriw)

18 Anna Farion, 'Homestead Girlhood,' in Piniuta, *Land of Pain, Land of Promise*, 86

19 *Svoboda*, 15 Jan. 1903

20 *Manitoba Free Press*, 8 June 1916

21 Panko Michalczuk, 'A Brief Autobiography of Panko Michalczuk in Canada' (manuscript, Vancouver 1957), 9; and Mundare Historical Society, *Memories of Mundare: A History of Mundare and District* (Mundare 1980), 380

22 For a discussion of changes in the structure of the Ukrainian family as a result of immigration to Canada see Halyna Muchin, 'The Evolution of the Ukrainian Family and Its Portrayal in Illia Kiriak's *Sons of the Soil*' (MA thesis, University of Manitoba 1978).

23 *Svoboda*, 28 May 1903

24 James S. Woodsworth, dir., 'Ukrainian Rural Communities' (mimeograph, Report of investigation by the Bureau of Social Research, governments of Manitoba, Saskatchewan, and Alberta, Winnipeg 1917), 5

25 Ibid., 102

26 Based on raw data, ibid., 62–73. At Prince Albert the average farm had 0.8 horses, 1.0 oxen, and small numbers of other livestock, compared with 5.0 horses and 1.6 oxen, plus other livestock, at Hafford.

27 Data from ibid., 5–6, and summary tables prepared from fieldworkers' reports on individual districts

28 Wellington Bridgman, *Breaking Prairie Sod* (Toronto 1920), 180–3

29 Two studies to touch upon the changes affecting women as Ukrainian peasant immigrants adapted to urban life took the Ukrainians, and not the Anglo-Canadian community or concerns of the general society, as their starting point. See Stephen W. Mamchur, 'The Economic and Social Adjustment of Slavic Immigrants in Canada: With Special Reference to the Ukrainians in Montreal' (MA thesis, McGill University 1934), and Charles M. Bayley, 'The Social Structure of the Italian and Ukrainian Immigrant Communities in Montreal, 1935–1937' (MA thesis, McGill University 1939).

30 Marjorie Harrison, *Go West – Go Wise! A Canadian Revelation* (London 1930), 80–1

31 *Manitoba Free Press*, 14 Feb. 1916

32 *Edmonton Bulletin*, 30 Oct. 1916; see also *Vegreville Observer*, 27 March 1918.

33 Constable J. Nash, Alberta Provincial Police, Vermilion, 31 Aug. 1917, Inquest Files, file 1012, Department of the Attorney General Records, Provincial Archives of Alberta, Edmonton

34 Ibid., file 599

35 Ralph Connor [Charles W. Gordon], *The Foreigner: A Tale of Saskatchewan* (Toronto 1909), 26–35. Basil d'Easum, 'A Galician Wedding,' *Canadian Magazine*, May–Oct. 1899, 83–4, uses an unkempt and light-fingered widower set on marrying the first available woman as a vehicle for exposing the folly of the Liberal government's 'pro-Ukrainian' immigration policy.

36 Miriam Elston, 'A Russian Wedding in Alberta,' *East and West*, 18 March 1916, 93; anonymous, 'Some Teacher Experiences' (manuscript, nd), William Martin Papers, 19165–7, Saskatchewan Archives Board, Saskatoon; J.S. Woodsworth, 'Foreign Immigrants and Temperance,' *Christian Guardian*, 13 April 1910, 8; and letter, Rev. W.H. Pike, Andrew, Alberta, *Missionary Bulletin*, March–June 1915, 390

37 Anonymous, 'Some Teacher Experiences'; Pike, *Missionary Bulletin*, 390; and Elsie M. Bishop, 'Some Teacher Experiences' (manuscript, nd), Martin Papers, 19430–1

38 Anonymous, 'Some Teacher Experiences'; and Pike, *Missionary Bulletin*, 390

39 James S. Woodsworth found this image to be wrong; girls married between the ages of seventeen and twenty, he said, while the average family had 4.72 children. *Edmonton Journal*, 2 Feb. 1916

40 Anonymous, 'Some Teacher Experiences'

41 Pike, *Missionary Bulletin*, 390. In 1910 infant mortality figures for two heavily Ukrainian electoral districts in Alberta (Victoria 117/1000 and Whitford 185/1000) compared unfavourably with nearby Scandinavian (Camrose 52/1000) and British-American (Wainwright 33/1000) districts; based on figures from the Vital Statistics Branch, in *Annual Report of the Department of Agriculture of the Province of Alberta for the Year 1910*.

42 Minutes, 15 Sept. 1913, Records of the Woman's Canadian Club of Calgary, Glenbow-Alberta Institute, Calgary; and minutes, 29 Sept. 1913, First Annual Convention (Alberta), Records of the Woman's Christian Temperance Union, Glenbow-Alberta Institute

43 *Svoboda*, 22 April 1897

44 *Edmonton Bulletin*, 19 Jan. 1912

45 Miriam Elston, 'The Russian in Our Midst,' *Westminster*, 1915, 531, in the Miriam Elston Papers, Provincial Archives of Alberta

46 J.H. Hardy, 'The Ruthenians in Alberta,' *Onward*, Elston Papers
47 This point is crucial to Eliane Leslau Silverman's *The Last Best West: Women on the Alberta Frontier, 1880–1930* (Montreal and London 1984). Proceeding from an initial bias towards the levelling influence of the frontier, which eroded not only objective differences but also social distance, and finding justification in the indifference of her informants, Silverman dismisses ethnicity as irrelevant outside a few formalized and symbolic rituals; it was neither an impediment to integration into the new society nor the source of personal and political identity (161).
48 *Kanadyiets*, 27 Sept. 1916; and *Ranok*, 7 Feb. 1912, 29 Jan. 1913, 25 Oct. 1916
49 *Robitnytsia*, 15 June 1924, 1–3; 1 June 1925, 15–17; 15 March 1927, 167–8
50 *Kanadiiskyi farmer*, 29 Oct. 1909. See also, for example, ibid., 1 Oct. 1909; and *Kanadyiskyi rusyn*, 1 Sept. 1915.
51 On the attitudes of the Ukrainian peasant to the Jews see John-Paul Himka, 'Ukrainian-Jewish Antagonism in the Galician Countryside during the Late Nineteenth Century,' in *Ukrainian-Jewish Relations in Historical Perspective*, ed. Peter J. Potichnyj and Howard Aster (Edmonton 1988), 111–58. For early immigrant attitudes toward the legacy of Polish and Jewish oppression see Frances Swyripa and Andrij Makuch, comps., *Ukrainian Canadian Content in the Newspaper 'Svoboda', 1893–1904* (Edmonton 1985).
52 On the general destructiveness of alcohol see *Kanadiiskyi farmer*, 12 Jan. 1910, 12 June and 18 Sept.–13 Nov. 1914, 25 Feb. 1916; and three lengthy series in *Kanadyiskyi rusyn*, 10 Jan.–7 Feb., 6 June–15 July, 18 July–29 Aug. 1914.
53 *Ranok*, 12 June 1912. See also ibid., 19 June 1912, 22 and 29 Jan., 19 Feb. and 23 July 1913, 6 May 1914; and *Kanadyiets*, 15 July 1915.
54 *Kanadyiskyi rusyn*, 31 March 1915
55 *Kanadiiskyi farmer*, 21 June 1907, 21 Feb. 1908, 9 March 1910, 17 May 1912
56 Himka, 'Ukrainian-Jewish Antagonism,' attributes tensions between the two groups in rural Galicia to this economic relationship, in which both were trapped. He also attributes the total absence of pogroms in this area to the politicization of the Ukrainian-Jewish conflict by the Ukrainian national movement, which stressed boycotts and the establishment of competing Ukrainian economic institutions, not violence.
57 *Kanadyiskyi rusyn*, 3 June 1911, 23 June and 25 Aug. 1915; *Kanadiiskyi*

farmer, 29 Dec. 1909, 26 Feb. 1915; and *Ukrainskyi holos*, 12 and 26 Oct. 1910

58 *Kanadiiskyi farmer*, 17 Aug., 7 and 21 Dec. 1905, 22 March 1906, 12 April 1907, 31 July 1908

59 Ibid., 16 July 1913

60 See, for example, *Kanadyiskyi rusyn*, 9 Dec. 1911, 16 Nov. 1912, 16 Aug. 1916, 4 Sept. 1918; *Kanadiiskyi farmer*, 7 Feb. 1908, 17 May 1912; and *Ukrainskyi holos*, 4 Sept. 1918.

61 *Kanadyiskyi rusyn*, 17 Aug. 1912, 12 July 1913, 5 Sept., 7 and 14 Oct. 1914; and *Ukrainskyi holos*, 3 Nov. 1915, 16 Aug. 1916, 7 Aug. and 4 Sept. 1918

62 The Presbyterian-funded *Ranok* (Dawn), for example, insisted that political and other rights Ukrainians shared with all Canadians meant little without the schooling and proper home upbringing that truly equalized people. *Ranok*, 15 May 1907

63 Ibid., 19 Feb. 1913. See also ibid., 7 Feb. 1912, and *Kanadyiets*, 1 Oct. 1919.

64 From the interwar period see two reviews of conditions prior to the founding of the Ukrainian Labour-Farmer Temple Association: *Robitnytsia*, 15 Nov. 1926, 2–4; 15 March 1933, 13–14.

65 *Holos robitnytsi*, Jan. 1924, 1–2; and *Robitnytsia*, 1 April 1931, 8–10. The second article, which criticizes the church's use of Easter to keep the working class in its place by exhorting it to emulate the suffering of Christ and await its reward in heaven, is not Ukrainian specific.

66 *Ranok*, 11 and 25 Aug. 1915, 12 and 26 Jan. 1916; and *Kanadiiskyi ranok*, 13 June 1922

67 *Kanadiiskyi farmer*, 22 Feb. 1907; *Kanadyiskyi rusyn*, 3 June and 26 Aug. 1911, 21 Sept. 1912, 28 Nov. 1917; and *Ukrainskyi holos*, 5 June 1912. The interwar labour-temple that pointed to the local replacement of 'Galician' with the cultured 'Ukrainian' as proof of enlightenment and successful propaganda shows that progressives, too, thought in similar terms; Tovarystvo ukrainskyi robitnycho-farmerskyi dim, *Almanakh Tovarystva ukrainskyi robitnycho-farmerskyi dim v Kanadi, 1918–1929* (Winnipeg 1930), 197.

68 *Kanadyiskyi rusyn*, 13 Sept. 1916. See also ibid., 9 and 16 Dec. 1911, 10 Aug. and 21 Sept. 1912.

69 Ibid., 3 June 1911, 5 Oct. 1912, 30 May and 4 Nov. 1914, 4 Aug. 1915 (the tongue-in-cheek 'Desiat zapovidyi ...'/Ten commandments ...), 25 Oct. 1916, 29 Jan. 1919

70 Non-Ukrainian Roman Catholic male orders initially financed and staffed private schools for boys; other schools, including the Sacred Heart Institute for girls opened in Yorkton in 1917, were run by the Ukrainian Sisters Servants of Mary Immaculate, who were praised in the community for their religious and patriotic work. See *Propamiatna knyha z nahody zolotoho iuvileiu poselennia ukrainskoho narodu v Kanadi, 1891–1941* (Yorkton 1941), 31–7; Claudia Helen Popowich, *To Serve Is To Love: The Canadian Story of the Sisters Servants of Mary Immaculate* (Toronto 1971), 81–91; and *Kanadyiskyi rusyn*, 17 Aug. 1912, 4 Aug. 1915.

71 Paul Yuzyk, *The Ukrainian Greek Orthodox Church of Canada, 1918–1951* (Ottawa 1981), 66–90; and *Iuvileina knyha Ukrainskoho instytutu im. Petra Mohyly v Saskatuni, 1916–1941* (Saskatoon 1941), 43–100

72 *Kanadiiskyi farmer*, 18 Oct. 1912; see also ibid., 14 March 1919.

73 *Ukrainskyi holos*, 17 June 1914

74 *Kanadyiskyi rusyn*, 11 Nov. 1914

75 Ibid., 26 Aug. 1911, 5 Sept., 7 and 14 Oct., and 4 and 11 Nov. 1914, 7 April 1915, 4 Sept. 1918

76 *Ukrainskyi holos*, 22 Dec. 1915. For two other female opinions see ibid., 16 Feb. and 8 March 1916.

77 *Kanadyiskyi rusyn*, 18 Nov. 1914; and *Kanadiiskyi farmer*, 6 Oct. 1916, 30 March 1917, 29 Aug. 1919

78 See, for example, *Robochyi narod*, 28 Feb. 1916, 30 May 1917, and *Robitnytsia*, 1 July 1924, 4–6.

79 *Robochyi narod*, 18 July 1917

80 Ibid., 1 and 22 Jan. 1914, 7 April 1915, 24 July and 14 Aug. 1918, 29 May 1919

81 *Ranok*, 28 Feb. 1912, 5 Jan. and 24 May 1916, 3 Oct. 1917

82 Ibid., 27 March 1912, 28 Jan. 1914, 25 July 1917; see *Ukrainskyi holos*, 11 July 1917, for the article that sparked the Wilchynsky letter in *Ranok*.

83 From the various camps see, for example, *Kanadyiskyi rusyn*, 15 Aug. 1914; *Robochyi narod*, 30 June 1915; *Kanadiiskyi farmer*, 30 Nov. 1915; and *Ukrainskyi holos*, 19 Jan. 1916.

84 *Kanadyiskyi rusyn*, 13 Jan. 1912. See also ibid., 24 Jan.–21 Feb. and 19 and 26 Dec. 1917, 16 Jan. 1918.

85 Ibid., 20 Jan. 1915

86 Ibid., 2 May and 10 Oct. 1917

87 *Kanadiiskyi farmer*, 8 Feb. 1906; and *Ukrainskyi holos*, 14 June 1911, 24 March 1915

88 *Kanadiiskyi farmer*, 8 Oct. 1909, 12 Jan. and 9 March 1910, 1 March
and 5 April 1912; and *Ukrainskyi holos*, 20 April 1910, 18 Jan. 1911, 22
May 1912, 9 Feb. 1916

89 *Ukrainskyi holos*, 21 Aug. 1912

90 Ibid., 5 Feb. 1919

91 *Svoboda*, 29 April 1897; *Ukrainskyi holos*, 20 April 1910, 21 Aug. 1912;
Kanadiiskyi farmer, 25 June 1915; and *Robochyi narod*, 28 Feb. 1916

92 *Svoboda*, 13 Feb. 1902; and *Ukrainskyi holos*, 25 March and 8 April 1914

93 *Svoboda*, 22 April and 20 May 1897, 25 Aug. 1904; *Kanadiiskyi farmer*,
5 March and 8 Dec. 1909, 16 Feb. and 9 March 1910; and *Ukrainskyi
holos*, 3 July 1918

94 Harrison, *Go West! Go Wise!* 82

95 *Svoboda*, 3 Nov. 1898

96 *Ukrainskyi holos*, 12 April 1916. Between the wars, Ukrainian men
would prefer the frugality of their peasant wives, whose savings helped
'progress,' to the spending habits of the English; Bayley, 'The Social
Structure of the Italian and Ukrainian Immigrant Communities in
Montreal,' 53–121.

97 *Kanadiiskyi farmer*, 9 March 1917. See also *Ukrainskyi holos*, 8 Nov.
1916, 15 May 1918; and *Kanadiiskyi farmer*, 2 Feb. 1917.

98 On the relationship between feminism and the frustrated nationalism
of subject or minority peoples see Jill McCalla Vickers, 'Sex/Gender
and the Construction of National Identities,' *Canadian Issues/Thèmes
Canadiens* 6 (1984): 34–49.

99 *Kanadiiskyi farmer*, 17 Jan. 1908, 23 April, 18 June, and 13 Aug. 1909,
14 April 1916; and *Ukrainskyi holos*, 1 June and 6 July 1910, 7 May
1913, 11 Aug. and 3 Nov. 1915, 3 Jan. 1917

100 *Ukrainskyi holos*, 7 Jan. 1914

101 Ibid., 28 June 1916

102 See, for example, ibid., 14 Oct. 1914, 17 May 1916. Also *Robitnytsia*, 1
Oct. 1924, 1–2; 15 Sept. 1926, 8–12, for progressive fears of the
street's snares.

103 James T.M. Anderson, *The Education of the New-Canadian: A Treatise on
Canada's Greatest Educational Problem* (London and Toronto 1918), 8, 9

CHAPTER 2   Jeopardizing the Future

1 *Vuikova knyha: Richnyk Vuika Shtifa v rysunkakh Ia. Maidanyka*, reprint
(Saskatoon 1974), 3. Jacob Maydanyk's cartoon of Nasha Meri is reproduced with the permission of the Maydanyk family.

2 *Ukrainskyi holos*, 31 May 1916

3 Maydanyk and his work are the subject of the National Film Board of Canada documentary, *Laughter in My Soul* (1983), directed by Halia Kuchmij.

4 *Kanadiiskyi farmer*, 21 Feb. 1908; *Kanadyiskyi rusyn*, 3 June 1911; *Ranok*, 19 Nov. 1913, 1 April 1914; *Ukrainskyi holos*, 29 April 1914; and the poem by I. Hashylnyk, 'Nashi khloptsi' (Our young blades) in *Humorystychnyi kaliendar Veselyi druh* (Winnipeg 1920), 149. Subsequent Ukrainian-Canadian historiography has largely ignored the Jacks and the problems of immigrant adjustment they represented. The major exception is Vera Lysenko, *Men in Sheepskin Coats: A Study in Assimilation* (Toronto 1947), 95–7. Michael H. Marunchak, *The Ukrainian Canadians: A History*, 2d ed. rev. (Winnipeg and Ottawa 1982), 90–1, maintains that the phenomenon vanished with the organization of Ukrainian community sociocultural life.

5 See, for example, Paul Yuzyk, *The Ukrainians in Manitoba: A Social History* (Toronto 1953), 190, 205–6; the wartime political expression of these ideas in Ukrainian Canadian Committee, *First All-Canadian Congress of Ukrainians in Canada* (Winnipeg 1943), 23, 34, 42, 93–4, 105; and their popular expression in *From Dreams to Reality: A History of the Ukrainian Senior Citizens of Regina and District, 1896–1976* (Regina 1977), 7, 13, 59, 69, 99–100, 120, 167, 178–83.

6 *Ranok*, 25 Oct. 1916

7 *Robitnytsia*, 15 Oct. 1936, 15; see also ibid., 1 July 1924, 4–6.

8 *Kanadiiskyi farmer*, 16 Aug. 1907, 23 June 1911. See also ibid., 28 Dec. 1905, 12 April 1906, 17 May 1912, 30 March 1917; and *Kanadyiskyi rusyn*, 16 Dec. 1911, 10 Aug. 1912, 5 Jan. 1916.

9 *Ranok*, 22 Jan. and 5 March 1919

10 Agnes C. Laut, *The Canadian Commonwealth* (Indianapolis 1915), 113; see also 118–19.

11 The percentages were 32.9 and 58.4; based on William Darcovich and Paul Yuzyk, eds., *A Statistical Compendium on the Ukrainians in Canada, 1891–1976* (Ottawa 1980), series 50.163–182, 525–6. The question of involuntary emigration for Ukrainian girls in Galicia, as part of a 'white slave trade' to Constantinople, Alexandria, India, and America, is raised by the Soviet Ukrainian historian, H.I. Khrobak, in 'Pro torhivliu zhinkamy v Halychyni naprykintsi XIX st. – na pochatku XX st.,' *Ukrainskyi istorychnyi zhurnal* 3 (March 1968): 123–4.

12 Wellington Bridgman, *Breaking Prairie Sod* (Toronto 1920), 178–9

13 Claudia Helen Popowich, *To Serve Is To Love: The Canadian Story of the*

Sisters Servants of Mary Immaculate (Toronto 1971), 32; and John Skwarok, *The Ukrainian Settlers in Canada and Their Schools, 1891–1921* (Edmonton 1958), 25

14 Based on Darcovich and Yuzyk, *Statistical Compendium*, series 40.156, 406. For the impact of interwar legislation on Ukrainians as 'non-preferred' immigrants see Myron Gulka-Tiechko, 'Inter-war Ukrainian Immigration to Canada, 1919–1939' (MA thesis, University of Manitoba 1983), esp. 136–244.

15 Bernard McEvoy, *From the Great Lakes to the Wide West: Impressions of a Tour between Toronto and the Pacific* (London 1902), 112

16 Figures based on Darcovich and Yuzyk, *Statistical Compendium*, series 40.15, 391; series 40.167 and 169, 407–8; and series 40.223, 425–6; see also Stephen W. Mamchur, 'The Economic and Social Adjustment of Slavic Immigrants in Canada: With Special Reference to the Ukrainians in Montreal' (MA thesis, McGill University 1934), 117–18.

17 *Lamont Tribune*, 27 April 1916

18 Justice of the Peace Files, file 74, Records of the Department of the Attorney General, Provincial Archives of Alberta, Edmonton; and *Manitoba Free Press*, 20 Oct. 1898

19 *Ukrainians in Alberta* (Edmonton 1981), 162; and *Promin*, Feb. 1978, 11. For Stechishin's contacts with the Canora branch of the UWAC, which she visited for many years as a representative of both UWAC headquarters and the Department of Extension at the University of Saskatchewan, see Olha Boichuk, comp., *Zolotyi vinets: Pivstolittia viddilu Soiuzu ukrainok Kanady imeny Marii Markovych u Kanori, Saskachevan, 1926–1976* (Canora 1981), 218.

20 Vuiko Shtif's wife, Evdokia, ran a boarding-house after she came to Canada, and proved herself a shrewd businesswoman.

21 Anna Arabska in *Ukrainskyi holos*, 25 April 1923

22 Ibid.

23 Based on Darcovich and Yuzyk, *Statistical Compendium*, series 32.1, 277; and series 32.76, 289

24 See, for example, the article by Sister Superior in *Kanadiiskyi ukrainets*, 9 Nov. 1927; and articles by Tekla Kroitor, Mariia Savchak, Anastaziia Troian, and Daria Iandova in *Ukrainskyi holos*, 11 April 1923, 26 March 1924, 30 Nov. 1927, 12 Dec. 1928, 26 Aug. and 2 Sept. 1931.

25 *Kanadiiskyi farmer*, 17 Jan. 1908, 23 April and 23 July 1909, 24 Nov. 1911 (reprint from *Narodnyi holos*); *Ukrainskyi holos*, 22 June 1910, 11 Aug. and 8 Sept. 1915, 28 June 1916, 1 Aug. 1923 (the reprint of an article by the Galician activist, Osyp Nazaruk); *Ranok*, 27 March 1912,

18 June 1913; *Kanadyiskyi rusyn*, 25 Aug. 1915, 10 Oct. 1917; *Kana-diiskyi ukrainets*, 3 Nov. 1920, 21 Sept. 1927; and Anna Arabska, 'Obra-zovykhovannia divchat,' *Kameniari*, 1 March 1919, 134–5

26 Nellie McClung, *The Stream Runs Fast: My Own Story* (Toronto 1945), 164

27 'Our New Immigrants – "The Galicians," ' *Great West Magazine*, Dec. 1898, 225

28 Letter, J.K. Smith, Edmonton, *Missionary Bulletin*, Sept.–Dec. 1915, 691–2

29 Emma Black, 'Kolokreeka – Home Work,' *Thirty-Fourth Annual Report of the Woman's Missionary Society of the Methodist Church* (1914–15), cxxviii

30 Letter, Rev. W.H. Pike, Andrew, Alberta, *Missionary Bulletin*, March–June 1915, 388–90

31 *Kanadiiskyi farmer*, 7, 14, and 28 Dec. 1905, 11 Jan. 1906

32 See, for example, ibid., 5 Feb., 26 March, and 13 Aug. 1909, 23 Feb. and 26 Oct. 1910, 13 March 1914; *Ukrainskyi holos*, 29 Jan. 1913; *Kana-dyiets*, 26 June 1918; and *Ranok*, 18 Nov. 1914, 4 Oct. 1916.

33 They included a Ukrainian translation (nd) of Mary Wood-Allen's *What a Young Girl Ought to Know*; *Poradnyk dlia zhenshchyn shcho khochut buty zdorovymy* (Advice for women who want to be healthy) (Winnipeg nd); Dr Mariian Dolynskyi, *Zhinka iak maty* (Woman as mother) (np [1923]); and Dr Mykhailo Kos, *Pro polovi spravy* (About sexual matters) (Winnipeg 1941).

34 *Svoboda*, 27 March 1902; and *Kanadiiskyi farmer*, 23 Aug. 1906

35 In forty years, the Basilians performed almost three thousand marriages, and, despite inevitable inconsistencies, their records contain a wealth of information on brides and grooms beyond the particulars of the ceremony – age, date and place of birth/baptism, legitimacy, parents, marital status, address, length of residence in Canada (for immigrants), and occupation. The marriage registers (1903–) are in the possession of the Ukrainian Basilian Fathers, Ss Peter and Paul Ukrainian Catholic Parish, Mundare, Alberta.

36 Alexander Royick, 'Ukrainian Settlements in Alberta,' *Canadian Slavonic Papers* 10, 3 (1968): 278–97; and Orest Martynowych, *The Ukrainian Bloc Settlement in East Central Alberta, 1890–1930: A History* (Edmonton 1985), 21–5

37 Vegreville United (Methodist) Register of Baptisms, Marriages and Burials, 1901–40, United Church Collection, Provincial Archives of Alberta

38 Records (microfilm) of St Josaphat's Ukrainian Catholic Cathedral, To-

ronto, Ontario, in the Ukrainian Collection of the Multicultural History Society of Ontario, Archives of Ontario, Toronto

39 In 1915, 42.9 per cent of weddings were performed on Sunday and 16.7 per cent on Saturday; in 1945, the figures were 26.2 and 41.0 per cent, respectively. As late as 1955, only 44.4 per cent of marriages took place on Saturday, but 91.7 per cent did by 1960.

40 Between 1910 and 1913, one-third of brides were under twenty-one; after that date, when reporting categories changed, between 25 and 30 per cent of brides were under twenty. Based on the annual reports of the vital statistics branch of the Departments of Agriculture (1905–17) and Public Health (1917–21) for the Province of Alberta

41 Based on parish records (1913–) of the Ukrainian Redemptorist Mission, St Mary's Ukrainian Catholic Church, Yorkton, Saskatchewan. Established in the 1890s by Latin-rite Belgian and French Redemptorists, the mission eventually became Greek Catholic under Ukrainian priests belonging to an Eastern-rite branch of the Congregation of Our Most Holy Redeemer. Early marriage registers do not contain the detail of those in Mundare, the inaccuracies and blanks in the entries a product of unfamiliarity with the language, customs, and homeland of the people the priests served.

42 In 1914 the average age of spinsters was 19.9 (compared with 17.3 in the Basilian sample), and a mere 3.5 per cent of brides were sixteen or younger; parish records, St Josaphat's Ukrainian Catholic Cathedral, Toronto.

43 In 1941, 22.9 per cent of brides in Alberta married before they were twenty (compared with 39.1 per cent in the Basilian sample); and a higher percentage married in the 20–24 and 25–29 age brackets (45.6 and 19.2 per cent compared with 37.7 and 15.9 per cent). Based on the annual report of the Dominion Bureau of Statistics for 1941

44 In 1941, 50.2 per cent of those aged 20 to 24 and 84.8 per cent of those aged 25 to 34 were married, compared with 38.5 per cent and 70.4 per cent, respectively, for all Canadian women; Jean E. Wolowyna, 'Trends in Marital Status and Fertility of Ukrainians in Canada,' in *Changing Realities: Social Trends among Ukrainian Canadians*, ed. W. Roman Petryshyn (Edmonton 1980), 169.

45 Charles H. Young, *Ukrainian Canadians: A Study in Assimilation* (Toronto 1931), 63

46 On continuity and change see Wolowyna, 'Trends in Marital Status and Fertility,' in Petryshyn, *Changing Realities*, 161–8; Marusia K. Petryshyn, 'The Changing Status of Ukrainian Women in Canada, 1921–1971,'

ibid., 189–209; and Nancy L. Penny, 'Marriage Patterns in an Ethnic Community in Rural Manitoba, 1896–1970' (MA thesis, University of Manitoba 1972).

47 While ethnic exogamy is miniscule in the parish records of the Basilian Fathers, they register the incidence of mixed marriage only among contracting parties who remained within the Ukrainian Catholic church. Convalidations, and by 1945 the increasing need to declare null and void marriages contracted by parishioners outside the church, suggest that religious ties were not always strong. Religious endogamy among Ukrainian Catholics in Alberta as a whole declined from 87.4 to 59.4 per cent between 1925 and 1945; based on Darcovich and Yuzyk, *Statistical Compendium*, series 60.337, 713.

48 Ibid., series 30.1–12, 177; series 31.34, 231; and series 60.275–292, 699

49 *Ukrainskyi holos*, 19 Nov. 1919

50 *Ranok*, 21 March 1917, 24 April 1918; *Svoboda*, 29 Sept. and 15 Dec. 1898; and *Kanadiiskyi farmer*, 19 July and 11 Oct. 1907

51 Anna Farion, 'Homestead Girlhood,' in *Land of Pain, Land of Promise: First Person Accounts by Ukrainian Settlers, 1891–1914*, comp. and trans. Harry Piniuta (Saskatoon 1978), 86–92

52 Eugen von Philippovich, 'Im Westen Kanadas,' *Österreichische Rundschau*, 13 April 1905, 494

53 *Kanadiiskyi farmer*, 11 Oct. 1907

54 *Robitnytsia*, 15 Dec. 1929, 762–3; and *Kanadiiskyi ukrainets*, 25 March 1925

55 See, for example, Ralph Connor [Charles W. Gordon], *The Foreigner: A Tale of Saskatchewan* (Toronto 1909), 160–70.

56 Lesia Ann Maruschak, 'The Ukrainian Wedding: An Examination of Its Rites, Customs and Traditions' (MA thesis, University of Saskatchewan 1985), 131–2. Vera Lysenko describes the headscarf ritual in a Ukrainian-Canadian context in her prairie novel, *Yellow Boots* (Toronto 1954), 119.

57 For a discussion of this phenomenon in the Canadian mainstream see Wayne Roberts, *Honest Womanhood: Feminism, Femininity and Class Consciousness among Toronto Working Women, 1893–1914* (Toronto 1976).

58 Ida Snyder, 'The Ruthenian Home and School, Edmonton,' *Thirty-Fourth Annual Report of the Woman's Missionary Society of the Methodist Church* (1914–15), cxix; see also letter, J.K. Smith, *Missionary Bulletin*, June–Sept. 1916, 522–3.

59 See Martha Bohachevsky-Chomiak, *Feminists Despite Themselves: Women in Ukrainian Community Life, 1884–1939* (Edmonton 1988), 98

60 *Ukrainskyi holos*, 31 May 1916
61 See, for example, *Ranok*, 24 April 1918, one of the few times the news-paper reprinted an article from *Ukrainskyi holos* without negative editorial comment.
62 *Ranok*, 1 April 1914
63 On the female nature see *Ukrainskyi holos*, 31 May and 26 July 1916, 19 Dec. 1917.
64 On parental responsibility for youth's character and behaviour, and therefore for their degree of 'civilization' and Ukrainian consciousness, see *Kanadiiskyi farmer*, 4 Jan. and 1 March 1906, 23 April 1909; *Ukrainskyi holos*, 6 July 1910, 3 Sept. 1913, 25 Nov. 1914, 16 Aug. 1916, 4 and 25 Sept. 1918, 26 March 1924; *Kanadyiskyi rusyn*, 7 and 14 Oct. 1914; and *Kanadiiskyi ranok*, 21 March and 29 Dec. 1922.
65 *Robochyi narod*, 18 July 1917; and for a later period, when nationalist women's organizations were accused of serving the Ukrainian-Canadian capitalist class and ignoring farm and working women's real needs, *Robitnytsia*, 1 Sept. 1933, 3–4
66 *Kanadiiskyi farmer*, 10 Sept. 1909
67 *Ukrainksyi holos*, 22 June 1910
68 Ibid., 29 July 1925, 12 Dec. 1928, 19 April 1933
69 What follows is a random sampling of this type of article or reporting. On child abuse and neglect, *Kanadiiskyi farmer*, 8 Feb. 1906. On sexual immorality, a girl's ruin by an unscrupulous adventurer, and poor judgment in choosing a husband, *Ranok*, 28 Feb. 1912; and the short story by A. Novak in *Ukrainskyi holos*, 22 April 1914. On bigamy, *Kanadiiskyi farmer*, 29 March 1906, 29 May 1908; and *Svoboda*, 28 Nov. 1901, 17 July 1902. On alcoholism, *Kanadiiskyi farmer*, 12 Nov. 1909, 12 Jan. 1910; *Kanadyiskyi rusyn*, 20 July 1912; *Ukrainskyi holos*, 6 Sept. 1916; and *Robitnytsia*, 15 Oct. 1926, 8–9.
70 Dmytro Hunkevych, *Zhertvy temnoty: Drama na 5 dii zi spivamy i tantsiamy z zhyttia ukrainskykh pereselentsiv v Kanadi* (Lviv and Winnipeg 1923), 'Slovo do chytachiv'
71 *Svoboda*, 14 Aug. 1902
72 'Another Wartime Casualty,' in Gloria Kupchenko Frolick, *The Green Tomato Years* (Toronto 1985), 103–12
73 Most of this work is unpublished, often only fragments of manuscripts. See the Vera Lysenko Papers, National Archives of Canada, Ottawa, particularly vol. 1, file 14; vol. 2, files 1–2; and vol. 3, files 1–2 and 5.
74 *Robitnytsia*, 15 Sept. 1924, 3–4; see also ibid., 15 Oct. 1936, 9, 11.
75 *Svoboda*, 31 Oct. 1900, 14 March 1901; *Kanadiiskyi farmer*, 28 Dec. 1905, 10 Sept. 1909; and *Ukrainskyi holos*, 3 Sept. 1913, 25 Nov. 1914

76 *Svoboda*, 10 July 1902. See also ibid., 16 April and 28 Aug. 1902, 20 Aug. 1903, 1 Sept. 1904; and *Kanadyiskyi rusyn*, 13 Jan. 1912

77 *Chervonyi prapor*, 5 Jan. 1908; the author also stressed the necessity of enlightenment and organization.

78 See *Kanadiiskyi farmer*, 13 April 1910.

79 Nestor Dmytriv, 'Assimilation,' *Svoboda*, 14 March 1898, in Piniuta, *Land of Pain, Land of Promise*, 51

80 *Ukrainskyi holos*, 6 Jan. 1926, 14 Oct. 1931, 23 May 1934

81 *Vuikova knyha*, 7

82 *Kanadiiskyi farmer*, 1 March 1906, 11 Oct. 1907, 13 July 1910

83 *Svoboda*, 3 June 1897

84 Ibid.

85 Robert England, *The Central European Immigrant in Canada* (Toronto 1929), 90

86 *Ukrainskyi holos*, 22 June and 14 Dec. 1910, 18 Jan. 1911; and *Kanadiiskyi farmer*, 12 Jan. 1910

87 *Robochyi narod*, 22 Jan. 1914, 18 July 1917; and *Robitnytsia*, 15 Feb. 1931, 7–8; 1 Sept. 1930, 27–8; 1 Oct. 1930, 18–21

88 Nationalist community historians would subsequently not even mention female wage-earners, concentrated in low-status and poorly paid jobs, when they discussed employment: Yuzyk, *Ukrainians in Manitoba*, 62–5; and Marunchak, *Ukrainian Canadians*, 184–9.

89 She is discussed in Martha Bohachevsky-Chomiak, 'Feminists Despite Themselves: Women in Ukrainian Community Life, 1884–1939' (Canadian Institute of Ukrainian Studies Archives, University of Alberta), 157–8.

90 *Ranok*, 27 March 1912, 18 June 1913; *Ukrainskyi holos*, 22 Sept. 1920, 21 March 1923; and *Kanadyiskyi rusyn*, 7 April 1915. In *Ukrainskyi holos*, 20 Dec. 1911, the girl acts as a foil for the denationalized young man.

91 *Ukrainskyi holos*, 19 Dec. 1917. See also ibid., 28 June 1916, 6 Aug. 1924, 18 Aug. 1926; *Kanadiiskyi ukrainets*, 10 July 1929; and for similar sentiments by the progressives, *Robitnytsia*, 1 Oct. 1924, 1–2.

92 *Ukrainskyi holos*, 26 July 1916

CHAPTER 3   Models for Their Sex

1 Iaroslav B. Rudnytskyi, 'Kanadiiski heohrafichni nazvy ukrainskoho pokhodzhennia,' in *Propamiatna knyha Ukrainskoho narodnoho domu u Vynypegu*, comp. Semen Kovbel and ed. Dmytro Doroshenko (Winnipeg 1949), 802

2 Dmytro Doroshenko, *A Survey of Ukrainian History*, ed. and updated by Oleh W. Gerus (Winnipeg 1975), 29–30

3 James T.M. Anderson, *The Education of the New-Canadian: A Treatise on Canada's Greatest Educational Problem* (London and Toronto 1918), 211

4 See, for example, 'Women's Work in Home Missions,' *Presbyterian Record*, June 1909, 226.

5 'A Message,' in fact, was the title of the short story published anonymously in the Woman's Christian Temperance Union collection, *Canadian National Prize Medal Contest Book* (np, nd), 39–42.

6 Robert England, *The Central European Immigrant in Canada* (Toronto 1929), 146. See also Anderson, *Education of the New-Canadian*, 143–50; Elsie M. Bishop, 'Some Teacher Experiences' (manuscript, nd), William Martin Papers, 19425–31, Saskatchewan Archives Board, Saskatoon; Miriam Elston, 'Ruthenians in Western Canada: School Teaching amongst the Russians,' *Onward*, 19 April 1919, np; and Mabel E. Finch, 'Christmas in a New Canadian School,' *Grain Growers' Guide*, 8 Dec. 1920, 66–7.

7 On the programs of the Protestant medical missions and school homes for Ukrainian girls see Vivian Olender, 'Presbyterian Missions and Ukrainians in Canada, 1900–1925' (PhD dissertation, University of Toronto 1984), 122, 133, 136–7, 144, 162, 167–8, 173–80, 192–4, 201–5, 217, 220–4.

8 P. Code, 'Everyday Life at Kolokreeka, Alberta,' *Missionary Outlook*, Jan. 1914, 16; also 'The Work of the WHMS,' *Home Mission Pioneer*, Nov. 1912, 118

9 Frank Yeigh, 'New Canadians Making Good,' *Canadian Magazine*, July 1922, 231–2; and Olender, 'Presbyterian Missions,' 144, 220–1

10 *Kanadiiskyi ranok*, 11 May 1928

11 *Vegreville Observer*, 14 March 1919

12 See, for example, Nellie L. McClung, *The Stream Runs Fast: My Own Story* (Toronto 1945), 167–9; and W.H. Pike, *Ruthenian Home, Edmonton, Alberta* (Toronto nd).

13 Comments attributed by J.H. Hall, 'Sifton School Home,' *Missionary Messenger*, April 1919, 12

14 M.J. Sproule's 'On A Russian Trail' was published with other contest winners in the *Edmonton Journal*, 22 Dec. 1914.

15 *Vegreville Observer*, 13 Jan. 1915

16 Jessie M. Deverell, 'The Ukrainian Teacher as an Agent of Cultural Assimilation' (MA thesis, University of Toronto 1941), 93–5

17 *Kanadyiskyi rusyn*, 17 July 1918; see also 4 Jan. 1913.

18 See the short story, 'Summer of '38,' in Gloria Kupchenko Frolick, *The Green Tomato Years* (Toronto 1985), 37–67; also Vera Lysenko's auto-biographical novel, 'The Torch' (Vera Lysenko Papers, vol. 1, file 14, National Archives of Canada, Ottawa), concerning Anglo-Canadian women teaching Ukrainian girls in North End Winnipeg.

19 United Church Collection, UC 172/24 and 172/95, Provincial Archives of Alberta, Edmonton; all three photographs were probably taken before 1914. See also Pearl Malayko's warm memory of schoolteacher and Woman's Christian Temperance Union worker, Mary Howard, in Andrew Historical Society, *Dreams and Destinies: Andrew and District* (Andrew 1980), 235–7.

20 Woman's Canadian Club of Calgary, *Year Book 1913* (Calgary 1913), 9; *Alberta Club Woman's Blue Book* (Calgary 1917), 8; and Nellie McClung to Robert Borden, cited in Howard Palmer, *Patterns of Prejudice: A History of Nativism in Alberta* (Toronto 1982), 44

21 *Ranok*, 24 May 1916

22 *Ukrainskyi holos*, 6 July 1910, 5 June 1912, 8 Sept. 1915; *Ranok*, 5 Jan. 1916; *Kanadiiskyi farmer*, 14 Sept. 1917; and for a later period, *Ukrainskyi holos*, 9 May 1934

23 For feature articles on prominent female revolutionaries see *Holos robitnytsi*, Jan.–Feb. 1923, 9–11; March 1923, 10–12; and *Robitnytsia*, 15 Jan. 1925, 3–4; 1 April 1930, 25; 15 Jan. 1935, 2–4.

24 See, for example, *Holos robitnytsi*, April 1923, 11–2; and in *Robitnytsia*: 1 Sept. 1924, 1–2; 15 Aug. 1925, 1–2; 1 Aug. 1928, 466–8; 15 Dec. 1934, 4–5; 1 Dec. 1935, 13–15; 1 April 1936, 10; 1 July 1937, 2–3.

25 See the remarks of Milena Rudnytska in Martha Bohachevsky-Chomiak, *Feminists Despite Themselves: Women in Ukrainian Community Life, 1884–1939* (Edmonton 1988), 144–6; Bohachevsky-Chomiak is generally critical of male attitudes towards women's participation in community life.

26 *Ukrainskyi holos*, 16 July and 9 Nov. 1919

27 Ibid., 6 Jan. 1926, 26 Feb. 1930

28 *Novyi shliakh*, 25 Oct. 1932, 12 Feb., 21 May, and 4 June 1935, 10 Nov. 1936, 21 Dec. 1937

29 Alexander Motyl, *The Turn to the Right: The Ideological Origins and Development of Ukrainian Nationalism* (Boulder 1980), esp. 153–61

30 *Novyi shliakh*, 27 June 1933

31 Ibid., 8 Jan. 1931, 19 Feb. 1935, 13 Oct. and 3 Nov. 1936, 26 Dec. 1938

32 Ibid., 3 May 1932, 11 Dec. 1934, 13 Aug. and 15 Oct. 1935

33 Claudia Koonz, 'Mothers in the Fatherland: Women in Nazi Germany,' in *Becoming Visible: Women in European History*, ed. Renate Bridenthal and Claudia Koonz (Boston 1977), 445–73

34 Ruth Roach Pierson, 'Women's Emancipation and the Recruitment of Women into the Labour Force in World War II,' in *The Neglected Majority: Essays in Canadian Women's History*, ed. Susan Mann Trofimenkoff and Alison Prentice (Toronto 1977), 125–45; *Canadian Women and the Second World War* (Ottawa 1983); and *'They're Still Women After All': The Second World War and Canadian Womanhood* (Toronto 1986)

35 *Novyi shliakh*, 1 Dec. 1936

36 See articles by Savella Stechishin in *Ukrainskyi holos*, 19 Jan. 1927, 24 Jan. 1934, and *Promin*, Feb. 1976, 3–6 (for International Women's Year and the ninetieth anniversary of the Ukrainian women's movement); also *Zhinochyi svit*, Feb. 1981, 2–5.

37 Stephanie Sawchuk, 'Our Women in Ukrainian and Canadian Life,' in Ukrainian Canadian Committee, *First All-Canadian Congress of Ukrainians in Canada* (Winnipeg 1943), 162

38 *Ukrainskyi holos*, 25 Feb. 1931; *Novyi shliakh*, 12 Feb. 1935, 31 March 1936, 21 Dec. 1937; and from a later period, *Promin*, Feb. 1976, 3–6

39 Sawchuk, 'Our Women in Ukrainian and Canadian Life,' 162

40 *Novyi shliakh*, 13 Aug. 1931. For a discussion of women during the revolutionary years by a post–1945 immigrant, described by the UWAC (which she joined) as one of the revolution's heroines, see *Promin*, Oct. 1967, 5–7; Nov. 1967, 18–21. The article is a good example of the continuity of ideas and their similarity among Ukrainian women on both sides of the ocean.

41 Cautious concerning twentieth-century Ukrainian gender relations, Bohachevsky-Chomiak accepts the view that Ukrainian women historically enjoyed considerable rights and liberties, although she does not actually examine their position in Ukrainian society prior to the nineteenth century; *Feminists Despite Themselves*, 3–8.

42 In Michael Chomiak Papers, file 504, Provincial Archives of Alberta. From Eastern Ukraine, Natalia Polonska-Vasylenko came to the West after the Second World War; her *Vydatni zhinky Ukrainy* (Winnipeg 1969) on prominent women of Ukraine was published by the UWAC.

43 Bohachevsky-Chomiak, *Feminists Despite Themselves*, 126–47

44 From the UWOC press see *Novyi shliakh*, 19 Feb. and 4 June 1935, 3 March 1936, and 29 Dec. 1936 (reprinted from *Zhinka*).

45 For a North American priest's tribute to the strength and contribution of the ordinary peasant woman during the recent war and in the struggle over Galicia see *Kanadiiskyi ukrainets*, 17 Nov. 1920.

46 *Promin*, Oct. 1971, 12–13

47 See the reprint from *Zhinka* in *Novyi shliakh*, 29 Dec. 1936. In the progressive camp, Peter Krawchuk credits Roxolana with freeing many Cossacks from Turkish slavery; *Ukrainian Canadian*, March 1972, 14.

48 In *Narodnyi iliustrovanyi kaliendar Kanadiiskoho farmera* (Winnipeg 1923), 140, Zavisna is used to illustrate heroism among Ukrainian women but she is not identified as a specifically female model and source of inspiration; on Mazepa's mother see *Promin*, May 1965, 15–16.

49 *Kanadyiskyi rusyn*, 7 Feb. 1917

50 Ibid., 9 Jan. 1918; *Ukrainskyi holos*, 27 Nov. 1929, 10 June 1931, 19 April 1933; *Novyi shliakh*, 11 Dec. 1934, 29 Sept. 1936, 30 Nov. 1937; and *Promin*, Feb. 1961, 14–15; May 1975, 4–8

51 *Svoboda*, 16 Oct. 1902

52 Bohachevsky-Chomiak, *Feminists Despite Themselves*, 300

53 On direct ties between the Women's Section of the ULFTA and Soviet Ukraine see *Robitnytsia*, 1 May 1926, 5–6; 15 Nov. 1926, 2–4; 1 June 1927, 329–30; 1 March 1937, 1–2, 8; 15 April 1937, 20–1.

54 Ibid., 1 July 1926, 1–2; 15 Feb. 1927, 100–1; 15 Oct. 1927, 612–15

55 *Ukrainian Canadian*, March 1972, 14–15

56 *Novyi shliakh*, 19 Feb. 1935, 24 July 1941; *Promin*, July 1960, 17–8; July 1969, 15 (also the special anniversary editorial); Feb. 1970, 20; July 1971, 1–4; and *Nasha doroha*, Jan.–March 1970, 17–18; July-Sept. 1979, 1–2; July-Sept. 1981, 102

57 *Robitnytsia*, 15 Sept. 1934, 9–10

58 *Ukrainian Canadian*, March 1972, 16–17

59 *Ukrainskyi holos*, 23 Jan. 1929, 25 Feb. 1931 (which focuses more on Kobrynska's feminism than her nationalism); *Promin*, June 1964, 15–16; and *Nasha doroha*, July-Sept. 1975, 4–7; July-Sept. 1984, 1–2

60 *Novyi shliakh*, 24 April 1939; *Nasha doroha*, May-June 1973, 7, virtually repeats these sentiments.

61 For two articles from different periods and camps, yet sharing the opinion of Pchilka's outstanding achievement as a Ukrainian mother, see *Novyi shliakh*, 21 April 1936; and *Nasha doroha*, Oct.–Dec. 1975, 23–4.

62 *Robitnytsia*, 15 Jan. 1925, 13–14; 1 March 1930, 13–14; 15 Feb. 1937, 29–30. For a Soviet assessment of Ukrainka's sociopolitical views see P.O. Zahorodniuk and I.F. Nadolnyi, 'Suspilno-politychni pohliady Lesi

Ukrainky,' *Ukrainskyi istorychnyi zhurnal* 2 (Feb. 1971): 14–18, written on the centenary of her birth.

63 *Novyi shliakh*, 22 Feb. 1938

64 Ibid., 11 Dec. 1934

65 *Promin*, Feb. 1960, 13; also the editor's note, ibid., Feb. 1973, 3, describing Ukrainka as 'a symbol of the national idea' whose 'great faith in the victory of our national righteousness' was a motivation for Ukrainians in the present. From UCWL circles see *Nasha doroha* Jan.–March 1976, 4; Oct.–Dec. 1981, 15, which also stress the power and influence of the poet's works for subsequent generations, including Ukrainians across the ocean.

66 Quoted in Bohachevsky-Chomiak, *Feminists Despite Themselves*, 122

67 For a later male perspective, in which Ukrainka's nationalism and uncompromising struggle are an example not only for Ukrainians but for anyone who loves his or her country, people, and culture, see the article by literary historian and critic Leonid Biletsky in *Promin*, Feb. 1960, 4.

68 *Robitnytsia*, 15 June 1924, 23; 15 July–1 Aug. 1924, 41

69 *Kanadiiskyi ukrainets*, 19 March, 30 April, and 16 July 1924; *Ukrainskyi holos*, 26 March 1924; and for a later period, *Promin*, Feb. 1960, 14–15. Basarab's year of birth is disputed; sources in 1924 gave 1889, others since have also given 1890 and 1899.

70 *Novyi shliakh*, 25 Oct. 1932, 20 March 1941

71 Oleksander Luhovyi [Oleksander Ovrutskyi-Shvabe], *Olha Basarabova: Drama v 5-okh diiakh* (Saskatoon 1936); and Charles M. Bayley, 'The Social Structure of the Italian and Ukrainian Immigrant Communities in Montreal, 1935–1937' (MA thesis, McGill University 1939), 223–35

72 *Nasha doroha*, April–June 1987, 22

73 Ibid., Jan.–March 1981, 10–11

74 See, for example, *Kanadyiskyi rusyn*, 10 Oct. 1917; and *Nasha doroha*, Oct.–Dec. 1972, 7–8.

75 Claudia Helen Popowich, *To Serve Is To Love: The Canadian Story of the Sisters Servants of Mary Immaculate* (Toronto 1971); and, on the order's pioneer work specifically, *Propamiatna knyha z nahody zolotoho iuvileiu poselennia ukrainskoho narodu v Kanadi, 1891–1941* (Yorkton 1941), 73–7, 81–3

76 In the interwar press see *Kanadiiskyi ukrainets*, 15 Aug. 1923, 12 Nov. 1924, 24 and 31 Jan. and 12 June 1929.

77 *Visnyk*, 1 May 1938, also 15 Jan. 1940; and from the Ukrainian Protestant camp, *Kanadiiskyi ranok*, 17 May 1921

78 See, for example, *Nasha doroha*, Oct.–Dec. 1981, 1. Marina Warner's *Alone of All Her Sex: The Myth and the Cult of the Virgin Mary* (London 1976) does not examine Mary as intercessor and protectress in national mythologies, particularly of oppressed peoples like the Ukrainians. The political-national role of the Virgin of Guadalupe in Mexico and of the Madonna of Czestochowa in Poland is discussed in James J. Preston, ed., *Mother Worship: Theme and Variation* (Chapel Hill 1982), 5–24, 335.

79 For early immigrant use of the idea see *Kanadiiskyi ukrainets*, 19 Dec. 1923, 12 Nov. 1924; for contemporary examples see *Nasha doroha*, July–Sept. 1978, 1–2; Oct.–Dec. 1981, 1–2.

80 *Novyi shliakh*, 23 April 1935; *Kanadiiskyi ukrainets*, 15 April 1923; and *Nasha doroha*, April–June 1971, 57–8; April–June 1984, 2

81 *Visnyk*, 1 May 1933, 1 June 1943

82 *Promin*, May 1980, 1–2. The following indicate the variety of inspirational motherhood articles in the nationalist women's press: *Ukrainskyi holos*, 20 June 1928 (local Mothers' Day observances in Saskatoon), 20 Feb. 1929 (Pchilka as Ukrainka's mother), 24 May 1933 (heroic Ukrainian mothers), 9 May 1945 (motherhood in former times); *Kanadiiskyi ukrainets*, 8 May 1929 (Olena Kysilewska on the first Mothers' Day in Galicia); *Novyi shliakh*, 1 Feb. 1938 (Ukrainian mothers in the national struggle), 8 May 1941 (Mothers' Day); *Promin*, May 1965, 15–16, on great mothers; and *Nasha doroha*, April–June 1982, 6, on Ukrainian mothers.

83 See, in particular, the UWOC press for February.

84 This particular reference comes from a UWOC Mothers' Day report from Bienfait, Saskatchewan; *Novyi shliakh*, 14 June 1938.

85 *Kanadiiskyi ukrainets*, 8 May 1929. See also *Ukrainskyi holos*, 5 June 1912, 9 May 1934; *Novyi shliakh*, 7 May 1935; *Nasha doroha*, April–June 1987, 8–10; and *Promin*, July–Aug. 1980, 8. A melodramatic allegory of the mother as Ukraine, by a delegate to the Third National Convention of Ukrainians in Canada, is recounted in *Kanadiiskyi farmer*, 31 Jan. 1919.

86 *Ranok*, 10 March 1920

87 *Visnyk*, 1 May 1938

88 Joanna Hubbs, *Mother Russia: The Feminine Myth in Russian Culture* (Bloomington and Indianapolis 1988)

89 See, for example, *Promin*, Feb. 1976, 3–6; and *Nasha doroha*, April–June 1981, 18.

90 Peter Krawchuk, *Shevchenko in Canada* (Toronto 1961), 64

91 On Shevchenko and women see *Robitnytsia* 15 March 1924, 3–4; 15

March 1928, 167–73; 15 March 1937, 7–8; *Holos robitnytsi*, March 1923, 4–7; and *Ukrainian Canadian*, 1 May 1961, 12–13.

92 The following are taken randomly from the UWAC press: *Ukrainskyi holos*, 9 March 1927, 11 March 1936, 8 March and 10 May 1939; and, more recently, illustrating Shevchenko's message for Mothers' Day, *Promin*, May 1961, 18–19.

93 *Robitnytsia*, 15 May 1931, 7–8

94 *Promin*, Feb. 1963, 3–4; Feb. 1978, 4–5; and *Zhinochyi svit*, Feb. 1972, 2–3

95 *Nasha doroha*, Jan.–Feb. 1975, 7–8; July–Sept. 1975, 16–18; Jan.–March 1976, 20–1; and *Promin*, Jan. 1972, 15–16; June 1972, 9–10; May 1979, 18–19. The author of the last article comments on meeting former political prisoner, Nadia Svitlychna, when she visited Winnipeg.

96 Dmytro Hunkevych, *Sered hradu kul abo neustrashyma heroinia* (Winnipeg nd)

CHAPTER 4   Putting the Models to Work

 1 *Novyi shliakh*, 28 May 1935, 5 May 1936; and for the postwar period, *Nasha doroha*, July–Sept. 1970, 138–9; April–June 1971, 57–8; April–June 1979, 1–2; and Anna Mariia Baran, 'Zavdannia ukrainky chlenkyni LUKZh,' in *Iuvileina knyha ukraintsiv katolykiv Saskachevanu 1905–1955*, (Saskatoon 1955), 188–90

 2 *Nasha doroha*, Jan.–March 1976, 16. See also, for example, M. Vala, 'Ukrainska kultura i molod,' in Komitet ukraintsiv Kanady, *Druhyi vsekanadiiskyi kongres ukraintsiv Kanady* (Winnipeg [1946]), 63–5, as Ukrainian-Canadian women faced their postwar tasks as mothers in the home and as participants in community life.

 3 *Robitnytsia*, 1 May 1929, 261–3

 4 Nataliia L. Kohuska, *Pivstolittia na hromadskii nyvi: Narys istorii Soiuzu ukrainok Kanady* (Edmonton and Winnipeg 1986), dedication page

 5 See Olha Swystun's speech to the Third Ukrainian National Convention in Saskatoon, in *Ukrainskyi holos*, 5 Feb. 1919; the speech by Mrs Baran in *Kanadiiskyi ukrainets*, 19 Feb. 1930; and Rozha Kovalska's article in *Novyi shliakh*, 1 Dec. 1936.

 6 *Kanadiiskyi ukrainets*, 19 Sept. 1923; *Ukrainskyi holos*, 17 Oct. 1923, 16 July 1924, 17 Nov. 1926, 12 Jan. 1927, 19 April 1933; and *Novyi shliakh*, 11 Dec. 1934, 12 Feb. and 13 Aug. 1935

 7 *Novyi shliakh*, 1 Dec. 1936

 8 Ibid., 17 May 1932, 5 June 1934, 11 Dec. 1934, 19 and 26 Feb. 1935,

10 Nov. 1936, 23 March, 12 Oct., and 28 Dec. 1937, 17 April 1941, 10 Nov. 1945

9 *Ukrainskyi holos*, 5 Dec. 1928, 12 June and 27 Nov. 1929

10 Ibid., 3 May 1933

11 Quoted in Kohuska, *Pivstolittia na hromadskii nyvi*, 605

12 N. Kohuska, 'Woman's Part in the Life of a Nation,' in Ukrainian Canadian Committee, *First All-Canadian Congress of Ukrainians in Canada* (Winnipeg 1943), 156–60

13 *Nasha doroha*, Jan.–Feb. 1973, 10–11; see ibid., July–Sept. 1977, 5–6, for the thoughts of another priest.

14 Kohuska, *Pivstolittia na hromadskii nyvi*, 620–8

15 See, for example, *Ukrainskyi holos*, 16 July 1919; reprinted in *Kanadiiskyi ukrainets*, 10 July 1929.

16 For the persistence of this attitude see the discussion on the need for women's organizations in *Nasha doroha*, Jan.–March 1987, 10–13.

17 *Robochyi narod*, 18 July 1917

18 *Robitnytsia*, 15 June 1930, 17–18; 1 Oct. 1930, 18–21. See also ibid., 1 March 1926, 14; 15 July 1926, 3–4; 15 Feb. 1931, 7–8; 15 April 1935, 12–13; 15 Oct. 1936, 9, 11; 15 June 1935, 9–11; 1 Feb. 1937, 2–3.

19 Ibid., 1 Sept. 1930, 27–8

20 Ibid., 1 May 1924, 3–4; 15 Aug. 1924, 2–3; 15 July 1926, 3–4; 15 June 1935, 9–11; 1 July 1937, 2–3

21 Ibid., 15 March–1 April 1929, 162–5, 190–1

22 Petro Kravchuk, comp., *Zhinochi doli* (Toronto 1973), ix; English translation by Michael Ukas, *Reminiscences of Courage and Hope: Stories of Ukrainian Canadian Women Pioneers* (Toronto 1991), 23. See also Petro Prokopchak, ed., *Almanakh piatdesiatyrichchia zhinochykh viddiliv Tovarystva obiednanykh ukrainskykh kanadtsiv* (Toronto 1976), 280.

23 The series, 'Chy potribno zhinkam organizatsii?' (Do women need organizations?), appeared in *Robitnytsia* between 1 April 1928 and 1 Feb. 1929. In June and July 1931 a series of discussion articles on whether the Women's Section should be liquidated raised many of the same points.

24 Cited in Donald Avery, *'Dangerous Foreigners': European Immigrant Workers and Labour Radicalism in Canada, 1896–1932* (Toronto 1979), 127, 182

25 *Holos robitnytsi*, Sept. 1923, 1–2

26 The editors of *Robitnytsia* were Myroslav Irchan, Mykhailo Lenartovych, Petro Prokopchak, and Petro Chaikiwsky; see Petro Kravchuk,

Piatdesiat rokiv sluzhinnia narodu: Do istorii ukrainskoi narodnoi presy v Kanadi (Toronto 1957), 147–59.

27 *Robitnytsia*, 15 Sept. 1925, 21; see also the memoirs of Mary Vinohradova in *Ukrainian Canadian*, March 1972, 24.

28 *Robitnytsia*, 1 Sept. 1929, 547–8

29 Ibid., 1 Sept. 1926, 9–10; 15 Feb. 1928, 97–8; 15 March–1 April 1929, 162–5; 1 March 1930, 2–3; 1 June 1931, 10–11; 1 July 1931, 2–5; 15 Jan. 1936, 16–17

30 Iryna Pavlykovska, ed., *Dlia Boha, tserkvy i narodu: Liga ukrainskykh katolytskykh zhinok edmontonskoi ieparkhii v 1944–1966 rokakh, pochatky i diialnist* (Edmonton [1966]), 177

31 *Ukrainskyi holos*, 17 May 1933

32 See the accounts of the establishment of UWOC branches in Fort William, Port Arthur, Windsor, and Sydney in Irena Knysh, ed., *Na sluzhbi ridnoho narodu: Iuvileinyi zbirnyk Orhanizatsii ukrainok Kanady im. Olhy Basarab u 25-richchia vid zaisnuvannia, 1930–1955* (Winnipeg 1955), 68, 213–29, 283–6, 288–9.

33 See 'Liga ukrainskykh katolytskykh zhinok/Ukrainian Catholic Women's League,' in *Iuvileina knyha ukraintsiv katolykiv Saskachevanu*, 63–79; and branch reports in the following eparchial histories: Pavlykovska, *Dlia Boha, tserkvy i narodu*; Vira Buchynska, ed., *Slidamy dyiakonis: 25 rokiv pratsi Ligy ukrainskykh katolytskykh zhinok Kanady u Manitobi* (Winnipeg 1973); and Iaroslava Vynnytska, ed., *Nacherk istorii Ligy ukrainskykh katolytskykh zhinok Kanady torontskoi eparkhii* (Toronto 1975).

34 For a concise statement of the involuntary nature of membership in the Ukrainian nation and its implications see the 'ten national commandments for Ukrainians' in *Kanadiiskyi ukrainets*, 28 Jan. 1925.

35 *Holos robitnytsi*, July 1923, 2–3

36 Ibid., Aug. 1923, 1–2; and *Robitnytsia*, 15 June 1926, 1; 15 Sept. 1926, 8–12; 1 April 1927, 193–4; 1 April 1928, 209–13; 1 Aug. 1928, 449; 1 July 1930, 28–9; 1 May 1935, 23

37 *Robitnytsia*, 15 March 1924, 17–18; 1 March 1926, 17–18; 15 Jan. 1928, 33–4

38 Ibid., 1 Oct. 1924, 1–2, is one of few instances.

39 For interwar attitudes see *Ukrainskyi holos*, 14 Jan. and 29 July 1925, 4 July 1928; *Kanadiiskyi ukrainets*, 22 Jan. 1930; and *Novyi shliakh*, 17 June 1933, 13 Aug. 1935, 19 Oct. 1937, 8 Feb. 1938.

40 *Ukrainskyi holos*, 23 Jan. 1924, 6, 13, and 20 Dec. 1933, 30 Dec. 1936. Kohuska, *Pivstolittia na hromadskii nyvi*, 628–33, describes the UWAC's

interwar work in home economics and health on the prairies; in 1930 it was instrumental in the appointment of a rural Ukrainian public health nurse.

41 Soiuz ukrainok Kanady, *Na storozhi kultury* (Winnipeg 1947), 3; see also *Nasha doroha*, April–June 1987, 8–10. From the postwar period see another UWAC publication, Tonia Horokhovych's *Batky i dity* (Winnipeg and Toronto 1965).

42 Specifically on the physical appearance of the interwar Ukrainian-Canadian home and its Ukrainian atmosphere see *Kanadiiskyi ukrainets*, 10 July 1929; and *Ukrainskyi holos*, 2 March and 6 April 1927, 22 Feb. 1928, 6 March and 10 April 1929.

43 For the contemporary significance of Tweedsmuir's speech see the nationalist press at the time of his death in Feb. 1940; Paul Yuzyk, *Ukrainian Canadians: Their Place and Role in Canadian Life* (Toronto 1967), 85, illustrates its political use since 1940.

44 See the official thinking in the editorial, 'Moloda generatsiia' (Young generation) in *Ukrainskyi holos*, 25 Feb. 1925; and the communication from the Ukrainian Canadian Committee in *Nasha doroha*, April–June 1970, np. For women on Tweedsmuir see *Novyi shliakh*, 16 June 1945; and Olha Boichuk, comp., *Zolotyi vinets: Pivstolittia viddilu Soiuzu ukrainok Kanady imeny Marii Markovych u Kanori, Saskachevan, 1926–1976* (Canora 1981), 240.

45 This fraction is based on the ULFTA, UWAC and UWOC membership figures for the late 1930s discussed in the introduction, and the population breakdown by age and sex in William Darcovich and Paul Yuzyk, eds., *A Statistical Compendium on the Ukrainians in Canada, 1891–1976* (Ottawa 1980).

46 *Robitnytsia*, 15 March 1937, 28; Aug. 1937, 8

47 Ibid., 15 Jan. 1937, 27; 15 March 1937, 26

48 Ibid., 1 April 1937, 26. For a later period see the history of the UWAC branch in St Julien, Saskatchewan, in Kohuska, *Pivstolittia na hromadskii nyvi*, 937–8; similar concerns are raised in other branch histories in this volume and Kohuska's earlier *Chvert stolittia na hromadskii nyvi: Istoriia Soiuzu ukrainok Kanady, 1926–1951* (Winnipeg 1952).

49 *Ukrainskyi holos*, 17 May 1933

50 *Robitnytsia*, 1 April 1937, 24. In 1931 the Women's Section reported that most of its members were mothers in the home; ibid., 1 May 1931, 8–10.

51 Based on Kohuska, *Pivstolittia na hromadskii nyvi*, and local histories from the Vegreville bloc settlement.

52 *Ukrainskyi holos*, 14 Feb. 1934, 25 Jan. and 8 March 1939

53 Charles M. Bayley, 'The Social Structure of the Italian and Ukrainian Immigrant Communities in Montreal, 1935–1937' (MA thesis, McGill University 1939), 102–3; the opposite was true for Italian women in the study.

54 *Robitnytsia*, 1924 and 1925, for Fedorah; Kohuska, *Chvert stolittia na hromadskii nyvi*, 195–7, and her *Pivstolittia na hromadskii nyvi*, 851–2

55 *Robitnytsia*, 1 Jan. 1930, 1–2; and *Ukrainskyi holos*, 12 Aug. 1931

56 See, for example, UCWL branch summaries for Hamilton (St Nicholas), Thunder Bay (Transfiguration), Welland, Chatham, and St Catharines in Vynnytska, *Nacherk istorii*.

57 Bankend, Prelate, and Candiac in Saskatchewan, Smoky Lake and Waskatenau in Alberta, and Transcona in Manitoba are only some of the UWAC branches to describe national affiliation as a stimulus; see Kohuska, *Chvert stolittia na hromadskii nyvi*, and her *Pivstolittia na hromadskii nyvi*, 785–7, 800–1, 846–7.

58 Tovarystvo ukrainskyi robitnycho-farmerskyi dim, *Almanakh Tovarystva ukrainskyi robitnycho-farmerskyi dim v Kanadi i bratnikh organizatsii, 1918–1929* (Winnipeg 1930), 213

59 See, for example, the accounts of the Bonnyville, Codette-Aylsham, Melfort, and Flin Flon branches of the UWAC in Kohuska, *Pivstolittia na hromadskii nyvi*, 804–5, 857–8, 951, 968–9.

60 The UWAC branch in New Toronto falls into this category (Kohuska, *Chvert stolittia na hromadskii nyvi*, 361–2); in the farming community of Itonia, Saskatchewan, it took the UWAC seven years to raise the funds for a *narodnyi dim* (481).

61 Boichuk, *Zolotyi vinets*, 221. On the introduction and popularity of the *pyrohy* supper in rural communities in the prairie provinces see the UWAC branch history from Thorhild, Alberta, in Kohuska, *Pivstolittia na hromadskii nyvi*, 803. By the tenth anniversary in 1972 of the '*pyrohy* industry' run from the basement of the Protection of the Blessed Virgin Mary Church in Thunder Bay, the local UCWL had raised $61,362.18 for the parish; Vynnytska, *Nacherk istorii*, 276.

62 Buchynska, *Slidamy diyakonis*, 190

63 Kohuska, *Pivstolittia na hromadskii nyvi*, 641; see also *Ukrainskyi holos*, 25 Oct. 1933.

64 E. Iankivska, comp., *Liga ukrainskykh katolytskykh zhinok Kanady: Vira – nadiia – liubov* (Toronto 1985), 278

65 Eugene W. Ratsoy, *Into the New Millennium: Ukrainian Orthodox Parish-*

ioners Explore Future Directions – A Descriptive Report of an Urban Parish and Its Needs (Edmonton 1990), 20–2

66 See, in particular, UWAC branch histories in Kohuska, *Pivstolittia na hromadskii nyvi.*

67 *Propamiatna knyha z nahody zolotoho iuvileiu poselennia ukrainskoho narodu v Kanadi* (Yorkton 1941), 74

68 Tovarystvo ukrainskyi robitnycho-farmerskyi dim, *Almanakh*, 63–227

69 See, for example, *Robitnytsia*, 15 Sept. 1927, 545–7; 15 June 1928, 353–5; 1 Sept. 1928, 519–20, an appeal from Kharkiv to readers of *Robitnytsia* on behalf of the Soviet Red Cross in Western Ukraine; 15 Feb. 1929, 113–14; 1 Nov. 1930, 15.

70 *Novyi shliakh*, 16 April 1935, 31 March 1936, 19 Oct. 1937, 21 June and 26 Dec. 1938, 3 April and 29 June 1939

71 Kohuska, *Pivstolittia na hromadskii nyvi*, 606; and *Ukrainskyi holos*, 18 Feb., 18 March, and 1 July 1925, 4 Sept. 1929, 24 Dec. 1930, 22 March and 25 July 1933

72 Kohuska, *Chvert stolittia na hromadskii nyvi*, 299

73 The remainder supported miscellaneous Ukrainian community projects and institutions, primarily sponsored by the Ukrainian Greek Orthodox church; Boichuk, *Zolotyi vinets*, 180–1, 275–6.

74 The remainder was divided among unspecified religious and cultural activities and charity; Bohdan Kazymyra et al., eds., *Spilnym zusylliam i napolehlyvoiu pratseiu: Iuvileina knyha ukrainskoi katolytskoi parafii sv. Vasyliia Velykoho, 1925–1975* (Regina 1975), 206.

75 Knysh, *Na sluzhbi ridnoho narodu*, 306–12, 325–34

76 *Kanadiiskyi ukrainets*, 14 Nov. 1928, 3 Dec. 1930; and *Ukrainskyi holos*, 24 Feb. 1932

77 Knysh, *Na sluzhbi ridnoho narodu*, 464; and *Ukrainskyi holos*, 15 March 1939. On the international contacts and activity of organized Ukrainian women in Europe between the wars see Martha Bohachevsky-Chomiak, *Feminists Despite Themselves: Women in Ukrainian Community Life, 1884–1939* (Edmonton 1988), 262–80.

78 *Robitnytsia*, 15 Sept. 1929, 551; 1 Dec. 1929, 707–8

79 See, for example, Kysilewska's visits to Saskatoon, Montreal, Winnipeg, Toronto, and Regina reported in *Ukrainskyi holos*, 16 and 23 Oct., and 6 and 13 Nov. 1929.

80 The Catholic senator and activist also touched Ukrainian Catholic women, and a local Women's Union created in the Catholic stronghold of Mundare under her stimulus to broader outreach remained outside

the Orthodox UWAC network; Pavlykovska, *Dlia Boha, tserkvy i narodu*, 16–20.

81 On the UWAC delegate to Stanislaviv see *Ukrainskyi holos*, 21 Feb. 1934; see also its reports on the congress from the Galician daily, *Dilo* (Deed), and the account in Bohachevsky-Chomiak, *Feminists Despite Themselves*, 175–9.

82 Knysh, *Na sluzhbi ridnoho narodu*, 464–5; and Kohuska, *Pivstolittia na hromadskii nyvi*, 639–42. On the need to cultivate Anglo-Canadian circles to propagandize the Ukrainian cause see also *Novyi shliakh*, 3 April 1939.

83 See Irena Knysh, *Patriotzym Anny Ionker* (Winnipeg 1964); and Anna Ionker, 'Moi vrazhennia z podorozhi do Halychyny i z pobutu na mizhnarodnim zhinochim kongresi u Vidni,' in Knysh, *Na sluzhbi ridnoho narodu*, 481–3.

84 Bohachevsky-Chomiak, *Feminists Despite Themselves*, 273, attributes the intransigence of the ICW's stand not to accredit Ukrainian women to its dependence on influential Polish women/connections in its disarmanent work (which received priority).

85 *Ukrainians in Alberta* (Edmonton 1981), 162

86 *Kanadyiskyi rusyn*, 29 March, 5 and 12 April 1916; *Ukrainskyi holos*, 12 May 1926, 2 March 1927, 28 March 1928, 23 May 1934, 5 April 1939; the reprint from *Zhinocha dolia* in *Kanadiiskyi ukrainets*, 5 March 1930; and *Kanadiiskyi ranok*, 26 July and 16 Aug. 1921, 20 June 1922

87 *Novyi shliakh*, 16 March 1937; and Kohuska, *Chvert stolittia na hromadskii nyvi*, 34

88 Following national affiliation, the UWAC encouraged its provincial wings and local branches to join the appropriate council. For the official UWAC perspective on its involvement in the NCWC see Kohuska, *Pivstolittia na hromadskii nyvi*, 646–60.

89 Ol'ha Woycenko, conversation with Frances Swyripa, 6 Oct. 1987

90 *Robitnytsia*, 1 Jan. 1929, 24–5

91 For a retrospective see *Ukrainian Canadian*, 15 Sept. 1966, 7.

92 *Robitnytsia*, 1 April 1937, 4–5; 15 June 1937, 18

93 Ibid., 15 Sept. 1930, 7–8; 1 Sept. 1933, 3–4; 15 Sept. 1934, 9–10; 15 May 1935, 7–8

94 Ibid., 1 Sept. 1933, 3–4; 15 Feb. 1937, 22; 15 July 1937, 2–3

95 On the fortunes and activities of UWOC branches during the Second World War see Knysh, *Na sluzhbi ridnoho narodu*.

96 *Novyi shliakh*, 8 Jan. 1931, 6 Oct. 1936, 10 Aug. 1937

97 Stephanie Sawchuk, 'Our Women in Ukrainian and Canadian Life,' in Ukrainian Canadian Committee, *First All-Canadian Congress of Ukrainians in Canada*, 163; see also *Novyi shliakh*, 25 April 1942, 8 May 1943, 16 June 1945.

98 *Novyi shliakh*, 14 March 1942

99 *Ukrainskyi holos*, 7 Oct. 1936; and *Novyi shliakh*, 13 Oct. 1936

100 The Orthodox women's group in Portage la Prairie, Manitoba, affiliated with the UWAC in 1942 at the behest of its Winnipeg priest and his wife, 'because of the appeal through the press and other media for help in the war effort'; Kohuska, *Pivstolittia na hromadskii nyvi*, 852.

101 The UWOC and UWAC pages in *Novyi shliakh* and *Ukrainskyi holos*, respectively, are the best contemporary sources for participation by the two organizations in the Canadian war effort. For the UWAC's assessment of its contribution see Kohuska, *Pivstolittia na hromadskii nyvi*, 658–64; Knysh, *Na sluzhbi ridnoho narodu*, 94–110, contains the official UWOC account.

102 John Kolasky, *The Shattered Illusion: The History of Ukrainian Pro-Communist Organizations in Canada* (Toronto 1979), 33, 109

103 *Ukrainskyi holos*, 7 and 14 Feb. 1940; and E. Sytnyk, 'Zavdannia ukrainskoho zhinotstva v Kanadi v systemi diialnosty KUK,' in Komitet ukraintsiv Kanady, *Tretii vse-kanadiiskyi kongres ukraintsiv Kanady* (Winnipeg [1950]), 86–90

104 Mariia Dyma, 'Znachennia Komitetu ukrainok Kanady,' 34–6; Mariia Dyma, 'Pochatky i diialnist Komitetu ukrainok Kanady,' 53–8; and Nataliia Kohuska, 'V ooboroni trevaloho myra i prav liudyny,' 59–62, in Komitet ukraintsiv Kanady, *Druhyi vse-kanadiiskyi kongres ukraintsiv Kanady*

105 Dyma, 'Znachennia Komitetu ukrainok Kanady,' 34–6

106 *Nasha doroha*, April–June 1975, 20. For the interwar and postwar periods see *Ukrainskyi holos*, 1 April 1925, 3 March 1933, 4 July 1934; *Novyi shliakh*, 7 May 1935, 25 April 1942, 24 March and 2 June 1945; Kohuska, 'Woman's Part in the Life of a Nation,' 156–60; Sawchuk, 'Our Women in Ukrainian and Canadian Life,' 163; the speech by Nadia Malaniuk in Natalia Lewenec-Kohuska, *Forty Years in Retrospect, 1926–1966*, trans. Sonia Cipywnyk (Hamilton 1967), 23; and *Nasha doroha*, July–Sept. 1970, 138–9; Jan.–March 1980, 7–8; Oct.–Dec. 1981, 23–4.

CHAPTER 5   Canadianizing a Legacy

1 See Evheniia Sytnyk, 'Ukrainske zhinotstvo na skytanni i nasha pomich iomu,' in Komitet ukraintsiv Kanady, *Druhyi vse-kanadiiskyi kongres ukraintsiv Kanady* (Winnipeg [1946]), 66–71; and her 'Zavdannia ukrain-skoho zhinotstva v Kanadi v systemi diialnosty KUK,' ibid., 86–90, for contemporary attitudes towards Ukrainian-Canadian women's responsibilities. For retrospective views of their aid to the displaced persons see Nataliia L. Kohuska, *Pivstolittia na hromadskii nyvi: Narys istorii Soiuzu ukrainok Kanady* (Edmonton and Winnipeg 1986), 666–75; Irena Knysh, ed., *Na sluzhbi ridnoho narodu: Iuvileinyi zbirnyk Orhanizatsii ukrainok Kanady im. Olhy Basarab u 25-richchia vid zaisnuvannia, 1930–1955* (Winnipeg 1955), 470–9; and Vira Buchynska, ed., *Slidamy dyiakonis: 25 rokiv pratsi Ligy ukrainskykh katolytskykh zhinok Kanady u Manitobi* (Winnipeg 1973), 148–68.

2 William Darcovich and Paul Yuzyk, eds., *A Statistical Compendium on the Ukrainians in Canada, 1891–1976* (Ottawa 1980), series 50.62–77, 513; series 50.94–103, 516; and series 50.163–182, 524–6

3 Oleh Romanyshyn, 'The Canadian League for the Liberation of Ukraine and Its Women's Association,' *Polyphony* 10 (1988): 163–6

4 *Promin*, April 1961, 13–15; May 1961, 3–5

5 Kohuska, *Pivstolittia na hromadskii nyvi*, 666–75

6 Ibid., 741–69

7 This list, based on UWAC branch summaries, is perhaps incomplete (see ibid.). The figure of five thousand members comes from Olha Boichuk, comp., *Zolotyi vinets: Pivstolittia viddilu Soiuzu ukrainok Kanady imeny Marii Markovych u Kanori, Saskachevan, 1926–1976* (Canora 1981), 190, 202.

8 The 180 figure (for 1964) comes from Iryna Pavlykovska, ed., *Dlia Boha, tserkvy i narodu: Liga ukrainskykh katolytskykh zhinok edmontonskoi ieparkhii v 1944–1966 rokakh, pochatky i diialnist* (Edmonton [1966]), 223; and Buchynska, *Slidamy dyiakonis*, 146. Provincial totals are from Pavlykovska, *Dlia Boha, tserkvy i narodu*, 77; Iaroslava Vynnytska, ed., *Nacherk istorii Ligy ukrainskykh katolytskykh zhinok Kanady torontskoi eparkhii* (Toronto 1975), 44 (for 1963); and UCWL branch histories in Buchynska, *Slidamy dyiakonis*. The only available figure for Saskatchewan is twenty-nine branches in 1955; *Iuvileina knyha ukraintsiv katolykiv Saskachevanu, 1905–1955* (Saskatoon 1955), 79.

9 On the UCWL in the Toronto eparchy (which includes Quebec and the Maritimes as well as Ontario), see Vynnytska, *Nacherk istorii*.

10 Conversation with Frances Swyripa, June 1987

11 Vynnytska, *Nacherk istorii*, 224, 229, 304–5, 318; and Kohuska, *Pivstolittia na hromadskii nyvi*, 874–7, 885 (Montreal and Hamilton). *Zolotyi vinets*, a history of the UWAC branch in Canora, Saskatchewan, was the work of Olha Boychuk, a displaced person married to the local Orthodox priest, himself a displaced person; her imprint on the book, in an aggressive Ukrainianness and its backward projection onto pioneer women, is pronounced.

12 Knysh, *Na sluzhbi ridnoho narodu*, 202–7, 348–70

13 Ibid., 306–24

14 See Bylaws, Records of the Ukrainian Women's Organization of Canada, vol. 1, Ukrainian Cultural and Educational Centre, Winnipeg.

15 For branch activities between 1956 and 1980 see *Na sluzhbi ridnoho narodu*, vol. 2 (Toronto 1984), 110–417. In Feb. 1985, *Zhinochyi svit* reported sixteen branches with approximately five hundred members in Ontario, but did not identify them by location.

16 See Martha Bohachevsky-Chomiak, 'The Women's Movement in the Camps,' in *The Refugee Experience: Ukrainian Displaced Persons after World War II*, ed. Wsewolod Isajiw, Roman Senkus, and Yury Boshyk (Edmonton 1992), 179–97.

17 For the UWAC's own explanation for its failure to join the WFUWO, see *Promin*, April 1968, 9–12.

18 All figures in this paragraph come from John Kolasky, *The Shattered Illusion: The History of Ukrainian Pro-Communist Organizations in Canada* (Toronto 1979), 177–99.

19 Petro Prokopchak, ed., *Almanakh piatdesiatyrichchia zhinochykh viddiliv Tovarystva obiednanykh ukrainskykh kanadtsiv, 1922–1972* (Toronto 1976), 51–109

20 E. Iankivska, comp., *Liga ukrainskykh katolytskykh zhinok Kanady: Vira – nadiia – liubov* (Toronto 1985), 182, 193, 280. The closure or inactivity of other rural branches was attributed to the absence of a resident priest.

21 Kohuska, *Pivstolittia na hromadskii nyvi*, 954–6

22 Knysh, *Na sluzhbi ridnoho narodu*, 230–42

23 Both Winnipeg and Toronto, for example, had 'Young Women's Clubs'; *Ukrainian Canadian*, 1 May 1949, 10; 15 Feb. 1950, 10.

24 Knysh, *Na sluzhbi ridnoho narodu*, 243–6, 264–5, 346–8

25 Pavlykovska, *Dlia Boha, tserkvy i narodu*, 121–6, 217; and Mykhailo Khomiak, ed., *Propamiatna knyha: Ukrainskyi katolytskyi soiuz – Ukrainskyi narodnyi dim, 1906–1965* (Edmonton [1966]), 366–71

26 *Nasha doroha*, Dec. 1972, 6–7

27 Pavlykovska, *Dlia Boha, tserkvy i narodu*, 127–31, 219; and Khomiak, *Propamiatna knyha*, 371–4

28 *Nasha doroha*, Jan.–March 1975, 16; Jan.–March 1984, 25–7

29 See Kohuska, *Pivstolittia na hromadskii nyvi*, 646–60.

30 Cited ibid., 716

31 *Nasha doroha*, Oct.–Dec. 1983, 28–9

32 Buchynska, *Slidamy dyiakonis*, 148–68; on UCWL initiatives to obtain mainstream funding for projects to help Ukrainians in Argentina and Brazil see Iankivska, *Vira – nadiia – liubov*, 251.

33 Nataliia Kohuska, *Chvert stolittia na hromadskii nyvi: Istoriia Soiuzu ukrainok Kanady, 1926–1951* (Winnipeg 1952), 61–88. On UCWL eparchial museums see Pavlykovska, *Dlia Boha, tserkvy i narodu*, 88–4; and Vynnytska, *Nacherk istorii*, 113–22.

34 See UWAC branch histories from Alberta, Saskatchewan, and Manitoba in Kohuska, *Pivstolittia na hromadskii nyvi*.

35 Prokopchak, *Almanakh*, 146–64, 280–8

36 *Ukrainian Canadian*, March 1972, 9–10; see also ibid., 15 May 1962, 13–14.

37 Ibid., 15 Dec. 1955, 5; 15 Jan. 1956, 8–9

38 Ibid., 15 Nov. 1949, 3; 15 April 1948, 3; 1 May 1949, 10; and Kolasky, *Shattered Illusion*, 8. See also Prokopchak, *Almanakh*, 240–55.

39 See the correspondence between the UWOC executive and the NCWC, 23 March 1948–21 March 1949, vol. 50, Records of the Ukrainian Women's Organization of Canada, Ukrainian Cultural and Educational Centre; the date of 1947 in Knysh, *Na sluzhbi ridnoho narodu*, 182, must be incorrect.

40 National Council of Women of Canada, *Year Book 1950–51*, 152–3; see also Knysh, *Na sluzhbi ridnoho narodu*, 179–83.

41 W. Kossar, 'Ukrainian Canadians in Canada's War Effort,' in Ukrainian Canadian Committee, *First All-Canadian Congress of Ukrainians in Canada* (Winnipeg 1943), 46

42 *Promin*, Oct. 1961, 15–16. Kohuska, *Pivstolittia na hromadskii nyvi*, 646–60, illustrates the UWAC's sense of pride in the executive achievements of its members on the NCWC and ICW; see also Hnatyshyn's biography at pages 767–9 of this book.

43 *Nasha doroha*, Jan.–March 1976, 17; July–Sept. 1970, 101–2

44 See, for example, the April 1956 issue of *Zhinochyi svit* on Kysilewska's death. Also ibid., March 1957, 1; July–Aug. 1957, 13; March 1966, 1, on the tenth anniversary of her death; June 1966, 9, reporting a local

UCWC commemoration in Hamilton; *Ukrainskyi holos*, 22 May and 12 June 1957; and *Nasha doroha*, July–Sept. 1975, 15.

45 *Ensign*, 20 Oct. 1951

46 *Ukrainskyi holos*, 8 Aug. 1923

47 Ibid., 30 July and 27 Aug. 1930

48 Ibid., 5 Sept. 1956. See also the eulogy of Mary Ortynsky, whose daughters and daughters-in-law all belonged to the UWAC, and whose grandchildren all belonged to the Ukrainian Canadian Youth Association, in Boichuk, *Zolotyi vinets*, 297.

49 This is amply demonstrated in the recitation of the accomplishments of UWAC presidents in Kohuska, *Pivstolittia na hromadskii nyvi*, 741–69. See also, for example, *Zhinochyi svit*, Sept. 1967, 13; and 'The Funeral of a Meritorious Pioneer' in *Postup*, 27 June 1982.

50 *Ukrainskyi holos*, 22 July 1936; Paul Yuzyk, *The Ukrainians in Manitoba: A Social History* (Toronto 1953), 158; and F.A. Macrouch, comp., *Ukrainian Year Book and Ukrainians of Distinction, 1953–1954* (Winnipeg 1953–4), 52

51 In the major standard histories see Yuzyk, *Ukrainians in Manitoba*, 52–7, 140–1, 166–9, 201, 204; Michael H. Marunchak, *The Ukrainian Canadians: A History*, 2d ed. rev. (Winnipeg and Ottawa 1982), 120, 529, 669–74, 690–8, 705, 709–10, 756–9, 772–87, 803–4, 859–67; Ol'ha Woycenko, *Ukrainians in Canada*, 2d ed. rev. (Ottawa and Winnipeg 1968), 33–4, 42, 52, 95–6, 155–6, 177–9; Leonid Biletskyi, *Ukrainski pionery v Kanadi, 1891–1951* (Winnipeg 1951), 65–8, 75–94; and Semen Kovbel, comp., and Dmytro Doroshenko, ed., *Propamiatna knyha Ukrainskoho narodnoho domu u Vynypegu* (Winnipeg 1949), 605–27.

52 Woycenko, *Ukrainians in Canada*, 155–6

53 On Grescoe alone see, for example, Vera Lysenko, *Men in Sheepskin Coats: A Study in Assimilation* (Toronto 1947), 272; Yuzyk, *Ukrainians in Manitoba*, 106–7; Marunchak, *Ukrainian Canadians*, 456; and, for community press commentary, *Novyi shliakh*, 2 May 1942, and *Opinion*, Nov. 1946.

54 See *Winnipeg Tribune*, 16 Oct. 1965, for an appearance by Juliette in that city and the positive Ukrainian response. She performed to boos, however, at the UCC congress in Winnipeg in 1968, purportedly because of the non-Ukrainian content of her songs; the Ukrainian Canadian University Students' Union accepted the blame and apologized. *Winnipeg Free Press*, 15 Oct. 1968

55 *Nasha doroha*, April–June 1976, 25–6; and Buchynska, *Slidamy dyiakonis*, 160

56 *Notable Saskatchewan Women, 1905–1980* (np 1980) was published by the Women's Division of Saskatchewan Labour.

57 See *Zhinochyi svit*, March 1968, 3, on the receipt by Mary Dyma and Mary Wawrykow of Centennial medals; and *Promin*, Oct. 1976, 14–15, and Jan. 1977, 4–5, on the naming of multiculturalism activist, Emily Ostapchuk, to the Order of Canada.

58 *Promin*, Jan. 1960, 12–13; April 1960, 9; Nov. 1963, 18–20; July 1967, 11–12; Dec. 1970, 9–10; May 1980, 1–2

59 Ibid., Feb. 1967, 1–5; *Winnipeg Tribune*, 26 Nov. 1966; and *Zhinochyi svit*, March 1966, 6–9

60 See Alison Prentice, Paula Bourne, Gail Cuthbert Brandt, Beth Light, Wendy Mitchinson, and Naomi Black, *Canadian Women: A History* (Toronto 1988), 189–211; the Icelandic Suffrage Association in Manitoba is mentioned.

61 *Zhinochyi svit*, June–July 1967, 6–7

62 *Promin*, Dec. 1963, 13

63 Marlene Stefanow, 'A Study of Intermarriage of Ukrainians in Saskatchewan' (MA thesis, University of Saskatchewan 1962); and Charles W. Hobart, 'Adjustment of Ukrainians in Alberta: Alienation and Integration,' *Slavs in Canada* 1 (1966): 77, 82–3. Alan Anderson, 'Generation Differences in Ethnic Identity Retention in Rural Saskatchewan,' *Prairie Forum* 7, 2 (1982): 188, found that both Catholic and Orthodox respondents looked more favourably on ethnic than religious out-marriage. For attitudes of the offspring of displaced persons in Toronto towards marriage see Nadia Skop, 'Ethnic Singlehood as a Sociological Phenomenon: Ukrainian-Canadians as a Case Study' (PhD dissertation, University of Toronto 1988).

64 See the remarks of Anna Balan in *Promin*, Dec. 1973, 15.

65 On intermarriage see o. dr. A. Redkevych, *Moderne supruzhe i kontrolia porodu* (Calgary 1927), 13–20; *Ukrainskyi holos*, 14 Oct. 1931, 23 May 1934, 6 Dec. 1944; *Promin*, May 1974, 2–5; Dec. 1974, 1–2; and *Nasha doroha*, July–Sept. 1980, 2–4; April–June 1983, 9–10; Jan.–March 1984, 6–7.

66 *Zhinochyi svit*, May 1981, 3–4, 23; Sept. 1981, 3–4, 21–2

67 Ukrainian Community Development Committee, Prairie Region, *Building the Future: Ukrainian Canadians in the 21st Century, A Blueprint for Action* (Edmonton 1986), 12–13. Concern was also expressed at the Ukrainian-Canadian divorce rate and the effect of the growing number of single-parent families on the culture retention of Ukrainian-Canadian children.

68 Based on Bohdan S. Kordan, *Ukrainians and the 1981 Canada Census: A Data Handbook* (Edmonton 1985), tables 5.1, 5.4, 5.6, 5.11

69 Ibid., tables 4.3, 4.4

70 Bohdan Bociurkiw, 'Ethnic Identification and Attitudes of University Students of Ukrainian Descent: The University of Alberta Case Study,' *Slavs in Canada* 3 (1971): 15–110

71 *Nasha doroha*, July–Sept. 1984, 25–7

72 From the UCWL press alone see *Nasha doroha*, Jan.–March 1978, 7–8; April–June 1983, 25–8; Oct.–Dec. 1984, 25–6; Jan.–March 1987, 9–13.

73 *Student*, Nov. 1979, 8

74 See, for example, Norma Baumel Joseph, 'Personal Reflections on Jewish Feminism,' in *The Canadian Jewish Mosaic*, ed. M. Weinfeld, W. Shaffir, and I. Cotler (Toronto 1981), 208. An outgrowth of American Jewish feminism, the Canadian movement was smaller, less well organized, and not as confrontational or involved in dialogue with religious leaders.

75 *Student*, March–April 1978, 6, 12 (reprinted from *New Directions*, spring 1973)

76 Taped-recorded proceedings of the Second Wreath Conference, available from the Second Wreath Society, Edmonton

77 Ukrainian Community Development Committee, *Building the Future*, 14–15, 33–4. See also Sonia Maryn, 'Ukrainian-Canadian Women in Transition: From Church Basement to Board Room,' *Journal of Ukrainian Studies* 10, 1 (summer 1985): 89–96.

78 Of forty-one past and current members, seven were women (five of whom came from Alberta).

79 Sofiia Kachor in *Nasha doroha*, Oct.–Dec. 1984, 8–10

80 See Claudia Helen Popowich, *To Serve Is To Love: The Canadian Story of the Sisters Servants of Mary Immaculate* (Toronto 1971).

81 *Nasha doroha*, Jan.–March 1984, 7–12

82 Parish histories in *Zbirnyk materiialiv z nahody iuvileinykh sviatkuvan u 50-littia Ukrainskoi hreko-pravoslavnoi tserkvy v Kanadi, 1918–1968* (Winnipeg 1968)

83 Stefan Semchuk, 'Vstupne slovo,' in Buchynska, *Slidamy dyiakonis*, 10–12; see also the remarks of Fr Mykhailo Shchudlo in *Nasha doroha*, Jan.–Feb. 1972, 10–11.

84 Neither the Ukrainian Self-Reliance League nor the Ukrainian Catholic Brotherhood has published national histories; the Ukrainian National Federation did so only in 1978.

85 Compare the accounts of UCWL branches in Alberta and Manitoba to

those in the Toronto eparchy, in Buchynska, *Slidamy dyiakonis*; Vynnytska, *Nacherk istorii*; and Pavlykovska, *Dlia Boha, tserkvy i narodu*.
86 *Nasha doroha*, April–June 1983, 27
87 Ibid., Oct.–Dec. 1984, 27–8
88 *Promin*, Dec. 1961, 20–1
89 *Ukrainian Canadian*, 1 April 1957, 13
90 Ibid., 15 May 1962, 13–14
91 Letter, UCWC (Toronto), 6 Oct. 1972, in Report No. 14 of the Committee on Parks, Recreation and City Property, Appendix A, Council
Minutes, City of Toronto, 4040
92 Enclosure to letter, UCC (Saskatoon), 17 Aug. 1976, to R.W. Begg,
President, University of Saskatchewan, Saskatoon, in Presidential Papers, Series V, General Correspondence, 1976, Archives of the University of Saskatchewan; and Council Minutes, City of Saskatoon, 1974–7
93 Minutes, Canora and District Chamber of Commerce, Canora, Saskatchewan, 1977–80; see also the special issue of the *Canora Courier*, 10
Sept. 1980, on *Lesia*'s unveiling. *Ukrainskyi holos*, 18 Oct. 1982, explic-
itly identifies the statue with Ukrainka.

CHAPTER 6   Rehabilitating the Peasant Immigrant

1 Gabrielle Roy, *Garden in the Wind*, trans. Alan Brown (Toronto 1977),
174
2 Eliane Leslau Silverman, *The Last Best West: Women on the Alberta Frontier, 1880–1930* (Montreal and London 1984), 74
3 See 'Our New Immigrants – "The Galicians,"' *Great West Magazine*,
Dec. 1898, 224; also Petro Kravchuk, *Vazhki roky* (Toronto 1968), 43,
citing the Saskatchewan educator, Edmund Oliver, no friend of
Ukrainian political aspirations in western Canada, who spoke admir-
ingly of the Ukrainian women who brought to their labour on the land
nothing but their 'pure hearts and willing hands.'
4 Robert B. Klymasz, 'Ukrainian Folklore in Canada: An Immigrant
Complex in Transition' (PhD dissertation, Indiana University 1970),
29, 48–51; also his *Folk Narrative among Ukrainian-Canadians in Western
Canada* (Ottawa 1973), 10–11, 23–5
5 See, for example, Natalia Kryhirchuk's 'Na chuzhyni' (Abroad) and
Magda Shcherba's 'Tuha zheny emigranty' (The sorrow of an emigrant's wife) in *Kanadiiskyi farmer*, 20 Sept. 1906 and 6 Sept. 1907, respectively.
6 Klymasz, *Folk Narrative among Ukrainian-Canadians in Western Canada*,

24–5. Klymasz also describes funeral laments as a specifically female genre, often with sexual overtones, where women protested against male dominance in Ukrainian peasant life; see his 'Speaking at/about/ with the Dead: Funerary Rhetoric among Ukrainians in Western Canada,' *Canadian Ethnic Studies* 7, 2 (1975): 52.

7 *Ukrainskyi holos*, 12 April 1916

8 James S. Woodsworth, dir., 'Ukrainian Rural Communities' (mimeograph, Report of investigation by the Bureau of Social Research, governments of Manitoba, Saskatchewan, and Alberta, Winnipeg 1917), 48

9 See 'Ethnicity and Femininity as Determinants of Life Experience,' *Canadian Ethnic Studies* 13, 1 (1981): 39–40.

10 Anna Bychinsky, 'Ukrainians' Pioneering,' *Grain Growers' Guide*, 1 Sept. 1920, 35

11 *Kanadiiskyi ukrainets*, 3 July 1929 (reprinted from *Ukrainskyi emigrant*)

12 Anna Bychinsky, 'Ukrainian Women at Home,' *Grain Growers' Guide*, 16 June 1920, 40

13 Although he would not so label it, the Ukrainian-Canadian senator and historian, Paul Yuzyk, was in the forefront of the cultivation of the peasant pioneer myth. See his *The Ukrainians in Manitoba: A Social History* (Toronto 1953), 40–5, 52; *Ukrainian Canadians: Their Place and Role in Canadian Life* (Toronto 1967), 11–12; and '75th Anniversary of Ukrainian Settlement in Canada,' *Ukrainian Review* 14, 1 (spring 1967): 81.

14 For a sense of the myth's popularity at elite and grassroots levels in nationalist circles see Ukrainian Canadian Committee, *First All-Canadian Congress of Ukrainians in Canada* (Winnipeg 1943), 178; Michael Luchkovich, 'The Achievements of Ukrainian Pioneers in Alberta,' in *Propamiatna knyha: Ukrainskyi katolytskyi soiuz – Ukrainskyi narodnyi dim, 1906–1965*, ed. Mykhailo Khomiak (Edmonton [1966]), 430–5; S. Semczuk, *Centennial of Canada and 75 Years of Ukrainian Catholic Church* (Winnipeg 1967), 5–7; B.L. Korchinski, 'Ukrainian Pioneers,' in *From Dreams to Reality: A History of the Ukrainian Senior Citizens of Regina and District, 1896–1976* (Regina 1977), 178–83; and Ukrainian Community Development Committee, Prairie Region, *Building the Future: Ukrainian Canadians in the 21st Century, A Blueprint for Action* (Edmonton 1986), 2–10. In progressive historiography see Association of United Ukrainian Canadians and Workers Benevolent Association, *A Tribute to Our Ukrainian Pioneers in Canada's First Century* (Winnipeg 1966), 1, 15–18, 42, 48, 54–6, 66–7, 73–6, 100; and two works by Petro Kravchuk: *Na*

novii zemli: Storinky z zhyttia, borotby i tvorchoi pratsi kanadskykh ukraintsiv
(Toronto 1958), 88–91, 101–7, 379–81; and *Vazhki roky*, 100–3. The
titles alone of Zonia Keywan's *Greater Than Kings* (Montreal 1977),
and her 'Women Who Won the West,' *Branching Out*, Nov.–Dec. 1975,
17–19, reveal the internalization of the peasant pioneer myth by the
displaced persons immigration.

15 Yuzyk, *Ukrainians in Manitoba*, 33

16 See the relevant sections in the surveys by Yuzyk, ibid.; Michael H.
   Marunchak, *The Ukrainian Canadians: A History*, 2d ed. rev. (Winnipeg
   and Ottawa 1982); and Leonid Biletskyi, *Ukrainski pionery v Kanadi,
   1891–1951* (Winnipeg 1951). The same approach characterizes works
   focusing exclusively on the period of first immigration: Vladimir J.
   Kaye, *Early Ukrainian Settlements in Canada, 1895–1900: Dr. Josef Oles-
   kow's Role in the Settlement of the Canadian Northwest* (Toronto 1964);
   Iuliian Stechyshyn, *Istoriia poselennia ukraintsiv u Kanadi* (Edmonton
   1975); and Jaroslav Petryshyn, *Peasants in the Promised Land: Canada
   and the Ukrainians, 1891–1914* (Toronto 1985).

17 Marunchak, *Ukrainian Canadians*, 96; overall mention of pioneer
   women is brief (34, 46, 50–2, 83–5, 88, 93–6). See also Stechyshyn, *Istoriia poselennia ukraintsiv u Kanadi*, 201.

18 Jars Balan, *Salt and Braided Bread: Ukrainian Life in Canada* (Toronto
   1984), 88–9; and Keywan, *Greater Than Kings*, 65–70, 88–98, 106–10,
   115–20

19 Marunchak, *Ukrainian Canadians*, 83

20 Stechyshyn, *Istoriia poselennia ukraintsiv u Kanadi*, 217

21 For examples of the way these volumes treat women within the family,
   the homesteading experience, and community life see three local histories from Alberta: Andrew Historical Society, *Dreams and Destinies: Andrew and District* (Andrew 1980); Steve Hrynew, ed., *Pride in Progress:
   Chipman-St. Michael-Star and Districts* (Chipman 1982); and Mundare
   Historical Society, *Memories of Mundare: A History of Mundare and District*
   (Mundare 1980).

22 Keywan, 'Women Who Won the West,' 19. See Maria Adamowska's
   reminiscences (published in *Kalendar-almanakh Ukrainskoho holosu* in
   1937 and 1939) in *Land of Pain, Land of Promise: First Person Accounts by
   Ukrainian Pioneers, 1891–1914*, comp. and trans. Harry Piniuta (Saskatoon 1978), 53–78.

23 Dorothy Cherewick, 'Woman in Ukrainian Canadian Folklore and
   Reminiscences' (MA thesis, University of Manitoba 1980), ii. Over half

of seventeen individuals interviewed for the study were not 'ordinary' women but identifiable as members of the elite – teachers, nuns, priests' wives, community activists, and teachers' wives.

24 Ibid., 13
25 Helen Potrebenko, *No Streets of Gold: A Social History of Ukrainians in Alberta* (Vancouver 1977). The book rather breathlessly combines autobiography, pioneer reminiscences (many by women from the progressive *Zhyttia i slovo*), general Ukrainian-Canadian history, and provincial and national developments. It nevertheless creates some powerful visual images, particularly of women's lot.
26 Ibid., 78
27 Ibid., 46
28 From the Alberta Culture government publication, *Alberta's Local Histories in the Historical Resources Library*, 6th ed. (Edmonton 1986). Joanne Stiles makes many of the same observations in 'Gilded Memories: Perceptions of the Frontier in Rural Alberta as Reflected in Popular History' (MA thesis, University of Alberta 1985).
29 Although proud of the work of Ukrainian pioneer women, one commentator claimed that emotionalism and physical weakness caused them to live 'in greater fear and anguish in the wilderness' than Ukrainian men; Peter Humeniuk, *Hardships and Progress of Ukrainian Pioneers: Memoirs from Stuartburn Colony and Other Points* (Steinbach 1976), 201.
30 Nancy Mattson Schelstraete, ed., *Life in the New Finland Woods: A History of New Finland, Saskatchewan* (Rocanville 1982), 41–3. Stiles, 'Gilded Memories,' 59, corroborates that women's work on the land is generally viewed as having been exceptional, but she fails to appreciate the Ukrainian differences.
31 Hrynew, *Pride in Progress*, 49–50
32 Ragna Steen and Magda Hendrickson, *Pioneer Days in Bardo, Alberta, Including Sketches of Early Surrounding Settlements* (Tofield 1944), dedication page; see also chapter 21, 'Our Pioneer Mothers,' 165–79. A glorified local history, the Norwegian volume in the Generations Series does tie Norwegian women to nation building, paying homage to their working courageously beside their strong partners in the 'titanic struggle to conquer the new land'; but it relies on the Bardo description for its primary image, and identifies women's role as mothers raising worthy citizens and leaders as their major function and contribution. See Gulbrand Loken, *From Fjord to Frontier: A History of the Norwegians in Canada* (Toronto 1980), 217–19
33 *Promin*, March 1982, 4

34 Telephone conversation, Martha Bielish to Frances Swyripa, 23 June 1987

35 Letter, John Weaver, Hope, British Columbia, to Frances Swyripa, 12 June 1987; also telephone conversation, 2 June 1987. Gloria Ferbey of the UWAC Alberta executive and an influential voice behind the portrayal of the pioneer woman reported of the unveiling that everyone was 'very pleased' with the result; *Promin*, March 1982, 4.

36 Stephanie Sawchuk, 'Our Women in Ukrainian and Canadian Life,' in Ukrainian Canadian Committee, *First All-Canadian Congress of Ukrainians in Canada* 161–3

37 *Novyi shliakh*, 12 May 1945; and *Zhinochyi svit*, Feb. 1966, 1

38 See 'Poklin ukrainskykh pioneram i pionerkam Kanady!' typescript, Olena Kysilewska Papers, vol. 9, file 4, National Archives of Canada, Ottawa.

39 *Promin*, May 1981, 5

40 *Nasha doroha*, April–June 1980, 2. The UCWL image of the Ukrainian pioneer woman as homemaker, nation builder, mother, and member of her church and community is captured in Anna Pryima, 'Zhinka-pionerka,' in *Dlia Boha, tserkvy i narodu: Liga ukrainskykh katolytskykh zhinok edmontonskoi ieparkhii v 1944–1964 rokakh, pochatky i diialnist*, ed. Iryna Pavlykovska (Edmonton [1966]), 13–15.

41 *Promin*, May 1960, 11–12; ibid., June 1961, 18–19, makes essentially the same points. For two male perspectives on the lessons of the pioneer mother for contemporary Ukrainian-Canadian women, see ibid., May 1963, 8–9; May 1966, 16–17.

42 Ibid., May 1960, 11–12

43 *Nasha doroha*, Jan.–Feb. 1975, 7–8

44 *Promin*, Feb. 1962, 1–3

45 See Mary Prokop in *Ukrainian Canadian*, March 1972, 9.

46 Peter Krawchuk, ibid., 15–19

47 Ibid., 15 April 1952, 9; and the speech by Anne Lapchuk, 'A Tribute to Our Women,' in Association of United Ukrainian Canadians and Workers Benevolent Association, *Tribute to Our Ukrainian Pioneers*, 92–4

48 *Ukrainian Canadian*, March 1972, 20–1; also ibid., June 1978, 15–19

49 Ibid., 1 May 1958, 9–10. See also ibid., 1 May 1957, 14; March 1972, 5.

50 Association of United Ukrainian Canadians and Workers Benevolent Association, *Tribute to Our Ukrainian Pioneers*, 94; see also *Ukrainian Canadian*, 15 May 1962, 12.

51 *Notable Saskatchewan Women, 1905–1980* (np 1980), 29. On the direct

line drawn between the Great Women of Ukraine and major organizational figures in Canada see Oleksander Luhovyi [Oleksander
Ovrutskyi-Shvabe], *Vyznachne zhinotstvo Ukrainy* (Winnipeg 1942);
and *Zhinochyi svit*, Oct.–Nov. 1954, 2–6.

52 *Robitnytsia*, 1 March 1937, 48

53 *Visnyk*, 1 Aug. 1935

54 Irena Knysh, *Patriotyzm Anny Ionker* (Winnipeg 1964), 181, 186; see
also, for example, *Zhinochyi svit*, June 1962, 13–14.

55 Petro Kravchuk, comp., *Zhinochi doli* (Toronto 1973); translation by
Michael Ukas published as *Reminiscences of Courage and Hope: Stories of
Ukrainian Canadian Women Pioneers* (Toronto 1991)

56 See, for example, the biographical sketches of the presidents of the
UWAC in Nataliia L. Kohuska, *Pivstolittia na hromadskii nyvi: Narys istorii
Soiuzu ukrainok Kanady* (Edmonton and Winnipeg 1986), 741–69. The
sections on the community activist in Cherewick, 'Woman in Ukrainian
Canadian Folklore and Reminiscences,' should be read in this context,
although Cherewick's composite does not correspond to any one individual.

57 From the three pioneer nationalist organizations see the biographies of
Maria Hultai and Evheniia Sytnyk in *Zhinochyi svit*, Nov.–Dec. 1968,
22–3; Feb. 1969, 9–11; those of Anna Pryima and Nellie Woytkiw in
Nasha doroha, April–June 1975, 9–10; Oct.–Dec. 1975, 17–18; and
those of Savella Stechishin, Hanka Romanchych-Kovalchuk, and Ste-
fania Paush in *Promin*, April 1977, 3–4; Feb. 1978, 11–13.

58 William Kurelek, 'Development of Ethnic Consciousness in a Canadian
Painter,' in *Identities: The Impact of Ethnicity on Canadian Society*, ed. Wsevolod Isajiw (Toronto 1977), 52

59 The Kurelek paintings in the Ukrainian Museum of Canada are *A First
Meeting of the Ukrainian Women's Association*, *Women Feeding Threshing
Gang*, *A Boorday – The First House*, *Ukrainian Canadian Farm Picnic*, *Blessing the Easter Paska*, *The Second House*, *Clay Plastering*, *Teaching the Sign of
the Cross*, *Making Easter Eggs*, *Ukrainian Christmas Eve Supper*, *Teaching
Ukrainian*, and *Teaching Embroidery*. The paintings are reproduced, with
short annotations, in the booklet, *Ukrainian Pioneer Women* (Saskatoon
1991), published by the Ukrainian Museum of Canada for the Ukrainian Canadian Centennial.

60 Ramsay Cook, 'William Kurelek: A Prairie Boy's Visions,' *Journal of
Ukrainian Studies* 5, 1 (spring 1980): 40

61 *Ukrainian Canadian*, 1 Feb. 1968, 11

62 The 'Baba bell' and doll are the creations of Edmontonians, Sandi
    Skakun and Donna Marchyshyn, respectively.
63 In Canada her type was found in the satirical-humorous press of the
    1920s and 1930s; this image was not always complimentary and often
    showed the peasant woman, like Vuiko Shtif and Nasha Meri, as the
    immigrant interacting with an unfamiliar new world. For examples see
    Vuiko, 1918–27, *Vuiko Shtif*, 1927–29, and *Tochylo*, 1930–47.
64 Maara Haas, 'Baba Podkova,' *Canadian Woman Studies* 4, 2 (winter
    1982): 6–7
65 Raymond Serwylo, 'Baba: A Day in the Life,' in *Student*, June 1978, 8
66 Haas, 'Baba Podkova,' 6–7. Serwylo (8) likewise condemns baba's treat-
    ment by a subsequent generation, in this case an uncaring non-Ukrain-
    ian daughter-in-law. In her unpublished manuscripts, writer Vera
    Lysenko returns repeatedly to baba as a tragic and unwanted figure;
    her old peasant women are also often deliberately ugly and uncultured
    – with fat rumps, loose breasts, flabby bellies, warts and whiskers, pipes,
    barefeet, and gaudy clothes. Vera Lysenko Papers, vol. 1, file 15; vol.
    2, file 5; vol. 3, files 8–9, National Archives of Canada
67 Designed and made by Gee Bee Buttons, Saskatoon
68 *Ukrainskyi holos*, 16 July 1919
69 Maara Haas, 'In Search of Multicultural Woman,' *Canadian Woman
    Studies* 4, 2 (winter 1982): 5
70 Wsevolod Isajiw, 'Symbols and Ukrainian Canadian Identity: Their
    Meaning and Significance,' in *Visible Symbols: Cultural Expression among
    Canada's Ukrainians*, ed. Manoly R. Lupul (Edmonton 1984), 119–28.
    In the same volume see also Zenon Pohorecky, 'Ukrainian Cultural and
    Political Symbols in Canada: An Anthropological Selection,' 129–41,
    and Jars Balan, 'The Search for Symbols: Some Observations,' 162–6,
    both of which refer to food and the Balan article also to baba.
71 Sylvia Shaw, 'Attitudes of Canadians of Ukrainian Descent toward
    Ukrainian Dance' (PhD dissertation, University of Alberta 1988), ex-
    plores the role of dance in Ukrainian-Canadian ethnic identity within
    the organized community, comparing attitudes in AUUC, Orthodox,
    and displaced person circles.
72 See, for example, *Edmonton Journal*, 6 Jan. 1966, 31 Dec. 1987; also
    24, 30, and 31 Aug. 1991 for the Glendon 'perogy.' Myrna Kostash,
    'The Ukrainian Easter Egg,' *The West*, April 1990, 11–12, gives a fem-
    inist perspective on the role of *pysanky* in Ukrainian-Canadian culture.
73 Maxine Seller, *Immigrant Women* (Philadelphia 1981), 287–8

74 Semen Kovbel, *Sviatyi Mykolai v Kanadi* (Winnipeg nd)

75 *Promin*, April 1969, 15; and *Nasha doroha*, Nov.–Dec. 1974, 13

76 Joyce Meyer, 'Why the Perogy Went W.A.S.P.,' *Edmonton Report on Dining*, 28 Nov. 1978, 20–1

77 Emily Linkiewich, *Baba's Cook Book*, 2 vols. (Vegreville 1981 and 1984)

78 Helen C. Kozicky, comp., 'Summary of U.C.S.A. Diary for the Month of Jan. 1945,' typescript, 11, 7, in Ol'ha Woycenko Papers, vol. 35, file 7, National Archives of Canada. See also 'The Plight of the Perih' in William Paluk, *Canadian Cossacks: Essays, Articles and Stories on Ukrainian-Canadian Life* (Winnipeg 1943), 61–7, which equates the *perih* with Ukrainian national identity, peasantness, and the family.

79 Robert Kroetsch and Andrew Suknaski in 'Ethnicity and Identity: The Question of One's Literary Passport' (panel discussion), in *Identities: Ethnicity and the Writer in Canada*, ed. Jars Balan (Edmonton 1982), 75

80 Natalia Aponiuk, 'Some Images of Ukrainian Women in Canadian Literature,' *Journal of Ukrainian Studies* 8, 1 (summer 1983): 39–50, contends that Ukrainian pioneer immigrant women, 'the only propagator[s] of joy and spiritual beauty in a harsh existence,' have had a more positive image than their male counterparts in Canadian literature. She also notes that in Margaret Atwood's *Life before Man* (1979), Lesje's Jewish and Ukrainian grandmothers battle for her ethnic allegiance.

81 Carlo Levi, *Christ Stopped at Eboli* (New York 1947). Jan Noel, 'New France: Les femmes favorisées,' in *The Neglected Majority: Essays in Canadian Women's History II*, ed. Susan Mann Trofimenkoff and Alison Prentice (Toronto 1985), 18–40, argues that the absence of men on fur trading, military, and exploring expeditions gave women unprecedented independence in New France; Micheline Dumont disputes this in 'Les femmes de la Nouvelle-France: Etaient-elles favorisées?' *Atlantis* 8, 1 (autumn 1982): 118–24.

82 In 1931 Ukrainian males in their thirties outnumbered Ukrainian females in the same age bracket by 18,537 to 11,600; in 1971, 57.8 per cent of Ukrainian Canadians sixty-five or older were men. Based on William Darcovich and Paul Yuzyk, eds., *A Statistical Compendium on the Ukrainians in Canada, 1891–1976* (Ottawa 1980), series 22.17–56, 133–5

83 Joanna Hubbs, 'The Worship of Mother Earth in Russian Culture,' in *Mother Worship: Theme and Variation*, ed. James J. Preston (Chapel Hill 1982), 123–44; see also her *Mother Russia: The Feminine Myth in Russian Culture* (Bloomington and Indianapolis 1988).

84 *Edmonton Journal*, 22 Dec. 1914

85 Miriam Elston, 'Our Little Russian Brother,' in *Chinook Arch*, ed. John

Patrick Gillese (Edmonton 1967), 46–54 (reprinted from *Christian Guardian*, 1916)

86 The importance of the matrilineal voice to native women and of matrilineal descent to emergent Métis identity is explored in Barbara Godard, 'Talking About Ourselves: The Literary Productions of the Native Women of Canada,' CRIAW *Papers* 11 (1985), and Jennifer S.H. Brown, 'Woman as Centre and Symbol in the Emergence of Metis Communities,' *Canadian Journal of Native Studies* 3, 1 (1983): 39–46.

87 See also, for example, the first-prize poem, 'Tradition,' by grade-eleven student, Kerri Froc, in *Saskatchewan Multicultural Magazine*, winter 1989, 5; and Ellen Bazdell's third-place essay, 'My Favourite Ukrainian,' typescript, in the 1976 high school essay contest sponsored by the Ottawa branch of the UCC, Woycenko Papers, vol. 70, file 7.

88 Ted Galay, *'After Baba's Funeral' and 'Sweet and Sour Pickles': Two Plays by Ted Galay* (Toronto 1981), 36

89 *Globe and Mail*, 18 Jan. 1986

CONCLUSION   Baba Meets the Queen

1 See *Invincible Spirit: Art and Poetry of Ukrainian Women Political Prisoners in the USSR* (Baltimore 1977).

Index

Illustration Credits

Ukrainian Cultural and Educational Centre, Winnipeg Ivan Bobersky Collection *appearing on page 27* (23/01/21–2/F84E222); *41* (19/06/21–5/F156E239); *48* (Ba182). Tovarystvo Ukrainy Collection *129* (11). UWOC Collection *130*. *Novyi shliakh* Collection *138*. Vogue Studio Collection *165* (7059); *192* (7037)

Provincial Archives of Alberta, Edmonton United Church Collection *29* (UC172/95); *30* (UC172/24); *51* (UC172/80); *82* (UC172/69); *85* (UC172/24); *111* (UC172/99). Nicholas Gavinchuk Collection *40* (G184); *72* (G1404); *73* (G1151); *147* (G408); *154* (G1092); *164* (G251); *167* (G865); *172* (G2202); *173* (G1954). Miriam Elston Collection *66* (A1614); *110* (65.55/3). Ukrainian Cultural Heritage Village Collection *71* (UV556); *76* (UV414); *77* (UV238); *83* (UV504); *89* (UV547)

Provincial Archives of Manitoba, Winnipeg William Sisler Collection *31* (N11586); *32* (N9697); *40* (N9601). Andrew Malofie Collection *49* (N11910); *75* (N5482). Legislative Building/Broadway Collection *231* (N13048)

The United Church of Canada / Victoria University Archives Immigration Collection *33, 43, 84, 86*

Estate of Jacob Maydanyk *63*

Ukrainian Women's Association of Canada *126* (courtesy of Ann Hluchaniuk), *137*

Olexa Bulavitsky *134*

St Andrew's College, Winnipeg *135*

Archives of Ontario, Toronto Association of United Ukrainian Canadians Collection *156* (AO444); *169* (AO446); *179* (AO448); *193* (AO447). Daria Temnyk Collection *153* (AO431). Albina Pypalowski Collection *146* (AO429). St Mary's UCC (Sudbury) Collection *166* (AO438). St Volodymyr's UGOC (Sudbury) Collection *189* (AO437)

National Archives of Canada, Ottawa CNR Collection *168* (C45102). V.J. Kaye Collection *174* (C74137)

Association of United Ukrainian Canadians *235*

Edward and Anne Topornicki *239*

The Edmonton Journal/Jim Cochrane *246, 250*

Ukrainian Senior Citizen's Centre, North Battleford *247* (courtesy of Julian Sadlowski)

Every attempt has been made to identify and credit sources for the illustrations. The publisher would appreciate receiving information as to any inaccuracies in the credits for subsequent editions.